TAKING LAND
BREAKING LAND

TAKING LAND

Women Colonizing the American West and Kenya, 1840–1940

BREAKING LAND

Glenda Riley

University of New Mexico Press
Albuquerque

First Edition

Library of Congress Cataloging-in-Publication Data

Riley, Glenda, 1938–

Taking Land, Breaking Land: Women colonizing the American and Kenyan frontiers, 1840–1940 / Glenda Riley—1st ed.

    p.   cm.

Includes index.

ISBN 0-8263-3111-4 (cloth : alk. paper)

ISBN 0-8263-3112-2 (pbk. : alk. paper)

1. Women pioneers—West (U.S.)—History—19th century.
2. Frontier and pioneer life—West (U.S.)
3. West (U.S.)—Social conditions—19th century.
4. West (U.S.)—Race relations.
5. Women pioneers—Kenya—History—19th century.
6. Women pioneers—Kenya—History—20th century.
7. Frontier and pioneer life—Kenya.
8. Kenya—Social conditions.
9. Kenya—Race relations.
10. Kenya—Colonial influence.
  I. Title.

F596 .R4155 2003

967.62'01'082—dc21

2003012648

9 8 7 6 5 4 3 2 1

Printed in the USA by Edwards Brothers Inc.

Typeset in Granjon 11/14

Display type set in Future condensed

Design and composition: Robyn Mundy

Production: Maya Allen-Gallegos

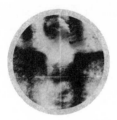

For Agneta and Gervase Akhaabi, and Peter Njoroge, who helped me catch a glimpse of Kenya through the eyes of black Africans

Contents

Photographs

Images

Acknowledgments

During the winter of 1987, I spent a month in East Africa. Kenya especially intrigued me. At that time, Kenya was a relatively prosperous country. Moreover, Kenyans were known for their hospitality to the tourists who underwrote the country's major industry. As a traveler, I happily took advantage of the sunshine, the safety, and the sights. As a scholar, however, I came to recognize how closely the colonial era in Kenya resembled the pioneer period in the American West. Moreover, the women who came to colonial Kenya appeared much like those who had helped populate the American frontier.

The existence of similarities, as well as differences, between frontier Kenya and the American West begged for further examination. Upon investigation, I learned that although scholars had compared the American West with South African, Argentinian, and even Russian frontiers, no one had contrasted the pioneer periods in the United States and Kenya. Certainly, no one had juxtaposed the roles, experiences, and impact of women in these regions.

As I set out to fill this void, I benefited from encouragement from a number of other historians. As early as 1977, W. Turrentine Jackson used his Western History Association presidential address to make a strong case for the comparative study of frontiers, including women on frontiers. Later, Sandra L. Myres not only argued for such comparative studies, but, before her death she inaugurated a comparison of English-speaking women settlers in Australia, New Zealand, the American West, and the Canadian West. Both Jackson and Myres gave me personal support in the form of cheering words and insightful comments. In addition, Howard R. Lamar, formerly Sterling Professor of History at Yale University and now Emeritus, encouraged me from the outset. As a practitioner and advocate of comparative frontier history, Lamar thought this project worth doing and, despite its challenges, kept after me to pursue it.

The American side of the project was relatively undemanding. Because I have spent some three decades researching women in the American West, I have accumulated plentiful women's sources and other information. To list the various archivists and librarians who have helped me would literally consume pages. From Iowa to California, and from Minnesota to Texas, I have found knowledgeable, dedicated professionals who steered me toward useful materials. The dozen file cases in my farm's outbuilding stand as testimony to those people's ability and commitment to assisting researchers.

The Kenya part of the project, however, required extensive time and travel. One major collection of women's writings and other documents is located in the Rhodes House Library in Oxford, England. At Rhodes House, deputy librarian Allan Lodge, U.S. Studies Librarian Linda E. Williamson, and library assistant Penny Brumfitt pointed me in the right directions. Other invaluable resources are found in the Kenya National Archives in Nairobi, Kenya. There, assistant director Agneta Akhaabi proved an invaluable resource and became a friend. And, always with smiles, archives assistant Richard A. J. Ambani helped me locate documents, while clerical officer Peterson Kithuka brought books and photocopied for me. In addition, women's letters, diaries, and published writings are found in everything from the imposing British Library in London, England, to the more modest Elsamere Conservation Centre in Naivasha, Kenya.

In 1998, a research grant from the Fulbright Association's African Studies Program allowed me to spend an extended period in Kenya, working primarily at the Kenya National Archives, but also traveling and pursuing interviews with black, white, and Asian Kenyans. Along the way, I also accrued many obligations to those Kenyans—black, white, and Asian—who filled in gaps in my knowledge, as well as supplying understanding of their country and its history. Some took me to dinner, others on drives into the countryside, still others to their homes. The eldest son of white settlers, D. M. Rocco, came to my assistance on many occasions by answering questions and sharing his own documents with me. In addition, a young black Kenyan, Edward Muigua Chege, served as a research assistant, especially conducting interviews in rural towns and areas. And Satish Shah, owner of Nairobi's Antiquity Shoppe, pursued rare books for me and gave me helpful leads on documents. Farther afield, Kikiyu Peter Njoroge of Loldia House in Naivasha set up interviews, acted as interpreter, and related to me local history anecdotes. Also in Naivasha, ecology manager Ian Marshall took me on a tour of the Delamere Estate, Elly Gramaticas of Loldia House shared her family's story with me, and director Velia Carn opened Elsamere's materials to me. Numerous other people in Kenya, as well as in Zanzibar, in Tanzania, the islands of the Seychelles, and Mauritius also helped. In Zanzibar, one person even gave me a much-appreciated lift in the back of a pickup truck from the archives to Zanzibar's Old Town.

Many people read all or parts of the manuscript. My appreciation goes especially to Agneta and Gervase Akhaabi, Stephanie Beswick, Anne M. Butler, Richard W. Etulain, N. Jill Howard, Shirley A. Leckie, Jay Spaulding, and several anonymous readers. Elizabeth G. Dulany gave me encouragement and Margaret Strobel expanded my awareness of issues regarding African women and African history.

Two people made special contributions. An exceptional graduate student, Deborah L. Rogers, contributed to this project. She not only kept my office and home running while I was in Nairobi in 1998, but turned up a huge number of sources. Since then, Rogers has taken time out from her doctoral program to apply her editorial talents to parts of the manuscript and to offer invaluable suggestions. In between times, Rogers supplied a lap for my dogs and cat, and fed the horses. Obviously, Rogers's support for this project went far beyond what one might expect from an assistant or even from a friend. To Samuel E. Griffet, I also owe a bigger debt than I can repay. Besides being patient and supportive, he kept the barn going, occasionally made dinner for me, and answered the telephone, all invaluable services when one is trying to write.

To all of the above I am everlastingly grateful. Certainly, people who furthered my work bear no responsibility if my own perceptions clouded my vision or for any other flaws I may have introduced into this study.

INTRODUCTION

THE adaptation, attitudes, and impact of women in the early American West beg for comparison with women in another frontier setting. In the West, women played a crucial role in aggrandizing lands not their own. They also helped shape the region that molded American character in a distinctive way. Still, scholars who now know a good deal about women migrants to the American West have not contrasted them to similar women. Among other possible frontiers, that of colonial Kenya clearly reprises the time and place that Americans refer to as the Old Wild West. A void exists here as well. Although scholars have compared the American West to South African, Argentine, and even Russian frontiers, no one has contrasted the pioneer periods in the United States and Kenya. Also, sources left by female migrants have not been systematically tallied against those of other women.

The goal of this treatise is to at least partially fill the void. By using the experiences of migrating women—both white and of color—to the West and to Kenya, it illuminates the course of women's relocation to, and settlement in, two comparable frontiers that are not usually studied together in traditional areas of historical analysis. Although this book draws upon postcolonial theory and incorporates some of its language, it is aimed at a larger audience, including teachers, students, scholars, and laypeople who are interested in understanding the lives and impact of female migrants on frontiers, as well as the vestiges of colonialism that continue to exist today. A comparison and synthesis of women colonizers on the American and Kenyan frontiers demonstrates that gender and race—and to a lesser extent social class—generally had greater weight in shaping women's frontier experiences than did the location, types of indigenous peoples, or time period of any specific frontier. Although the West and Kenya lay half a world apart, had racially different indigenes, and developed during disparate eras, the lives of women colonizers showed remarkable parallels.

The process of contrasting the American West and Kenya has many potential benefits. For one, the existence of similarities offers a challenge to the long-standing assumption that America's history was exceptional, that is, different from all other nations.[1] Recently, historians Ian Tyrrell and Michael Kammen pointed out that Americans have not stood alone in touting their supposed exceptionalism. Throughout world history, all national groups have interpreted events in light of their own values and perspectives. Virtually all peoples believed they stood apart—and perhaps above—others. The analysis presented here demonstrates that neither the demands of the American frontier nor women's adaptation to them were singular.[2] At least in the United States and Kenya, women's attitudes and experiences reveal not only similarities but a strongly related cadence and rhythm.

For other Americans, who like to think of their nation's history as atypical among world civilizations, discovering that an analogous frontier existed may be unsettling. After all, what is more distinctive to United States history than the American West? Because the West has served as a widespread mythology and a national symbol, it can be disillusioning to learn of another similar phenomenon. Yet for some Americans the existence of historical parallels may be reassuring. Such similarities indicate that contemporary problems are not peculiar to either the United States or Kenya and that much is to be gained by cooperation in confronting them.

More specifically, this methodology for the study of women on frontiers puts American women's frontier migration in historical context. A number of comparative scholars point out that factual information—in this case, the data that reconstructs women's experiences—answers the questions concerning who, when, and how. At the same time, comparison brings out characteristics of the American and Kenyan frontiers that might otherwise be misinterpreted or go unremarked.[3] Both regions, for example, had some form of slavery and, at least among white women, the beginnings of an environmental conservation movement. For another thing, this narrative indicates that individual frontiers changed over time, perhaps through improved technology or by the arrival of immigrants from such countries as China or India, which helped diversify the population of a particular frontier.

Additionally, the historian Peter Kolchin argues that comparison allows an investigator to "test the relative impact of various social, economic, demographic, political, or intellectual factors," which in turn provide the basis for generalizations. These generalizations lead to an awareness of alternatives, which inform the formulation of causal hypotheses. To Kolchin, this is as close as historians can get to "scientific method" or "experimentation," where the investigator studies a given phenomenon in two or more different situations.[4]

Similitudes also supply a wider framework of analysis. From Robert F. Berkhofer, Jr., during the late 1960s to George M. Fredrickson during the 1980s and 1990s, historians have maintained that contrasting two or more countries suggests larger research questions. The process of answering such queries addresses the crucial "why" issues, such as women's roles in the continuance of colonization (as in the American West) or in its collapse (as in Kenya), or why colonizers in these two regions tended to be white, whereas the colonized were peoples of color.[5] In Fredrickson's view, such a research design also enlarges appreciation of, and insight into, established principles. In this instance, principles are constructions of gender, race, and class.[6] Considering the earlier American West in relation to Kenya shows that white women's constructions of race and gender were not only alike, but were widespread and long lived. According to their beliefs, white women were inferior to white men, whereas people of color were inferior to white men and women. Thus, a white man stood above all women, but a white woman ranked above black men. In this system, white women played gendered roles in the frontier process, yet frequently seized opportunities to enlarge those roles.

As the twenty-first century unfolds, the results of expansionism based on this gender and racial ranking become increasingly conspicuous. Native Americans and black Kenyans try to solve the problems that beleaguer them. Hispanics, many of whom were indigenous to parts of the American West, also struggle with a difficult historical legacy. At the same time, white people attempt to assess—and compensate for—their inherited responsibility. As the historian David Thelen remarks, comprehending such historical developments can lead to improved problem-solving.[7] Thus, members of every group need to look to the past—especially to the evolution of colonialism, or the philosophy and system involved in the domination of one group over others—to understand the forces that brought them to the present point.

Lastly, from the viewpoints of world-systems analysis and of bio-history—or ethological history—comparison of these two frontiers reveals thought-provoking parallels in human conduct and may prove an important step in moving toward a synthetic history of the world. Early practitioners of the first, the world-systems approach, defined it as the investigation of "an intersocietal system marked by a self-contained division of labor." A particular "world," such as an imperial state, has a certain amount of internal cohesion and functions as a unit. More recent advocates of world-systems methodology stress its interdisciplinary nature and its focus on "trends with embedded continuing cycles." Among others, these include commodification (exchange based on currency), state formation, and capitalism. Hegemonic progressions are another type of trend, in which one group dominates a world-system primarily through political and economic power. The social scientist Thomas D. Hall explains that hegemony creates associated sequences, such as war, colonization, decolonization, and a need for social reform.[8]

In terms of this book, the pertinent world-systems are the United

States, especially the American West, and the British empire, notably Kenya. Both progressed through the hegemonic phases of war, colonization, decolonization, and social repair, including expressions of guilt and figurative hand-wringing.[9] Here, these two are captured in their colonial periods before substantial decline begins. The idea of predictable stages in a world-systems development helps explain why British imperialism in Kenya followed a similar route as Manifest Destiny in the American West, even though Americans had already shown a number of policies to be unworkable or even calamitous.

Rather than assessing societal patterns, the second approach, that of bio-history, focuses on people. The classicist Walter Burkert takes issue with the idea that "there is no human nature apart from culture." He proposes that there are "phenomena common to all human civilizations," which "may be but need not be called characteristics of human nature."[10] Stated simply, bio-historians argue that culture is not the sole determinant of people's thoughts and actions. The real diversity of cultures derives from nature using a template of flexible human universals, which are adaptable to different needs and environments, yet related to basic principles, including hierarchy, reciprocity, curiosity, and xenophobia. In other words, a certain amount of species-specific behavior exists across cultures and across centuries, such as "display"—perhaps conquerors pounding their chests or firing cannons—to enforce their power or influence. Sometimes, biology can help explain why people seem driven to behave in comparable ways, even if that behavior appears destructive or has already been proven so by an earlier cultural group.

Regarding this point, the historian Abel Alves maintains that history "does not benefit from ignoring psychological studies of human beings." He adds that human ethology and comparative ethology can help illuminate "fundamental human characteristics beneath the trappings of culture."[11] Rather than saying that the need to dominate is "natural," so that humans might as well put aside their notions of equality and peace, ethology indicates not only why equality and peace are so hard to attain, but suggests some ways to achieve them. Biology can also clarify some gender differences. For instance, recent studies, ranging from medical to bio-sociological, indicate that women and men employ their brains differently, express themselves in dissimilar ways, and see the world from distinct perspectives.[12]

Understandably, many people fear such thinking. Admittedly, during the 1950s and 1960s the application of Freudian thought to history generated more heat than light.[13] More recently, critics have charged that the bio-historical outlook smacks of biological determinism. Thus, it is especially difficult for historians of women to accept the bio-historical perspective. After all, feminists and feminist scholars have spent the last thirty-five years or so destroying stereotyped gender roles based on supposed biological characteristics of women and men. Similarly, literary analysts, or deconstructionists, have devoted entire careers to revealing how such concepts as male and female are culturally constructed rather than derived from some immutable biological source.[14] Both feminism and deconstructionism have contributed revolutionary methods and theories, which bio-historians have no wish to weaken or destroy. They do not propose a return to gender expectations based on biological determinism. Rather than human reductionism, they suggest that *some* human actions can be understood in terms of biological makeup, especially similarities in DNA, the universality of the Alpha factor, sharing of the flight-or-fight response, and gender differences.[15]

Even though most bio-historians study humans and "apes," meaning chimpanzees, gorillas, and orangutans, whose DNA are comparable,[16] human actions also can be related to other members of the animal world. For example, the natural scientist Richard Dawkins points out that people and horses are both mammals.[17] Horses, however, are a precocial species; they are neurologically developed when born and immediately begin learning at a speed faster than humans of any age. Also, much like elephants, horses have uncanny memories and seldom forget anything. What they experience imbeds lifelong attitudes and perceptions in their minds. Some experts even argue that horses have a psychic sixth sense, whereas others attribute horses' eerie abilities to their heightened sensory perceptions, notably sight, hearing, and smell.[18]

One only has to watch on a daily basis a herd of horses, which are, after all, more appropriate than chimpanzees to frontier history. Like people, horses establish hierarchies based on variables including seniority, forcefulness, and experience. According to the noted veterinarian Robert M. Miller, "the horse is the only domestic animal that exerts dominance and determines the hierarchy by controlling the movement of its peers." On the top side, one horse, often a stallion, dominates others through what Miller calls "threatening movements." The leader enforces authority chiefly through "display"—approaching another horse with its ears pinned back and snorting—or through violence, including shoving, nipping, and kicking. Subordinate horses respond (like people) by bowing their heads to authority, as well as by making chewing movements and smacking their lips to indicate submissiveness.[19] Alpha horses may also confine some horses to a less desirable section of the pasture, thus creating a horse-ghetto.

On the lower end, subjugated horses often resist control, usually (like people) through passive-aggressive action. Although subordinate animals appear to accept their fate, lesser horses express agency by sneaking grain or hay behind a leader's back, forming coalitions with other subaltern horses, and, when put into a different herd, becoming dominant themselves. Some will look for opportunities to show active resistance, perhaps by nipping or kicking dominant horses. At the same time, mares establish sub-hierarchies consisting of themselves and their children. Upon occasion, females—especially older, well-seasoned mares—will challenge the upper echelons, thus taking over leadership and becoming the "boss mare." Once in power, a lead mare is almost as active as a lead stallion in keeping the group together for safety and moving it in different directions through pinned-back ears, a raised tail, and nips on sensitive hocks and upper hind legs.[20]

In time of outside stimuli, however, a herd closes ranks and acts as a unified group. They can—and often do—demonstrate aggression and violence toward another herd. If given the opportunity, a group will follow its leader or leaders to displace another herd of horses, appropriating (like humans) their grazing area and water supplies for themselves. Because horses are prey animals they prefer to flee. They will bolt together from a threat, but if flight is not feasible, they will, like humans (who are predators), stand their ground and fight. Horses, like humans, can also be kind and cooperative, a point which Social

Darwinists overlooked. Occasionally, horses show care and altruism, especially by demonstrating warning behavior. Several might protect a mare who is about to foal, or one horse will "stand guard" while the others sleep in a vulnerable lying-down position. In addition, two or three horses will exhibit bonding behavior by becoming buddies. The leader especially cultivates several pals, who help enforce his or her regime. Such coalitions can be identified by looking for horses who habitually graze within a short distance of each other. If one of these is removed from the pasture, the others will wail and moan, letting the responsible human know that he or she has interfered with an alliance.[21]

In the case of two actual horses who have been together for nearly six years, first in a herd setting and later in a pasture of their own, the above conduct is very evident. On their home range, the older and more experienced horse is dominant. He demands to be fed first, released from the barn first, and to have his choice of hay flakes out in the field. He keeps the other horse in line by nipping his backside or kicking his legs. That the subordinate horse occasionally resists this arrangement is demonstrated by bite and kick marks on the body of the dominant horse. Because the subaltern horse is younger, more inquisitive, and more intelligent, his role is to make their shared environment as hospitable as possible. He accomplishes this by what the horse behaviorist Moyra Williams calls problem-solving. Williams points out that while people do this through reasoning, horses use the trial and error method.[22] Consequently, the younger horse often initiates what people define as acts of mischief. These include unfastening the gate with his nose so that he and his chum can graze on the front lawn, or noticing that someone left the barn door unsecured so that they are able to raid hay supplies and especially bags of horse cookies, which they leave empty on the barn floor.

Yet they can also be the tightest of friends. When things are going well for them, the two, both geldings, show their benign sides. They graze nose to nose and literally "scratch" each other's backs with their teeth. If one is left behind in the pasture, he wails and runs up and down the fence line until the other returns. When the younger horse developed a foot problem that required veterinary care, he refused to load into the trailer until his companion was also loaded, thus accompanying him on the unnerving journey. Upon return, the ailing horse had to remain in his stall for three days and nights. During this time, the healthy horse passed his time standing at the barn door with his head inside so he could see his pasture-mate.[23]

Translating horse actions into terms of nineteenth- and twentieth-century colonialism indicates a number of likenesses. "Controllers," who were frequently but not always white, displaced indigenous peoples, who were often but not always of color, and seized their resources. Once in power, white men constructed echelons that put some of them at the top. These men looked for opportunities to enforce their power, perhaps through laws or policies, and through "display" of their dominance, notably with military parades or by constructing formidable buildings and huge statues. The social scientist James C. Scott explains that "parades, inaugurations, processions, coronations, funerals provide ruling groups with the occasion to make a spectacle of themselves in a manner largely of their own choosing."[24] At the same time, whites, especially women, showed signs of benevolence and wanting to "help" the very indigenes they controlled. Many hoped to do "good" for conquered peoples, bringing them better education and improved health. They built schools and hospitals, as well as acting as teachers and medical personnel. Meanwhile, white women established their own sub-echelons, which included their children and domestic servants. White women who had not had servants at home and moved from lower to middle class when they migrated to a frontier also learned how to organize a domestic hierarchy. Regarding the male system, white women alternately supported or opposed it. Occasionally, white women (like boss mares) challenged male classifications and seized a customarily male leadership position.

In the role of "controllees," indigenes also acted much like horses. This is not meant to suggest that dominated peoples exhibited immutable characteristics. Rather, because structures of dominance operated in similar ways, they elicited similar responses. According to James Scott, "every subordinate group creates, out of its ordeal, a 'hidden transcript' that represents a critique of power spoken behind the back of the dominant." In addition, reactance theory maintains that because humans have an innate desire for freedom and self-rule, they respond to domination with opposition.[25] Indigenous peoples demonstrated a wide range of resistive conduct, including jokes, rumors, subtle insults, grumbling, and even shunning. Some used poaching and theft, forms of resistance that allowed the dominated to recoup some of the fruits of their labor. Additionally, they attempted to weaken existing white ranking systems. Some "buddied-up" with others, occasionally with "renegade" whites. Like subordinate horses, many found ways to sabotage white power, particularly by laboring inefficiently and by acting inept. A significant number of them opposed white benevolence, including schools and hospitals, preferring instead ways that gave them a measure of autonomy and independence. Indigenes undermined displays of white dominance, perhaps by acting up during a parade or other public ceremony, or by vandalizing government buildings and statues of white leaders. Some controllees also worked to create the necessary conditions for revolt, which might offer them the chance to usurp leadership for themselves.

The correspondence between horses and people who participated in colonial systems may be arguable. Ethologists, for example, raise issues of homology versus analogy. Homology indicates shared characteristics due to common ancestry, as between apes and people. Analogy suggests resemblances in physical form or in behavior as a result of adaptation to similar environmental forces, as between horses and people.[26] Although analogous parallel evolution may or may not explain the similarities between horses and humans, it will be invoked occasionally. Because multi-causal approaches are usually more enlightening than mono-causal, world-systems analysis and bio-history add yet other perspectives and help point out resemblances between groups of controllers and controllees.

Certainly, basic similitudes between the western and Kenyan frontier experiences are becoming increasingly clear to scholars. In 1966, a scholar of British policy in Kenya, Marjorie R. Dilley, remarked almost casually, "Kenya reminds one of the development of the American frontier." From the perspective of the 1990s and 2000s, however, congruence appears to be obvious. In 1995, an expert on colonialism, Jürgen Osterhammel, resolutely stated, "Only Britain and the United States have been imperialist powers in the full sense of the term." Two years later, the American historian Gregory H. Nobles suggested that rather than exploring what the noted western historian Frederick Jackson Turner called the "closing of the frontier," researchers should think instead in terms of "the colonization of the Great West." The historian Walter Nugent added that during the late nineteenth and early twentieth centuries, "the frontier impulse and the imperial impulse were related in source and performance" so that imperial ventures "appear to be a special type of frontier." Most recently, the western historian Patricia Nelson Limerick commented that "the United States's imperial history and, say, Britain's imperial history, is underdeveloped, neglected, even concealed."[27]

Corresponding traits between the American West and Kenya were indeed numerous. In both, the peoples of a "mother" country thought themselves superior enough to impose their ways on others. The opening of the American West and Kenya to outsiders was based upon colonialist thinking—called Manifest Destiny in the American West and imperialism in Kenya. Thus, both the West and Kenya had a historical background of exploration and settlement by Great Britain. After the United States declared independence from Britain, the new American government administered its frontiers from afar, first as government-owned lands and territories, later as states, with expanding rights for white American men and women. Similarly, Britain ruled Kenya indirectly, first as a protectorate, later as a colony, with growing representation for white British men and women. In both cases, local leeway existed. Although the American West was under the jurisdiction of federal statutes, it had unusual flexibility in establishing state and county provisions. In Kenya, local custom and rules also influenced such matters as marriage, divorce, and inheritance.

The American West and Kenya had other characteristics in common. The development of the two regions overlapped the epoch between 1840 and 1940. The hundred-year period witnessed first a sharp rise in white expansion in the American West—meaning the Great Plains, the Southwest, California, and the Pacific Northwest—and later in Kenya. Both frontiers were primarily English-speaking "settler" societies grounded mostly in agriculture and commerce. Because such settlement depended upon the inclusion and support of women, the roles of women and their children were enhanced. In addition, the American West and Kenya contained frontier conditions. Both were geographical territories in which two or more groups of people met and were involved in the process of resistance by native peoples to intruders intent on imposing their own economic, political, religious, and cultural forms, whether welcome or not (see below for further discussion of what constitutes a frontier).[28]

Even the physical terrains of the two regions were similarly vast and varied in their physical and cultural characteristics. Both had deserts; the West especially became known for its tumbleweeds and dryland vegetation. Both also had wet areas; Kenya was often thought of as a tropical clime with exotic plants, which, in fact, flourished mostly along the muggy coast. In neither case did these images characterize the whole. Clearly, the American West and frontier Kenya were established more according to American and British government definitions and needs rather than such natural demarcations as geographical unity, similarities of peoples and cultures, or kin and ancestral allegiances. Once designated, the West and Kenya became accepted geographical denotations and governing units. The two not only gained identity in people's minds as unified regions, but they offered such gorgeous visual panoramas that they became tourist destinations even as they were being colonized.

Besides general similarities between the American and Kenyan frontiers, white women's attitudes and adaptation show a number of corresponding characteristics. For instance, white female settlers on these frontiers typically subscribed to the colonialist and racialist beliefs in vogue during the nineteenth and early twentieth centuries. White female migrants to these two frontier regions carried with them the gendered conviction that they had a duty to help "deprived" and "primitive" native peoples by bringing them "up" to the level of their own culture and civilizations. In part, helping others had to do with patriotism. The Asia scholar Benedict Anderson points out that emergent nationalism not only aroused a love of country, but of duty as well. Spread and recapitulated in the new print media, notably newspapers and novels, nationalist discourse inspired men to die in battle and women to migrate to far-flung lands in the name of service.[29]

This pervasive belief in helping others, or "genteel conceit," bored a few white women and inspired many others, but for most it constituted an omnipresent responsibility. Women's homogeneity on this point is unsurprising given white women's common heritage of evangelical Christianity, Darwinian social theories, and long-standing convictions regarding white superiority. Both western and Kenyan white migrants used the genteel conceit as a convenient rationale for settlement. It allowed white women to push—uninvited—into other peoples' countries. It gave them what they judged a satisfactory reason to appropriate land, to establish homes and such institutions as schools and churches, and to develop a feeling of ownership for the areas they seized. Regarding such other important issues as the reforms women promoted, how they appeared to others, and changes they sustained as a result of migrating to a frontier, a close reading of white women's documents shows that a number of them questioned imperialistic values. Colonized themselves by gender, and frequently by ethnicity or social class, some women became suspicious of doctrines based upon the inherent superiority of one group of people over another. They especially developed sympathy for indigenous females who, to them, seemed too much under the thrall of men.

White women's occasional hesitation made them no less effective as colonizers. White women often outdid men in insinuating their culture's values into native societies. Although white men frequently used the schoolroom and church to get their messages across, they were a small proportion of all white men, the majority of whom conquered and colonized by force, economic dominance, and legislation, all of which drew protests from indigenes. Women did their conquering and colonizing on a less conspicuous level, innocuous enough to raise relatively little resistance. Also, a high proportion of white women were involved in sensitive cross-cultural interactions related to domestic life, educational endeavors, and the intricacies of daily culture. It might be said that most men excelled in colonizing the body, whereas most women became especially adept at what the Kenyan writer and activist Ngũgĩ Wa Thiong'o calls conolonizing the mind.[30]

Thus, it is argued here that women provided the real glue of empire, from attitudes and folkways to domestic consumerism.[31] Because women had closer relationships with indigenes than did men, they had more influence on them. It was women, after all, who were primarily responsible for instruction in manners, language, clothing, food, material goods, and, along with those, beliefs and aspirations. In public settings, women missionaries, teachers, and nurses formally taught the rudiments of white civilization. In the home and on the farm, white mother figures modeled white ideals on a daily basis. As employers and supervisors, white women insisted on white standards of behavior. From properly setting a tea table and developing an appreciation for certain commercial products to feeling guilty if a piece of cloth did not cover one's nakedness, women subtly subverted the values of Native Americans and black Kenyans.

In the face of resistance to their offerings, some white women grew more determined and convinced of the superiority of their ways. They seemed to have a number of handy rationales, including the argument that indigenous people were too "primitive" to recognize the value of white people's offerings. When aboriginal men and women expressed displeasure with the situation by slackening at their work, appropriating foodstuffs and other goods for themselves, and accepting some white ideas while ignoring others, white women attributed such actions to a lack of sophistication rather than purposeful rejection.

This long list of similarities is not meant to argue that the American and Kenyan frontiers were clones. Besides sharing certain characteristics, the two regions differed from each other in crucial ways. The two locales lay thousands of miles away from each other and encompassed racially disparate indigenous populations. Much of the American West was arid, whereas Kenya experienced wet and dry seasons. Wildlife was often dissimilar as well. In the American West, such animals as bison and wild horses graced the landscape, while in Kenya giraffes and wildebeests roamed the countryside.

In addition, beginnings and endings came at slightly different times in the West and in Kenya. The American West underwent extensive growth between 1840 and the early 1890s,[32] whereas the Kenyan frontier sprouted much later—between the 1890s and 1940s.

More specifically, in 1840 the first big wagon trains of settlers headed toward the Oregon country, at the same time that explorers and traders began to invade Kenya. After fifty years of vigorous westward migration, the era of the frontier West appeared to be finished. Despite the fact that sizeable numbers of settlers continued to move westward during the 1880s and 1890s, in 1890, the U.S. Bureau of the Census declared the American frontier "closed" by virtue of its population, an average of two people per square mile.

During the early 1890s, the British in Kenya were on a different trajectory. The British government built a railroad and urged white settlers to take up land. After World War I, Britain renewed its commitment to colonize Kenya by supporting a soldier settlement scheme in which veterans drew lots that allowed them to claim land in Kenya. According to the Kenyan historian E. S. Atieno-Odhiambo, the eruption of World War II, which began for Kenyans in July 1940 when Italian troops attacked Moyale in northern Kenya, marked the beginning of a new epoch. The historian Margaret Strobel agrees that imperialism reached its height in Africa before World War II.[33] Although black Kenyans had long resisted imperialism in a wide range of ways, after the war's end they—especially the Kikuyu—stepped up their opposition of the British. As white settlement continued and even grew significantly after World War II, black Kenyans demonstrated increasingly vocal and violent defiance to white incursion, especially white settlers who took additional land. Because compliance no longer seemed a useful or appropriate strategy, the same black Kenyans who had worn a veneer of western civilization, education, and religion before the war became, after the war's end, supporters and leaders of Kenya's emerging independence movement, known throughout the world as the Mau Mau Emergency or Mau Mau Rebellion.

Because of these date differentials, the American West and Kenya also experienced separate technological innovations. In the American West, the nineteenth-century Industrial Revolution supplied steamships, railroads, the telegraph, sophisticated weaponry, and improved printing presses, which made newspapers and magazines widely available. Between 1840 and 1890, these and other new technologies eased travel, communication, and defense for western settlers, at the same time making it more difficult for Native Americans to resist. That American Indians realized they were fighting a battle against people *and* technology is demonstrated by stories of Indians damaging railroad track, cutting telegraph lines, and chopping down telegraph poles. In Kenya, new generations of technological advances aided white settlement. Although black Kenyans also destroyed or carried off what they could, between 1890 and 1940, canned foods, improved medicines, and pasteurization made it possible for white Europeans to relocate in a land different from the one to which they were accustomed. Internal combustion engines, wireless communication, and airplanes gave white settlers an advantage that helped compensate for their small numbers in comparison to huge numbers of black Kenyans.

Other variations occurred in political and economic structures. The American West was one region in an independent nation, the United States, whereas Kenya was part of a far-flung empire, Great Britain, which never granted white Kenyans self-rule. According to the historian William G. Robbins, the American West was highly accessible and extremely rich in land, mineral resources, and potential transportation routes.[34] In Kenya, climatic extremes and a basically agrarian economy presented barriers to capitalist innovation and the introduction of some technology.

In addition, distance constituted an important variable. While the American West was physically attached to the eastern United States and remained under the sometimes tenuous control of officials in Washington, D.C., Kenya lay an ocean away from Great Britain. Even though technology had improved, notably rail and steamship transportation, British officials sometimes found it difficult to send adequate supplies, remain abreast of the issues that engaged white Kenyans, or encourage large numbers of white settlers to undertake the arduous trip. As a result, Kenya's white settlers had little political or numerical power and were more of a transient than a permanent population.[35]

Labor systems differed as well. Although white westerners sometimes employed Native Americans and other peoples of color, they did not become dependent on such help. Rather, white westerners usually supplied their own workforce or "hired-out" to others. In Kenya, white settlers imposed a coercive labor scheme on black Kenyans. Consequently, a relatively small number of white settlers felt extremely reliant on black Kenyans to work their farms and plantations.

Settlers also fared differently in the two regions. In the American West, settlers received constant boosts from immigration and high birthrates. In addition, westerners had at their disposal a huge land area over which to disperse the native population. In Kenya, whites received some reinforcement, especially from soldier-settlement schemes after world wars, but it was not enough to offset large numbers of black Kenyans. Eventually, the imbalance in the white/black population and the growing dissatisfaction of both sides created great potential for revolution by black Kenyans. In other words, settlers in the American West constituted a moving frontier, a mobile society that encompassed many groups, but in Kenya the settler population was generally static, both numerically and geographically.[36] The American West remained part of its mother country, but in 1963 black Kenyans proclaimed themselves free and independent of British authority. Black Kenyans moved beyond their hidden derision of whites to public insubordination, ranging from clear refusal to accept the white system to violent acts of defiance. Although American Indians were unable to reclaim their lands and hegemony, black Kenyans were able to do so.

Women of Color

Because white women were highly visible and left ample written sources behind, they have claimed the bulk of historians' attention—and will be a major focus here, largely because they were the leading group of female colonizers in the American West and Kenya. According to modern standards, white women were admirable on some levels, as in their adaptability, whereas on other levels they were despicable, especially regarding their racialist attitudes. White women were not the only female newcomers on frontiers, however. In the

American West, Hispanic frontierswomen predated white women settlers, whereas such other groups as African American and Asian women came with, or after, them. In Kenya, Asian Indian women formed the largest—but not the only—female-settler community of color.

Women settlers of color are included here when materials are available or have been collected by the author. As the western historian Richard White says regarding evidence that is "scattered, partial, and difficult to decipher," the "trick is to work with what you have."[37] Thus, rather than pretending to be a full ethnographic history of these women, their inclusion is an attempt to avoid ghettoization—meaning frontier history that assesses *either* white people *or* those of color. The postcolonial scholars Frederick Cooper and Ann Laura Stoler warn that pitting white colonizers against the colonized results in one-dimensional history. According to them, "the Manichaean world of high colonialism that we have etched so deeply in our historiographies" is inaccurate.[38] Nor is anything gained by leaving out of the narrative female migrants of color. Consequently, in an effort to present more of a textured tapestry, this book presents several points of view, including some evidence of what the literary critic Gayatri Chakravorty Spivak calls the "subaltern voice."[39] Along the way, it is argued that women of all ethnicities and races developed a variety of coping and resistance mechanisms, thus exercising more influence and agency than is usually attributed to them.[40]

Keeping in mind the warning of the women's historian Joan Scott that many differences existed *within* groups, some generalizations can be made.[41] Shared characteristics of female migrants of color often included poverty, prejudice, marginalization by their home societies, previous colonization, or even enslavement. Ordinarily, these women hoped to attain a better economic and social status than they had at home. Once on a frontier, however, they found themselves caught somewhere between white settlers and indigenes. Migrants of color tried to adapt to changeable conditions and to develop mechanisms to prevent their control by whites. Also, much like white women, female migrants of color struggled to preserve their own customs and beliefs in a land strange to them. Because the details of women's frontiering process frequently transcended place, the makeup of indigenous peoples, and time period, both white women and those of color developed analogous solutions in such matters as food, housing, and clothing. Other concerns, however, notably education, employment, race, or religion, created an unbridgeable chasm between groups of women.

Indigenous women were also part of these frontiers, or colonization processes, albeit unwillingly. Because groups like American Indians and black Kenyans frequently relied on oral tradition and group recollections, written source materials are sparse. Even written documents have been excluded from what the Canadian anthropologist Michael G. Kenny calls "collective memory," usually by white colonialists who wrote histories and controlled archives.[42] Yet writing frontier history that totally ignores indigenous women is a kind of scholarly imperialism, in that it explores the history of white people in lands originally inhabited and controlled by peoples of color, and applies "white" research questions to historical developments there. Scholars in many disciplines are working to right these imbalances, in part by utilizing source materials that relate to indigenes, such as court records, wills, employment files, and tax receipts, and in part by developing a strong indigenous perspective in their research designs.

All this and more has evolved in less than fifty years. Women's studies, Native American studies, and African studies date back only to the turbulent 1960s. In that decade, practitioners in these areas had first to demonstrate that women, Indians, and Africans had an impact on historical events. During the 1970s and 1980s, researchers retrieved sources, experimented with a variety of approaches, and developed an array of interpretations. During the 1990s and early 2000s, scholars demonstrated growing sophistication, exploring such issues as race, gender, ethnicity, class, migration, and types of colonialism. Thus, the history of the conquered is being told, from its beginnings through colonial eras and on to more recent developments.

To fill the gaps, researchers frequently rely on oral history, often in the form of what the scholar Claire C. Robertson terms "life histories."[43] This study not only draws on existing transcriptions, but uses oral interviews conducted with black Kenyans, especially those who worked for white settlers. Of course, there is a measure of risk in oral history. The editor of *Comparative Studies in Society and History*, Thomas R. Trautman, comments that although oral recollections give a human flavor and immediacy to historical investigation, interviews must be used judiciously because people "adjust" their remembrances as they age.[44] In addition, collective traditions, including family lore and orally transmitted tales, are often invented.[45] But interviews do show what people choose to remember, as well as reflecting a group's oral traditions.

From available resources, several aspects emerge regarding aboriginal women's lives under white occupation. Although original residents possessed the land and resources that white colonists wanted, they were at a disadvantage. In many ways, early inhabitants of the American West and of Kenya were in a pre-modern stage of development. Rather than forming united and strong nation-states, members of indigenous societies lived in a wide range of kin- or lineage-based systems, which were sometimes hostile to each other. Although indigenes were not isolated from the rest of the world and had long engaged in trade, the rise of the West, especially Europe, beginning around 1400 and the decline of the East beginning around 1800 made it possible for capitalistic and industrialized European invaders to bring with them to North America and East Africa the latest technology in tools and weapons. In the major textbook used in Kenya today, W. R. Ochieng' explains this happening by saying that iron-age Africa had "fallen behind the strong powers of the rest of the world in the ability to produce goods, whether for war or for peace."[46]

As a result of white conquest, indigenous women found themselves pushed to the margins culturally and economically. Most suffered from poverty and racial prejudice. They saw their cultures sustain irreparable damage. Yet they were not victims or dolts. Rather, they combined passive-aggressive resistance, which historians now recognize as forms of agency and defiance, with increasingly outward and even violent resistance.

The Nature of Frontiers

In addition to perspectives and source materials, another topic that needs to be addressed at the outset is the meaning of the term *frontier*. In both the American West and Kenya, the existence of frontiers pre-dated the arrival of white settlers. In writing about African frontiers, for example, the anthropologist Igor Kopytoff points out that they occurred regularly in African history and did not always involve racial differences. Throughout Africa's history, kin- or lineage-based groups moved to new areas where they overpowered, usually through force, people born in the area. These conquests were often by, and of, black Africans. According to Kopytoff, such factors as "famines, civil wars, ethnic rivalries, despotic regimes, and conflicts between polities" made Africa and its migrating populations a "frontier continent."[47]

This study, however, concentrates on frontiers initiated by the appearance of white conquerors. Even with this limitation, frontiers are difficult to define. Regarding the American West, in spite of a rich and varied literature, its historians have long disagreed on what constitutes a frontier. This heterogeneity is easier to comprehend if one thinks of history as another form of social discourse (usually white dominated), vulnerable to changing attitudes and beliefs. Three recent books are especially useful in understanding the debate. The historian Richard W. Etulain's *Re-Imagining the Modern American* explores the fiction, history, and art of the American frontier, whereas historian Richard W. Slatta's *Comparing Cowboys and Frontiers* demonstrates ways to deconstruct frontier images. The historian Walter Nugent's *Into the West: The Story of Its People* indicates the complexity of the West and its varied inhabitants.[48]

In recent decades, western historians have reached an uneasy compromise about the term *frontier*. For one thing, they agree that a frontier is a *place*, that is, a definable territory with set boundaries. In the American-history tradition, this place is usually defined geographically. Although frontiers and regions might be cultural, economic, or political entities, American historians ordinarily view them as physical. Even *Webster's Dictionary* describes a frontier as a geographical place: "the border or confine of a country abutting on the territory of another; the part of a settled, civilized country nearest to an unsettled or uncivilized region."[49] Thus, a frontier generally takes in a sizeable amount of terrain with such distinctive characteristics as aridity and scattered aboriginal populations.

Because the movement of peoples across these places is key, a frontier might also be a moving place.[50] One example is the farmers' frontier, meaning the introduction of white-style agriculture into such areas as Iowa and Kansas, and across the West to California and the Pacific Northwest. Or a moving frontier might refer to the zone of contact between invaders and indigenes as it ebbed and flowed across an area. Thus, mini-frontiers may exist within a macro-frontier and locations of specific frontiers may change over time. Also, frontiers may be short lived, as was the Appalachian frontier in the mid-eastern United States during the late 1700s.

Western historians also generally agree that the second element of a frontier is *process*, meaning that people from another region or nation migrate to a place where they attempt to control and dominate original residents, exploit resources, and direct political, economic, and cultural life. According to Nugent, these newly arrived people, often whites, attempt to change and destroy thousands of years of tradition, imposing their own ways instead. These include forcing their language and religion on conquered people, building towns and cities, and establishing market agriculture and other aspects of capitalism.[51] At the same time, other groups of immigrants, often peoples of color, arrive. Although they have more modest aspirations, they are caught in the cultural crossfire between conquerors and conquered. The frontier process, then, was one of social change and volatility for many groups.

In this inquiry, the widely accepted two-part definition of frontiers as place and process is expanded to include four phases of frontiering, both for the American West and for Kenya. The first addition is *philosophy*, which takes into account the ideology, attitudes, and values of frontierspeople. Well before migration, men and women, again usually white, had to accept a philosophy that underwrote migration and potential settlement. They had to believe that for some reason—such as their group's perceived moral superiority, advanced technological know-how, or emergent capitalism—they not only had the right, but the responsibility to seize another group's territory and show its former inhabitants how to run it in ways whites thought better. "Better" meant proceeding according to invaders' standards and might include the exploitation of natural resources or the imposition of a mandated labor system on indigenous people. Better might also include barring people from growing competing crops, at which they had often become proficient.

Such migrants either had to believe their group's rationales or at least espouse them. Even if individuals recognized that they were about to pillage and exploit, ultimately at great cost to the land and its original inhabitants, they seldom admitted their misgivings. Rather, they typically cloaked their inner feelings with outward bravado, such as declaring the responsibility to spread "advanced white civilization" to other countries, or of ridding the world economy of what they regarded as inefficient production in certain regions, such as parts of the American West and of Africa. On their journeys, migrants used their time to reinforce the rightness of their philosophy. By assessing the indigenes they met as "barbarians," or repeating exaggerated rumors regarding "hostiles" and "attacks," migrants convinced themselves that their particular frontier would indeed benefit from their presence and ministrations. They not only reassured themselves that they would survive and conquer, they practiced the necessary skills, including handling firearms.

In a sense, this first stage of a frontier—the development and espousal of beliefs and attitudes—was the most important one, for it underwrote the remaining three phases. When migrants finally reached their frontier *place*, the philosophy that rationalized their endeavors thus far helped keep their backs straight and their trigger fingers steady. Their convictions also allowed migrants to bemoan the "primitive" nature of the place and the "backward" condition of its inhabitants, including immigrants of color. With confidence, they initiated the process of "settling" their frontier. Philosophy also sustained white settlers during *process* when blood was shed, homes demolished, family members scattered, and cultures damaged or destroyed. During this third phase of a frontier, one faction of people, often the invaders, assumed authority over others. This ascendancy might be uneasy and soon toppled, or it might stay in place for so many generations that it became the accepted way of doing things.

The definition of a frontier cannot stop here, however. Philosophy, place, and process always culminated in a *product*. Typically, product began to emerge during a frontier "period." Moreover, product remained in existence long after a given frontier closed. Comparison indicates that in the American West and on the Kenyan frontier the impact of values, beliefs, and ideology played a pivotal role in frontier interactions. In both regions, however, white values underwrote a philosophy that led to a faulty product. Much of frontier product resulted from white settlers' racist standards and policies. Although white migrants instituted their ideas during the frontier era, those beliefs linger on, even during the early twenty-first century. Racist beliefs continue to influence such matters as who is hired for what job, who lives where, and who marries whom. Related "products" are the bitterness and even hatred that many aboriginal peoples hold toward the invaders. The other side of this product is that people of color have spoken up and fought back, making contemporary white people more aware of their tendency to "colonize" others.

Because these and other frontier products lasted for generations, their perceived value frequently changed over time. In most instances, initial praise gave way to criticism and opposition. Indigenous peoples, who often welcomed early waves of whites, usually expressed the first objections, especially in the form of defiance, including verbal complaints, armed revolution, or far more subtle forms of protest. In other words, when indigenes' grievances were ignored and their charges went unanswered, they found other ways to express their disapproval of the system.

Dissatisfaction from conquered peoples is unsurprising, but protests also came from less predictable sources. In some cases, censure flowed from the people who stayed home in mother countries, who had at first viewed migrants as national heroes and heroines. After they became disillusioned with expansionism and realized the costs, they labeled migrants as greedy spoilers. Another group of critics were white travelers who toured the West or Kenya, often with the intention of writing books, articles, and newspaper columns. Even though some visitors lauded pioneers, others blasted them verbally. Nor did reproach cease when a particular frontier "ended." In numerous cases, denunciation increased as time passed. A frontier might close, but its product lived on, as did criticism of the product.

Combining the above four elements—philosophy, place, process, and product—in studying a frontier gives a fuller understanding of the scope and effects of mass migrations by "pioneers" to areas they viewed as "unsettled." This is not meant to suggest that aboriginal peoples would define frontier development in the same way or with similar stages. For example, Ochieng' presents the Kenyan frontier as a bipolar struggle: "at one pole stood industrial Europe, at the other stood the disinherited." For Ochieng', this contest led to a final stage—"a world order founded on conquest and maintained by force."[52]

The four-part definition of a frontier is still useful, however. It encourages discussion of the interaction between indigenes, white settlers, migrants of color, and folks back home, for it was such interaction that shaped a specific frontier. Perhaps most importantly, the four stages of a frontier indicate how transitory phases turned into modern social issues.

Organization and Terms

Because all four elements of the expanded definition of a frontier apply to the American West and to Kenya, chapters are arranged in four parts: a frontier as philosophy, place, process, and product. The theme of identifying similarities and differences between women on the two frontiers runs throughout the book, but women's expectations, responses, contributions, and reputations are grouped according to the four-part scheme.

More specifically, philosophy is the organizing principle of the first two chapters, which consider women's reasons for migrating, as well as the use they made—or did not make—of their journeys as a time of transition. The next set of two chapters falls under place: what women discovered in terms of urban and rural landscapes when they arrived on a frontier, how they established their personal and domestic space, and what impact their endeavors had on others. The following sequence of two chapters relates to process: how women entered the public realm, what they wanted in terms of reforms, and how their programs affected indigenous peoples. The last two chapters speak to a frontier as product: they explore how female migrants appeared to others, what indigenes thought of them, and what women endured from the very structures they helped create.

Several notes on terminology are in order. Throughout, the term *scholars* refers to historians, anthropologists, and other social scientists. For the American West, Manifest Destiny means the belief of Americans, Canadians, Europeans, and others that they had a divine right to migrate to and settle in the American West. Although white Americans of the time considered native-born Indians as foreigners with whom they had to make treaties, here they are identified as Americans, either American Indians or Native Americans. Hispanics are also called peoples of Spanish heritage. White people are sometimes Anglos. Blacks are also termed African Americans. Those from Asia are Asians. Settlers usually meant people who took up residence in the American West for a finite period or for a lifetime.

Because most readers are likely to know little about Kenya's frontier period and its female settlers, Kenya receives more attention throughout than does the American West. Each chapter also includes coverage of the earlier frontier period, 1840 to 1890, in the American West, compared to similar situations in Kenya. Examples used relate to all areas of the trans-Mississippi West, ranging from what many Americans think of as the Old Wild West—the prairie and Plains— to the Southwest and Pacific Northwest.

Regarding terminology relating to Kenya, imperialism indicates a broad, inclusive concept supporting a transcolonial empire. Colony denotes an organizational body, as in the Kenya Colony. Although Kenya was called the British East Africa Protectorate from 1895 to 1920, and became Kenya Colony in 1920 (until 1963), the name Kenya is used generically to designate the area in both time periods. Other terms that need explanation describe the peoples of Kenya. Blacks are called black Kenyans or, when possible, identified by such group names as Kikuyu, Maasai, or Nandi. Whites are termed whites, Europeans, or white Kenyans. Those from India are Asian Indians. In Kenya, the term *settler* was more limited than in the West; it meant white farmers or other entrepreneurs who came to stay. Missionaries and officials were not usually considered settlers, nor were Asian Indians. Where appropriate, sources used are identified according to group.

The desire to be inclusive has obviously complicated some things, but it has also produced a richer and more textured scholarship. It is far better to have a small amount of confusion than a good deal of exclusion, as in the past.

A Frontier as Philosophy

ONE
A Genteel Conceit

WHY would women—white or of color—agree to relocate on frontiers geographically and culturally worlds apart from their own homes? The customary answer has been that women followed men to frontiers. After all, what could be more appealing and romantic—or typically female—than allowing men and relationships to shape one's life?

In fact, numerous women did go to the American West, as well as to Kenya, alongside men, in the paths of men, and in search of men to marry. Yet many women—single and married—went to these frontiers for many other reasons, as varied as those that motivated men. Far from being immune to frontier philosophies that urged men to migrate, women listened to the arguments, rationales, and theories of their eras, adapting them to female value systems. Although women were sometimes aware of government machinations behind the scenes and of arguments against expansion, they could still relate to pleas based upon what appeared to be morality and justice. Altruistic migration especially appealed to white women, who reassured themselves they would be entering a reciprocal relationship with indigenes; they would trade their skills and assistance for what they thought of as open and unclaimed land.

As postcolonial scholars note, white women's motivations do not make their views moral or excuse the damage they did. Still, as the historian Margaret Strobel posits, it is unlikely that white women would reject their era's values and beliefs, replacing them with more modern attitudes. In other words, the historical reality is that Manifest Destiny did sweep over the American West, just as an imperialistic British empire did exist.[1] To understand women on frontiers, it is necessary to explore white women's adaptations of the myths of unoccupied lands and unoccupied minds to rationalize their intrusion into the West and Kenya.

For white women, two widely touted beliefs proved compelling. Both shared the underlying—and unquestioned—assumption that "superior" white people had the right to invade lands held by "inferior" peoples of color. The first belief urged people to migrate to a frontier to help someone, perhaps by providing medical care or religious education. The second claimed that even people who migrated to advance themselves, financially or otherwise, would still help others, perhaps by providing models of entrepreneurship or of monogamous marriage. These two themes were the major components of the frontier philosophy that prevailed in the nineteenth-century United States, as well as in early twentieth-century Great Britain. Called "Manifest Destiny" in America and "imperialism" in Britain, high-flown rhetoric assured potential white pioneers that they had a duty to carry their religion, technology, and "civilized" values to aboriginal peoples.

Helping Others in the American West

During the nineteenth century, American women grew up hearing patriotic messages urging citizens to reach out to others, especially the poverty stricken, the non-Christian, and the ill. As adults, literate white women were subjected to pro-frontier hyperbole through magazines and books, as well as printed sermons and speeches. Because imperialism had already begun to peak during the mid-nineteenth century, when Manifest Destiny caught the American imagination, justification for expansion had to be ardent and convincing. Leaders had to persuade themselves and others that the imperialist dream was not only alive and well, but was "right." Consequently, arguments drew heavily on long-standing and widely accepted Anglo-American traditions of racism and domination of others, asserting that the rich should assist the poor and the "superior" should lift up the "inferior." At the same time, such theories espoused eventual liberty for colonized populations. These objectives seemed so right and selfless—at least to white people—that critics seldom spoke out publicly.[2]

Meanwhile, gendered discourse assured women that outreach was particularly a female obligation. White women of the middle and upper classes especially adopted these attitudes, which might be called "a genteel conceit." It was widely believed that these women should use their "domestic seclusion" as a base from which to promote virtue, preserve their cultures, and inculcate others with their values. Nineteenth-century communities increasingly expected women also to act as conservators of family, tradition, and beliefs, and to serve as municipal housekeepers who organized society much as they ordered their own homes. Consequently, such endeavors as teaching Sunday school and organizing volunteer civic-improvement organizations attracted significant numbers of women. Additionally, as health givers, religious models, and ethical advisors of their families, women had skills to help peoples they believed to be needy.

In the American West, however, white women's desire to be of assistance often created chaos. What one scholar has called "conquest through benevolence" seldom turned out the way women hoped.[3] In the West, maternal domination took many forms. Between 1840 and 1890, Christianity and its missionaries appeared early. Women missionaries believed they had a "female" duty to spread Christianity, along with American-style democracy. Although these women aided American Indians in many ways, they constituted part of the wedge being driven between Indians and their lives, lands, and cultures. By teaching Native Americans the principles of Christianity, the "three Rs," and basic white customs and beliefs, white women often helped damage native cultures, traditions, and self-esteem.

Another group who wanted to "do good" in the West were abolitionists. Although the West is usually thought of as "free" territory, some white settlers brought slaves westward with them. Before the Emancipation Proclamation of 1863 abolished slavery in the United States, taking slaves westward was legal, except in the Northwest Territory where the Northwest Ordinance of 1787 had outlawed slavery. The rest of the West generally had little use for the institution because of philosophical or economic reasons, or both. Notable exceptions were the present-day states of Missouri, Texas, and Oklahoma.

Besides missionaries and abolitionists, a significant number of white women hoped to serve in other ways, especially as teachers and nurses. Of the helping professions open to nineteenth-century women, teaching was regarded as a natural concomitant to women's domestic duties. Women supposedly possessed inbred talents for child care and nurturing. Also, they supposedly had high character and a capacity for tenderness for their charges, which would be improper for the "other sex," as men were called during the late nineteenth century. As male teachers learned that they could earn higher wages and hold year-round employment in factories, stores, and offices, teaching jobs throughout the West opened for women. One observer noted that women teachers were willing to "elbow aside" male teachers. Women teachers, who accepted less pay than men, soon outnumbered male teachers in the trans-Mississippi West.[4]

Unlike teachers, female nurses were not prominent in the West. In the United States, women who nursed as a career were few. During the 1840s and 1850s, nursing had not yet professionalized. Rather, women were expected, as part of their domestic duties, to serve their families and neighbors as nurses, midwives, and apothecaries. Sometimes, women were "neighborhood nurses," who received payments ranging from a verbal thank-you to cash or goods. Gradually, however, nursing separated from women's domestic duties, especially during the Civil War. Because the number of male nurses proved insufficient, women were recruited and hastily trained. Although these women received pitifully low wages, they demonstrated that women made excellent nurses and that schools must be established for them. Consequently, by the 1880s a number of trained nurses went West, such as widow Jean Todd. After Todd arrived in South Dakota in 1887, she not only practiced nursing but acted as midwife and mortician.[5]

Even though the mythology of the region overlooks them, female doctors also migrated to the West. In novels, films, and television programs, the kindly country doctor, a hardy old gentleman making his rounds by wagon or buggy during a blizzard or dust storm, is prominent, while women doctors are virtually invisible. Yet women doctors went to all parts of the West. During the 1880s, German-born and trained Dr. Friede Feige established herself as a physician in Dakota Territory, while her husband homesteaded. Farther west in Sacramento, California, Dr. Lavinia Goodyear Waterhouse became a successful hydropathic physician.[6]

Clearly, the concept of "civilizing" and helping native peoples constituted a powerful motivator. White women believed that the willingness to give of oneself for the good of the nation demonstrated that American society had a high moral tone. Moreover, in an era of industrialization that raised fears about ethics and integrity, Americans who migrated westward to help others offset fears regarding the declining morals of Americans.

Despite the presence of so many benevolent women, the American West was far from a benevolent place. White women usually thought of their own ways as peerless. For instance, although some came to see the Native American point of view, others were arrogant and insulting, so that Indians rejected their help or learned to take from them only what they could use. As a result, the West's peoples of color still mistrust whites and blame whites for their misfortunes.

Helping Others in Kenya

A similar scenario played itself out decades later in Kenya, where white women who intended to do good found themselves, in the long run, doing evil. The historical experience of women in the American West was lost on them. They also apparently discounted negative input from what one historian termed "a momentous debate" regarding imperialism. Beginning as early as 1870, anti-imperialists made their arguments known through every medium available. Citizens opposed to the high taxes needed to fund colonial developments stood against expansion. Cultural relativists maintained that Great Britain did not have enough to offer to justify seizing other nations. The "free trade" advocates felt that economic gains would be few. Yet, even in the face of growing criticism that imperialism and its "racial theory" were wrong headed and potentially harmful for indigenes and their cultures, Kenya-bound migrants seemed undeterred.[7] If one accepts the argument of bio-historians, it would have been impossible for white settlers to learn anything from their predecessors. Rather, a biological need to aggrandize others kept them going.

Certainly, the contention that English-speaking societies were innately superior and that it was women's duty to spread white "civilization" and "truth" around the world were more meaningful to women than were the negative arguments of anti-imperialists. Not only did women's culture dictate service, but women's conceptions of "savages" and "inferior" peoples had a long history in Europe, dating back at least to the sixteenth century. Over the years, the notion grew that white Christians could retrieve from the depths of depravity non-white peoples, who after all were noble in heart. In addition, the image of Africa exerted a powerful hold on Europeans. To Anglo-Europeans, the continent appeared mysterious and unfathomable, and its people "primitive" and "barbarous." Rather than recognizing that European civilization had its roots in Africa, European thinkers and writers viewed their cultures as distinct and exceptional. Their view of Africans as lesser "others" underwrote what the African scholar V. Y. Mudimbe calls Britain's "will to power," or "negative paradigm," that allowed colonialism to develop.[8]

Social constructions regarding what women were supposed to be and do especially affected literate, leisured white women. These women internalized a number of maxims that although gendered, were increasingly wide-ranging: "civilize" wherever you go, do good (as you understand it), and provide a model of womanhood and of the "civilized" world for those you meet. Apparently, women could leave the confines of their homes, or even cross national borders, to pursue charitable and benevolent works.[9] Thus, thousands of these women supported Great Britain's earliest avowed reason for involvement in East Africa—the abolition of the slave trade along the coast and in Zanzibar, the British center for their intercession in the area. Beginning in the 1770s, the English evangelical movement urged the abolition of slavery, especially in the African and Caribbean holdings of the British empire. By the 1830s, abolition of slavery became a British cause and abolitionist leaders a political force. Yet Britain itself had once engaged in an active slave trade, a fact that was far from forgotten. In 1836, in the midst of Britain's abolitionist efforts, an American writer reminded the British that they held "the first guilt of the introduction of slavery" into the United States.[10]

British reformers seemed determined to respond to such criticisms. Government leaders passed the British empire's first abolition provisions, which were to take effect between 1834 and 1838.[11] Having cleansed itself, Britain wanted to purge others, especially the major source of slaves, Africa. During the 1830s and 1840s, the British government inaugurated a crusade to abolish the slave trade along the East African coast. British leaders hoped to block Arab and other slave traders from going about their centuries-old business, especially from their Zanzibar base. To achieve this, British officials based antislavery fleets at the southerly islands of Seychelles and Mauritius, British controlled since 1794 and 1810, respectively. The British government emancipated all slaves in the Seychelles and Mauritius in 1835. Moreover, during the next few years it relocated on the Seychelles twenty-five hundred freed slaves.[12]

Of course, business-minded Britons recognized that their industrializing nation stood to profit from a free Africa that produced raw materials and consumed manufactured goods. The scholar Andre Gunder Frank points out that because the East declined around 1800, Europe easily entered the expanding Asian trade network and soon devised a complex imperial system. Aggressive white Europeans intended to make the most of the situation.[13] Englishman Cecil John Rhodes, who made a fortune from mining diamonds in South Africa, put it succinctly: "I would annex the stars, if I could." Yet reformers emphasized the glory of emancipation and the moral righteousness of the abolition of slavery in Africa, proclaiming that only by working within the boundaries of Christian morality would capitalism revolutionize the world's undeveloped areas.[14]

By the mid-1800s, white Victorians obviously believed in their ability to change the world, especially halting the East African slave trade. As an 1860 antislavery tract published in London put it, Christian nations, especially England, had "shouldered the responsibility" of freeing the world from slavery.[15] Although these reformers included women, many of whom hoped to carry antislavery views to British East Africa (B.E.A.), the British Foreign Office doubted that European women and their children could survive in Africa. A number of Britons had long protested the Foreign Office's attitude as untenable, yet during the 1890s neither it nor any other government agency had as yet advocated white migration to East Africa.[16]

The situation began to change in 1895 when, hoping to offset other nations' interest in the area, the British government declared the British East Africa Protectorate, including Kenya and Zanzibar. The following year, at least in part to insure the empire's access to Egypt and the as-yet-unexplored source of the Nile River, British officials launched the Uganda Railway. Within months, Africa's savannahs, rivers, and mountains turned the project into a costly nightmare. The sheer immensity and expense of the protectorate and the railway, as well as the military force needed to guard government and railway workers from violence at the hands of what some British leaders called "recalcitrant tribes," created huge expenses. Exasperated British taxpayers dubbed the railroad the Lunatic Express. Hoping that white settlers would turn a loss into a profit, British citizens cried out for white settlement to justify the cost of the protectorate and the railroad.[17]

The completion of the Uganda Railway in 1901 marked the beginning of a dramatic turning point in government policy. Much as American officials, who had once viewed the Great Plains as an uninhabitable desert, changed their minds, so did British officials rethink their position on British East Africa. In 1901, they agreed that white migration to B.E.A. was possible after all. The following year, the 1902 Crown Lands Ordinance provided for the purchase, granting, or leasing of unoccupied lands in B.E.A., notably Kenya. Between 1901 and 1904, Sir Charles Eliot, commissioner of the protectorate, argued vociferously for white settlement. For Eliot, the case of Kenya was one of pure Darwinian theory played out in real life. The fittest had survived and they were—unsurprisingly to him—the British. In Eliot's view, Britons had all the necessary components for colonization. An expanding population could supply the demand for settlers. Wealth from trade, industrialization, and resource exploitation in other parts of the British empire would provide the funds to develop yet another British colony. Advanced technology, medicine, and such institutions as schools and courts would demonstrate that Britons were not only superior to black Kenyans, but had a moral responsibility to help them. In a typically white, open-handed way, Eliot assumed that elements of British "civilization," as well as British capitalism, would bring black Kenyans into the modern world, whether they wanted to be there or not.

As potential "white settlers," Eliot and others like him had in mind farmers, plantation owners, business magnates, and international traders. To Eliot, white settlers were developers, capitalists, industrialists, and financiers who would make Kenya more British than Britain itself. Falling outside the category were such people as missionaries, teachers, and medical personnel. In addition, because the bureaucrats and soldiers sent to keep order in Britain's latest acquisition seldom took up permanent homes in Kenya, they and their families stood somewhere between white settlers and black Kenyans.

In a strange way, early abolitionists and Christian missionaries had made possible this reversal of policy. Much as had happened in the American West, they "softened" up indigenes who failed to see white missionaries as the advance guard of a threat to their way of life. As a result, the establishment of the British East Africa Protectorate came as a shock to black Kenyans. Although they attempted to regroup and resist during the late 1890s and well into the 1900s, their efforts proved largely ineffective against what one described as British "bayonets and machine guns," as well as "the help of regiments from India."[18]

After the British government announced white settlement as a goal, numbers of missionaries in Kenya increased. Church officials recognized that white settlement created new moral dilemmas for indigenes. Missionaries even hoped to diffuse the military situation between the British and Kenyans. Thus, establishing missions and sending missionaries to Kenya attained a prominent place on the agendas of sects in locations ranging from Scotland to Ireland and even from Kansas to California.

Clearly, a strong strain of reformism existed among white women who settled in Kenya between 1890 and 1940. The goal of helping others implied that an individual had the ability and altruism to help others. As in the United States, such motivation not only affirmed a woman's strength of character, but also validated the nation from which she came. Among other things, women migrants demonstrated that Europeans were willing to forfeit a life of comfort and relocate in a "primitive" place for the good of others. Soon, additional white women wanted to "come out" to Kenya to "serve humanity." Many migrated as teachers and nurses, professions generally open to women because of their similarity to child raising. Especially during the protectorate's early years, many of these teachers and nurses–often one and the same person—worked at religious missions. During the 1890s and early 1900s, *The Taveta Chronicle*, voice of the Church Missionary Society, stated that such women would assist the "poor benighted natives of Taveta," insuring that the "civilising of East Africa goes on apace."[19]

In addition to working in mission stations, teachers and especially nurses and female doctors who hoped to combine paid work with altruism increasingly came to Kenya in pursuit of nonecclesiastical positions. For example, in 1922, a Sussex woman inquired of a Kenyan official whether two vacancies might exist, one for herself and a friend who hoped to come to Nairobi to nurse black patients.[20] Also in 1922, a woman doctor queried the colonial secretary about a post working with Asian Indians in Kenya's population.[21] Although other reasons, including getting away from home and gaining a modicum of freedom, influenced these women to migrate, they probably would not have thought of such a far-off place had it not been for frontier propaganda.

Helping Oneself in the American West

Of course, not all women, even those in the helping professions, went to frontiers out of compassion. The second motivation for migration also derived from prevailing frontier philosophy, which dictated that people migrate to the American frontier to improve their financial situations or to broaden their minds through adventure. Such beliefs, often referred to as Manifest Destiny, rationalized for white Americans the seizing of land inhabited and controlled by others.

As a result, an industrial society that measured achievement in terms of financial gain found itself sending men *and* women to frontier regions to invest their time and labor, to work hard, and eventually to profit, even if such profit came at the expense of the region's original peoples. Women who were perhaps a bit less selfless or introspective than some of those mentioned above sought far-flung jobs not only to serve students or patients, but to better themselves. Because frontiers implied independence and financial rewards, many women intended to capitalize on the need for their services.

During the nineteenth century, one of the ways women could better themselves was through marriage. Consequently, thousands of white women converged on the American frontier in hopes of improving their lot by finding spouses. Anxious to become wives and mothers, many went with or followed men. Meanwhile, because of the steady flow of men going West during the nineteenth century, single women who stayed behind found themselves on the wrong end of a supply-demand imbalance. They soon proved themselves creative, including initiating correspondence with single men in the West, placing personal advertisements in western newspapers, and showing a willingness to go west as mail-order brides.

As a result of women's openness to nontraditional courtships, letters flowed in a steady stream between East and West or between Europe and the American West. In one case, a Norwegian woman, Emma Odegaard, corresponded with a man she had known briefly before he migrated to the American West. When he proposed in 1889 and asked her to join him in the Dakotas, she willingly picked up and left for the West.[22] To find potential husbands, other innovative women placed notices in western newspapers and magazines. In 1860, one young woman in central New York advertised that she was "desirous of opening a correspondence with some young man in the West, with a view to a matrimonial engagement." The writer, as in modern personal advertisements, listed her attributes: "She is about 24 years of age, possesses a good moral character, is not what would be called handsome, has a good disposition, enjoys good health, is tolerably well-educated, and thoroughly versed in the mysteries of housekeeping."[23]

Mail-order brides took even more of a risk to obtain a western husband. The writer Mari Sandoz, daughter of a Nebraska immigrant homesteader, explained that male homesteaders carried "heart-and-hand" publications around until "they wore the pictures off the pages."[24] When a prospective bride and groom reached a satisfactory settlement, she began to pack and he sent a railroad or steamer ticket. The next step for her was to travel west and discover if her intended had honestly described himself and his situation.

Besides marrying to better their status, numerous ambitious white women went west to establish businesses, notably boardinghouses, restaurants, and shops, or to seek paid employment in such capacities as domestics and dairy maids. Although some western settlers employed American Indians, Hispanics, and African Americans as "hired help," the number of white settlers was so great that native labor could not meet the demand. In addition, white female settlers often preferred to hire white men and women rather than workers of color. Thus, white women created their own female-driven labor market within the larger white economy, in that the greater the number of white female settlers who arrived, the more women's paid domestic services were needed.

As a result, a number of women went west to hire out as domestics. This work was considered suitable for women (but not for women of the upper classes) because it involved "home" duties. Many women found domestic service attractive because it required no specialized training and allowed them to live in a family situation. One Swedish woman who went to Dakota Territory thought housework and farmwork "taxing," yet she did not regret her decision to migrate.

"Have a good home here," she wrote to her family, "and have no wish ever to return to Sweden."[25]

Between 1840 and 1890, thousands of women from the eastern United States, Canada, and Europe, especially Ireland, migrated to take positions as nursemaids, general house servants, and cooks. Hired help was especially in demand during spring and summer when farmwives needed assistance with such seasonal chores as canning or cooking for threshing crews. Despite white women's complaints that paid workers were impossible to find, domestic service continued to be a common employment in the West. Although it is true that women regularly "married out" of domestic service and established homes of their own, other women took their places. In Kansas in 1870, for example, 4,002 women out of 162,175 females worked as domestic servants, while 1,285 out of 52,568 females did so in Nebraska.[26]

Besides domestic duties, western women needed other women to help in chicken houses and dairy barns, as well as in cheese- and butter-making. Because many Scandinavian women already had dairy-associated skills, they migrated to the West as dairy maids. Others established their own enterprises. Confident in her competency as a milk maid, Bertha Anderson migrated in 1899 from Sweden to Glendive, Montana, where she bought ten cows. Soon, she produced one hundred pounds of butter a week, which she sold at nearby Fort Bufford.[27]

White women in the West also entered male-dominated aspects of the western economy, notably by helping establish white-style agriculture, which constituted a colonizing force in the West. Women filled such jobs as farm operators, day laborers, or helpers with such seasonal tasks as threshing and planting. Women also cleared forests and plowed-up prairies, thus stamping their presence on areas that had once run wild or that aboriginal peoples had farmed.[28] In spite of their obvious presence, women on the land did not see themselves reflected in guidebooks and other promotional literature. Called "boomer" literature, these publications promoted areas of the West, praised certain crops or types of stock, and offered advice. They featured men and male occupations, giving only cursory notice to women's interests.

One pamphlet promoting Laramie, Wyoming, declared, "No place offers more inducements for men who are willing to work."[29]

White women also entered another area thought to be for men only. Female adventurers went west for the splendid vistas, wild game, and astonishing mountains. Some used the West as inspirations for their work, whereas others hoped to regain health or to find a personal "cause." In 1867, for example, writer Helen Hunt Jackson moved from her native Massachusetts to Colorado Springs, Colorado, so she could climb mountains, explore nature, and write essays, poems, and travel sketches about the Colorado landscape.[30] Like their male counterparts, such women viewed the American West as theirs for the taking.

Helping Oneself in Kenya

As in the United States, the industrial age in Britain imbued its citizens with such goals as seeking improved opportunities and higher wages. At the same time, frontier philosophy urged people to "better" themselves, to "make good," to "succeed" in capitalistic terms. In 1895, the British prime minister, Lord Salisbury, explained that the British government had only opened a "path" to East Africa; that individual English men and women would supply the "energy, initiative, the force" that colonization demanded. Salisbury was quite certain that in British East Africa within a few years "it will be our people that will be masters, it will be our commerce that will prevail, it will be our capital that will rule."[31] Along with men, women not only listened to these sentiments, but acted on them.

As in the earlier American West, one of the most acceptable means for a late nineteenth- or early twentieth-century woman to better herself was to marry and follow the profession of wife and mother. At the time, writers of prescriptive literature stressed that marriage and motherhood were the ultimate goals of a woman's life. Consequently, most women expected not only to marry, but to follow their husbands wherever they could, frontiers included. Others appear purposefully to have chosen mates who would introduce them to travel and new experiences—what one described as the "wandering life."[32]

Certainly, the stunningly successful 1985 film *Out of Africa* focused on this popular, if rather stock, situation by showing Karen Blixen fleeing to Kenya in 1914 to escape a tragic love affair. Blixen convinces the twin brother of the man who spurned her to run away to Kenya and wed her there. In spite of Hollywood's rendition of Blixen's life, in reality she married a man who had courted her for years. Karen and her betrothed fled Denmark not because of tragic love, but to make a fortune growing coffee in Kenya. Blixen claimed that she also hoped to carry what she viewed as the benefits of European civilization to black Kenyans.[33]

The pattern of women following men started very early. Even though they are often overlooked, a number of white women accompanied the first white men in East Africa. For instance, during the building of the Uganda Railway, Florence Preston lived in tents with her husband, Ronald O. Preston, who in 1897 took charge of rail-laying gangs. Usually wearing a straw boater hat, white shirtwaist, dark ankle-length skirt, and carrying a parasol, Florence appeared in numerous railway photographs. Also, it was Florence who on December 20, 1901, hammered the last peg into the final rail of the so-called Lunatic Express.[34]

Between the 1890s and the early 1940s, thousands of other women followed fathers, lovers, husbands, and sons to Kenya. Those who came as wives of officials expected to leave Kenya after their husbands' tours of duty. Wives of white settlers usually intended to stay. In 1919, for example, Lady Francis Scott followed her career-politician husband from India to Kenya where she helped manage their landholdings, the Deloraine Estate.[35]

Besides marrying to improve her fortunes, an ambitious woman settler, much like a man, might invest her labor, her money, or both. Becoming a "successful" woman in Kenya was a bit more difficult than in the American West, however. In Kenya, white women had to keep up appearances for the cause of the empire, including modeling domestic roles for women. Still, a significant number of enterprising women established boardinghouses, restaurants, and shops. When the British administration expanded in Kenya after World War I, ambitious women sought civil-service jobs. Also, a number of white women came to Kenya to obtain farmland. Early in the twentieth century, coffee, first planted and harvested in 1896 by the Holy Ghost Fathers, was the promising crop. As world demand for coffee increased, coffee plantations became paying propositions. Later, between the two world wars, the British government promoted the cultivation of cotton, sisal, maize, flax, and wheat. Stock farming and dairying also offered great returns. Thousands of men seized upon the idea of farming in Kenya as the answer to their financial problems. Others responded to the soldier-settlement scheme that offered free land to those who had served in World War I.[36]

Little wonder that, despite prejudice against female farmers, some women also tried their hands at farming in Kenya. At least as early as 1908 women applied for land grants, although not all applicants received land. When a Miss Plowman asked for one thousand acres in the Ukambi Province, officials remonstrated that there were already too many white farmers in the area, native labor was insufficient, and the soil was poor and rocky. It seems likely, however, that male authorities objected to the presence of a woman farmer.[37]

After World War I and into the 1920s and 1930s, Kenya booster literature proliferated, yet none of the guidebooks, directories, or handbooks published to attract white settlers, especially farmers, to Kenya directed articles to women farmers. Neither did the Kenya Land Settlement Advisory Committee, formed in 1924, include women members or issue appeals to women interested in farming.[38] Frequently, Kenya's white women farmers, like those in the American West, were also overlooked by census takers who failed to perceive women as full-time farmers.

Another important, but very different, factor that drew women to frontiers is seldom mentioned. Much as people had trouble perceiving of women as farmers, they overlooked women who sought adventure. In spite of inaccurate stereotypes of passive and fearful late nineteenth- and early twentieth-century women, the desire to take a risk enticed some women to relocate. In 1924, a female visitor to Kenya remarked that although some "ultra-feminine" and "clinging vine" type women existed, they were usually socialites belonging to a "smart set."[39] Although women who shot lions and elephants seldom appeared in newspapers or other media, Kenya had numerous women, single and married, who liked to camp and to hunt.

Why did women venture so far from their supposed sphere? A woman who in 1927 traveled from the Cape to Cairo, visiting Kenya on the way, explained that she did so because "wanderlust, and an unsatiable spirit of adventure" had always been her "ruling passions."[40] After returning home, some of these women wrote books encouraging others to think of, and use, Kenya as a playground. Others ended their wanderings by taking up land. Thus, adventurers and tourists contributed to colonialism in their own ways.

Frontierswomen of Color

There is, however, far more to the story of frontier migration. Although white women have dominated the mythology of the American West, women settlers of color—Hispanic, African American, and Asian— were found everywhere. The earliest and largest group was Hispanic, who deserve a place in what the historian Emma Pérez calls the "decolonial imaginary," meaning new and more inclusive ways of thinking about such categories as "the West" and "frontier."[41] Many Hispanic women came to areas like New Mexico and California long before white Europeans had arrived on the East Coast of North America. In New Mexico, Hispanas not only migrated, but formed settlements; soon Hispanic people were indigenous.[42] In California during the era of the American Revolution, well before white Americans thought about expanding their nation to the West Coast, families like the Castros, Picos, Bandinis, Vallejos, and Yorbas established themselves as the conquerors and settlers of a frontier they called El Norte.

Some Hispanic women went to the frontier to Christianize others, especially at the Spanish missions scattered throughout El Norte. Although much of the impetus for Christianizing Indians originated with male priests, early Hispanic frontierswomen also intended to spread their religious and cultural beliefs to others, particularly to

California Indians. The literary scholar Virginia M. Bouvier argues that the "role of female newcomers to Alta California was initially an ideological one." As role models and teachers, they hoped to instill in California Indians European values regarding personal hygiene, gender relations, sexuality, and a work ethic.[43] For instance, at California Mission San José during the early nineteenth century, Mexican matrons required young women and men to follow Spanish courting procedures. Couples could court only through iron-barred windows mounted in thick adobe walls, where women waited for men to approach the windows.[44] Overall, however, Hispanic women did not appear to have the idea of "civilizing" other peoples implanted in them in the same intense way that white women did. Neither did Hispanic women enjoy long tenure in "civilizing" roles. When El Norte became part of the United States in 1848, Mexican women found themselves cast in the role of civilizees rather than civilizers.

Much like white women, numerous Hispanas also went to the western frontier to make money, alone or with families and friends. Some homesteaded, while others worked in factories, fields, and shops. Many Hispanic women, like white women, migrated with their husbands. Others hoped to escape onerous conditions at home, or to gain freedom and autonomy. In early New Mexico, for example, a Hispana could own property and control her wages. In the Spanish-derived legal and cultural system, women were not assumed to be totally subordinate to men.[45]

A smaller and later western group of women found different reasons for migration. Before the abolition of slavery in the United States in 1863, African American slave women were taken west by their owners like so much baggage. In 1822, a party of settlers moving from Virginia to Missouri included four black men and a woman called "Mammy." During following decades, other women followed "Mammy's" trail, especially to Missouri, Arkansas, Texas, and Oklahoma.[46] Also prior to 1863, other slave women fled westward in hopes of escaping slavery. Even free blacks migrated in hopes of outdistancing racial prejudice and discrimination. After 1863, thousands of other southern blacks headed west. Groups called Exodusters left the South looking for what they hoped would be a "promised land." They took up farms in Kansas, Oklahoma, and Colorado. Among them were black women who wanted the freedom they hoped existed in the West, and also wanted to find paid employment as washwomen, cooks, nursemaids, and teachers. For example, in the Exoduster town of Nicodemus, Kansas, in 1848, one woman taught a class of forty-five children in her dugout home.[47]

During the 1870s and 1880s, newly freed black women moved west with husbands, to take up homestead land, open boardinghouses or other small businesses, and enter the professions. In spite of state and local attempts to prohibit blacks from attending school or to limit them to poorly funded, segregated schools, teaching continued to draw black women to the West. Frequently, these women, who took positions in segregated schools or founded their own schools, outnumbered black male teachers in most western regions.[48]

At the other end of the professional spectrum was the prostitute. Some African American women went west with this moneymaking venture in mind or, after arrival in the West, discovered the need of men, including black cowhands and black soldiers, for women. Some worked in black brothels, whereas others joined racially mixed establishments. Although poverty and lack of job opportunities pushed black women toward this activity, neither observers nor census takers noted unusually large numbers of black prostitutes in the West.[49]

Also during the post–Civil War decades, a small number of Asian women began to arrive in the American West, many coming against their will. Poverty-stricken Chinese families sold daughters into wage slavery, including prostitution. Chinese prostitutes served Chinese "coolies," or manual laborers, who were brought in to help build the continental railroad in the 1860s. Rather than regarding the West as a land free of slavery, such women saw it as the worst place they had ever known. In addition, many other Asian women came as wives (including mail-order brides), workers, and entrepreneurs. Some settled in Asian fishing villages along the coast or clustered around mining and lumber camps. Others worked in California fields or western sweatshops. A few ran shops of their own. These women hoped that the land known as "Golden Mountain" would remove them from poverty and give them an opportunity to work and utilize their talents. Rather than returning home, a majority of them stayed, forming a transnational community by sending home funds that improved the lives of their families in China.[50]

Later, in Kenya, a comparable process took place. Although white women were themselves varied, including English, Scotch, Irish, French, Germans, Austrians, Polish, Canadians, South Africans, Australians, and New Zealanders, other disparate types of women also took part, as happened earlier in the West, in developing Kenya. Women of color who stamped their presence and cultures on Kenya included African-born Swahili women. Usually with their families, they migrated throughout the 1800s either overland or by sea to the prosperous trading area along Kenya's southern coast, notably in and around Mombasa. Many were Muslims, who believed in the seclusion of women from men. One Swahili woman, Bi Kaje, explained that during the 1890s women of the middle and upper classes escaped men's notice by wrapping themselves in a huge cloth called a *rumba*. According to her, the concealing black dress and head wrapping known as a *buibui* appeared among Mombasa's Muslim women sometime during the early 1900s.[51] Then—as now—many Swahili women adopted the buibui, which immediately set them apart from Kenya's other women.

By far, however, the most numerous and ubiquitous of Kenya's women of color were Asian Indians, who during the early 1800s came to Hindu and Muslim trading settlements on the coast of what would become B.E.A., especially near Malindi and Mombasa, and on the island of Zanzibar. Asian Indians not only continued to migrate throughout the century, but began to settle inland from the coast. Gradually, small traders and merchants established centers at Nyeri, Limeru, Thika, and Meru. Other Asian Indian migrants were skilled employees. One was Alibhai Mulla Jeevanjee, who came to Kenya in 1890 to work for the Imperial British East Africa Trading Company in Nairobi; his wife Jenabai soon joined him. A few years later, in 1896, Indian immigration received a boost when the British brought 350 "coolies" to East Africa to help build the Uganda Railway. Asian Indian immigration increased rapidly during the early 1900s, especially when British officials encouraged merchants and even farmers to move to East Africa. Other Indian men entered technical trades and the professions. Typically, Asian Indians became urban people, who established self-sufficient communities.

Even though it might seem odd that Asian Indians would travel from one British colony to another, they had good reasons. Because their own homeland had been usurped and colonized, Indian women were part of a displaced population desperate to find a place in the world that would sustain them and their families. Also, generations of Indian women living under the rule of the British Raj saw their rights and opportunities reduced. Muslim women who could inherit land generally lost that right. Also, because communal lands were abolished, women no longer could plant vegetable plots. Instead, women worked in factories for pitiful wages.[52]

At the same time, white British women increasingly characterized Indian women as degraded, vulgar, and exploited by eastern religions. The worse Indian women could be made to appear to outsiders, the greater the achievements that white female "saviors" could claim. It seemed to Indian women that intrusive white women could leave nothing alone. Without investigating, they summarily interfered with the Muslim practice of purdah (segregation of women by a space known as *zenana* and by veiling) and the Hindu belief in *suti* (a widow burning to death on her husband's funeral pyre). Although Indian women may have had reservations about certain religious practices, they resented the interference of white colonialists in private matters.[53]

Asian Indian women had many other reasons to be restive. Unlike white women, they migrated more as a result of pushes at home than pulls from abroad. Women left India for Kenya in the 1870s and 1880s to escape plague, poverty, and political oppression. More came during the 1890s as economic conditions deteriorated in India. For example, around 1890 a widow left Junagar State, bringing her three children to Kenya in hopes that she could find a job and support her family, which she was unable to do in India.[54] As jobs opened up for Indian men on the Uganda Railway during the 1890s, some women migrated to Kenya with men or joined them later. One woman came to Kenya with her husband and son, who sought jobs with the railway. In 1899, she rode in the construction train that her engineer son guided into

Nairobi. Until her death in Nairobi at age 112, she was known as "Grandmother of the Railways." Eventually, some thirty-two thousand Asian Indians came to Kenya to work on the railway; of those, approximately six thousand chose to remain, often bringing mothers, wives, and daughters to join them.[55]

During the early 1900s, Asian Indian women went to Kenya in growing numbers. Many migrated with their menfolk or joined them. For instance, in 1903, Mathra Devi moved to Kenya to be with her stationmaster husband in Port Florence, the present-day Kisumu. Similarly, in 1910, a Goan woman traveled to Kenya to be with her husband. Also, the pull of family members other than husbands was a strong force. In 1928, another Indian woman came to Kenya because she had a sister already there. One woman said that "relatives following the first pioneers" was a common settlement pattern in Indian communities. Yet others migrated to practice professions. In 1919, Dr. Mary de Souza went to Kenya to doctor her people. In 1931, the twenty-four-year-old daughter of a well-to-do Parsee family, Freny Mehenwanji Sidpra, overcame her parent's opposition and sailed from India to Africa to become headmistress and teacher for forty Ismali children in the Janat Khana, or Ismali Mosque, in Kisumu.[56]

Even though Asian Indian women were not "civilizers" in the white sense, they frequently altered conditions by their very presence. When a Hindu woman named Maniben joined her husband in Nyeri, Kenya, in 1912, he ordered that every male servant be given shorts and shirts in place of the loose *shukas* they had worn in an all-male household. In other cases, the arrival of Indian women led to more complete meals and authentic Indian dishes being served. Household protocol also became more formal and language more polite.[57]

Internal Colonization

Unquestionably, most female migrants of color went to the American West and Kenya in hopes of finding relief from financial, political, and economic turmoil. Many had allowed themselves to listen to frontier philosophy suggesting that frontiers offered more autonomy than did their homes. One of these was the black abolitionist Mary Ellen Pleasant, who went to San Francisco in 1852 to make money and help other African Americans. The historian Quintard Taylor notes that Pleasant "subscribed to the quintessentially American belief that anyone, including African Americans, could improve one's life by migrating west."[58] Because Asian Indian women came from societies based on castes, autonomy was more chimerical for them. Yet, in 1901, even one young Asian Indian latched onto a bit of white frontier rhetoric, citing "freedom and independence" as her symbols of hope.[59]

After arriving, however, peoples of color soon learned that white people were more autonomous and they were less so. Men and women of color soon found themselves inhabiting smaller colonies within the larger colonies of the American West and Kenya. Just as white migrants colonized indigenes, they internally colonized migrants of color. White women were very much a part of the development and enforcement of this internal colonization.[60] They felt they had migrated to help indigenous peoples, not those of color who originated from places outside the frontier's borders. Nor did white women expect to deal with mixed-heritage children who resulted from cohabitation or marriage between members of different racial groups. Yet, by implication, the frontier creed had led non-white peoples to believe they might share with white settlers a frontier's bounty. Whites, however, had no intention of furthering or accepting migrants of color or of racially mixed backgrounds. Rather, whites pushed aside these intruders of color, forcing them to live and work separately, as well as to accept lesser standards of living.

Obviously, frontiers did not turn out quite the way that migrants of color had hoped. Although they usually found more freedom than they had experienced in their former homes, it was still less than they expected. Even on the job front, the situation was often dismal. Internally colonized peoples of color became economically dependent, usually working for white settlers at low wages. Women were especially impoverished. Because frontier philosophy had failed to provide for them, such peoples became, by default, part of a social system that, despite its indefensible nature, still hangs on in the modern West and in contemporary Kenya.

Conclusion

Clearly, white women especially migrated to the American and Kenyan frontiers in response to a similar frontier philosophy. In spite of the decades separating the settling of the American West and of the Kenyan frontier, arguments and rationales remained much the same. In addition, the dictates of women's culture differed little from one situation to the other. Blending frontier philosophy with women's culture created a frontier situation far more complex than is usually recognized.

For one thing, although women may have adapted frontier philosophy to suit the needs of their gender, they frequently acted on its tenets as vigorously or more so than men. For example, women who went to the American West to homestead often showed themselves more dedicated than men, who had a lower rate of "proving up" (completing requirements for ownership) on their land than did female homesteaders. This determined mind-set positioned white women to become effective colonizers of everyone and everything in sight. Underwritten by a belief in white supremacy, the tenets of frontier philosophy led to the establishment of hierarchies, norms, and policies, all of which elevated some people above others.

In the long run, however, ideas that appeared constructive to white women proved to be paternalistic and destructive for indigenous peoples. By contemporary standards, these women represented an arrogant and racist frontier philosophy. They accepted a belief system that encouraged them to view other people's lands as their own. White ethnocentrism had not only reached a high state; it ran rampant. Similarly, because whites thought of indigenes' minds as unoccupied, they "civilized" indigenous peoples according to their own beliefs.

Even though many, if not most, white women went to the American and Kenyan frontiers with helping on their minds, their efforts and beliefs were too often misguided and insensitive. Moreover, white women's ideas did not affect just indigenous peoples. For migrants of color, white women helped create an oppressive societal strata. The dynamics that resulted from the daily intermingling of all these groups—and from resistance by peoples of color—shaped the American and Kenyan frontiers in distinctive, yet essentially similar, ways.

TWO
The Journey as Transition

THEORETICALLY, travel to a frontier offered a period of transition from the known to the new. Journeys supplied migrants with abundant time to bring their attitudes and beliefs into closer harmony with the reality of the land and peoples that lay ahead. In practice, most white travelers failed to take advantage of these opportunities. In part, the duress of the journey consumed travelers' physical and psychic energies. Even when they had a chance to reflect, the very travelers who willingly learned new skills, including hunting wild game and cooking outdoors, clung to their original frontier philosophy.

For most female travelers, the strain of their trips caused them to clutch their beliefs as a rationale. The stress of travel and relocation to an unknown region made most people insecure; hardly the time for adjusting one's values. Rather than attempting to make a mental compromise, travelers quieted their anxieties by repeating old shibboleths. For white women, this meant keeping in mind their supposed moral and cultural superiority over indigenous peoples. Furthermore, white women who came into contact with indigenous peoples along the way stilled their misgivings by judging them as primitive and backward—definitely in need of "civilizing" by white migrants.

Despite using portions of frontier philosophy to keep their spirits up, women's tempers became edgy and their nerves frayed from anticipating the unknown. Consequently, most white women arrived at their particular frontier without adequate mental preparation. Women's worn-down condition created the worst possible situation for an initial meeting between travelers and original inhabitants. People on the other side were not at their best either. For instance, no one had given black Kenyans transition time or offered them information about the newcomers. As a result, black Kenyans, who had not invited white people to enter their homeland, were curious and resentful. For example, a Mombasa woman, Bi Kaje, said that the city's Swahilis regarded whites as "foreigners" and Asian Indians as "strangers." She added, "This is not their place."[1] Thus, contact between groups was a less than ideal blind date.

"Seeing the Elephant" on the Way West

Between 1840 and 1890, westward migration became almost a mania in the United States. Women were clearly part of the westward movement, which was largely a family migration to agricultural areas. As one early chronicler said, wagon trains contained "cattle and hogs, men and dogs, and frequently women and children."[2] Growing numbers of women were about to "see the elephant," which meant they would have an outlandish experience they would never forget.

Just to ready themselves, women spent months and sometimes a year in planning and preparation. Many took advantage of goods offered by a growing migration industry. Such products as ready-made packing crates, food tins, and two basic types of wagons could be purchased. Of these, the most important was the wagon. The larger of the two wagons available was the Conestoga wagon; the smaller, the emigrant wagon. People chose one or the other depending on the amount they wanted to carry and the speed they hoped to travel. Of the two, the Conestoga wagon has become a predominant symbol of westering. It must have been an impressive sight indeed as it stood fully loaded, ranging from fifteen hundred to two thousand pounds or more, farm stock tied to its back end and chickens in crates lashed to its sides.

Unfortunately for women, the American publishing industry failed to meet their need for information regarding westward migration. Although a spate of guidebooks became available, they were usually written by men for men. Apparently, most people assumed that men made all decisions of importance regarding migration. Thus, female migrants who pored over guidebooks seldom learned anything of use to them. Advertisements and newspaper articles were not much better. They were frequently aimed at farmers and small entrepreneurs, both presumed to be male. Because much of this propaganda originated with land companies, newly built transportation lines, and various media, it shared the single objective of selling frontier land to farmers and anyone else interested in buying property or starting a business.

In addition to ignoring females, migration literature perpetuated a large, unintended hoax that the West was a veritable Garden of Eden. Advertisements and newspapers urged people, as one journalist proclaimed in 1855, to migrate in the name of "progress, civilization, and Christianity," to multiply, and to work hard. People had only to bring "strong minds and willing hands to work" and they would "be abundantly blessed and rewarded."[3] Thus was the American frontier idealized as offering a spirit of hope to the poor and despairing. Although in reality it took capital to go West, Americans were urged to believe, in the words of a typical mid-nineteenth-century magazine article, that the West was "the paradise of the poor."[4] Few pointed out that covered wagons and other supplies cost money, to say nothing of western land. Undoubtedly, the endless tributes to the West encouraged people who lacked the necessary resources to move west and to find themselves among the poor rather than in paradise.

By the late 1850s, booster organizations, designed to promote immigration from outside the United States to a specific western state, formed to promote the American West in other countries. Some of this literature eventually reached out to women, at least in a limited way. During the late 1860s and 1870s, Scandinavian dairy maids were invited to come to the American West, where freedoms like the existence of coeducation or the impending passage of woman suffrage in some western territories and states were dangled in front of women.[5] For migration within the United States, however, authors generally ignored potential appeals to women and continued through the 1880s the trend of writing western guidebooks largely for men. Consequently, a woman who wondered what to take with her to the western frontier or how she would take care of personal bodily needs on the vast plains without trees or bushes behind which to hide found no practical guidance. Instead, she received maps, information on flora and fauna, climate and temperature data, and lists of crops to plant.[6]

When it came to a choice of routes and transportation, overland trails and covered wagons dominated. Perhaps the most traveled was the Oregon-California Trail, initiated in 1841 by the California-bound Bidwell-Bartelson party. In 1843, the trail helped begin Oregon emigration when a company arrived at Oregon City in November. The following year, the route, which began in Independence, Missouri, led a wagon train to Sacramento. Between 1843 and 1873, approximately 400,000 men, women, and children made use of the trail.[7]

Migrating by wagon was serious work with hardship and potential danger involved. What travelers learned and experienced on the trail might spell the difference between success and failure in their new lives. Wagon travelers applied their attentions to four areas: performing tasks necessary for daily living, but with the stress of the trail added; moving themselves, their families, stock, and goods safely and efficiently; honing such skills as hunting and cooking over open fires that would stand them in good stead in the West; and giving their minds a chance to readjust so that instead of looking backward to their old homes they looked forward to the new.

White women found the trail extremely demanding, but life in the nineteenth century *was* arduous. One woman explained that her parents survived difficult conditions because "their early lives had been spent amid such surroundings."[8] In addition, many were farm women who already knew how to churn butter and bake bread. The majority were not upper-class wives and daughters, disadvantaged at the start by a surfeit of servants in their former homes. Also, trail women often proved competent and creative. During her 1848 trip to Oregon,

Kitturah Belknap prided herself on having the only dinner table in the wagon train with a tablecloth. To get such necessities as fresh vegetables and fish, Kitturah traded with farmers, other emigrants, and Native Americans. Despite her son's serious illness, Kitturah entered in her journal the upbeat comment that "the road is good and I am standing the riding fine."[9]

For other women, the trail was an ordeal. One of these was a young woman, Mary Ann Hafen, a member of the Church of Jesus Christ of Latter-day Saints, who migrated with her family in 1860 from Switzerland to Nebraska. In Omaha, men built handcarts—two-wheeled vehicles with canvas covers—which they intended to pull to the Mormon Zion in Utah. Accompanied by three provision wagons, the family set out walking with their handcart. After trudging across the desert, Mary Ann recalled the day when the party reached Emigration Canyon, overlooking Salt Lake, and released a shout of triumph and joy.[10]

Clearly, a majority of migrants preferred wagons, yet railroads also proved important for western settlement between 1840 and 1890. Because rail travel provided a more pleasant and safer trip than did wagons, many pioneers chose the railroad for portions of their journey. In 1858, for example, when Hosea and Mary Anne Newton left Connecticut for the West they took a stagecoach from Fair Haven to the dock where they embarked on a steamboat to New York. There they boarded the railroad "cars" for Chicago. After spending a few days sightseeing in Chicago, they rode the railroad again, this time to the end of the line in Louisa County, Iowa, where they hired a man with a wagon and team to take them to their land in Keokuk County.[11]

Company executives quickly realized that railroads could play a crucial part in the migration industry. Settlers, once established, would do business with railroads, which could ship manufactured goods from the East to the West and settlers' produce from the West to the East. Consequently, railroad lines made a concerted effort to attract migrants through expanded advertising, improved facilities, and enlarged routes. In 1869, the first transcontinental railway, the Union Pacific and Central Pacific, provided a rail route from the East to California. Railroads also had disadvantages. Space limitations made it impossible for travelers to transport necessary domestic goods, farm equipments, seed, stock, and even clothing. Because these items were more expensive in the West, poorly equipped arrivals could expect difficulty in finding what they needed, as well as paying inflated prices. In addition, rail fares were expensive; first class on the Union Pacific/Central Pacific ran one hundred dollars from Omaha to Sacramento in 1869. For most people of the era, such fares were beyond their means. For instance, in 1861, San Francisco carpenters earned eighty dollars to one hundred dollars a month; in 1869, army privates drew sixteen dollars a month; in 1873 female domestic servants in Helena, Montana, received less than sixty dollars per month; and in 1880 California farm laborers got forty-one dollars each month. Even if pioneers chose third class, which cost forty dollars from Omaha to Sacramento, such fares became prohibitive for a family of more than two or three members.[12]

Railroad companies, including the Southern Pacific and the Northern Pacific, tried to offset these liabilities by offering free trips to visit a frontier area, professional touring lecturers about specific locations, and special discounted fares to settlers. Eventually, railroads even provided "emigrant cars," in which settlers could load their goods, stock, and family. After arrival, usually somewhere on the Great Plains, family members could continue to live in the boxcar until they built their own homes.[13] Still, on wagon trips migrants transported more and learned more, whereas traveling by rail made migration seem more like a vacation than part of a pioneer trail. Passengers ran to windows to spot unusual sights, disembarked to eat meals and visit local attractions, and even collected trinkets and souvenirs. Although railroad travel had definite attractions, it did not provide the seasoning that most pioneers needed.

Besides wagons and trains, a wide range of vessels also brought pioneers to the American West. Within the United States, steamships carried people from coastal New England to the docks of New York City, where they began their wagon journeys. In addition, riverboats took settlers from locations like Pennsylvania to prairie states like Iowa. Riverboats provided a relatively inexpensive means of transportation with plenty of cargo space for settlers' goods. Also, riverboat routes connected to one another so that some westward trips could be made entirely by water. When the Harris family—James, his wife, and seven children—left Pennsylvania in the 1850s they chose water travel all the way. First, they went down the Allegheny River to the port of Pittsburgh, where they switched to the "Diadem," a Cairo, Illinois, steamboat that carried them down the Ohio River. Finally, they took the "New England" up the Mississippi River to the Iowa port city of Keokuk.[14]

External water routes led to the West as well. A number of female settlers sailed from New York to South America, where they steamed "around the horn" and up the western coast to San Francisco. After 1849, even more went from New York City to Chagres, Panama, where they crossed the isthmus, in the late 1840s and early 1850s by mule and after 1855 by railroad. From Panama City or Acapulco, Mexico, they sailed for San Francisco. The Panama Trail, which took six weeks if everything worked, often carried women and children joining a husband and father in California or leaving California to return to the East. One of the earliest of these was Jessie Benton Frémont, who crossed Panama in 1849. From Chagres, she rode in dugout canoes and slept on the ground in huts. Frémont also survived a dangerous two-day mule trek to Panama City, which she termed "a nightmare." Because the steamship's crew had abandoned the ship to go themselves to the California goldfields, Frémont spent seven miserable weeks in Panama City waiting for transportation to California.[15] After 1855 and the coming of the trans-isthmian railroad, the Panama Trail became somewhat easier. In 1863, Angelina Harvey wrote her cousin that she had experienced "a prosperous passage of 10 days to the isthmus; the crossing of which was truly an oasis in the desert of waters and another equally prosperous [journey] of 14 [days] to the bay of San Francisco."[16]

Harvey complained only of the throngs of passengers that clogged the port of San Francisco and made arrival a distressing experience. Although it was an American city, San Francisco was not the usual city. Its streets zigzagged up hillsides, while its houses perched precariously over the bay. San Francisco overflowed with dirt, noise, and the presence of curiosities. In its early years during the 1850s, San

Francisco's population was largely male, many of whom lived a raucous life in saloons and theaters, which featured infamous female performers like Lola Montez.[17] Even after the Civil War, the city continued to offer an abundance of saloons, theaters, and brothels. In sum, San Francisco provided a peculiar experience for settlers headed for the western frontier.

At the same time, women of color also traversed the various trails leading to the American West, often under radically different conditions than white women. During the mid-nineteenth century, wagon trails to the West carried a variety of people, including African American slaves. A former Missouri slave woman remembered that sometime before the American Civil War "we rides the wagons all the way, how many days, I dunno." This female slave recalled that "the country was wild most of the way" and that she was sold at auction to a white female slaveowner in Texas, where she stayed until the Civil War led to the emancipation of slaves in 1863.[18] After the war's end in 1865, numerous free blacks chose to go west. Often called Exodusters, many went in groups that established farm communities in the western states of Kansas, Oklahoma, and Colorado. Others migrated as individual families. One woman explained that during the 1860s, "We keeps hearin' talk of Texas and me an' my ole man, I'd done been married several years den and had one little boy, well we gits in our covered wagon wid our little mules hitched to it and we comes to Texas."[19]

On the way to the West, Asian women usually suffered the worst conditions of all. Often stopping in Hawaii first, primarily to work on sugar plantations, Asian people later migrated to California or the Pacific Northwest. They typically clustered in Chinatowns, Little Tokyos, and fishing villages, or worked as railroad or agricultural laborers. During the period between 1840 and 1890, the number of Asian women remained low compared to Asian men. The trip from Asia to the American West was long and expensive. In addition, because of the 1882 Chinese Exclusion Law, Chinese women were unwelcome. Asian women who did migrate to the American West frequently came as "proxy" brides. After the 1882 act, some Chinese men, swearing the women were their own wives, brought women through U.S. immigration for other men.[20] Asian women traveled by ship, often in steerage class and segregated by anti-Asian prejudice from other travelers, which left them with unpleasant memories.

For all female migrants, then, the trip itself was so demanding that it left little time or energy for soul-searching. Women under pressure held tightly to their assumptions. Given the deep-seated nature of prejudice, there was little likelihood that under even the best of circumstances women would let go of their attitudes.

"Coming Out" to Kenya

Kenya-bound women had comparable experiences. Between 1890 and 1940, the chance to "come out" to Kenya, as migration was called, seemed to present an unparalleled opportunity. In England, Scotland, Wales, Ireland—and in other parts of the British Empire, especially South Africa, Australia, and New Zealand—migration became a national ethic. Such exotic-sounding place-names as Mombasa and Nairobi peppered conversations, radio newscasts, and legislative debates. Again and again, Britons quoted Governor of the Protectorate Charles Eliot, who described an interior section of Kenya, which he called the "white highlands," as perfect for white settlement because of the area's cool, malaria-free climate and fertile land.

Because British officials hoped that the acquisition of East Africa would benefit the empire, they considered importing various groups of people to Kenya to act as "managers." These groups ranged from Finns to Jews to Asian Indians. While British policymakers investigated possibilities, a small group of white British settlers gained a foothold in Kenya. British officials soon gave up the idea of managers, giving in instead to white settlers' demands to open British East Africa to white immigration. Because they hoped to avoid creating a class of "poor whites" in Kenya, they targeted primarily the middle and upper classes with their pro-migration messages. As early as the 1890s, the commissioner of British East Africa warned that, because of the difficulties of frontier life, only the "best type" of immigrants should go to Kenya.[21] By 1900, official British policy also welcomed shopkeepers and other entrepreneurs, teachers and medical personnel, and civil servants, whose numbers grew exponentially as settlement increased. A large number of these were efficient, ambitious Asian Indians. Also, because the British government could not exercise control over people who migrated to Kenya from other parts of Europe or Africa, a sizeable number of white migrants came to Kenya from South Africa. These were the Boers, or Afrikaners, who were white South Africans of European, usually Dutch, ancestry. They were not welcomed by other white migrants, who thought of Boers as slothful and ignorant.

Regarding immigration from Britain, the government's policy created a top-heavy migration in terms of social class, at least in the early days. Although the British philosophy differed from that utilized years earlier in the American West, in many ways it was realistic. Relocation to a far-off frontier in Africa was not an undertaking for the financially unstable, the inexperienced, or the worldly. Middle- and upper-class people possessed the necessary capital to invest in a trip, land, housing, and equipment. Some well-to-do families even viewed Kenya as a proper "starting-over" place for "black sheep" sons. Naturally, there were drawbacks to class-based migration. People from the middle and upper classes, especially those who had agricul-tural-management experience, viewed Kenya as an expanse of empty and unclaimed land—free for the taking—very much unlike England's meager and restricted estates. They had little comprehen-sion of the needs of the peoples who already inhabited the land. In addition, because elite people thought of themselves as "top drawer," they were unlikely to modify their attitudes.

During the 1890s and early 1900s, then, a trickle of migrants set sail for British East Africa. Some of these were from the upper classes, but a sizeable number of others hoped to advance a class or more by virtue of moving to the Kenyan frontier. As early as 1902, white settlers formed an organization in Kenya, the Farmers' and Planters' Association, which in 1903 became the Colonists' Association. This group lobbied the British government to support white British migra-tion and to establish policies favorable to white settlers. One member clearly stated the group's intentions: "The goal of this generation is the establishment in East Africa of a new, loyal, white dominion, securely founded in the principles of British Tradition and Western civilisation."[22] By 1910, Kenya contained approximately three thousand white Europeans. The following year, the British Parliament granted a loan for internal improvements, notably the Thika tramway. Meanwhile, the coffee market rose internationally. The resulting enthusiasm for Kenya encouraged white settlers to clear more land, buy additional agricultural implements, and purchase more speciality goods than ever before. In 1912, the British Treasury made what it said would be its last grant; from then on Kenya was no longer to be a debtor.[23]

Karen Blixen (Isak Dinesen) was representative of early middle- to upper-class white settlers. In 1913, Blixen traveled with her mother and youngest sister Ellen largely by train from Denmark to Naples, Italy, where she took first-class passage aboard the *Admiral*, a well-outfitted steamship belonging to the German-East Africa line. The sea voyage, which lasted nineteen days, took Blixen through the Mediterranean Sea, the Suez Canal into the Red Sea, the Gulf of Aden to the Indian Ocean, and finally to Mombasa in British East Africa, or Kenya. Although the route was typical of people going by sea to East Africa, Blixen's life aboard ship was not. Twenty-seven-year-old Blixen sailed with distinguished company, including a German scientist on his twenty-seventh foray to Kenya and a colonel bound for Dar es Salaam to take charge of German forces. These men's conversation helped relieve Blixen's nervousness, as did a German stewardess named Martha, who Blixen hired as a lady's maid. In Aden, Blixen acquired a Somali servant named Fara, who her future husband Bror had sent to accompany her on the rest of the trip.[24]

During subsequent years, migration to Kenya was erratic. Unlike travelers to the American West, Kenya-bound migrants were relatively small in number and far more vulnerable to world events. For instance, World War I slowed Kenya's apparent success. Although white settlement continued, the numbers of settlers declined. After peace in 1919, the British government appealed to returning military personnel to migrate to Kenya as farmers. Under the government's soldier-settlement scheme, introduced in 1919, male or female military personnel could enter a lottery, in which they drew numbers entitling them to plots of land in the Kenya highlands. Although something like the Homestead Act of 1862 that offered free land to western homesteaders, the soldier-settlement plan did not attract the same large numbers. The plan created a boomlet during the 1920s, which ended abruptly with the stock-market crash of 1929 and the following economic depression of the 1930s.

Like the American West, Kenya's migration included a significant number of women. As single women, as wives, and as mothers, women helped populate British East Africa. Because some women were wives of officials, they did not plan to spend their entire lives in Kenya. White female settlers usually had more long-range plans. In 1918, records of the B.E.A. Protectorate indicated that "white settler" provinces included about one-fourth to one-third women. Yet other women came to Kenya as travelers and as adventurers anxious to participate in safaris and hunt wild game, either traveling on their own or with husbands or other family members.[25]

As the white settlement of Kenya became a British national undertaking, an industry sprang up around it and related products appeared, including guidebooks. As in the West, such books offered advice and smacked of boosterism. Text, photographs, and advertisements portrayed Kenya as a Shangri-la of sorts. White settler Alyse Simpson recalled that an advertisement headed "Come to Kenya" inspired in her and her husband "new hopes and conjured images of untold happiness and success." In addition, promotional advertising reinforced the frontier philosophy that white people, whatever their purpose, had a right to enter East Africa. Like their earlier western counterparts, women generally found such books worthless, for most authors were men who wrote for male readers. Topics ranging from which animals to shoot and where to plant coffee were staples, but clothing, domestic management, and child care were often ignored or covered in limited, biased ways.

As early as 1897, for example, a guidebook titled *British Central Africa* was published in London. Since few women went to British East Africa at the time, its author, Harry Johnston, offered advice primarily to men. Johnston's guidebook contained only one small section of interest to visiting women, concerning appropriate clothing. He advised them to pack silk or wool underclothing; evening clothes would also come in handy. Kenyan settlers, Johnston warned, are not "rough pioneers who chiefly dress in red flannel shirts and buckskin breeches." When visiting settlements, travelers would need dress clothes for dinner parties and church.[26]

In 1912, a book titled *A Colony in the Making, Or, Sport and Profit in British East Africa* finally took account of women because its author, Lord Cranworth, asked his wife to prepare a chapter directed to women. Much like Johnston, Lady Cranworth apparently had in mind well-to-do women who would reside in Nairobi or on nearby plantations and who expected to carry on lifestyles similar to the ones they had known at home. Among the important questions on a woman's mind, Lady Cranworth rightly presumed, were what to take with her in the way of clothing and domestic items. Cranworth assured women that each year the shops in Nairobi improved; thus, most clothing and household goods could be bought after arrival. Between what a woman brought with her and what she purchased in Nairobi, a woman should assemble the following "useful outfit" of apparel:

> Plenty of cotton and muslin frocks; linen coats and skirts; two khaki-colored coats and skirts; a divided skirt for riding about the farm; silk shirts; a riding-habit for Nairobi; plenty of brown boots and shoes; tweed coats and skirts for the rainy season; a large double Terrai hat or Pith Helmet; two or three evening dresses of crepe de chine, satin, or velvet; one or two smart hats.[27]

In the 1919 edition of *A Colony in the Making*, Lady Cranworth eliminated the riding-habit and suggested that evening dresses be made of uncrushable materials like brocade or chiffon.[28]

Cranworth also gave advice regarding servants, which was heavy with not only elitist but racist overtones. Cranworth pointed out that women would have to manage servants, which was "an art in itself." In her view, an adequate house staff for a husband and wife consisted of "a Goanese cook, cook's helper (native), head boy (Swahili), and two under boys (native)." Additional servants might be useful in overseeing children and in creating a English garden, which Cranworth noted "grew in Kenya with wonderfully little effort." She assured readers that when "one becomes accustomed to the sight of black faces, native servants will be found fairly good." She added that women would learn from experience when "to have a servant beaten for rubbing silver plate on the gravel path to clean it," especially after the servant had received "several previous warnings."[29] Cranworth's recommendations revealed that upper-class women not only expected homes run by trained servants, but deemed servants as vastly inferior to themselves.

During the 1920s, additional manuals appeared, but their contents ran toward the usual topics of climate, vegetation, and health conditions. These guides, which one woman described as "sketchy reading," increasingly included advertisements, often with photographs. From these, a reader could cull some information regarding the banks, hotels, and other amenities available in British East Africa.[30]

During the 1930s, some guidebooks still appealed to what one called the "man" of means. Others, however, increasingly aimed their pitches at tourists and middle-class whites. In a 1931 advertisement, Mombasa's Tudor Hotel described itself as "the select retreat, at the coast, for the settlers of Kenya" and pictured three decidedly un-pioneer-looking women with short haircuts and revealing modern bathing suits. From such advertisements, a woman planning to migrate to Kenya must have derived a decidedly fanciful view of the Kenyan frontier.[31] Like Lady Cranworth, the author of the 1931 book sandwiched in some useful information. The book cautioned women to wear old clothes when traveling on the Uganda Railroad: "Ladies will find it desirable to wear a light dust coat or pullover and a head wrap to prevent dust lodging in the hair, and a duster and towels to supplement those supplied in the carriages will be found useful." The guide also suggested that housekeepers pack cutlery, crockery, and glass in well-padded barrels, but leave their heavy furniture at home. Bolts of cloth to make curtains and furniture covers would be useful. Rugs were preferable over carpets, which retained dust and insects. A medicine chest was a necessity for ministering to oneself, family members, and black Kenyan employees. In addition, a woman might want to take along her favorite dog or horse, her tennis racket, and a musical instrument, although not anything the size of a piano, which could be bought locally.[32]

Promotional literature of the 1930s indicated that Kenya was quite "civilized" by white standards. Facilities included everything from churches and schools to taxis and automobile dealerships, while private clubs offered libraries, game rooms, tennis courts, and gourmet cuisine. The climate was perfect, expenses low, and schools good. White women would find that the "social life of Kenya is the social life of England transplanted," yet "freed from much formality and convention." Near the end of the decade, one author even claimed that Kenya was a "country for women," where they would find "space geographically" and "space mentally." Without being too blatant, the guide seemed to court single women, especially those of a feminist persuasion. The book assured such women that they could travel alone in safety, discard "hide-bound customs," and share in the colony's "progressive" nature.[33]

In other words, potential female settlers found in guidebooks little helpful information, much misinformation, and a misleading portrait of the Kenyan frontier. As a consequence, a woman had to make her own decisions. As one explained, "we attended lectures given by old settlers . . . we read all the literature we could get hold of—there was not much—that would give us useful information . . . and we collected what we thought (and what proved to be) a suitable outfit of household gear."[34] When packing, some women chose wisely, others not so well. Uninformed and cursory advice contributed to women bringing with them huge crates of furniture and other household items, such as settees, desks, dining-room sets, outfits of bedroom furniture, silver and linens, and paintings.[35] More women appeared over-prepared, taking too much rather than too little so that they had to pay additional freight charges or leave goods behind. Unfortunately for them, they did not discover their ignorance until well after their departures.

Besides women's pre-trip efforts, the choice of a specific type of transportation and trail counted for a great deal. As in the American West, these two factors helped determine women's physical and emotional states when they reached their chosen frontiers. Despite the importance of transportation and trail, women had little voice in the selection of either one. Men usually made such decisions, selecting a conveyance according to their point of origin, destination, finances, and social class. As with westward migration, the much-vaunted covered wagon was a natural choice for overland travel, especially during the early years of settlement before railroad lines reached remote destinations. Typically, Kenya-bound parties combined several types of transport, including ships, covered wagons, railroad cars, and occasionally automobiles.

A group of Afrikaners who departed for Kenya during the early 1900s combined wagon travel with other modes of transportation. When the group started for Kenya's Uasin Gishi plateau in June 1908, it contained forty-seven families and three single men; all except two families had their own wagons. Near Pretoria, the group's "Kommandant," a Mr. van Rensburg, herded people, wagons, and stock onto a chartered German ship that sailed in seven days to the port of Mombasa. From there, equipment and animals were transferred to five special trains, while people rode in the back of trucks. When the company reached Nakuru in Kenya on July 18, some of its men bought additional wagons and untrained oxen, which they had to introduce to yokes and drill. Meanwhile, a smaller group of men followed a narrow track through Eldama Ravine to a flat and treeless area, devoid of human habitation, but full of game for hunting. After the expedition members returned to the main company, their excited retelling of what they had seen daunted only four families. On August 4, the rest began their march.[36]

More than fifty covered wagons, each pulled by a span of sixteen oxen, lumbered toward the Afrikaner's homestead land in Kenya. To discourage attacks by wild animals or by local people, at night the travelers created defensive circles of wagons around cooking fires. Men threw up hasty *bomas* (corrals) of thorn bushes for the oxen and other stock, while women prepared sleeping arrangements, women and children in the wagons and men on the ground outside.[37] Above the Eldama Ravine the company confronted its first real challenge. A chronicler of colonial Kenya, Elspeth Huxley, wrote, "To get heavily-loaded wagons up this steep escarpment along the rough, narrow, treacherous track, with inexperienced oxen and in a wet year, was a truly remarkable feat, and only Afrikaners could have performed it." A few more days of steep climbs and laying brush causeways over swamps brought them to their destination, today known as Eldoret.[38]

Travel conditions improved only slowly. Near the settlement of Eldoret, where white people remained few, roads were sparse and so poorly maintained that for several rainy months each year heavy vehicles such as automobiles, which became available during the 1910s, could not get through. Railroad lines finally came to the Eldoret area. In 1920, when white settlers Eve Bache and her husband took advantage of the soldier-settlement scheme to obtain a tract near Eldoret, they took a ship to Mombasa and the railroad to Eldoret's nearest railhead, Londiani. There they waited for the post carts, teams, and drivers they had ordered. A post cart was a smaller, lighter version of a covered wagon, having four wheels, a canvas cover, and a team of eight oxen. The Baches' caravan spent seven hours fighting knee-high mud bogs interspersed with drier, but bumpier hills, while Eve tried to immerse herself in what she called "the beauty of the landscape."[39] When the Baches finally arrived in Eldoret, a tired and dismayed Eve described Eldoret as "the wilds." On the positive side, the Baches found a more developed place than had the Afrikaners in 1908. In 1920, Eldoret boasted tin-roofed bungalows and grass huts and a butcher's shop on the one main street.[40] After yet another wagon ride, the Baches finally found their own remote piece of the Kenyan frontier.

For several more years, until the railroad reached Eldoret early in the 1920s, the gumbo mud that surrounded Eldoret, Meru, and other highlands destinations continued to impede settlers and commerce alike. Even during the late 1920s and early 1930s, women settlers often found highlands roads lonely and the surrounding countryside frightening.[41] Much to women's dismay, the Kenyan frontier bore little resemblance to the happy photographs and slick advertisements in the guidebooks. Traveling in Kenya proved demanding. Mud and isolation were only two of the hurdles that women settlers faced. One traveling in a small cart wrote of rivers full of "open-mouthed crocodiles" and bush full of "grunting lions."[42]

Such overland journeys had advantages and disadvantages. Like the trails of the American West, the greatest benefit of land routes lay in giving women an opportunity to refine new skills, including cooking over an open fire and using weapons. Their greatest drawback stemmed from encounters with terrain, climate, and wild animals. Within a few years, however, railroad travel became widely available. Although railways were relatively fast and easy, passenger fares and rates for shipping cargo were high and cargo space was limited. Yet the railroad provided a crucial link in the Kenya-bound trail, both in Europe and in Kenya itself. By bringing settlers from all over Europe, railroad lines diversified the social class and ethnic makeup of white settlers headed for Kenya. Railways took white Europeans to such ports as Naples or Marseilles, where they embarked on the ocean portion of their trips. Once in Kenya, travelers again boarded railroad cars, usually night trains on the Uganda Railway to Nairobi, where they changed for a destination in the highlands or another interior area. First-class cabins accommodated Europeans, their servants, and well-to-do Asians; second class served less affluent Asians; and third class carried penurious travelers who brought with them baskets of food.

Unsurprisingly, age and responsibilities were important in how travelers perceived their journeys. Children tended to remember the railroad portion of their trips as more fascinating than they seemed to their elders. One five-year-old girl, who traveled in 1909 with her family and her nanny, recalled her two-day ride from Mombasa as filled with sights of long-necked giraffes nibbling at acacia tops and "sparks from the wood-burning engine going up into the dark night like fireworks."[43] Adult women more often recollected heat, dust, and inconvenience. Stops at stations made up largely of tin sheds to take on fuel, water, and passengers seemed innumerable. In between stops, the necessity to keep windows closed—to shut out sun with a blue glass window, mosquitoes with a perforated zinc screen, and lions and other intruders with shutters—was enough to make women claustrophobic and nervous. Despite complaints, railroad accommodations continued to be minimal and trying to even the most experienced traveler. In 1920, one woman remarked that on the Mombasa-Nairobi line "there were no such doubtful refinements as corridor trains, and we had meals in the restaurants of certain stations." Even during the early 1930s, when dining salons were provided, passengers had to test their mettle in getting from passenger cars to the dining car while the train was moving.[44]

As in the American West, ships of all types transported thousands more people to Kenya. The difference was that the majority of white settlers had to use ships to reach Kenya, while westerners could choose them or not. During the 1890s, few passenger lines ran to East Africa and the first women to sail to Kenya had appalling crossings. In 1896, Dr. Henry Albert Boedeker brought his bride from Tilbury to Mombasa on the *Goorka*, a poky vessel that stopped at nearly every port to resupply itself. At Aden, the Boedekers transferred to the *Goa*; what Helen Boedeker termed "a frightful passage" to Mombasa followed.[45]

During the early 1900s, shipping lines improved vastly, adding ticketing agents, baggage handling, larger water and food storage facilities, and more comfortable cabins. Still, "dull" and "tedious" were two words women often used to describe their voyages. Neither did sea travel prepare people for the Kenyan frontier. Social activities designed to relieve the tedium of sea travel masked the actuality of the frontier and allayed passenger's anxieties as long as possible. Travelers played games and danced on shipboard, or on shore ran into what Lady Daphne Moore disparaged as the "usual seething mass of tourists and touts" and thus hastened back to their ships, which they hardly fit the pioneer profile. Moore, an official's wife, later admitted that because she was apprehensive about arriving in Kenya she welcomed "any postponement."[46]

During the years of World War I, these relatively favorable circumstances deteriorated. Due to the large numbers of wives and children returning to Europe while husbands and fathers served at the front, shipboard life could be what one woman termed "horrific." The threat of submarines and sea raiders, which set off alarms during the day and at night, forced ships to keep fully battened down until they reached the Red Sea. The result was steaming cabins, whining children, and widespread dehydration. Past Port Said, the weather became impossibly cold for people supplied only with light clothing.[47] After the war ended, ships destined for Kenya were also crammed, largely with government officials, intending settlers, and people returning from home leaves. These people formed cliques, each with their own set of concerns. Officials and their wives speculated about assignments and housing, settlers compared ideas about crops and stock, and returnees to Kenya expressed anxiety about their families and homes in Kenya.[48]

Conditions improved somewhat during the late 1920s and 1930s. Settlers and civil-service employees comprised the majority of travelers. Ship lines again tried to improve their facilities, including offering private "saloons," or suites, as well as organizing excursions and tours in ports of call. One government official's wife traveling with her husband, two small children, and a nanny in 1929 still found the ship "not conspicuously clean," the service "rotten," and cabins "not very good." She thought the majority of other passengers dull and the climate increasingly "sticky." Despite her distress, at the end of the voyage she concluded, "We have got through very well on the whole."[49]

On these voyages, it continued to be true that social class and family standing could determine the details of a traveler's experience. When white settler Esther Nash sailed to Kenya in 1930, her father arranged for his young, betrothed daughter to share a cabin with two female missionaries. In the hold of the ship, Esther's family deposited fourteen pieces of luggage, mostly trunks, along with linens, books, furniture, and an upright piano. During the trip, people watched out for Esther and reminded her to wear her *terai*, a thick double-felt hat with flannel lining, which she explained "was obligatory for women in those days against the sun." Esther duly arrived in Mombasa in satisfactory health and in reasonably good spirits. When Esther's fiancé, Jack Hopcraft, and his Kikuyu servant, Gatharia, met her, Jack had to undergo an hour-long interview with the captain before the man would release Esther.[50]

Like Esther, virtually all sea travelers entered Kenya through the port of Mombasa, which comprised as colorful and unexpected a point of entry for backcountry pioneers as did San Francisco. Because Mombasa harbor, topped with giant baobab and mango trees, could not accommodate ocean-going ships, travelers stopped first in Kilindi harbor on the south side of Mombasa Island. Travelers boarded small boats to approach Mombasa, with its bustling marketplaces and wrought-iron verandahs curtained with hanging vines. Upon disembarking, travelers entered the impossibly hot and noisy customs sheds. In 1920, one cranky woman remarked that customs was a "fair imitation" of "the infernal regions."[51] Under the custom shed's corrugated iron roof, white people waved bills of lading and shouted in English at Kenyan porters who knew no English.

Once out of customs and on the streets of Mombasa, new arrivals encountered waves of heat. Their eyes swung from the ruins of Fort Jesus to the extravagant tropical foliage growing everywhere. In 1929, one young woman exclaimed out loud when she saw bananas growing in bunches on a tree.[52] Another woman in the party, Lady Daphne Moore, noted in a condescending way that she felt like Mama in Swiss Family Robinson. Moore was no less amused when she arrived at the chief commissioner's home, which she described as a jumble of "leopard skins and masses of brass and rich silk cushions." Moore thought it luxuriant and remarkable, yet "somewhat loud,—no half tones."[53]

To white arrivals, Mombasa *was* loud; not at all what pioneers expected to find as the portal of their frontier. Although white Europeans had tried to subdue Mombasa and impose their staid presence on the gaudy city, they had generally failed. True, rickshaws pulled by black Kenyans along narrow-gauge lines transported European officials to their offices or to hillside bungalows surrounded by lush gardens.[54] Yet, despite such attempts to tame Mombasa's exuberant personality, Europeans had not subdued the city. Even the dignified and very English Mombasa Club, which dominated a portion of Mombasa's shoreline, could not overshadow nearby market-places, ancient Arab buildings, and the looming hulk of Fort Jesus. All of this intrigued some new arrivals and shocked others, who concluded that they had a lot of "civilizing" to do in this unfamiliar land.

Because not all female travelers were white, however, very different stories can be told. For women of color the migration experience was also marked by hardships, but, unlike white women, women of color lacked a strong frontier philosophy to sustain them. Rather than relying on false concepts of racial superiority, they looked to the promise of economic opportunity to help them endure. Kenya's single largest contingent of people of color, Asian Indians, typically went to

Kenya by *dhows*. These were sail-powered ships that offered cheap passage to people willing to camp out in the hold of the vessel or on its open deck. There were no bathrooms or fresh water for bathing. Aboard ship, each community of Asian Indians cooked its own food and followed its own customs. Seasickness and food shortages were rife. In a sense, travel by dhow resembled the Mormons crossing the desert pulling handcarts. Although dhows were used much longer than handcarts, both migrations involved terrible conditions endured by people desperate to reach a new land. Women did what they could to survive. In 1901, for example, one young woman traveling by dhow concentrated on the "vastness of the ocean and the largeness of the sky," which, although frightening to others, sustained her.[55]

In following decades, conditions remained bad on dhows, which were, after all, essentially cargo or fishing vessels rather than passenger ships. Although men and women sometimes had separate compartments in the hold, they had just enough room to lay out a bedroll for sleeping and no space in which to walk around. By the late 1930s toilets were still just slimy holes for squatting at the edge of the deck. In such circumstances, seasickness and other diseases were prevalent and drowning was common.[56]

Even Asian Indian women who sailed to Kenya by steamer experienced a very different voyage than did most white women. Unless they were unusually affluent, women of color traveled steerage class, meaning they traveled in the hold of the ships, which generally had no rooms or even partitions. Men, women, and children lived in the hold together, each family picking a spot where it would cook and sleep. Some people slept on benches, but most chose the floor. In such a situation, illness and especially seasickness were rife. One thirteen-year-old girl who sailed from India to Kenya in 1913 was so seasick during the voyage that at ninety years of age she said just thinking about the trip made her "giddy."[57]

In spite of the tribulations of the voyage, between 1890 and 1940 Asian Indian women thronged to Kenya. Their willingness to make the difficult trip suggests that the political and economic circumstances in India were dire. In 1938, one population estimate indicated that about eighteen thousand Europeans, or white people, resided in

Kenya, as compared to twenty-seven thousand Asian Indians, of which perhaps one-third or more were female.[58]

Traveling with Tourists to the American West and to Kenya

Migrants to the American West and Kenya shared a number of experiences, one of the most curious and unsettling of which was that they often traveled with tourists. As early as the mid-nineteenth century, transportation companies promoted the American West as a tourist destination. For pioneers, it could be dismaying to know that other passengers would enjoy the best of an area and soon return home, while one's own party was committed to staying. In fact, the presence of tourists could be so upsetting to migrants that they clutched all the harder at the philosophies that rationalized them taking to the trail in the first place.

During the middle and late nineteenth century in the United States, steamship travel to the American West remained important and even grew, carrying both tourists and settlers. In 1890, American sightseer Septima M. Collis declared that she toured the northwest coast without the "slightest fatigue or discomfort."[59] Female ship passengers who intended to become settlers might not have had such fond memories. The multitude of European and Scandinavian women who went to the American West during the Civil War era and afterward traveled in the cheapest classes, especially steerage.

American railway companies also vied for their share of the tourist business. Railroads offered safety and comfort to women who were anxious to see the wild West of the prairie and Plains, the Southwest, the Far West, and the Pacific Northwest.[60] Amenities ranging from the Pullman sleeping car to observation and dining cars made a cross-country journey attractive to even the most fastidious travelers. Additionally, the growing identification of western areas with improved health led to increased tourism. Americans came to believe that the western climate and its water improved one's health, so that during the 1870s and 1880s easterners went by rail to Denver, Colorado, in hopes of curing tuberculosis, whereas Californians took the train to the Nevada mountains seeking relief from catarrh. Railroad tourism and searching for improved health became so appealing that settlers often went west along with tourists *and* health-seekers. Most settlers, tourists, and others remained in their own parts of the train and associated primarily with each other. In 1890, when easterner Martha Long and her family journeyed from Hingham, Massachusetts, to Yellowstone National Park, Long's family traveled in the relative ease of a tourist car, first through the Bad Lands of Dakota and finally to Yellowstone, while would-be settlers traveled second or third class.[61]

Near the end of the nineteenth century, a comparable development took place in Great Britain. Such travel companies as the Uganda Railway and Thomas Cook & Son recruited the well off. Advertising broadsides urged aristocrats to build winter homes in the superb highlands of British East Africa, to travel and hunt large game in Kenya, and to find restored health there.[62] Such advertising drew tourists to Kenya along with pioneers, giving an odd twist to an already surreal situation. As had western settlers, Kenya migrants reacted to tourists by reassuring themselves that they were on a "serious" mission and by refusing to mix with adventurers. Although variety relieved the sameness of a ship's passenger list, travelers stayed locked in social sets. It is understandable that similar types of people shared interests and topics of conversation, but the degree of cohesion that passengers experienced during sea voyages was often remarked upon by travelers, one of whom found her voyage a bit "gloomy."[63]

Once in Kenya, rail passengers also had the tension of traveling with tourists, especially hunters who were usually men intending to shoot Kenya game rather than photograph it. Despite increasing numbers of advertisements saying "Shoot Your Game With a Kodak," railroad propaganda promoted Kenya as a "Hunter's Paradise." In 1931, the Uganda line claimed that although "a greater number of lions has been shot annually for the past 20 years in Kenya than anywhere else," lions were "still plentiful as ever in some of the outlying districts."[64] Talk of lions and other marauding animals could have done little to calm the fears of women headed for a long-term home on the Kenya frontier.

Meeting Indigenous Peoples

Besides its similarities, travel to the Kenyan and American frontiers had pronounced differences. Perhaps the most important was that white western pioneers often mentioned conflicts with Native Americans, whereas Kenya-bound travelers seldom remarked on troubles with indigenous peoples. For one thing, the very nature of overland travel in the United States made possible frequent contact between white travelers and Native Americans. For another, the area of the West was so great that U.S. troops had trouble keeping Indians under their control. Between 1840 and 1890, the U.S. government tried tactics ranging from military force, forts, removal, and reservations to outright genocide against practitioners of the Ghost Dance (a pro-Indian and, by implication, an anti-white ceremony). Federal officials had millions of people and acres of land to administer, all with slim financial resources. United States troops also had other engagements, notably the Mexican War in 1846 and 1847, the Mormon, or Utah, War in 1857, and the Civil War between 1861 and 1864. During the 1880s, American officials still sought to regulate what it had long categorized as "hostile" Indians.

Consequently, westward-bound migrants' diaries and letters often included statements regarding their fear of Native Americans, rumors about the "marauding" natives in their immediate area, or details of an attack. Accounts of scalpings appeared in eastern newspapers, as did inflated stories regarding burnings of settler's cabins and captivities of white men, women, and children. These episodes also provided fodder for dime novels, stage plays, songs, paintings, advertisements, and sermons. As a result, before taking to the trail migrants were well steeped not only in a racist frontier philosophy, but in anti-Indian lore.

If Manifest Destiny ordained anything, it was that meetings between peoples of two very different cultures would be troubled and highly volatile. On the trail, contact between white travelers and Native Americans became contests. People from both sides acted in a rude manner, staring at others, touching pieces of their clothing, and handling such implements as knives or quivers of arrows. At the same time, each side had definite objectives in mind. Because of their gender,

Indian men were charged with protecting their families and villages, resisting the invaders, and saving their crops, stock, and lands. Similarly, white male migrants were determined to defend their women and children as they pushed Indians aside, destroyed buffalo or other resources, and took Indian land. Unsurprisingly, conflict often resulted. Because white migrants had better technology and massive numbers, conflict turned into outright conquest of Native Americans.

Women of all sorts reacted strongly to this sequence of contact, contest, conflict, and conquest. Indian women trembled at the implications for their families and villages, whereas white American women feared Indians. After hearing stories at home and rumors on the trail, white women thought about disfigurement and death at the hands of Indians, as well as the possibility of their children being scalped, killed, or taken into captivity. Charged with child care, women were horrified at tales of Indians who seized white children and tortured them. Making matters worse were migrants themselves, most of whom believed that a woman's weak, nervous nature as opposed to a man's calm, steady disposition put women travelers at a disadvantage. Women received the message that they were expected to behave in a hysterical way and that it was acceptable for them to do so. Naturally, many women responded by becoming, according to former easterner Catherine Haun, on her way to California in 1849, "nearly paralyzed with fear." She explained that seeing "nothing but Indians, lizards, and snakes" for weeks was "trying, indeed, to feminine nerves."[65] Other women rejected the idea that women should be anything but plucky and composed at the possibility of an Indian attack. In 1853, Harriet Ward and some of her co-travelers conducted themselves admirably in the face of danger and lent aid to their weaker sisters. With equanimity, Ward explained, "I hardly think we ever suffer quite as much when anything of this kind really happens as we do in the anticipation."[66]

Perhaps the most unfortunate aspect of Indian anxiety is that it had little to do with real Native Americans. Rumors and alarmism accounted for more distress than did genuine confrontations, whereas journalists inflated or invented incidents. In addition, scholars have demonstrated that white people killed more Indians than vice versa.[67] Fear and killing were an inevitable result of a frontier philosophy that cast American Indians in the role of "primitive heathens" likely to act in "barbaric" ways.

In Kenya, a different situation existed. Traveling over an ocean insulated white Europeans from black Kenyans. In addition, in Kenya white military power was used in a more concerted way. Reportedly, the British in East Africa committed one-third of their budget to military purposes during their first ten years. Also, beginning in 1895 with the proclamation of the British East Africa Protectorate, officials like the consul general at Zanzibar, A. H. Hardinge, made intense efforts to impose British rule on a region considerably smaller than the American West. Although indigenes resisted the loss of their independence, the British had a technological advantage in their weapons, including rifles and machine guns. Between 1895 and 1914, the British government built forts and launched a series of attacks on black Kenyans, who gradually gave way.[68]

The process of rule by force began on the Kenya coast and moved inland. Even the Nandi of West Kenya, whose superb guerilla fighters gave British forces the most opposition, finally collapsed in 1905. Nandi warriors, who had harassed the British for years by carrying away British supplies and executing mail parties, agreed to removal to a reserve.[69] Although the Maasai tried a different tack, passive resistance, they could not halt large-scale removals of their people to the Southern Reserve in 1909. Britain continued well into the 1910s its "punitive expeditions" to bring about "pacification" by force. British troops burned homes and villages, confiscated cattle, and shot black Kenyans, especially the Abagusii and the Marakwet who fought British rifles and cannon with spears, swords, and poisoned arrows. One British officer rationalized these actions by saying that black Kenyans had to "learn submission by bullets—it is the only school, after that you may begin more modern and humane methods of education."[70] When in 1913 the Mumbo cult, an anti-missionary and anti-European movement, broke out in Gusii country, batches of young Gusii men were taken to live and work outside their district.[71] In British eyes, black Kenyans had no choice but to accept the fact that the Kenya highlands were perfectly suited to become "a white man's country." As a result, female migrants met few indigenes, much less faced conflict with them.

Conclusion

For all women, whether white or of color, preparations were daunting and the matter of trails and transportation critical. Even among white women, differences existed. Although some traveled first class, a host of others migrated in lower classes or in steerage. A female pioneer's trip might include anything from stagecoaches and railroads to covered wagons and automobiles.[72]

In spite of very different settings and time periods the process of women leaving their homes to settle somewhere else was comparable. Rather than adapting, women hung on to their versions of frontier philosophy. White women depended on their supposed superiority to get them through, whereas women of color dared hope that the frontier offered them some opportunities. After tiring and even dangerous trips, few women were ready to put their best selves forward. Nor were they ready to look for the good in their new homes. Although women hoped "place" would make their sacrifices worthwhile, they were set up to be impatient and disillusioned with their frontiers.

On the other side, no one wrote guidebooks for indigenes giving them information regarding the people trespassing their homeland. In Kenya, no one explained what the coming of white colonists would mean to them; for example, that in a few years white settlers would establish a legislative council composed of whites only. Nor did black Kenyans have time to "adjust" by adopting new attitudes and learning new skills. Thus, displaced black women farmers would have to learn by experience how to be market traders in Nairobi and other urban areas. As a result, the historical stage was set for a calamity.

A Frontier as Place

THREE
Arriving in "White Man's Country"

WOMEN knew what they hoped to find when they reached their frontiers, but in an era that largely predated film and well before television, they had few actual images to draw upon. Although such media as art, photographs, and illustrated advertisements gave women a visual sense of frontiers, these were largely interpretive or freely embellished. After all, the idea of a frontier was a culturally constructed symbol intended to ignite enthusiasm and generate enterprise. Consequently, when women entered a frontier region, often through a busy city bloated by migration-related industries, they were shocked. Where were the scenic landscapes and grateful indigenous peoples they had been led to expect?

For newly arrived women, who had tremendous interest in four features of their new environment—towns and cities, available housing, peoples and social classes, and land/labor systems—cities and towns were provided as their initial introduction to the frontier. White female migrants, who adhered to a frontier philosophy encouraging them to "civilize" frontier places and frontier peoples, recognized that places had their own demands and peoples their own minds. In experiencing portals, women learned that the country they intended to shape would, in turn, shape them.

Confronting Frontier Towns and Cities in the West and in Kenya

Towns and cities in the American West spread rapidly and grew quickly in size. During the decades between 1840 and 1890, most white urban dwellers in the West believed that bustle and enterprise affirmed the dynamic spirit of white settlement and fulfilled white conceptions of progress. With the exception of such holdouts as Santa Fe in New Mexico and El Paso and San Antonio in Texas, the towns and cities that fanned out from the Mississippi River to the West Coast became symbols and beacons to white migrants. As hubs of commerce, mining, or cattle trading, these places heralded the spread of white-style capitalism throughout the West. They often utilized "white" street names, like Main Street and Central Avenue, and included statues of early white male luminaries like California promoter John Sutter.

Yet many western towns and cities reminded people more of the netherworld than of a Garden of Eden. Women who lived on the Great Plains used the phrases "roaring towns," "tough town," and "hell on wheels." One woman remembered that after the first railroad line came through in 1881, Aberdeen, South Dakota, "became a town almost over night," boasting "dozens of false-front store buildings" that "rubbed elbows with tar paper shacks and sod shanties."[1] Noise, dirt, and crowding caused by carriages, freight wagons, and other vehicles made streets unsafe and unpleasant. Oceans of mud made streets impassable for long-skirted women, whereas the lack of night lamps forced women to go out only when escorted. According to some women, crime, ranging from petty theft to murder, constituted the worst urban problem.[2]

At the same time, Plains towns offered certain advantages to white women. Economic opportunities included paid jobs and chances to become small entrepreneurs. For well-off white women, urban areas offered schools and colleges, women's clubs and organizations, a pool of hired help, and a rich social life. A Pierre, South Dakota, woman of the 1880s said that the social columns of newspapers told "of the gay life, ladies' afternoon teas and elegant evenings, ladies and gentlemen's parties in full dress."[3] Other typical events included shopping trips, singing lessons, parties and receptions, balls, and card parties.

In virtually all Plains towns, types of women were divided by race, ethnicity, and social class. Typically, downtowns and upscale suburbs were white; fringe areas and undesirable sections housed peoples of color. Urban residents referred to sections of a city as "white town," "Mexican town," or "black town." Substandard housing and lack of services characterized the latter two, whose residents knew because they would be refused service in "white town" they had better find housing, meals, entertainment, haircuts, and other goods and services in their own sections.[4]

White people failed to recognize the consequences of pushing those of color to live in urban ghettoes, which they found amusing and "colorful." Along the West Coast, Mexican *barrios* and Chinatowns became tourist attractions where white visitors saw the superficial side of life rather than its harsh realities. White people who patronized merchants in Chinatowns found shopkeepers pleasant, respectful, and willing to serve. In 1869, one white San Francisco tourist said, "The merchants welcome all of our citizens." Of course, whites could not read the Chinese scrolls hanging on shop walls that read, "Customers coming like clouds" and "Let rich customers continually come." Had white people been able to do so, they would have understood why the very Asians they shunned and insulted welcomed them so warmly.[5]

For the most part, however, white women of the middle and upper classes stayed in their own part of town. Within a year or two of settlement white merchants carried calico and gingham, as well as luxury items, including polka slippers, fancy gloves, and false hairpieces. After studying editions of *Godey's Lady's Book* or *Peterson's Magazine* for the latest fashions, women consulted dressmakers and milliners about styles and materials. In the decades following the Civil War, white women's purchases included perfume, face powder, hair pins, curling irons, ribbons, lace, pearl buttons, corsets, hoop skirts, bustles, hats, gloves, stockings, and shoes. For their homes, women bought everything from books, magazines, paper, ink, postcards, and postage stamps to stoves, sofas, and pianos.[6] Most white women thought of consumerism as necessary to keep up "standards" on the frontier, but the goods they purchased also established high expectations for non-whites. Rather than letting themselves slip or becoming "barbarized" by frontier living, white women fully intended to transplant society as they knew and liked it, and to persuade others to aspire to their ways as well.

During a later era, 1890 to 1940, Kenya's frontier developed urban centers much like those in the American West. Kenya's towns and cities reassured some white women settlers and frightened others. According to white women's beliefs, they were supposed to "civilize" this wild frontier place. How would they accomplish such a task? many wondered. Many women arrived first in the port city of Mombasa, which proved either upsetting or enchanting. Because of an imperious attitude now referred to as Orientalism, women saw Mombasa as more like a place out of the *Tales of Arabian Nights* than a portal to the Kenya frontier.[7]

Most women hoped Nairobi, a city established by white Europeans that lay inland from Mombasa, would be more familiar to them. Nairobi was the first "white" city women would see; it would continue to be their base city as long as they remained in Kenya. Yet Nairobi was not much more malleable than Mombasa. The city was relatively young, dating to the late 1890s, when white colonialists who could not work effectively from Mombasa decided to create a new capitol. Mombasa was neither well-situated nor historically suited for the purposes of colonization. For one thing, Mombasa lay on Kenya's coast, while most white migrants headed for the country's more temperate interior. For another, Mombasa was too old and established, the city's history too connected with its Swahili inhabitants, with ancient forts and mosques. None of these people or things provided symbols for white people, especially the British who came from a land of Anglo-Saxons, Gothic buildings, and Protestant churches.

Thus, in 1899, Uganda Railroad equipment and workers carved out from a swamp the city of Nyrobi, meaning, in the Maasai language, the place of cold water. In 1907, the capitol of British East Africa moved from Mombasa to Nairobi, as whites spelled it. Nairobi was far from a garden spot. It sat in the south-central area of a country slightly larger than France, approximately the same size as Texas, or twice the square mileage of Great Britain and the Republic of Ireland. Nairobi caught the "big" rains each year from March to May and the "small rains" in the late fall. Thus, Nairobi was frequently full of mud. Nairobi was also isolated and feral. Wild game ran thick across the Athi Plains, surrounding Nairobi with zebra, wildebeeste, and antelope. During the late 1890s, Lady Whitehouse, wife of the Uganda Railroad's chief engineer, and Florence Preston, wife of the chief of plate-laying (iron rails) gangs, both commented on the abundance of game.[8]

At the turn of the twentieth century, Nairobi was a crude frontier town, a place where white hunters—and later locals and tourists—strode into the outdoor cafe of the New Stanley Hotel and left messages for each other on the massive tree in the cafe's center. Under its white surface, another Nairobi existed. Nairobi was simply a British form inflicted upon a centuries-old, durable culture. As black Kenyans flowed into the city looking for work, the result was a melange, a hodgepodge of black practices vying with white ones. Although black Kenyans swelled Nairobi's population, white men and women pushed blacks to the city's geographical and economic margins. Moreover, as Asians established their communities, another culture enriched the city, yet found itself marginalized and colonized.

White people intended to make Nairobi into a city of which they could be proud, a place filled with manifestations of British pride and power, including wide avenues bearing illustrious British names like Victoria Avenue and Kings Way. Gradually, Nairobi did become a hallmark of British colonialism, or in terms of bio-history, a manifestation of "display." Like an ape who beats his chest or a stallion who pins his ears back, Nairobi's existence told the indigenous population who was in charge, that the British government intended this to be a "white man's country." Nairobi's main streets eventually held classical buildings, while their precise lines divided the city into "white" areas and those of color. This display was also meant to reinforce white people's sense of superiority. Because white people needed heroes to emulate and leaders to follow, officials erected statues, virtually always of white men. A special icon was the farmer and settler, Lord Delamere, also known as Hugh Cholmondeley.[9]

Even though white people might have considered Nairobi's main streets neutral territory, black Kenyans saw them as dangerous, white-controlled spaces. Streets, parks, and green spaces were contested terrain for Nairobians of color. White discourse took no account of these people's feelings. In British parlance, Nairobi was the outpost that stood between "the Queen's peace and Uganda," the city to which settlers carried "the Flag and the Faith."[10] Despite such rhetoric, to many female arrivals the situation did not look promising. During the early 1900s, Nairobi was little more than a jumble of structures, including railway headquarters and houses for its personnel. White settlers had hastily erected tin buildings, tents, and lopsided shacks.

Nairobi was also home to a wide variety of peoples—primarily white, Asian Indian, and black. The latter were allowed no say in city government and found themselves restricted—sometimes by city codes and other times by informal practice—to poor jobs, low pay, and inadequate housing.

For example, near the end of World War I, Nairobi politicians used sanitary concerns to segregate the city into racial districts. In 1918, the Municipality of Nairobi Council (MNC) claimed it could retard the spread of venereal disease by separating black Kenyans from white Europeans. Accordingly, the MNC designated housing areas for whites, for Asian Indians, and for blacks. In a sense, the creation of black housing areas criminalized Nairobi's blacks; they had to be of "good character" to live in the district, with its small houses, communal bathing and toilet areas, and lack of recreation space. After 10 P.M., only residents could enter. By conflating sanitary provisions with segregation, the MNC, much like officials in South African towns and cities, created a black ghetto and an unpleasant one at that. A number of black women responded to this situation by selling sex, home-cooked meals, and home-brewed beer to members of the heavily male population, both white and of color. Nairobi prostitute Margaret Githeka, a Kikuyu, claimed that early prostitutes got a certain amount of respect. They worked for a wage and some even earned enough profit to invest in property. Although white women saw prostitution as a moral crisis, black women proved themselves successful frontier entrepreneurs, full of "pioneering spirit."[11]

At the same time, *dukas*, or Indian-owned shops, sprang up to supply Nairobi's growing population with such goods as cotton goods, blankets, and enamelware. By 1907, white Nairobi officials had burned down the bazaar on three occasions, they said "to avoid plague." One Indian who spent most of his days there recalled that "it wasn't very sanitary, and there were lots of rats." After each fire, Asian Indian merchants rebuilt the bazaar. Meanwhile, Asian Indians made their presence felt in other ways. In 1904, the National Bank of India erected its first Nairobi branch, a one-room, corrugated-iron shed on Government Road. Only two years later, the National Bank company replaced it with a substantial stone building and in 1931 erected the imposing structure that now serves as the Kenya National Archives.[12]

Clearly, Nairobi was a growth industry, especially for whites. They soon replaced the shacks and crude buildings with permanent structures. In 1901, several Britons founded the Nairobi Club and laid out a racecourse. In 1904, the aristocratic Norfolk Hotel opened its doors to white Europeans. Identifiable streets appeared and houses sprang up in the residential district of Parklands. During these early years, Nairobi's white population included a small number of women, each of whom reacted to frontier Nairobi in her own way. Just outside Nairobi at Rhino Farm, in what is today the suburb of Karen (named after Karen Blixen), Mary McQueen took a traditional female route, educating her children by reading from the Bible or from *Pilgrim's Progress*. Other more entrepreneurial-minded women exploited Nairobi's economic opportunities. A Mrs. Sandbach-Baker at Muthaiga sold fresh butter to the European community, while Mayence Bent (later Tate) established a millinery business and ran such hotels as Tommy Woods's and the Stanley.[13]

Because Nairobi changed so rapidly during the 1910s, 1920s, and 1930s, it gained a contradictory reputation among newly arrived white women. Some described the city as "modern, full of vim and bustle," but others dismissed it as "an uninspiring collection of tin roofs scattered about the plain."[14] Among the latter was white settler Alyse Simpson, who remembered that when she arrived in Nairobi during the mid-1930s, the city "took the sheen" off "her enthusiasm."[15] Still, Nairobi of the 1930s presented an increasingly sophisticated face to arriving settlers. At least on its surface, Nairobi appeared European and suitably capitalistic. The city had grown tremendously and gained renown as the center of European dressmakers, hairdressers, milliners, and furniture shops. In addition, local produce, including fresh fish and vegetables, replaced stacks of imported tinned goods. On Government Road, European shops specialized in silks and curios. The Indian bazaar, which had become something of a tourist attraction, offered thousands of additional items, including jewelry, embroidered caps, and inexpensive clothing. Late in the decade, a white female visitor was moved to write, "Nairobi has the appearance of some of our western cities."[16]

The transformation of Nairobi into a commercial center was critical to white women in Kenya. By the 1920s and 1930s, women's duties in countries like England included consumerism, a function that white women expected to continue in Kenya. Although some selective borrowing of the black Kenyan and Asian Indian cultures was inevitable, especially in matters of food, clothing, and housing, white women intended to transplant their own civilization, including consumer goods. White women sent such items as Asian Indian shawls, jewelry, curry powders, and even cookbooks as "exotic" gifts to friends at home, but they intended to recreate their own households as they had known and loved them.[17] Thus, the more white-style articles that were available, the more comfortable white women felt.

Nairobi was not the only city to experience white female influence or to respond to their desires. Town after town felt the hands of white women wielding the twin hammers of "civilization" and "colonialism." Nyeri is a good example. About ninety miles north of Nairobi between Mt. Kenya and the Aberdare Mountains, Nyeri was established as a British administrative center in 1902, just after British troops sent a punitive expedition against the Tetu people, who reportedly attacked a wagon train and killed its members. In 1909, a Church of Scotland mission located nearby. About the same time, administrators' bungalows appeared on the edge of town, and white farm families took up land in the district. During the early 1930s, the Tree-Tops Hotel opened its doors to white visitors.[18]

In their efforts to make Kenya towns into white towns, some women noticed the similarity to developments in the American West. Was Kenya the West all over again? One women maintained that Eldoret could "only be likened to the towns of the old American West,

with its single street lined haphazardly with buildings." A.
judged Nairobi a disappointing town as no better with its "reckle
Wild West atmosphere" than a western frontier town."[19]

Finding a Home on the Range in the West and in Kenya

Besides having great interest in urban areas, female migrants wanted
to know about the homes in which they would live and work. This was
not just a matter of desiring comfort and niceties, but of being able to
function as domestic artisans. Especially in agrarian frontier settings,
men produced the raw materials in the field, while women trans-
formed them into usable goods within the home. Although this system
was effective in terms of production, it is questionable whether it
contributed to family harmony. From the Marxist-feminist point of
view, the family included two disparate types of workers. Although
they needed each other, women and men had different interests
regarding means of production, redistribution, use of income, capital
investment, and the employment and training of laborers.[20]

Because women trained and supervised the child workers who
usually provided an important source of labor in home and field, they
tried to instill their values in these young workers. When male children
went into the field or family business, fathers took over their training
and supervision. Also, men usually prevailed in the use of income and
capital investments. Arguing that the fields or business brought in cash,
they ignored women's role in everything from translating raw
materials to finished goods to feeding gangs of workers at threshing
time. The need for a new piece of farm equipment usually eclipsed a
woman's desire for an inside water pump or an improved stove.

Little wonder that white women worried about the housing that
would also serve as their workplaces. Women's minds raced with
questions. Would a frontier house be livable? Could a woman perform
as a domestic artisan in one? Could she raise happy and healthy
children? Could she maintain white standards and set a model for
others? For women, these were complex issues with far-reaching
import. Yet women often had to take what was available. The easiest

and cheapest home for settlers who arrived by wagon was the wagon itself. Thousands of women began life on the frontier calling a wagon their home. In addition, wagons served as spare bedrooms for children, as pantries for kitchen equipment and food, as root cellars for supplies of meats and vegetables, and as storage sheds for clothing and tools. Other families took up residence in abandoned corncribs, stables, sheds, and diverse outbuildings.[21]

New arrivals on the American frontier saw these shelters as temporary. As soon as possible, they erected sturdier houses of logs, usually sixteen by eighteen feet, with floors made of packed dirt or hand-hewn puncheons (split logs with smoothed surfaces). They added root cellars, loft bedrooms, and lean-to kitchens. In treeless areas, pioneers erected tarpaper-covered shacks or plowed strips of sod from the ground and built sod huts with sod roofs and dirt or wooden floors. Regional variations appeared as well, including Norwegian homes with ramp roofs and porches in Minnesota and the Dakotas, adobe haciendas with *vigas* (open wooden beams) in New Mexico and Arizona, and fanciful Victorian houses in San Francisco.[22]

During the early years of settlement, housing acted as a leveler of women in the West. White and black women, native born and foreign born, Hispanic or Asian, lived in similar dwellings. In 1885, an African American woman settled in Cherry County, Nebraska, where, just like women all over the West, she lived in a cabin and helped in the family endeavor to raise cattle and mules. About the same time, Chinese settler Polly Bemis of Idaho lived in a cabin and became a homesteader, just like white women all over the West.[23] Such frontier egalitarianism was a temporary stage, however. Especially after the Civil War, when many parts of the West became more cosmopolitan, fashionable homes appeared. In such western states as mineral- and timber-rich Minnesota, silver-loded Nevada, and gold-blessed California, estates of the wealthy demonstrated the success of their owners. For instance, during the 1870s the stylish Ramsey home in St. Paul provided its mistress, Anna, with comfortable living and its bevy of servants with plenty of work to do.[24] On the West Coast, San Francisco's Nob Hill boasted opulent homes belonging to those who had made fortunes in gold, railroads, or land speculation.

Conditions were much the same in Kenya between 1890 and 1940. Even the most aristocratic English women realized that they needed appropriate workplaces. In their homes/workplaces, women would produce such staples as clothing and foodstuffs, or would oversee black Kenyan helpers. In either situation, white women had to possess knowledge regarding the home manufacture of domestic goods and have dedicated spaces in which to operate. In addition, most white women equated a decent home with enlightened living. Women asked themselves how they could "civilize" their own children, much less the black Kenyans with whom they came into contact, if they lived in a makeshift dwelling lacking what they thought of as necessary accouterments, such as windows and curtains. Although they could bring curtain material with them, walls and roofs had to come on site.

These factors explain why women experienced shock, or even went into a swoon, when they saw their first "home." How a woman viewed her first house depended on her personality, age, state of health, expectations, even the quality of her marriage. Being optimistic or young could bias a woman in favor of whatever type of dwelling she found, whereas being pregnant or expecting a typical English cottage could turn her against a particular abode. One lighthearted white woman who arrived in Meru in 1910 discovered a two-story house with a mud floor and a leaky roof, yet, in her diary, she emphasized the glorious view of Mt. Kenya from the log-and-clay verandah.[25]

In 1920, another woman and her mother survived their surprise that the family-farm home was a tent. In an instance of cultural borrowing, the kitchen was a separate lean-to with a grass roof and an open African fireplace. Eventually, the woman's father built a *banda* with mud walls, a thatch roof, and wooden floor.[26] The banda, a hut made of wattle and daub like black Kenyans built, was a near relation to the sod hut of the American West's prairie and Plains. Early bandas might have only one room or several, topped with wild grass or reeds. Kenya settlers built additional bandas as individual bedrooms, kitchens, or guest houses, and often added such improvements as wooden floors, doors, and shutters and walls plastered with a mixture of cow dung and ashes. One woman who lived in such a house for two years during the early 1920s remembered it as "very comfortable."[27]

Other women moved into English-style homes. In 1914, a district commissioner's wife was delighted to find a stone house with a thatched roof and windows instead of shutters. Other similar homes belonged to settlers, like a model, if rustic, English-style farm near Gilgil during the early 1920s.[28] Also, settlers of means like Lord and Lady Delamere built more substantial houses, whereas some urban homes, notably the Macmillan estate northeast of Nairobi, provided space, style, and comfort. One especially elegant house was built in 1922 in the white highlands. Its owner, Lord Francis Scott, was, along with Lord Delamere, an Eton alumnus, a man of wealth, and a steward of Nairobi's Jockey Club. His two-story stone house had a verandah on each level, floors of local cedar wood, and furnishings from a London residence, including black and gold Italian furniture, which had arrived at Njoro railway station twenty miles away and came the rest of the way in ox wagons. The Scotts named their estate Deloraine, where during the 1920s they hosted such dignitaries as the Duke and Duchess of York.[29]

Still, even as late as the 1930s, it was more common to find white settlers living in simple houses. Although promotional literature suggested that houses could be built of local materials, including timber, stone, or brick, small mud or log houses constituted many a family's first home. One woman who arrived in Kenya in 1931 and found only a small hut awaiting her on a farm near Gilgil recalled, "My spirits sank to a low ebb." To replace it, she helped erect a modified banda with a thatched roof and log walls chinked with mud.[30]

Women were not stuck forever with these first domiciles. In 1906, Emmaline Hopcraft moved into a rough stone house with her husband and infant son. Later, she lived in a number of farmhouses. After World War I, she ended up in a substantial stone house, which featured a gracious verandah, a spacious living and dining room, a large kitchen, and several nice bedrooms. That Emmaline had moved up in social class was also demonstrated by the large number of domestic servants she commanded. Her daughter-in-law Esther followed a similar, yet not quite as difficult, route. In 1930, Esther started out on the Hopcraft's "back farm," later known as Kongoni Farm, and in 1931, moved to a larger house on Baharini Farm by the lake. Eventually, Esther also lived in the big stone house at Loldia.[31]

The phenomenon of moving up to a better house might have been typical for white women in Kenya, but it presented a challenge for Asian Indian women, who often lived in houses attached to shops located in urban bazaars or rural duka towns. Even in the late 1930s, a Tharaka woman explained that "there was no difference between shop and home: it was all one." Her father improved the building, however, and added a bathroom. Later, he built a new shop and living quarters for the family.[32]

Yet other Asian Indian women, especially of the merchant and professional classes, not only left their original dwellings, but added Indian elements, including inside courtyards, wooden balconies with wrought-iron railings, and a special place, or *zenana*, for women to gather. Even in rural villages, women eventually utilized carved doors and windows brought from India on dhows or commissioned a local artisan to make them.[33] Only a few Asian Indian women lived in mansions. During the late 1920s, the wife and daughter of A. M. Jeevanjee, prominent Nairobi merchant and political leader, occupied the family's large stone house with spacious grounds on Second Avenue in the city's Parklands area.[34]

Meeting One's Neighbors in the West and in Kenya

A third and extremely important consideration for female settlers in the American West concerned the social classes and races with whom they might mix. Naturally, female migrants of all ethnicities and races hoped that they would find some compatible women on the frontier. But white women brought with them firm ideas regarding social echelons that they intended to recreate in their new homes.[35]

In the West, social classes soon appeared. Although popular mythology of the period depicted the West as "the paradise of the poor," social stratification developed.[36] Like horses, people resisted equality. Although one can temporarily change the pecking order of a herd by adding or subtracting a horse, a new hierarchy will form. People are much the same. In the West, competition for land and other resources underlay social divisions. The people who controlled land wielded power, whereas those who originally controlled the land had no power.

Among white women, domestic servants, hired help, and wage laborers fell at the lower end of the white class scale. Usually non-American born, they had migrated to the West to take advantage of its opportunities, but found themselves working as washerwomen, nursemaids, and field help. A step above white wage workers were two more groups, determined largely by economic factors. These were women of the middling classes, who typically began life in the West in cabins, sod huts, or frame farmhouses. Such women saw improvement in their economic and social status within two or three years. At the top of the white ladder were women from families of financial means to provide them with eastern-style homes, domestic servants, and some leisure time.[37] This social situation was somewhat fluid. Women who started out in log cabins often became mistresses of two-story cabins and eventually of brick or frame homes with store-bought furniture and luxuries. For instance, after Abbie Mott Benedict arrived on the Iowa prairie before the Civil War, she made twenty-one moves. Eventually, through her own hard work and that of family members, she progressed along the social-class yardstick and spent her last years living in financial stability and physical comfort.[38]

Farther west on the Great Plains, struggle and lack of material goods reduced almost everyone to the same level during the early days. One black plainswoman felt free of the usual social-class boundaries because, as she explained, "Debt was no disgrace . . . everybody was in debt: everything was mortgaged."[39] Such "leveling" disappeared rapidly on the Plains. With commercial development and prosperity came a social-class system, particularly in towns and cities. People like large farmers, ranchers, successful shop owners and miners, professional men and women, and leading government officials were in the top bracket. Among the upper classes, married women and their daughters seldom held paid employment. Rather, they supported literary societies and service clubs and worked to advance churches and schools. At the other end were those who failed to prosper on the Plains. Unproductive land, natural disasters, lack of effort, or the death of a spouse that left a destitute widow in its wake created the lower class. Women of this type survived by accepting help from relatives, churches, or charitable organizations, or worked at any job they could get to improve their situations.[40]

"Rising" and "leveling" were seldom available to Native Americans and other people of color living in the American West. Disenfranchised and dispossessed of land, these people received little notice from whites. According to white westerners, Indians and people of color occupied an amorphous category that hardly recognized them as a social class. Whites tended to enforce their domination through extolling their exalted status, while ascribing negative characteristics to peoples of color. This was especially true for Native Americans, whom most whites disregarded as ignorant "savages." Although whites neglected to learn about Indian customs, they were quick to laugh or criticize when misunderstandings occurred. In 1849, for example, American government officials issued rations to Native Americans at Fort Laramie, but gave no explanations as to their use or preparation. A Cheyenne woman, Iron Teeth, remembered that her people discarded the soda and beef, utilized the bacon in tanning animal skins, and threw away green coffee beans after they found they could not chew or cook them.[41] Although whites reinforced their own superiority by joking about the sanity and intelligence of the Cheyenne people, the Cheyenne had their doubts about whites as well.

Besides harboring ignorance, white women frequently applied their own value systems to others, criticizing them in uncomplimentary terms. More specifically, white women reinforced their status through ridicule, verbal insults, and shaming others. During the 1840s in Santa Fe, for example, an Anglo-American woman, Susan Shelby Magoffin, denigrated Doña Tules, also known as Gertrudis Barcelo, who was a saloon-keeper and well-known monte dealer. Magoffin called Tules a "stately dame" who possessed a "shrewd sense and fascinating manner necessary to allure the wayward, inexperienced youth to the hall of final ruin." More than a century later, a Hispanic priest, Fray Angelico Chávez, defended Tules, saying that "to the Latin there was nothing in the law of nature, or in the Scriptures, that labeled tobacco, liquor, or gambling, as sins in themselves." To him, Magoffin was at fault for superimposing what he called puritanical American value judgements on Tules.[42]

Not all white women held such negative attitudes about others. Missionaries and teachers often had empathy for Indians and other peoples of color. Even Susan Magoffin could see some good in them and went so far as to suggest that the postnatal procedures of American Indian women surpassed in wisdom those followed by "ladies in civilized life." Later, Leola Lehman stated that friendships were possible with Indian women, who initially hung back from white women because of the horrifying stories they had heard. When Lehman befriended an Indian woman she came to "like and respect her as one of the best women" she had ever known.[43] Of course, western women on both sides of the color line held prejudices. In the American West, Hispanas could be especially outspoken. In 1874, Rosalia Leese, a *Californio* living in Sonoma, disparaged California hero John Sutter. To her, Sutter was responsible in 1846 for the "wholesale robbery of California" from her people. Twenty-eight years after Sutter helped open California to white settlement, Leese not only disliked him, but harbored "large doses of hate" against "the white race."[44]

Later in Kenya, between 1890 and 1940, a similar pattern developed. White women helped establish and enforce analogous hierarchies to those in the West. They usually looked for, and categorized, white Europeans first. Women had a limited community to assess, for white Europeans were always the smallest group numerically. One source reported in 1921 that Europeans numbered almost 4,000, of whom 1,153 were women, whereas in 1931, there were not quite 17,000 Europeans, of whom 7,408 were female.[45]

Much like western Americans, Kenya boosters claimed that "friendship and hospitality" were "a striking feature" of the European community, but this was untrue.[46] White migrants who came from a highly class-conscious society could not be expected to turn egalitarian over the course of their journeys to Kenya. As elsewhere in the British empire, white settlers who gained a class or two by migrating to Kenya were anxious to maintain it by looking down on others. When Lady

Scott first arrived in Kenya in 1919, she judged a white Nairobi woman as a "cultured lady," but dismissed a Scotch rural woman as "a nice farmer's wife."[47]

Throughout the colonial period, the white social scale had numerous gradations. South African Boers, who preferred to live in rural areas and often disdained education for their children, fell on the low end. Jews were another group who were not only discriminated against, but were feared because of their ethnic backgrounds and religious beliefs. Somewhere in the middle were government officials and their spouses, along with settlers of average means and their mates. Neither officials, who enforced policy and relocated frequently, nor settlers, who disliked much of British policy and had a stake in staying put, thought much of the other. At the top in social standing, at least according to white values, were Anglo-Saxon, Protestant families of wealth. In 1924, one white woman remarked favorably on the abundance of rich Englishmen, usually younger sons of good families, adding that Kenya was "a country to which no man should hesitate to bring out a lady."[48]

During these years, white women of the "better" type worried that Europeans would "decline" in Kenya, even becoming "white trash." Despite the British policy of encouraging settlers of substance to migrate to Kenya, people of lesser means got through the government's erratically enforced restrictions. Thus, the fear of white degeneration haunted many white women who, in the words of the African writer J. M. Coetzee, were "apprehensive that Africa might turn out to be not a Garden but an anti-Garden, a garden ruled over by the serpent, where the wilderness takes root once again." As a result, middle- and upper-class white female settlers opposed what they called "mixing" of classes, whether it be in daily life or in marriage, and often judged the lower classes, especially Afrikaners, as rabble. In 1927, for example, one woman visiting Nairobi described white rowdies and toughs hanging around the entrance hall and other public rooms of the New Stanley Hotel as "annoying" men who could easily lapse into becoming "poor whites."[49]

Because most white settlers chose to work and socialize primarily within their own class, they had a limited number of associates and friends. Nor could they easily reach out to people of other races. Social convention forbid it, while the construction of the "other" was so complete that white women would have had a difficult time identifying women of color as potentially likeable human beings. Colonial discourse characterized the "other" as a uniform reality, so that all peoples of color were, to whites, at once exotic and alien, as well as different and thus threatening.[50] Apparently, concepts of the "other" had not changed much from the days of the American West. Racist attitudes still derived from Christianity, capitalism, and supposed white superiority so that Kenya's white women lived among unknown and, to them, scary faces.

These "others" included native-born and migrant Swahilis. Many were Muslims living in or around Mombasa, or in Kenya's inland western areas. One Mombasa woman, Bi Kaje, was born in 1890 to a fairly prosperous Swahili family. She remembered that, like most girls of her class and religion, her education was limited and she spent most of her time within her family's home. She received religious instruction from an aunt and, after she married, she returned home to have her first child. Another slightly younger woman, Mishi wa Abdala, was the granddaughter of slaves brought by Arab traders from Mozambique to Mombasa. They converted to Christianity at Freretown, during the tenure of the well-known missionaries Reverend Harry K. Binns and his wife, Mary Anne Katherine Ferrar Binns. Later, however, the family became Muslim.[51]

At the same time, Asian Indians were found everywhere, especially in towns and cities. According to one source, Asian Indians numbered approximately fifty-six hundred in 1921 and about seven thousand ten years later. By 1921, native-born and migrant Asian Indians totaled nearly twenty-three thousand and in 1931, close to forty thousand. Of these, one-fourth to one-third were women.[52] Because of their great numbers, Asian Indians, called Asians in Kenya, were a particular target of fear and scorn. White constructions of Asian Indians as alien and inferior to themselves helped drive Asian Indians together spatially, living in their own communities, often by choice. Although Indian merchants followed white settlements so they could supply whites, they lived separately. One Asian woman explained that, "few Indians sought the European way of life." Instead, they preferred to live within their own neighborhoods, where they could follow intricacies of sectarianism, caste, and religion. Although most Asian Indians who migrated to Kenya came from northwestern India, including the Punjab and Goa, each group spoke its own languages, ate its own types of food, and followed its own religious practices. These groups included Hindus, Muslims, Sikhs, and Catholic Christians. The only way they could be lumped together was with the term *Asian*. Yet lumping Asian Indians together is exactly what most white women did.[53] To them, Indians were good shopkeepers and artisans, but were not settlers in the same sense as whites. Certainly, white settlers were adamant that Asian Indians should never be allowed to farm in competition with them. Yet, unlike black Kenyans, Asian Indians could become citizens of Kenya and exercise certain political rights.

On the white social scale, indigenous peoples came last. Because black Kenyans were not considered citizens in their own land, there are no voting records or land deeds to give population figures. In addition, many believed that counting their children brought misfortune. Understandably, black Kenyans also disliked being enumerated for the payment of hut taxes and avoided getting on tax rolls whenever possible. In 1931, one count placed the indigenous population at about three million, but a white official commented that this figure should be multiplied by three to get a more accurate tally.[54] Obviously, black Kenyans formed the numerical majority, yet whites considered blacks important as laborers, but of minor consequence as people. To whites, blacks seemed an anarchic and amorphous mass.

In reality, black Kenyans, like Asian Indians, divided along many different cultural and religious lines. The largest group of black Kenyans were Bantu speakers, originally from the Nile-Congo area. They included the Kikuyu and Meru peoples. Among the smaller grouping of Cushitic-speaking peoples were the Somali and Boran. Nilotic speakers included the Nandi, Turkana, Maasai, and Luo.[55] Also like American Indians, each group had its own language, economic system, political structure, customs, and religious beliefs.

The arrival of white people and the interruption of the economy broke down the existing social order and the gradations found in black societies. Throughout Africa, white colonization caused a splintering of kin- and lineage-based groups. According to one expert, a variety of colonial schemes broke Africa into small, artificial units, seldom united by language, culture, or governing bodies. Rather than taking long-standing affiliations into account, officials placed Kenya's boundaries along latitude and longitude lines or such physical features as rivers. Although some groups remained intact under this plan, others were split, leaving shattered cultures and ineffective economies in their wake. In addition, the Maasai had lost the best agricultural land in Kenya to whites. Thus, for black women the frontier process meant a stripping away of female agrarianism and the status that went with it. Meanwhile, in white cities like Nairobi, British officials largely ignored the needs of indigenous peoples, even the Kikuyu who during the early twentieth century grew rapidly in numbers.[56] In addition, black Kenyans had neither the technology nor the economic sophistication of invading whites. Kenyan warriors who relied on clubs and spears were no match for British military technology. Although black Kenyans had the advantage of greater numbers, knowledge of the terrain, and adaptation to the climate, they eventually yielded to well-armed and usually hardened British soldiers. Recruited from the lower levels of British society, the average soldier drank hard, swore hard, and fought doggedly to expand the territory of the British empire. In addition, British military forces drew on the accumulated experience of maneuvers against indigenous peoples ranging from China to India and Africa. These wars included punitive expeditions, campaigns of conquest, and "expedient" attacks intended to demonstrate political power.[57] Nor were black Kenyans prepared to deal with white regulations, which kept, for example, black farmers from obtaining the training and financial assistance available to white farmers. Another prohibited black Kenyans from growing coffee so that they would have to work on white coffee plantations instead. Nor were black Kenyans eligible for the special rates that the Uganda Railway gave to white shippers. Thus, even though black Kenyans produced prime cows or coffee, they could not do so on a commercial basis.

Whites definitely looked down on black peoples.[58] At the same time that whites talked of "progress" for indigenes, they kept blacks on the edges economically and politically. Whites judged blacks as not quite human; a sub-species of people to be "brought along" by whites. Sometimes a white person, such as a missionary or educator, expressed interest or sympathy, but typically, whites described black Kenyans as inferior, lazy, and stupid. Despite the efforts of such organizations as the Race Relations Committee of Christian Tolerance, many white women gained little understanding of black Kenyans or developed any sensitivity to comparative cultures. As late in the British colonial period as the end of the 1920s and the beginning of the 1930s, when white women might have learned enough to know better, old prejudices hung on. One woman called black Kenyans "a primitive race" who were "inferior in intelligence." Another maintained that "the African does not work if he can possibly avoid it."[59]

These responses were unsurprising coming from women steeped in a culture that maintained the superiority of white people. Yet there was far more to white women's racial attitudes. To declare black people insignificant was a protective device. White women, who were in the numerical minority, strengthened their position by stamping blacks as inferior and inept. Women staring from train windows, sidewalks, and verandahs at hundreds of pairs of eyes containing wonder or hostility felt less vulnerable due to their own supposed superiority. For example, if a woman harbored a fear of rape, unreasonable or not, the belief that black males were incapable of carrying out an attack allayed her anxiety.

White people in Kenya, especially the British, further demeaned blacks and other peoples of color by judging them as frivolous, whereas whites were levelheaded and able to handle adversity. White women thought Somalis especially emotional and unstable. One said Somalis were the "Irish of Africa . . . quite fearless, utterly loyal, fiery-tempered and unpredictable." Another, a white farm woman, characterized her servant Omar Adam as "very temperamental." Because Omar Adam lacked the qualities of white settlers, he would "never survive the caprices of fortune that enliven the life of a settler in Kenya Colony."[60] Obviously, it would flesh out the story to know what Omar Adam thought of his employer. He probably felt disdain for his white mistress; for an Arab man to serve any woman would be demeaning.

Unfortunately, it is also difficult to determine what blacks had to say about whites. It seems reasonable to assume that, as in the American West, prejudice did not flow in just one direction. Like subaltern horses, dominated peoples seemingly accepted their status, while expressing their dissatisfaction in subtle ways. Their feelings manifested themselves in such physical acts as "stealing" food behind their employer's backs or "misbehaving" in a variety of other ways. Also, as early as 1922, black Kenyan women manifested explicit dissatisfaction by participating in a demonstration against the jailing of Kikuyu leader Harry Thuku in Nairobi. Black women taunted black men to take action on behalf of Thuku, known as "chief of women" for his support of women coffee pickers and other female laborers. As a result of subtle and not-so-subtle actions, whites feared blacks, judging them felonious, unstable, and dangerous.

Owning Land and Hiring Help in the West and in Kenya

In the American West, the ownership of land and hiring of laborers became highly contested issues. Calling their intrusion into American Indians' and Hispanics' lives "westward expansion," "economic growth," and "progress," white settlers established agricultural systems that exploited ecological resources, notably land.[61] Despite evidence to the contrary, white colonizers maintained that they brought prosperity and cultural enlightenment to indigenes. In fact, white people often impoverished Indians and Hispanics by seizing their lands. When the Mexican War ended in 1848, the Treaty of Guadalupe Hidalgo supposedly protected Hispanic land claims, yet, in practice, American interlopers demanded that landowners show titles or deeds, which seldom existed in the Spanish land-grant system. When a Hispanic landowner failed to produce a document, his or her land was considered open to white claimants. During the mid-1870s, Sister Blandina Segale, a member of a religious order, condemned such actions: "Nothing too bad for the native—nothing too good for the land-grabbers."[62]

Neither did white capitalistic ideas make much sense to indigenous westerners, who resisted them at every turn. In Minnesota, a Hidatsa woman, Buffalo Bird Woman, thought it immoral that Anglo-American farmers exhausted their farmlands to grow far more bushels of corn than they could use. She was further puzzled that, in spite of improved technology and methods, white farmers grew corn inferior to what she produced by cultivating "the corn exactly as in old times, with a hoe."[63] A different, yet similarly illuminating, case occurred in Arizona. A Yavapai woman named Nellie Quail explained that when her people had discovered a remote section of Arizona's Verde Valley and identified what they believed were tracks of Jesus Christ there, they set aside the place as sacred and attempted to preserve it. During the 1880s, when an Anglo-American heard the story, he fenced in the area and charged entrance fees. Quail could not understand how anyone could seek financial gain from a holy site.[64]

Despite differences in attitudes and beliefs, indigenes were essentially forced to work for whites who had appropriated the more fertile land, as well as water rights. Throughout the West, Indians and Hispanics were shoved onto poor, dry land where they had little opportunity to grow cash crops or to earn money to pay white taxes and buy white consumer goods. Other peoples of color also found it difficult to own land or find employment in anything but the most menial, poorly paid jobs. In California and the Pacific Northwest, Asians confronted signs in shop and restaurant windows saying "No Chinese Need Apply" or "No Japanese Hired Here." Consequently, westerners of color had to take jobs when and where they were available.[65]

White women who hired peoples of color usually approached employer-employee relations with minds full of stereotypes and horror stories, such as Native Americans taking white children captive. Despite such beliefs, white women hired American Indians and others of color to perform such household chores as chopping wood, drawing water, washing dishes and clothes, and even caring for their children. In 1840, Iowan Caroline Phelps employed an Indian man to help her in the house and with her children. Her case demonstrated that interaction could lead to understanding, as well as create change. When Phelps's Indian nursemaid died in an accident she wrote: "We felt his loss very much, my children cryed [sic] for poor John as we called him, as much as though he had been a relative."[66]

Farther west, a similar situation existed. Indian helpers worked for farmers, ranchers, and army officers' wives living in the forts strewn across the central West. From Ft. McDowell in Montana, Evy Alexander wrote her mother during the mid-1860s that she was "absolutely delighted" with her daughter's Indian nurse.[67] On the West Coast during the 1850s and 1860s, especially in California, a number of farms and ranches depended on the labor of male and female Indians. White women not only employed Indians to cook, clean, and care for children, but, like Alexander, wrote their families back east that these workers were responsible and smart.[68] Moreover, Rachel Wright of California's Napa Valley stated a basic rule of labor relations; that the key to getting along with Indian employees rested with white employers. Indians were "an advantage rather than otherwise," she maintained, "as they were not only willing but glad to work if they were left free, well treated and properly paid for their labor."[69]

After the Civil War, the situation deteriorated. Because the U.S. government relocated more Indians on reservations, they were unavailable as hired helpers. White employers on the Plains turned to African Americans, who where often Exodusters (refugees from the Reconstruction South). Farther west, in Texas, Arizona, New Mexico, and California, whites hired Hispanics and Asians; men as migrant field laborers and women as domestic help. Generally, wages were poor and working conditions bad. White women disparaged their helpers, whereas helpers criticized their employers. Due to the lack of white wageworkers and few economic opportunities for people of color, each group felt tied to the other.[70]

In Kenya, between 1890 and 1940, female migrants also found— and participated in—oppressive land and labor systems. White intruders grafted onto black Kenyan society procedures that alienated black Kenyans from ancestral lands and threatened them with becoming essentially slave laborers. Almost at once after declaring a protectorate in Kenya, British officials let black Kenyans know what to expect. On December 24, 1895, a proclamation stated that government representatives would seize land for the building of the Uganda

Railroad. Moreover, a special commission would determine the land's value and establish a fair rate of compensation. No provision appears to have been made for black Kenyans to contribute information or to appeal decisions. Later, the Ordinance of 1902 nationalized all Kenya land. The 1902 provision stipulated that government commissioners "would not sell or lease any land in the actual occupation of the natives." Black Kenyans who relocated would be compensated, but, in theory at least, lands presently occupied by them would be left alone.[71]

In following years, white settlers, including women, claimed thousands of acres of seemingly unoccupied land for themselves. As in the American West, white settlers saw "empty" land as theirs for the taking. In white eyes, such "undeveloped" lands connoted neglect or even failure. Because whites tended to see progress as linear, only the increasing use of land meant they were going forward. Black Kenyans held a different concept. They practiced usufruct, meaning that cultivation or other use of land established "ownership," at least for the period of usage. On a larger level, kin groups or lineages held rights to land, but did not own them in the white sense of the term. Although Kenyan leaders explained that they had prior claims on these areas, that unused lands served as reserves for future planting or grazing, or that empty land acted as buffer zones between kin- and lineage-based groups, British officials recognized only actual occupation as a valid claim. This policy encouraged John Dawson (J. D.) Hopcraft, an Englishman who had fought in the Boer War, to migrate by ox-wagon from South Africa and in 1905 to claim more than eight thousand acres and six miles of lake front on the west side of Lake Naivasha. The claim held even after a python reportedly ate the surveyor, along with his papers.[72]

From a black African point of view, however, such white occupation of Kenyan land was audacious. A Kikuyu woman, Charity Waciuma, later wrote stingingly about what she considered an absurd situation. She accused white authorities of making themselves "trustees and guardians of what they regarded as backward and uncivilised people." Africans, who "naturally resented this treatment," usually deferred to white power, saying, "Yes sir, yes sir," while thinking whites both arrogant and stupid. Although Waciuma admitted that language difficulties and the frequent transfers of white officials exacerbated difficulties between whites and blacks, she castigated the white government for refusing to respect land systems. "Every acre of land in Kikuyu country belonged to an individual family," she maintained. "How would a settler have felt if some other European had wandered in and taken possession of some of his land just because it looked undeveloped?"[73]

Gradually, the British government in Kenya became even more intrusive. Copying the South African model, whites moved groups of blacks from productive land to areas called "native reserves." Because four calamities struck the land around the turn of the nineteenth century—smallpox, rinderpest, drought, and locusts—the black Kenyan population was already in turmoil. Many had moved or died; those remaining were relocated on reserves. As with Indian reservations in the West, Kenyan reserves were small areas of marginal land incapable of supporting the number of black Kenyans transferred to them. At the same time, the government granted white men and women legal rights to develop land and other resources within reserves. In 1931, when gold was discovered in the Kavirondo area, black Kenyans became obstacles to white gold-seekers. With dispatch, the Crown relocated black Kenyans, compensating them meagerly for the loss of their lands, then issuing permits to white miners to exploit the mineral wealth of the land.[74] The message was clear: profits from Kenya's natural resources belonged to whites rather than to original inhabitants. As in the California gold rush, when American Indians and Hispanics lost their lands because they were in the way, black Kenyans could expect no government protection and could anticipate further upheaval at any time.

This government-sanctioned property grab obtained land for white settlers and provided them with a labor force. Because black Kenyans had to pay a cash tax on their huts, they had to work for wages. Although the hut-tax monies supposedly provided services and protection for indigenes, it also drove black Africans into the colonial economy at the lowest and most menial levels, thus creating one of the least expensive labor forces in the world. White men hired black Kenyans primarily as field laborers on farms and plantations; women employed them as domestic workers. Even though taxes, laws, and troops caused black Kenyans to work, white Kenyans maintained that this was not "forced" labor. In reality, however, tax "defaulters" were ordered to work and were accompanied by prison wardens as supervisors.[75]

White Kenyans rationalized their actions by pointing out that they allowed black Kenyans, usually Kikuyu, to farm unused land as squatters or sharecroppers. In the Naivasha area, formerly prosperous Kikuyu became largely squatters—on European land that their families had once controlled. Wambui Waiyaki Otieno explained that her relatives had done their best to adjust to the new system. Her grandfather sent a son to the Thogoto Mission School, newly built on land he had given the whites. The boy became a teacher and later a police inspector and, in 1925, married a mission-educated girl. Their first son, born in 1926, eventually became a medical doctor and political leader.[76]

Unfortunately, this case was more an exception than a rule. In liberating Africans from slave trade, the British had failed to create in its place a system of free labor, much less access to the professions. The noted Kenya scholars John Lonsdale and Bruce Berman point out that Kenya's labor system was more than an economic issue. Although the colonial administration had been able to maintain a shaky balance between peasant and settler production before 1914, after the end of World War I an increase in numbers of white settlers drove up the demand for black workers. Officials, who were charged with promoting white businesses, were no longer able to equalize peasant and capitalist production, yet they were hesitant to let such problems destroy what cohesion had developed among white colonists. Unfortunately for black Kenyans, British policymakers were committed to assisting white settlers and commercializing Kenya's land.[77]

For black Kenyan women, British land and labor policies had a further deleterious effect, in that it eroded female influence and autonomy. As in most colonies, British policies pushed black Kenyans into a cash economy and a commodification of nearly all resources, which weakened women's power and wealth without offering them any substantial benefits. Because whites believed that men should farm and women attend to domestic matters, they instituted policies that forced men to work for cash and left women at home in the villages, devoid of their former status as agricultural producers. For instance, prior to forced colonial rule in 1905, Nandi women had the right to farm communal plots of land. Beginning in 1905, the Nandi were put on small reserves. After World War I, the Nandi lost some of their reserve land to a soldier-settlement scheme. The paucity of land undercut the security and influence women had as a result of certain access to adequate land. In addition, men's pursuit of wage employment away from the reserve created larger workloads for women, who had to take on tasks formerly belonging to men.[78]

Even though whites argued that such policies elevated black Kenyan women and freed them from exploitation by men (who supposedly "forced" women to farm while they did little), Nandi women, as well as Maasai and Luo, lost some rights and stature. For example, women's usual role of gathering firewood was disrupted. European officials appointed black men to guard forests; these men sometimes robbed women of axes and wood, and on other occasions they forced sexual intercourse upon the women. Black women not only had to give up their role as wood gatherers, but were expected to stay in their villages under the "protection" of men.[79]

Hiring was problematic as well. White employers selected his or her own workers from labor pools of black Kenyans living on land reserves or as legal squatters on white plantations. Utilizing a comparative world-systems approach shows that this was a common ploy; temporary contract labor was the norm in imperial dominions. Because agricultural labor is seasonal, it has always included a high amount of temporary workers. In Kenya during peak periods, wages were extremely low and medical care was almost nil (except that given, usually gratis, by white women). One observer noted that black men could be hired at such low wages that it did "not pay employers to spend large sums in keeping them alive." Neither did white employers expect to support workers year-round, nor to offer them any fringe benefits that might see them through lean seasons. In between times, black workers were expected to supply themselves and their families from subsistence plots, where they grew such crops as beans and yams.

In order to pay their hut and poll taxes—which came due with regularity—black workers drew on other income sources, including charging tourists to enter their villages or selling women's craftwork, including clay pots, oiled sheep and goat skins, and (as American Indian women produced) fine beadwork.[80]

Unsurprisingly, white capitalism repulsed pre-capitalist black workers. For one thing, the system did not allow them to accumulate the capital necessary to farm efficiently. For another, although British government policies denounced the idea of colonies solely for profit and proclaimed fair treatment for black Kenyans, the enforcement of these policies proved inconsistent and favorable to white settlers. For example, with the exception of a few agricultural training schools established during the 1920s, the British government seldom offered any government aid to black Kenyan farmers. At the same time, few whites had intentions of teaching black Kenyans to become self-sustaining economically; many grew furious with those who tried to do so. Given the almost total lack of incentives and assistance, black Kenyans came to prefer wage labor rather than eking out an inadequate living from a small, unproductive plot. According to Lonsdale and Berman, the primary reasons the labor "system" worked, although usually ineffectively, was because black Kenyans and white Europeans shared an understanding of feudal hierarchies and principles.[81]

In this situation, white women became the trainers and overseers of domestic workers, who were black Kenyan men, and sometimes supervisors of field workers as well. Initially, white women found jarring the idea of black male workers as house servants. White women, who were used to reasonably well-trained white servants, judged black workers as nearly worthless. One, who came to Kenya in 1920, described black workers as having the "mentality of a backward child." She showed her lack of knowledge of black Kenyan culture when she added that black employees lacked affection, were "cruel to animals," and seldom helped each other. Had she understood intra-ethnic enmities, notably between the Kikuyu and Maasai, she would have known why they could not work together peacefully in one household.[82]

Much as white men established hierarchies, white women set up ranks and levels within their homes. At the top were white women. In part because of their lesser, and often ill-defined, position within white society, women made sure to exercise what little power they had. Although some white women had sympathy for black Kenyans, their own inferior ranking encouraged them to maintain, however they could, their supposed superiority over indigenes. Black servants seemed to accept their position, but they expressed agency subtly, perhaps by encouraging their mistresses to rely on them, or by protecting their mistresses on occasion, thus creating dependence. Helping a mistress rise in status could also be purposeful, as well as gratifying, because a servant's prestige increased as well.

Little wonder that black Kenyans were more often uncooperative and distant. Overwrought by seeing their land invaded and having their defiance quelled by Britain's superior military force made them churlish at best, bitter and disobedient at worst. Finding themselves conscripted as poorly paid domestic laborers further soured their relationships with white women. Increasingly during the years between 1890 and 1940, black Kenyans protested the white-imposed labor system by work slowdowns, misinterpreting orders, feigning illness, and pilfering. Dissembling and pretending ignorance became universal tactics to avoid work, especially chores that black workers found distasteful. When blacks resisted, frustrated whites judged them ignorant and slothful, as well as ungrateful. In 1939, one guidebook warned white female migrants that they would have to devote an enormous amount of time to training black servants, who would then "fulfil their duties in an almost automatic fashion."[83]

At the same time that whites misunderstood blacks, white men and women charged British officials with failing to understand their situation. White settlers pushed for the transfer of the protectorate from the Foreign Office to the Colonial Office, which occurred in 1905. The new colonial under-secretary, Winston Churchill, complained that matters regarding Kenya were "in confusion."[84] White Kenyans next expressed the desire to become a Crown colony with an elected legislative council. White Kenyans reminded British officials that the government had assured them that whites were superior and that colonization was a patriotic enterprise. They also represented themselves as unproductive and barely surviving, an inaccurate characterization designed to elicit official sympathy and aid. White farmers' labor-intensive operations demanded little capital outlay and proved to be, in the long run, reasonably efficient. Also, wealth accumulated in the hands of a few. By the era between the two world wars, two men, Gilbert Colvile and Brian Curry, controlled approximately one-third of European-owned cattle in Kenya. During the 1930s, a few large farmers grew approximately one-tenth of the grain exported. These were the people pleading for government assistance, invoking disparate production statistics to strengthen their own cases.[85]

Part of the problem was that some white settlers hoped to amass wealth rather than just making a living. They resented the "interference" of British officials, who dictated that settlers had to use the Uganda Railway and supply the British empire with the raw materials it most needed, chiefly maize, sisal, and coffee. Another part of the difficulty was the labor-intensive situation. Although labor was cheap and released white farmers from the risk inherent in high-capital equipment, they disliked hiring both individual workers and labor "gangs."[86]

Much like earlier white settlers in the American West, white Kenyan employers had deeply entrenched racist attitudes. One historian has stated that many "were hard men with hard prejudices, some from Britain and Europe, but a very large proportion from South Africa."[87] Additionally, potential employers were ignorant of black Kenyans' customs and folkways. Unaware that councils of elders rather than chiefs ruled groups like the Kikuyu and Embu, white men and women frequently tried to employ workers through black leaders who were not really chiefs or had been merely appointed to that position by the white district commissioner. Miscommunication and frustration often resulted. After watching a series of particularly trying, yet ultimately successful, negotiations, farmer Lord Francis Scott grabbed credit for whites: "It does really show the superiority of the white man; we are a wonderful nation." By engaging in a verbal ritual of solidarity, Scott at once elevated whites and deprecated blacks, condemning indigenes as inferior to whites in all ways.[88]

Clearly, white men and women developed an us-versus-them mentality, with "them" being black workers.[89] British officials said this was untrue; that inveterate complainers distorted the situation. One white official stated that a mere 10 percent of white farmers had "chronic" difficulties with black workers.[90] Whites responded in disbelief. To them, controversies over wages constituted chronic trouble, as did disagreements about the number of days of required labor. Underlying these debates were European attitudes toward work. Europeans had been brought up to believe that work was right and anything that smacked of idleness was wrong. Thus, too many of them disregarded black Kenyans' beliefs and spent little time in visiting Kenyan reserves and getting to know native habits. They also seemed oblivious to the heavy workloads of many black Kenyan men and women who eked out a living only by working for wages and for themselves on the side. As a result, much like earlier white westerners, white Kenyans urged black Kenyans to work in ways that were meaningless to them and for goals they did not understand or share.[91]

White men and women, especially those from Great Britain, had undergone far too much indoctrination to relent. Characteristics they labeled idleness and sloth held untold terrors for people who were heirs to Reformation and Renaissance philosophies decreeing that work was no less than an edict from God. Without work, people would relapse into sin and backwardness. During the 1600s in parts of Europe, almsgiving became a crime because it encouraged the poor to depend on Providence for sustenance. Legal provisions were put into place to end begging and vagrancy. By the Enlightenment, thinkers had begun to argue that people somehow owed work to themselves and to their kin, colleagues, and neighbors. Industrialization added a new spin; work had a potent moral force that could abolish poverty, while idleness resulted in the well-deserved punishment of poverty.[92] Although a number of white Kenyans, notably the Happy Valley crowd, understood and even revered leisure, most whites saw labor as moral, especially black labor that furthered white ambitions.

To avoid disputes over wages and hours, white men and women created a system that kept black workers insulated from any genuine interaction with white people and fully aware of their status as hired hands. Much of this constituted what bio-historians call "display," meaning, in this case, exhibiting power every day in many ways. For example, whites called black Kenyan men "boys," a demeaning title that made clear the low standing of a black male worker. White settlers set apart black workers in other ways as well. They expected employees to don clothing denoting their jobs and rank. White women employers wanted Somali house servants to wear their usual dress— a *kanzu*, a Muslim floor-length "shirt," and a red fez or embroidered cap. Gradually, the kanzu became customary for non-Somali "house-boys" as well. Some women, who did not trust their employees' hygienic practices, required house servants to wear white gloves. Women also sometimes supplied field-workers with loose shirts, trousers, blankets, and dresses to discourage black Kenyans' practice of wearing customary—and to white women—"scanty" dress.

Additionally, white employers expected black workers and their families to reside in a compound separate from the main house. There, house and field-workers lived in mud huts, or bandas, which they built themselves, along with additional huts for their wives and children. Typically, black women labored within these compounds, working in white homes only as *ayahs* (nursemaids) or washerwomen, or occasionally going into the fields as grossly underpaid members of all-female planting and weeding gangs.[93] Paradoxically, relocating workers in pseudo villages on farms and plantations created the time and social space for workers and their families to vent frustration and anger. Black women appear to have become especially adept at gossiping, making jokes, and telling demeaning stories about white employers. For every step that white conquerors took to confirm their power, black Kenyans initiated a counteroffensive to weaken it.

In another attempt to ensure their dominance, whites meted out corporal punishment to recalcitrant black workers. In the field, men used everything from whips to firearms to keep black workers in line. In the house, the merest infringement of duties might merit a slap or could bring a broomstick or kitchen implement down on a servant's head. In 1913, the settler newspaper, *The East African Standard*, recommended physical reprisals. The author of "The Native" claimed that kindness would only be seen as weakness. The employer who could not rule would lose face—as well as workers. White courts also supported this philosophy. When government officials attempted to bring white settlers to task, white juries usually acquitted employers or convicted them with a recommendation for leniency. Although not all white people felt or acted in these ways, enough did so to make Kenya's labor situation less than ideal.

Conclusion

Evidently, female migrants' expectations of a frontier place did not have much to do with what they actually found. They soon learned that the images of frontiers in which they believed were part symbol, part myth. Both white women and those of color had to face conditions as they were, including less-than-attractive towns and cities, inadequate housing, resentful neighbors, and destructive land and labor practices. In the American West and in Kenya, female migrants often failed to find the garden of Eden they had been promised. Disillusioned, some returned home. Others remained, some happily, others unhappily.

In frontier towns, both in the West and Kenya, white culture was more a veneer than a deep-seated reality. Still, white women did not easily desert their cause of "civilizing" frontier places and peoples. Among women's devices were consumer goods, as well as such institutions as libraries, social clubs, and white-style houses with tennis courts. In spite of such efforts, white women soon learned that frontier places were not as malleable and unformed as they had been led to believe. Perhaps the most significant thing white women discovered in the West and in Kenya was the presence of an enduring culture that would reassert itself the moment their attention wavered and their energies flagged. The task of making a frontier into a "white man's country" did not appear to them to be an easy one.

FOUR
Establishing Personal and Domestic Space

THE aspects of a frontier place that most interested female migrants were the specific bits that would form their own personal and domestic domains. In fashioning new lives, frontierswomen developed three tactics. First, women determined to carve out a spot for themselves learned to accept and deal with the facts of place. Because adapting to different ecological systems was an inherent part of pioneering, women who intended to stay had to adjust.[1] Women who could not adopt action-based mind-sets gave up and went elsewhere. For women who remained, invasions of locusts, unfamiliar crops and animals, unaccustomed soil types, and demanding climates were some of the new truths that they, whether white or of color, had to face.

Second, women drew on the human resources around them for support. Women turned to men, children, and other women, especially in times of childbirth, ill health, or crisis. Women might not have known the term *networking*, but they understood how it operated. Yet neither white women nor women of color extended their networks very far out of their own racial, class, or cultural groups.

The third technique—upholding "standards"—belonged almost exclusively to white women. Migration was not a move in which a family accepted new neighbors and a community as they were. On the contrary, the underlying philosophy of settlement urged pioneers to reshape their new locales. Also, because place played a crucial role in white women's self-images, they felt compelled to recast frontier areas to better fit what they believed themselves to be or aspired to become. To achieve this, women were willing to learn from others of their own social class and race, but not from members of disdained or conquered groups.[2] Rather than utilizing cultural borrowing to get along, white women hoped to layer their culture on top of others until they suffocated and disappeared. Quickly, white women established clear dividing lines between themselves and "others." In their former homes, women rarely invited their maids for tea and never their grocers; white women on frontiers applied similar boundaries to their personal lives. White women became the architects and enforcers of this domestic segregation. Although there is no evidence that women of color particularly wanted to mix with women of other races, white women made it very clear that they intended to hold themselves aloof from any meaningful interactions with women of color. Middle- and upper-class white women even distanced themselves from white women of the lower classes. As a result, although groups of frontierswomen shared much, they remained essentially apart from one another.

Women Facing the Realities of Place in the American West

A popular saying in nineteenth-century America stated that the West was good for men and horses, but was hell on women and dogs. White pioneer women soon learned which features of the West would make their lives hell. Some responded by fleeing, perhaps returning to their former homes or trying somewhere else. Others stayed, not always happily. One such woman saw failure everywhere she looked. She literally made herself sick by dwelling on the idea that women had become "mere verbs—'to be, to do, and to suffer.'"[3]

Certainly, the realities of life in the West could be dramatic and discouraging. One of these realities was hordes of locusts, which appeared in regular waves every decade or so. Usually referred to as grasshoppers, the insects ate clothing and bedding, gnawed away woodwork and furniture, destroyed foodstuffs, and chewed gardens to the bare ground. After a locust plague hit Kansas during the 1870s, Anne Bingham complained that the state had been "droughty Kansas, the state of cyclones, the state of cranks, the state of mortgages—and now grasshopper fame had come!"[4] Frenzied women did what they could, including lighting fires to smoke away the locusts or to burn the pests alive.

Fortunately for western women, all the demands on them were not this horrific. In establishing their first homes, early homemakers had only to show their inventive sides. For furniture, many relied on packing crates, turning boxes into kitchen cupboards, benches and chairs, tables, dressers, and desks. Women of varied backgrounds added their own touches, perhaps a carved figure of a saint or a dresser brought all the way from Norway.[5] Women also hung curtains over the fronts of these cupboards, covered them with wallpaper, and crocheted doilies for their tops. Female pioneers further dressed up homemade furniture by adding flowers in crocks or tins, papered walls with newspaper and magazine illustrations, and made curtains from muslin, cheesecloth, old sheets, or petticoats. To increase the feeling of Victorian elegance, women added rag rugs, family portraits, and even canaries in dainty cages.[6]

Shortly, manufactured goods not only lightened women's burdens, especially in rural areas, but allowed women to create homes that looked familiar and welcoming. In response to women's needs, itinerant traders and peddlers appeared, followed by the building of mercantiles and other shops. Rather than making soap from lye and ashes, women could purchase soap, along with other items such as dress goods and ready-made underclothing. Moreover, new mail-order houses, including Montgomery Ward and Sears, Roebuck, offered a line of furnishings and other domestic goods by mail.[7]

At the same time, technology held out to women the hope of further regulating their domestic realms. Although the introduction of domestic machinery never kept pace with the adoption of labor-saving devices in the field, shop, or store, the machine age did affect western homes, albeit slowly.[8] Eventually, however, the technology that thrilled women when it arrived actually increased their workloads. A woman with a water tap in her kitchen sink in place of her hand pump, discovered that, rather than cutting down time, she did a more thorough job of washing dishes. Also, people expected more of women who owned machines. One used her new sewing machine to make dresses for friends and produce shirts and overalls for sale in her brother's store. In the rare instance when technology actually relieved workloads, it failed to change the gender orientation of the tasks. Sewing machines belonged to women, as did crude clothes-washing machines. Water pumps made water easier to draw, but women still drew it.[9]

Despite the challenges involved, western women also learned how to give medical care. In a frontier society that lacked doctors and hospitals, women had to do what they could. During early years, women waited anxiously for the appearance of a Watkins "medicine man" or other salespersons to supplement their home remedies with patent medicines. Even when women had more supplies and became more accomplished, they usually provided medical treatment without pay. In 1871, one woman said that her "neighbors acted as doctors, nurses and housekeepers [for the ill], without a thought of reward."[10]

Besides all these "inside" duties, women frequently engaged in "outside" labor, especially gardening. Because women perceived the physical environment as new and unfinished, they colonized western landscapes, that is, made them look more like "home." Female migrants brought with them seedlings or sent home for seeds from which they planted grass, flowers, and trees.[11]

Women sometimes even went into fields and pastures as workers. Although western men hired male helpers, they often proved temporary, transient, unreliable, or a combination of all three. As a result, western women drove teams of plow animals, dropped seed, and harvested crops. Because they had worked in fields at home, eastern European women were more willing to tackle fieldwork than were white, native-born women. Yet, in 1862, native-born Sarah Kenyon took it stoically when the hired man quit before the fall harvest: "I shouldered my hoe and have worked out ever since and I guess my services are just as acceptable as his or will be in time to come to the country."[12]

Among their expanded duties, farm and ranch women also functioned in what were customarily men's spheres, even protecting themselves, family members, and farm stock. In Washington Territory, Susanna Ede evicted an Indian interloper from her kitchen by menacing him with a pan full of hot grease. In Arizona, a woman climbed to the top of the stable to protect her family's mules and horses; she spent a long night shooting at a group of Pima Indians from one end of the roof and then the other.[13]

Urban women had less need to take on military-type duties, but they worked equally hard to create economic niches for themselves and their families. They labored in family businesses and other enterprises, including subscription schools, orphanages, and missions. In the California gold town of Weaverville, Sarah Royce helped serve customers in her husband's store.[14] Other women learned to set type, cut hair, wait tables, survey land, assay gold, and deal blackjack, all to take the place of paid employees in their family endeavors.

Whether rural or urban, women's lives became even more complicated during times of national troubles. During the Civil War from 1861 to 1865, especially in the prairie and Plains states, women watched their menfolk forsake farms and businesses to join the war effort, leaving the care of them in the hands of women and children. During the late 1860s and 1870s, problems of national reconstruction and the settlement of thousands of freed slaves demanded the attention of Americans, including westerners. To survive, women reverted to earlier "make do" techniques, which again served them well.

Women did reap some rewards. Those who entered men's spheres as laborers and protectors, or kept things going during time of crisis, experienced three unexpected results. First, they felt empowered by being able to perform a wide range of tasks and to protect themselves and their children. Second, women enlarged their appreciation of their own abilities and worth. Lastly, other people, such as men and children, respected these women for what they accomplished.

At the same time, women of color in the West faced many of the same problems and devised many of the same solutions as did white women. The parallels can be seen by comparing African American women to white women. In 1870, approximately eight hundred African Americans, less than half female, lived in Minnesota.[15] Most black pioneers clustered in St. Paul and St. Anthony, later Minneapolis, where working-class women labored as domestics, nursemaids, washerwomen, and cooks. Although they established their own communities, organizations, and such churches as the St. Paul Pilgrim Baptist Church, and bore racial prejudice as an additional burden, in their private lives black women relied on procedures much like those white women used. As late as the 1880s, black families, like white families, lived in converted barns and other outbuildings, sat on upended crates in place of chairs, and stored their clothing in dressers made of packing boxes covered with calico.[16]

Western women of color also became medical practitioners. This was especially apparent among Hispanas. Known as *curanderas*, they provided medical care for members of their families and communities, either for free or for pay. These women were well versed in midwifery, plant medicine, and herbal treatments. They were highly respected, and essential, members of frontier Hispanic settlements in such locations as California and the Southwest—Arizona, New Mexico, and Texas.[17]

Women's willingness to contribute their labor also cut across ethnic and racial lines. One Hispanic woman in Arizona remembered her mother's life as filled with hard physical labor. Like her, many female pioneers of color contributed to the development of the American West by doing everything from drawing water to helping men harvest and grind grain.[18]

Women of color differed from white women in their attitudes toward the physical environment and in their use of land. Because whites had the wealth to control and plant large plots of fertile land, creating gardens and green spaces was largely an Anglo concept. By way of contrast, Native Americans were confined to reservation lands, usually low in agricultural productivity. Female Indians seldom had the money or the motivation to plant ornamental gardens and create parks. Also, they had more pressing problems, including medical care, education, alcoholism, and sustaining their cultural identity. Similarly,

Hispanic women in urban barrios fought low wages, poor health conditions, and substandard housing. Because Hispanas also waged a battle to conserve their culture and language, the Pro Raza Society and other similar organizations were a higher priority to them than environmental groups.[19]

Women Facing the Realities of Place in Kenya

Years later in Kenya, both white women and those of color confronted similar problems and devised similar solutions. In 1894, when white people in Kenya numbered slightly more than two hundred, the commissioner of B.E.A. agreed that women had to put up with "discomforts and anxieties," yet failed to understand the depth of women's reactions to frontier conditions.[20] One young Swiss woman who migrated to Kenya on her honeymoon wrote that she would have rather settled in England. When she discovered that their new farm was desolate land with a mud house topped with a corrugated iron roof, she was sure their venture was folly. Another woman who came to Kenya as a bride was repulsed by seeing white farm families living in mud-and-wattle huts, and was relieved to learn that her own home was brick. Others felt that Kenya lacked too many niceties, and counted the days until they could leave.[21]

Elspeth Grant Huxley's *The Flame Trees of Thika*, first published in 1959, revealed how critical women's immediate environments were to them. Huxley, born in England in 1906 to Major Josceline and Nellie Grant, joined her parents shortly after they migrated to Kenya in 1913 and traveled with them to Thika looking for "a bit of El Dorado my father had been fortunate enough to buy in the bar of the Norfolk hotel from a man wearing an Old Etonian tie." This sense of droll humor never deserts Huxley as she describes her family's first years establishing a coffee farm near Thika. Elspeth and her parents, called Robin and Tilly in Huxley's book, live in a grass shack rustling with insects, eat off a damask cloth spread over packing cases, and learn to function in a world dominated by Kikuyu. Huxley describes her mother, Nellie (Tilly), as a strong, optimistic woman, and her father,

Jos (Robin), as a "quester," always ready to start a new project. After World War I begins, Robin goes off to war, and Tilly and her daughter sail to England. They all return to Africa at the war's end and reunite in what they consider their real home, Kenya. Huxley resumes the Kenya portion of her experiences in *The Mottled Lizard* (1962).[22]

Like Huxley's mother, most white women came to Kenya expecting more in the way of amenities and less in the way of adversities. They, much like their counterparts in the American West, had never experienced such evils as locusts. As in the West, these insects came in droves, hordes, and blizzards, darkening the sky and filling the air with a roaring sound. When they landed, locusts gobbled everything: crops, vegetation, the mosquito netting on windows and doors, even sheets hanging on lines. One of the worst locust attacks in Kenya occurred between 1928 and 1930, leaving many settlers bankrupt before the great depression even began. Along with family members and hired help, women frantically fought locust invasions, one ringing a huge dinner bell in their midst, another pounding an empty tin can with a stick, others joining with husbands, children, and servants to spread poison or set fires to destroy them.[23]

Fortunately for Kenya's white women, the daily challenges they faced were more mundane. In founding a family home, women made do with what they found. When Margaret Elkington and her parents arrived in 1905 in Nairobi, the family set up housekeeping in an unlined tin bungalow with a dirt floor, furnished only with a few cane chairs and tables. On the table, a converted packing case, Margaret's mother laid out the six enamel plates, three enamel cups, and three sets of cutlery she had brought with her. In the nearby lean-to kitchen the Elkingtons found a "stove" made of three stones, on which Margaret's mother learned to cook.[24]

Women made do in other ways as well. The most recurrent domestic item derived from a *debbi*, a fourteen-by-nine-inch tin can that held four Imperial gallons of petrol or paraffin. Once cleaned, a debbi served as the standard measure for such liquids as linseed oil, ghee (liquid butter), and honey. The debbi also provided ovens, stoves, water carriers, and lamps. Beaten flat, it became roofing material, or bent, made good gutters. Also, much like the ubiquitous packing crate in the American West, the boxes that debbis came in proved handy when put together in geometrical patterns to form cupboards, desks, wardrobes, bookcases, and vanity tables, especially with curtains on their fronts and hand-made doilies on their tops.[25]

Other pieces of furniture were of local production. During the 1920s, one woman made temporary use of "Kavirondo" chairs with scratchy seats covered with goatskin, including hair. She explained that the "farm always came first," meaning seed, equipment, and workers' salaries. When her husband constructed a rudimentary bathroom with a concrete floor, a tin bathtub, no water taps, and a window facing the verandah, she pasted colored pictures from the *Illustrated London News* over the glass, thus preserving the privacy of the room's user.[26]

With slight variations, women repeated this "make do" cycle over and over again. After Vera Williams went in 1923 to Subukia, near the town of Nakuru, she learned the damage that wild animals could wreak. Once, when her soldier-settler husband was away, she grabbed a rifle and ammunition to dislodge water buffalo who had gotten in with the cattle. She dropped the lead buffalo, trading its hide for what she called a "much-needed iron bedstead and mattress."[27]

As white settlement grew, more manufactured goods became available in Kenya, but they were high priced due to shipping costs from Europe. Meanwhile, between 1890 and 1940, technology came slowly or not at all. Because it was expensive to import machines but very cheap to hire servants, white women kept the hands of black Kenyans busy stitching hems, washing clothes, emptying slop jars, and cleaning paraffin and kerosene lamps.

During the decades between 1890 and 1940, white women also struggled to establish rudimentary medical clinics in missions, in parlors, on verandahs, or in yards. When a Mrs. Watson arrived at the Kikuyu mission in 1899, she discovered widespread famine and smallpox. Although she and her husband treated the ill as best they could with the limited supplies they had brought with them, most of their efforts went to burying the dead and comforting the survivors.[28] As medical practitioners, other white Kenyan women treated black Kenyans with whatever they had at hand, usually cod-liver oil and

Epsom salts. According to one woman, such remedies were applied "inside and out with a small prayer."[29] Women also handled emergencies. On her way to church one Sunday early in the 1920s, Elspeth Huxley's mother, Nellie Grant, stopped to repair a black man's nearly severed right forefinger. Grant explained that she "seized the dangling bit, popped everything into a solution of permanganate of potash and strapped the two bits of finger together."[30] Women like Grant were relieved when medical goods from bandages to patent medicines became available in towns and cities, and in Indian dukas.[31]

In addition to domestically oriented duties, white women often worked outdoors, where they applied white ideas to Kenya's natural environment. Although they agreed that Kenya had the most gorgeous scenery in the world, settlers changed their immediate surroundings to suit themselves. Just as they colonized Kenya peoples, whites domesticated Kenyan land to meet white expectations. In a colossal affront to Kenya, they set about reshaping her natural beauty by planning gardens, directing gardeners, or gardening themselves. They turned Kenya into English countryside by replacing native trees with seedlings shipped from England and tearing up native shrubs and flowers to plant English-style gardens. As soon as possible, they planted rolling green lawns around their homes and on their golf courses. One woman explained that "it is proverbial of the English that they love to make two blades of grass grow where there was one before." In 1912, because lawn-mowing machines were not yet available, the golf course near Meru had to hire five hundred black women to cut the grass by plucking it with their fingers.[32] Even acres of grass were not enough. In lawns and around their edges, settlers planted varieties of familiar trees. One woman, who had asked her nephew to send her seeds, wrote to him that she had "nine or ten adorable little scotch firs." Female settlers also delighted in filling the borders with English flowers, including daffodils, hyacinths, petunias, phloxes, iris, and delphiniums, and in creating formal rose gardens.[33]

As in the earlier American West, Kenya's white women did more outside their homes than plant and garden. A woman who saw animals to be tended and fields to be harvested helped finish the job. Although black laborers were supposed to take care of such chores, many pioneers could afford only a few employees. Moreover, black workers were frequently unskilled in the ways white women wanted jobs done. As a result, women took over everything from sheep-dipping to running a family store.[34] Women also ran dairies, raised chickens and hogs, planted and harvested, and sometimes took over farming operations on their own. Women soon discovered that they could repair fences or construct dams as well as men. In the absence of men, women shod horses or changed tires, drove teams and freight wagons, and packed produce for shipping. Women's work even included scaring away from homes and fields a variety of predators, including porcupines that gnawed potatoes and maize, and lions. Because farm women could not afford to be apprehensive, they learned to shoot anything from rats to marauding animals. One woman slept with a dog on her bed and a rifle by her side.[35]

In times of crisis, notably the eruption of World War I in 1914, white women also relied on the "make do" mentality. Even though the war was an outside force occurring far from Kenya, it drained Kenya's male population by drawing white and black men to military service in East Africa, the Middle East, Europe, and on the high seas. In cities, white women kept businesses going and joined war-supply associations. In the countryside, women managed farms on their own, supplying foodstuffs like maize and milk to the troops.[36] At the war's end the British government recommitted itself to enlarging the white settler population in Kenya. As a result, increased production and prosperity marked the 1920s.[37]

Near the end of the decade, however, a new emergency struck. The year 1929 marked the beginning of a worldwide depression, another outside force, that damaged Kenya's booming economy. Margaret Nicholson's mother-in-law responded by raising poultry, putting in a garden, and planting swampland in vegetables and fruit trees. "Luckily," Nicholson said, "my mother-in-law was a woman of determination"; her work sustained the family for three years.[38]

Mairo Low Hopcraft, who came to Kenya as the young daughter of an Anglican minister and later married a farmer, summed up white women's labor, especially on Kenyan farms and plantations. She said, "it was fun to be a farmer's wife," but "it was also very hard work."

Among her jobs during the late 1930s, Mairo kept records of dairy cows, oversaw house workers and sometimes field laborers, and helped her husband in myriad farm tasks.[39]

Kenya's white women, like those in the earlier American West, reaped unexpected benefits from their efforts. In many cases, empoerment, autonomy, and respect accrued to women. In 1934, one observer stated that mothers of sons who went out to Kenya need not worry if their boys found wives there, for Kenya girls were "much less likely to lose their heads than the girl fresh out from home."[40] More recently, Dorian Rocco said of his mother that although her life near Lake Naivasha was "jolly tough," she managed to "do it and do it well."[41]

For Kenya's Asian Indian women, domestic life was much the same as that of white frontierswomen. They too faced a lack of household goods and furniture. At first, these women did a bit of cultural borrowing, living in mud huts and cooking over open fires. Yet, much like white women, they preferred familiar surroundings. Women turned to Indian dukas, which opened their doors as early as the 1890s. Although the first dukas offered limited selections, Indian settlers could purchase some of their favorite vegetables and spices. Also, like white women, they gratefully utilized the ubiquitous debbi.[42] In time, however, Asian Indian women could purchase from dukas such kitchen utensils as hand mills, brass pots and pans, and clay griddles for making chapatis. From *fundis*, or Indian artisans, they ordered pieces of furniture, often carved with Indian designs. Gradually, they could also order from India such items as plates and pillows and a range of spices, including those used to make a wide variety of curries.[43]

Even though Asian Indian women also faced a shortage of medicinal goods, they became accomplished apothecaries, midwives, and doctors, usually employing herbal remedies. A Muslim woman who came to Mombasa as a bride during the mid-1800s was a midwife skilled in the use of herbal medicines. Later, in Nairobi, a Parsi woman named Dhanbai seemed to have exceptional skill and knowledge of herbs, from which she produced nutritious foods and drinks, hair oils, and healthful cosmetics. Like white women, Dhanbai refused to accept pay, but the gift of an amber necklace or other token often came her way.[44]

Another means by which Asian Indian women took control of space and declared their permanency in Kenya was by contributing their labor to family businesses or farms. They were ever-present in Indian dukas, sometimes helping fathers or husbands, and other times running shops while men worked elsewhere. Other women condensed their household duties so they could produce items of clothing and craftwork for sale. Rather than being oppressed pieceworkers at home, these women exhibited agency by arranging their space and time to create a laboring environment in which they had some autonomy and freedom.[45]

Outside the walls of their homes, Asian Indian women were also proactive. Because they were largely urban people, Asian Indian women lived on some of Kenya's most expensive real estate and thus could plant only small gardens. They made the best of the situation. In Nairobi and in duka towns women grew vegetables, herbs, and trees around their houses. When they could, they campaigned for larger green spaces, notably Parklands in Nairobi. But green spaces were not a high priority of Asian Indian women. First-generation women especially placed more value on reestablishing the identities of their extended-kinship families and of community members. To them, social relationships between kin and neighbors were far more important than an individual's success in amassing and reshaping land.[46]

Women Seeking Support in the American West

As a second strategy, women in the American West relied on others to keep their homes, their families, and their minds in order. Between 1840 and 1890, white women turned to men for help and encouragement. Although a significant number of women thought western men treated women callously or that their own men were not "doing quite right" by them, many more described their fathers, brothers, spouses, and sons as industrious in the field and helpful in the home, willingly lending a hand with laundry, floor-scrubbing, or cooking.[47]

Women, especially among the lower and middle classes, also turned to children as helpers. Families with many children and little income "hired out" children to other families as workers or allowed them to labor for wages on farms, in mines, and in factories. Such practices were not thought unusual or cruel, but simply necessary to a family's survival and important to a child's training for future work roles.[48]

Children who worked within their own homes received training from their mothers in the tasks of food processing, soap-making, candle-making, spinning and weaving, knitting, and the like. Young boys and girls participated in these tasks, but as they grew older, boys assumed more outdoor chores and girls more indoor ones.[49] These gender-role assignments were not absolute, however. On a western farm or ranch, girls might herd stock, whereas children as young as six and seven went out to follow the sound of the bell hanging from the lead cow's neck and drive the animals home for milking. Girls also carried in wood for cookstoves, brought water, fed the calves and children, dropped corn and potatoes into rows at planting time, chased blackbirds away from crops, and pulled weeds.[50]

Besides relying on family members, western women found an enormous source of sustenance in female friends. Women traveled for miles by horseback or ox team to pay visits, or skied across snowbound Minnesota or Wyoming to visit female relatives or friends. Women gave each other physical help and psychological support, whether it be through the cookbooks they wrote, such as Mary B. Welch's *Mrs. Welch's Cookbook* (1884), or, more directly, by nursing a friend through a time of illness. During the 1880s, when ranch wife Nannie Alderson fell ill, her husband urged her to summon a doctor from Miles City. She replied: "I don't want a doctor. I want a woman!" She sent for a neighbor and later explained, "I simply kept quiet and let her wait on me, and I recovered without any complications whatever."[51]

In addition, when it came to religious, leisure, and sports activities, white women turned to other white women. With them, they spent time worshiping or attending church-sponsored social events. In addition, women sought out other white people to fill leisure time. Especially during the early years of an area's settlement, the home served as the primary social center, where women celebrated holidays, held dinners and picnics, and played euchre and bridge. They read, especially classics and the Bible, and sang and played the guitars, pianos, and small parlor organs that they had insisted on bringing with them. They organized taffy pulls, oyster suppers, and quilting bees, all of which they had relished in their former homes. Eventually, towns boasted hotels with dining rooms and ballrooms, as well as theaters, which offered puppet shows, dramatic readings, folk dancing, and vaudeville acts. At the same time, carnivals, circuses, and the Chatauqua appeared.[52]

In sports, which played an important role in western women's lives, white women also preferred other whites as companions and competitors. Sports were diverse, including tennis, golf, riding, camping, and shooting.[53] Some women regarded riding, hunting, and camping as the ultimate vacation. Athletic women also found excitement in mountain climbing. As early as 1858, twenty-year-old feminist Julia Anna Archibald Holmes ascended one of Colorado's most impressive elevations, Pikes Peak.[54]

At the same time, western women of color struggled to establish themselves in the American West. In their daily lives, they devised similar, yet slightly different, coping mechanisms in comparison to those of the West's white women. Hispanas provide one example. Although they differed from one another in many ways, some generalizations can be made. Family and motherhood were extremely important to Hispanas, who, as Catholics, gave their first allegiance to extended families, including godparents and *compadres*, or friends. Hispanas' values included the love of children, family well-being, and the collective good over personal gain.[55] Because family and friends were crucial in their culture, Hispanas could turn for help to the men and children of their tight-knit families. Not only could Hispanas depend on such people for assistance from day to day, they could also call on them in times of crisis. Women might get financial aid from, or even live with, a family member until they established personal and domestic lives.[56]

The Amador family of Las Cruces, New Mexico, embodied all these characteristics. During the 1860s, Don Martin Amador wed Refugio Ruiz. Although Doña Refugio was only thirteen or fourteen at the time of her marriage, she learned how to manage an extensive household. She bore fifteen children, of whom eight survived infancy. The older of the five girls raised the younger children, as well as helping Doña Refugio with family matters. Later, when the three oldest girls experienced emergencies in their adult lives, they returned to the household. During the 1880s, Don Martin praised Doña Refugio as a good wife and mother, as well as a capable woman who managed family affairs, business, and property in his absence.[57]

Besides family members, Hispanas also counted on other women to help and work with them. Together such women arranged parties, dances, and picnics. Women also actively conserved Hispanic forms of entertainment, including fandangos and fiestas. In addition, Hispanic church-centered organizations in which women were active held a variety of social events, picnics, and other outdoor outings.[58] Weddings were especially important, serving to tie together members of Hispanic families and communities. Women arranged weddings, which varied by social class. When fifteen-year-old Juana Machado Alípaz married her soldier husband in San Diego in 1852, a breakfast followed the morning wedding; later a dinner, and an all-night dance ensued.[59] During the latter part of the nineteenth century, well-to-do Hispanic families in New Mexico and Colorado expected a groom to provide the bride's trousseau, a lavish wedding, and a gala reception. Afterward, the bride's and groom's families exchanged gifts to cement a new family network.[60] Although it is widely believed that Hispanas frequently married Anglo men, this is largely untrue. In New Mexico's Río Arriba Valley and farther north in Santa Fe, only a small portion of Hispanas married Anglo men, perhaps two or three hundred of a community of four thousand Hispanics. Most Hispanas chose to tie their family and friends together through marriage rather than introducing a divisive element.[61]

Beginning in the 1890s, Kenyan women energized their spheres in much the same ways as women in the West. White women drew upon such assets outside of themselves as spouses, children, and friends and neighbors. Women said that when they undertook something, like cleaning a kitchen and pantry, everyone pitched in and helped out.[62] Unlike the West, however, Kenya's white women could not depend on children as laborers, for they were often away at school, either in

Kenya or in their former homes. Low-paid black Kenyan workers did the household tasks that fell to western children.

For help and personal support, most white women preferred to rely on other white women. In 1928, white women who had learned through experience compiled *The Kenya Settlers' Cookery Book and Household Guide* to assist other women. The guide, which combined recipes with suggestions for such domestic tasks as laundry and medical care, proved so useful that it went through many editions and is available today in updated form.[63] White women also joined with other women to create work teams. At quilting bees, female work groups produced attractive and useful bed coverings, while individuals shared information, gave psychological support, and bonded with each other. During World War I, two Australian women living in Kenya combined their farms and built cottages to house military convalescents as nonpaying guests.[64] Some women were lucky enough to find individual female mentors. In 1931, an Irish woman, Molly Ryan, discovered what she called "a guide, philosopher, and friend" in her neighbor, Pearl Poulton, who had come up from South Africa ten years earlier. Pearl taught Molly how to scrub a floor, letting disinfectant run in the cracks to chase away fleas; how to repair a broken window pane with a sheet of brown paper; and how to garden and raise sheep.[65]

Throughout the period of 1890 to 1940, white women also preferred to join other whites for social activities. Pioneers who played tennis at home or traveled to Nairobi for shopping and entertainment wanted more than a break from farm routine, however. They needed to reassure themselves that they retained their character as white women; that they still belonged to the white world. Thus, white women joined together for numerous activities. For spiritual comfort—and occasional social events—they turned to religious sects ranging from Anglicanism to Methodism. Especially in rural areas women organized "home" entertainments, including simple "carry-in" or potluck parties on such holidays as Christmas or someone's birthday. Other popular activities included playing chess or bridge, going on picnics, and joining in games of croquet and tennis. Families who lived on otherwise rough farms constructed tennis courts so they could continue the pastime that had given them so much pleasure in their former homes. During the night the grunting of hippopotami who came up from Lake Naivasha to graze could be heard, but during daylight hours the sound of tennis volleys might resound in the same spots.[66]

In towns and cities, the social scene offered much more variety, at least for white women of the middle and upper classes. Leisure activities included formal visits to friends, tea parties, receptions, balls, magicians, and traveling circuses. As early as 1902, Mombasa's white women ordered engraved calling cards and expected to receive printed programs and dance cards, complete with pencils, at balls. In Nairobi of the mid-1930s, one middle-class official's wife, Lady Lucy Marguerite Thomas, described social life as "very gay," replete with horse races, dances, and visits from up-country settlers. Yet hospitality could be a drain upon women. During the early 1930s, one government official's wife in Nairobi, said that entertaining oneself and others had grown to "a perfectly absurd scale."[67]

In the matter of sport, golf and tennis provided some of the tamest games in which white women engaged, whereas ladies' polo was more demanding. As white sport and jockey clubs sprang up, they accommodated athletic women. In 1927, Thomson's Falls country club opened, offering a nine-hole golf course. In 1935, Thomson's Falls polo club organized. These clubs reinforced class and racial lines by accepting only white, non-Jewish members and employing only black Kenyans.[68] Meanwhile, shooting, hunting, and going on safari constituted the most exciting—and most harmful to the environment—of white women's sports. White arrogance and feelings of owning Kenya rationalized women's actions. It was not uncommon for white women of all social classes to own firearms and to kill everything from lions, pythons, and elephants to game for the family dinner table.[69] A single woman farmer who loved to hunt and usually carried her rifle with her described Kenya as "an awfully sporting place."[70]

At the same time, Asian Indian women created personal and domestic lives largely separate from whites. In Nairobi and other cities, urban women established neighborhoods that resembled their villages in India, each with its own tiers of race, class, and religion. In the countryside, rural women of duka towns also clustered in Indian-style villages. Asian Indians did almost no socializing with white Kenyans. In the countryside, Asian Indians stayed in the duka towns they created; whites came into town only for shopping or official business. As an Athi River woman said, "They had to come to our store for shopping, but we had no reason to go to their farms, and we were too busy to be away from the shop."[71]

Within these villages/neighborhoods, the extended family was the locus of Asian Indian women's activities. Arranged marriages were common, especially among wealthier families who hoped to preserve their wealth and social status. Divorce was not permitted among Hindus and rare among Muslims. For both, motherhood was everything. One woman whose family settled in Eldama Ravine during the early 1900s not only bore fourteen children, but reportedly delivered them herself. She happily taught her children and grandchildren how to fish—and tie the hooks properly—and how to hunt, using her own double-barreled lady's shotgun.[72]

When children attained school age, mothers typically enrolled them in local Indian schools, often taught by women. As early as 1897, the first commissioner of the East Africa Protectorate, Sir Arthur Hardinge, suggested the establishment of a school in Mombasa that would offer religious and secular education, and would qualify young Asian Indian men for posts in the colonial administration. During the early 1900s, Qur'an schools that included religious instruction increasingly attracted students. Consequently, western education reached few Muslim children during these decades.[73]

Unlike white women, Asian Indian women usually kept control of their kitchens. Although Asian Indian women hired servants, especially Kamba and Kikuyu men, and supervised them in rudimentary Swahili, they stayed in the kitchen to oversee complicated dietary and hygienic rules. They called upon spouses and children, however, to assist with such other chores as laundry.[74]

Asian Indian women also leaned heavily on other women in support. Together, they preserved traditions regarding food, clothing, and religion. Although they had come to Kenya to escape conditions at home, they replicated in Kenya what they considered the good parts of India, such as weddings. In 1917, one splendid wedding in Nairobi lasted seven days and involved hundreds of guests, mountains of food, and gorgeous *saris* for the women of the wedding party. On the last day, the bride's father, a prominent Nairobi businessman, added an unusual touch by hosting a wedding dinner at the New Stanley Hotel, to which he invited white settlers. This was the first, and one of the few occasions, when Asians and Europeans celebrated a wedding together.[75]

Upholding Standards in the American West and in Kenya

Third, an important means that white women utilized in establishing personal and domestic space was a dedication to keeping up "standards" of their former societies. In a sense, all women manifested this belief by acting as cultural conservators wherever they went. Certainly, colonial discourse cast women as conservators of culture, families, and communities.[76] These female migrants had two or more communities: the ethnic and racial neighborhoods from which they came and the one in which they presently lived, as well as the larger ethnic and racial society that surrounded them back home and the one surrounding them on the frontier. Thus, they had to sort out the strands and eventually weave them back together into a usable fabric for their families and communities. To do this, women kept in touch with folks at home. Also, wherever they went, women took with them bits of material culture, such as embroidered tablecloths, china cups, and even pianos.

When white women referred to upholding standards, however, they meant something more rigorous and racially oriented. These women were dedicated to keeping themselves "civilized" by white measurements and modeling for others what they considered "proper" behavior. As a result, in the mid- to late-nineteenth-century American West, white women held tightly to their former homes and everything they represented. Letters flowed back and forth, sometimes resulting in home folks migrating westward as well. One remarkable collection, kept by Rebecca Ann Patillo Bass Adams of Fairfield, Texas, contains

260 letters, which reveal not only the lives of Rebecca's family and friends, but document the birth of her eleven children and her ordeal during Civil War, when she managed alone a large plantation with fifty slaves.[77]

In addition, western women kept in touch with current trends and styles back home by reading newspapers and magazines. Of the latter, *Godey's Lady's Book* was the most widespread and influential. Women joined together in subscription clubs, each contributing twenty-five to fifty cents to purchase one subscription which they passed from hand to hand. In 1849, the Philadelphia-based *Godey's* announced that it had "received a club of four subscribers" from the "rather remote settlement" of St. Paul, Minnesota. When an issue of *Godey's* arrived, eager women passed it around. Although white women might don men's trousers or split skirts when working or riding, they wanted to wear the very latest fashions on more formal occasions.

White women were also anxious to purchase the products they had known at home; thus manufactured goods quickly flooded the West. Western women soon found most of what they wanted, and at competitive prices. Women also used material goods to colonize American Indians and other peoples of color by encouraging them to adopt white products, ranging from white-style clothing to such foodstuffs as bacon, butter, and white flour. This strategy was not always successful, however. A comparison of world-systems indicates that non-white groups typically resented and resisted incorporation, usually by clinging to shreds of their own culture.[78]

Even though white women shared their products, they did not care to open their homes to peoples of color. In their personal and domestic realms, white women created a pattern of segregation that kept whites and peoples of color living in separate neighborhoods and attending different schools. Unlike slavery in the American South, which had vertical lines of domination, white over black, the line of control in the West was horizontal. Whites used force and intimidation to constrain other groups, who tacitly accepted white dominance and made the necessary accommodations. Marriage provided one example. White women were happy to arrange weddings as long as intermarriage was not involved. Most believed that white women should marry white men. The diversity in wedding styles, however, was tremendous, ranging from simple to elegant, from Protestant to Catholic, and from a city clerk's office to a cathedral. White westerners also contributed distinctive wedding practices. One of the most unusual was the shivaree (charivari), an informal party, usually outside the bedroom of a newly wed couple. Such accompaniment as cowbells, whistles, fiddles, and drumming on tin pans could enliven a neighborhood most of the night.[79]

Motherhood offered another chance to keep whites detached. The politics of exclusion can be seen very clearly in the realm of child raising, especially as children grew older and mothers encouraged them to spend time with members of their own racial group and social class. In the West, neither the rigors of the trail nor the demands of frontier living slowed the birth of children. Many westerners believed that families needed to have numerous children to provide laborers. In fact, the West generally had a higher white birthrate than the East, where some forms of birth control could be found, even after the passage of the restrictive Comstock Act of 1873. On the Great Plains during the late 1800s, the birthrate ranged from four children among American-born women to almost eight among non-American-born females.[80] Families also grew by taking in orphans or other homeless children.

White mothers wanted their children to grow up "white," rather than adopting attitudes and practices from the cultures around them. In children's early years or in isolated areas, white mothers who hired Native American and Hispanic nursemaids for their children seldom objected when the employees taught white girls and boys native customs, languages, food preferences, and games. During the late 1880s, Nannie Alderson of Montana was delighted that her baby's nurse crooned Indian songs to the baby, made beaded moccasins for her, and followed the Indian custom of avoiding spanking as a method of discipline.[81] But when children became of age to attend schools, white mothers wanted white schools, which appeared rapidly and in great profusion in the American West. Mothers often felt that pioneer schools did not go far enough, however, in implanting white gender expectations in students. The results of freedom for young women dismayed mothers who discovered they had daughters who threw back their sunbonnets and, contrary to nineteenth-century conceptions of beauty, let their faces get tanned and freckled, or declared that they had decided not to marry.[82]

Decades later, on the Kenyan frontier, white women emphasized "standards" even more than did western women. Kenya's white women seemed almost obsessed with transplanting and maintaining European ways, including having afternoon tea and "dressing" for dinner. Their relatively greater concern with white customs stems largely from two differences between the West and Kenya. In the West, the United States government backed white people through favorable legislation, building railroads, and other perquisites, whereas in Kenya the British government wavered in its support of white migrants. Although Kenya settlers asked for self-government, they felt that they increasingly received less, rather than more, encouragement from British officials. As a result, whites in Kenya believed that they constantly needed to assert themselves and protect themselves on points where the government left them vulnerable. In addition, huge numbers of whites migrated to the West, making clear that white culture had the force of numbers to become dominant. In Kenya, however, white settlers remained in the numerical minority, which convinced women that they would have to work very hard indeed to inculcate white ways.

The belief that Kenya's white women brought advancement to supposedly "backward" peoples permeated public discourse, through lean years and times of crisis, through prosperity and bankruptcy. In 1914, for example, Uganda Railway advertising told women settlers that they participated in the conversion of Kenya "from brutality and brutes to civilization and culture." A decade later, a Kenya booster assured white mothers that they raised their children "in an atmosphere of loyalty and service to infant peoples which breeds in them wisdom, patience and independence of spirit."[83]

Such discourse reinforced the resolution of white mothers to maintain close touch with their former homes and cultures. Consequently, the extension of postal services and the arrival of railroad lines took on new dimensions. Marjorie Pharazyn, the wife of a soldier settler, explained that when the railway reached Eldoret in 1924 and Kitale the following year, "the wild and woolly days of the Trans Nzoia came to an end." Soon schools, banks, hospitals, churches, and political meetings existed. According to Pharazyn, "'civilization' had arrived."[84]

Given this need for contact, "home leaves" became especially important to whites, who believed it was essential to spend some time at home every few years to renew their definition of "civilization" and to reassure themselves that "civilization" still existed "back home." Although such trips offered respite, renewed family ties, and restored health, their primary purpose was to keep a person's mind from becoming what one English woman described as "inert as a cabbage." She feared that if she were transplanted from Kenya to an English drawing room she would sit "bewildered and dumb."[85] Home leaves offered an additional opportunity in that some white families were able to take black Kenyans with them, showing them such technological wonders as elevators, taxis, and even wax models in shop windows, and sending them back to Kenya with plenty to tell family members and friends.[86]

Even though contact with "home" was important, white women felt that in Kenya they must set good examples and model the benefits of white "civilization."[87] One of women's major worries was dressing appropriately. In the course of their new duties, white women settlers soon discovered that they had to adapt their clothing. Instead of the full skirts and long-sleeved, high-necked shirtwaists of the 1890s and early 1900s, gradually sturdy shoes, plain white shirts, and long khaki skirts became the order of the day, with the skirts growing shorter during the 1910s and 1920s. Because white women hoped to retain such vestiges of white femininity as pale skin, they covered their faces with brimmed hats and their hands with gloves. Even this utilitarian clothing proved awkward for such tasks as riding a horse or sewing up a bloody gash in a worker's arm. As a result, by the 1920s and 1930s, a number of women adopted another innovation, the split skirt, which looked like a proper skirt yet gave the necessary freedom of movement for women's multiple tasks.[88] These same women were determined not to "regress" to what they considered a barbaric state. Like white western women, they kept abreast of fashions back home. In addition, on farms and plantations, white settlers "dressed" for dinner, either in gowns and suits or in fancy dressing gowns and pyjamas made for such occasions.[89] "It was essential that we kept high standards," one woman explained, "as it was only too easy to go native."[90]

At the same time, white women employed consumer goods in their campaign to uphold white standards. Women tried to offset Kenya's deficiencies by sending for such trappings of women's culture as treadle-sewing machines, books containing receipts (recipes) and household hints, and children's lesson and story books. One young woman commented that before the arrival of books and pictures, she was "quite stumped" when trying to tell children fairy tales. She thought it distressing that "little Joan, aged 5, knew all about milking & calving & farm things but nothing make-believe or fanciful."[91] The lack of fairy tales, nursery rhymes, and children's books left Joan and others like her without the fuzziest notion of white popular culture, or of women's traditions regarding everything from princesses and sleeping beauties to wicked stepmothers and witches. The absence of popular children's literature created a lamentable void for women who wished to pass on positive and negative models of white womanhood.

White women also relied upon certain products, along with their advertising and labeling, to impart a message to black Kenyans. Products to make things white abounded: body soap, laundry detergent, bleach, face creams, and powder, all associated with the female gender. Into their servants' work lives, white women introduced white uniforms, white gloves, and toothbrushes with white paste. In advertisements and product labels, the color white also predominated. White aprons, white dresses, white socks, white bread, white buildings, and white women, men, and children all seemed to be symbols of civilization, at least as white settlers knew it.[92]

White women were also adept at establishing clear dividing lines between themselves and others. Women's desire to conserve customary ways manifested itself in marriage ceremonies and celebrations. Unlike the American West, Kenya's white women had more control over marriage through the use of social sanctions. Because the white community was small in number, scorn and shunning could seriously affect a white man who had a relationship with a woman of color. In addition, weddings were celebrated as traditionally as possible, with an eye to white propriety. Often, weddings occurred immediately after a bride-to-be joined her betrothed in Mombasa. Women stepped from the deck of the ship that brought them to Kenya to find themselves whisked to the alter of Mombasa Memorial Cathedral, dedicated in 1905, and decorated for this occasion with oleanders and jasmine.[93] Despite the city's incredible heat, brides wore elaborate dresses and veils that wilted in Mombasa's humidity. After a choral service, with the bishop of Mombasa officiating, newly married women stood perspiring in receiving lines to accept congratulations. When the soldier-settlement scheme went into effect after World War I, so many engaged women arrived on the *Garth Castle* in 1919 to wed their fiancees that officials married three couples at a time.[94]

On other occasions, weddings were elaborate and constituted the white social event of the year. When Esther Nash arrived in Mombasa on April 10, 1930, her fiancee and his servant escorted her to the family farm on Lake Naivasha. On April 19, the couple wed in front of one hundred guests, a ceremony that the *East Africa Standard* duly reported. With the servant still in attendance, the couple went to Nairobi's Norfolk Hotel and to a honeymoon in Uganda.[95]

After marriage, Kenya's white women, like those in the American West, put a lot of energy into motherhood. Although some expectant mothers returned to England to give birth, others stayed in Kenya. In 1907, with the assistance of a black Kenyan midwife an Afrikaner women delivered a daughter near Kiambu. In 1908, an English woman bore a baby at Delamere's Florida Farm, which she claimed was the first white child born in the highlands area of Kenya. In 1912, a Quaker missionary from Wichita, Kansas, had a child at a far-flung mission station on the shores of Lake Victoria.[96]

Of course, women everywhere debated and studied child raising, but Kenya's white mothers viewed it as an especially troubling issue. Beginning during the 1890s, British officials and other observers hotly debated whether a white child could survive in Africa's climate. Most said no, at least not without suffering some decline in health and mental development. Some said yes; Europeans might "rear children without much, if any deterioration of race." By the 1920s, low infant-

and child-mortality figures among Europeans supported the latter point of view. Neither did statistics regarding lunacy or nervous disorders suggest that white children had anything to fear in Kenya besides the usual malaria and fevers.[97] To mothers, however, Kenya threatened children. In their eyes, every bush sheltered a poisonous puff adder, every ray of sun cast a debilitating flame. Thus, mothers took what might appear to be drastic measures. For example, between 8 A.M. and 4 P.M., mothers clad their children in flannel spine pads and pith helmets, both meant to keep the rays of the sun off children's delicate backs and heads.

In Kenya, place forced many mothers to make an accommodation seldom found in the American West. Because black employers lived on the farms and plantations where they worked, their children were available as companions to the children of white farm and plantation owners. In addition, there were few white schools and other white children often lived a considerable distance away. When one white woman recalled her childhood near Lake Naivasha in the years before World War I she said of herself and her siblings, "We cared nothing for the things that European children did" and "knew nothing of the taboos of sophisticated societies." Their toys came from bits of sticks and string; because their friends were black, for their first years they spoke Swahili. Other white children learned to speak Kikuyu, absorbing it from black children rather than through lessons.[98]

Mothers who wanted to help their children become, in their words, properly "civilized," started early by teaching young children at home or organizing small schools for white children only. As soon as children reached school age, they attended day schools and boarding schools in Kenya or went "home" for further education.[99] In some cases, white parents had to separate their children from their black playmates and set them on a "white" educational course. One white man could still feel the "bitter disappointment" he experienced when he started school. "My days as a barefoot white Maasai were over," he explained.[100]

Even during the 1920s and 1930s, when white settlement increased, a number of white children considered black children their friends. During the late 1930s, Robert R. McConnel, whose family had recently migrated from Scotland, recalled that he survived being the only child of a white farm family by playing with the children of black workers. McConnel added that when his parents sent him to a white boarding school, he "hated going away" from his friends and familiar ways of life.[101]

Also, unlike white women in the American West, Kenya's white mothers hesitated to employ local people for child care. Those who hired black women called ayahs (nursemaids) judged them incompetent and useful for only the most basic duties. Those who could afford it brought white governesses and nannies from Europe, at least in part to stand as sentinels for white society. Governesses and nannies instilled in white children things they needed to know, including sexual practices and customary white values. One frequently pointed out to her charges that a neighborhood bachelor needed a wife to "keep him up to civilized standards," whereas another told her youngsters that because whites were far different from blacks they dared not lose "a grip" on their "standards." White governesses and nannies also reassured white children that they would not grow up to be "a colonial, but just the same as any well-brought-up English child." At the same time, governesses and nannies, who were themselves socially inferior to the children for whom they cared, taught boys and girls how to dominate space through body language, tone of voice, and upper-class accents. These children did not whistle, wiggle, giggle, or spit. Rather, they commanded deference through dignity.[102]

Even though exceptions existed, most white women wanted their children to learn white-style discipline, self-control, and work habits so they could eventually pass British school exams. Because English people at home viewed colonial children as an asset on which the future of the British empire relied, they hoped for the same outcome. Proper motherhood and formal education thus became national duties. With the right mother and a good education, whites at home and in Kenya believed that children would make a success of their lives and become "worthy" Kenyan citizens.[103]

Conclusion

Comparing the first two strategies that women utilized on frontiers in establishing their personal and domestic space reveals that many similarities existed in spite of social class and race. The techniques that female migrants employed in "settling in" brought them closer than in any other area of their lives. A modicum of sharing and cultural borrowing occurred. For instance, women of one race who worked for women of another as seamstresses and cooks imparted patterns and recipes. Racial tensions and prejudices cannot be discounted, however. Most women—white and of color—preferred to create lives among people who appeared to them comfortable and reassuring. To achieve this goal, white women utilized a third strategy, upholding "standards," which purposely held at bay women of color.

Why do scholars know a great deal about white frontierswomen and relatively little about those of color? In part, white women's families saved their letters and diaries, eventually giving them to research archives who collected white women's documents, but seldom those of color. Also, white writers had far more access to publishers who would print their words. A prime example is Elspeth Huxley, who developed into the unofficial chronicler of the white experience in Kenya. In addition to writing *The Flame Trees of Thika* and other books, Huxley collected and published the reminiscences of Kenya's white pioneers, including a memoir and the Africa letters (1933–1977) of her mother, Nellie Grant.[104] Apparently, Huxley represented white settlers fairly, at least from the perspective of white settlers. In 1998, white settler Doreen Tofe Field, living in a retirement village in Malindi, said "that was us . . . there we were in Huxley's books."[105]

Unfortunately, however, because white women kept to themselves and carefully controlled their personal and domestic spheres, they lost track of the wider world around them. Kenyan Margaret Elkington said that her father believed that whites in general made a critical error: because black Kenyans seemed friendly and "learned to work," white settlers "took it for granted that everything was all right."[106] As the Elkingtons and others found out, everything was quite the opposite from "all right."

Although railroads and ships were important in migration to the American and Kenyan frontiers, many people relied on versions of the Conestoga wagon or the lighter immigrant wagon. The first wagon travelers in the American West are unidentified and undated; the second is the Percival family, probably in the Kenyan highlands during the 1910s.

Courtesy of the Museum of New Mexico, negative #15069, and the Bodleian Library, Kenya Settlers Photographic Collection, Oxford, England.

When female migrants arrived on the American and Kenyan frontiers, they found vast spaces and spectacular scenery. The upper photo is Nevada Falls in Yosemite National Park, undated, and the lower, which looks like Arizona, is in Kenya, place unidentified and undated.

Courtesy of the author and of the Bodleian Library, Kenya Settlers Photographic Collection, Oxford, England.

Potential settlers usually arrived on the frontier through a town, like Lake Andes, undated, in what is today South Dakota, or Gilgil, 1927, in Kenya, which served as supply centers and contact points with white civilization.

Courtesy of the author and the Bodleian Library, Kenya Settlers Photographic Collection, Oxford, England.

The majority of early white settlers hoped to become successful farmers, but had to start small, like this farm family in Morton County, today North Dakota, undated, and the Powys-Cobb family, during the 1910s, in the Kenya highlands. The latter adopted the houses and stick fences from black Kenyans.

  Courtesy of the State Archives and Historical Research Library, Bismarck, ND, and the Bodleian Library, Kenya Settlers Photograph Collection, Oxford, England.

On these early farms, white women worked inside and outside. A woman living in a frame homestead in Montana, undated, cooks on a wood-burning stove. During the 1910s, Vivien Percival, place unidentified, tends chickens.

Courtesy of the Montana State Historical Society and the Bodleian Library, Kenya Settlers Photograph Collection, Oxford, England.

Female migrants were not only white, but included those of color, some of whom farmed whereas others entered the local economy. Although this photograph of Polly Bemis was taken in 1910, she arrived in Warren, Idaho, in 1872, where she earned a living trapping, trading, and helping her husband work their mine. In Kenya, Asian Indian women sometimes supplied poorly paid factory labor, unidentified place and undated.

Courtesy of the Idaho State Historical Society and the Bodleian Library, Kenya Settlers Photographic Collection, Oxford, England.

Indigenous women continued to play important roles in colonial economies, often working at customary tasks, like the Chippewa woman who weaves a birch canoe, undated, and the Kenyan woman with a churn, undated.

Courtesy of the Museum of New Mexico, negative #90554, and the Bodleian Library, Kenya Settlers Photographic Collection, Oxford, England.

For white women, such frontier conditions as demanding climates, lack of capital, and numerous children forced them to adapt while also clinging to whatever traditions they could. An extended family in Arizona during the 1880s lived in log cabins, but the women hung curtains in the single window. Probably during the 1920s, the Powys-Cobb family began construction of a frame home to replace their straw dwellings. Their only concession to frontier clothing fashions is the addition of pith helmets, thought necessary for protection from the sun.

Courtesy of the Museum of New Mexico, Santa Fe, negative #15615, and the Bodleian Library, Kenya Settlers Photographic Collection, Oxford, England.

Settlers on frontiers also preserved their traditional celebrations and holidays. On February 20, 1881, William and Anna Belle Steintemp wed in Minnesota. Probably during the 1920s, a group of white Kenyans celebrated Empire Day, unidentified place.

Courtesy of Minnesota Historical Society and the Bodleian Library, Kenya Settlers Photographic Collection, Oxford, England.

Indigenous women also tried to preserve their cultures, as with the Indian potter at San Ildefonso Pueblo in New Mexico, undated, and the Lumbwa girl in Saigo Soi, 1914, who displays fine ceremonial beadwork.

Courtesy of the author and of the Bodleian Library, Kenya Settlers Photographic Collection, Oxford, England.

White settlers also had a penchant for enjoying the natural environment, as with the Engle family camping in a canyon near Utah's Lost Lake Valley, 1887, and a safari group of white Kenyans with black Kenyan helpers in the background at an unidentified place in 1926.

Courtesy of the Utah State Historical Society and the Bodleian Library, Kenya Settlers Photographic Collection, Oxford, England.

The invention of photography, especially portable Eastman Kodak cameras, encouraged whites to visit the homes and villages of indigenous peoples and to photograph them as tourist sites.

Courtesy of the Montana Historical Society and the Bodleian Library, Kenya Settlers Photographic Collection, Oxford, England.

A Frontier as Process

FIVE
Entering the Public Realm

F RONTIERSWOMEN seldom stayed in the personal and domestic spaces they established. In the American West and in Kenya, women participated in the larger public process of "settling" a frontier. During the development of frontier process, women influenced policymaking, as well as determining details. To rationalize such public involvement, supposedly home-oriented women expanded their definitions of personal and domestic spheres to include activities away from their homes. This was relatively easy on a frontier, at least for white women. A lack of strong governmental agencies, clear policies, and effective central control created openings for women, both paid and volunteer. As officials debated and dispatched numerous memorandums to home governments, women on the ground seized opportunities.[1]

Other openings existed as well in the public sphere. Because frontier settlers hoped to establish as soon as possible a market economy like the one back home, women's labor became acceptable; thus, a considerable number of other white women entered the world outside their homes by grasping economic opportunities. Yet others got involved in public affairs through such benevolent undertakings as establishing mission stations, nursing the ill, or organizing women's clubs. Some women's activities spanned both categories, the economic and the benevolent. Because virtually all these women agreed that frontiers should be white dominated, they also helped establish a public color line, which made it very clear that although white women ventured far away from their homes, they were still untouchable.

White Women Seizing Economic Opportunities in the West and in Kenya

On frontiers, a number of economic opportunities opened for white women who were willing to develop new skills or capitalize on old ones. This is not to say that these women lacked altruistic feelings; many of them also gave time to favorite causes, ranging from charity organizations to women's clubs. In fact, numerous women gained self-confidence and marketable abilities through volunteer work, including administering budgets, meeting the public, and supervising employees.[2] In addition, some women seemed to have been born with a fierce entrepreneurial spirit, which life on a frontier fostered. Because of preference or economic need, women helped establish a white-style economy on frontiers, but added to it the principle of women as paid workers outside their homes.

At least in part, because self-sufficiency was important to women in the American West the region had a generous share of female wage-workers and entrepreneurs, including milliners, dressmakers, merchants, and boarding-house keepers. Also, the West badly needed women's energies and skills. In 1849, in gold-rush California, one woman housed and fed ten male boarders. During the Colorado gold rush of the 1850s, a widow with children to support spurned such gender-related businesses. Instead, she dressed as a man and worked as a miner and saloon-keeper.[3] Other western women worked at paid jobs too numerous to list. Most gravitated to female-related jobs, including milliners, dress and cloak makers, and seamstresses. Because white female settlers were determined to remain stylish despite frontier living, female workers found that they could satisfy a need, make a reasonable wage, have steady work, and sometimes start their own businesses.[4]

A variety of other women made a living by providing another "domestic" service, one marketed to men rather than women. One example of a woman quick to take advantage of the boom years in Montana, when male miners dominated the population, was "Chicago Joe," or Josephine Welch, who left Illinois to open the Red Light Saloon in Helena. Others went to Kansas cattle towns or, during the 1850s and 1860s, to California gold camps. San Francisco especially drew "sporting" women from such faraway places as Chile, France, and China.[5] At the other end of the gamut of professions stood a variety of western women. Many were teachers. A few entered the law or the ministry. In 1869, Arabella Babb Mansfield of Iowa became the first woman to pass the bar exam in the United States. During the 1850s and 1860s, the Unitarian minister Marian Murdock held a pastorate in Humboldt, Iowa. Thousands of additional women became writers, editors, nurses, and doctors.[6]

Even though towns and cities provided numerous employment opportunities for women, rural women also worked. In towns, some women ran, or were employed in, millinery, dry goods, or other shops. Outside towns, many were farmers, who helped colonize western lands by imposing white agriculture on them. During the 1860s, a Norwegian settler in Minnesota, Bertha Sonsteby, who had begun to do farm labor at age eight, toiled alongside her husband building a house, planting trees, reaping, and threshing. She claimed there was no "kind of work which I have not done."[7] In 1886, Mary Olivette Taylor Bunton of Sweetwater not only helped on the ranch, but took part in an event that was usually men only—a trail drive.[8]

In addition, so-called girl homesteaders became a phenomenon of sorts. Although homesteading was usually thought of as a "male" undertaking, a significant number of women tried their hand at it. Such women took advantage of the Homestead Act of 1862 and later the Kincaid Act of 1904, which offered western land to "heads of households" without specifying gender.[9] Female claimants were primarily white, young, and single, and often took up land as an investment, sometimes to pay for their own or for others' educations, or to support themselves and sometimes their children after divorce, desertion, or a spouse's death. In 1870, a single woman, Abbie Bright, homesteaded in Kansas and wrote for the *Wichita Times*. Nor was she a unique case. During the early 1880s, a widow with two small children homesteaded after discovering that a number of her friends were leaving for Kansas to enter claims. "I jumped up," she recalled "saying, I am going to Kansas." She added, "I was soon on the train to join the western party."[10]

A number of women devised another way to utilize land to support themselves. Although such women would not have thought of themselves as colonizers of landscapes, that is what they were. For example, in the late nineteenth-century West, flower artist Alice Stewart combed the area around Colorado Springs for floral specimens, which she painted or used in teaching others. She ranged the mountainsides, picking live wild flowers as if they personally belonged to her. As an individual, Stewart could not have harmed the environment, but she demonstrated an attitude of white proprietorship of western resources.[11]

In Kenya, between 1890 and 1940, the economic situation was similar. As one Kenya settler put it, women's "self-sufficiency" was every bit as meaningful as "in the American West, where I was born."[12] Unsurprisingly, because the growing capital city of Nairobi offered many openings to women, it had a wealth of female entrepreneurs. One of early Nairobi's most colorful and epic figures, May (Mayence) Bent, like her predecessors in California, utilized her domestic skills by housing and feeding people for pay. When she and her husband, W. S. Bent, established a farm at Fort Smith on the outskirts of Nairobi early in the 1900s, May looked for ways to bring in cash to the struggling enterprise. In 1902, she took on the job of operating Tommy Woods's general store in Nairobi. Bent not only ran the shop and its post office, but followed the milliner and dressmaker trade on the side, as well as opening a hotel upstairs. From her Fort Smith farm, Bent supplied vegetables and butter for the hotel's dining table. Not being one to miss an opportunity, May Bent tried to reach a larger market by advertising in the *Mombasa Times and Uganda Argus*, later known as the *African Standard*. In August 1903, she ran the following advertisement: "Fort Smith Butter. Mrs. Bent Nairobi. It Takes the Cake. It Would Keep for Ages, But People Don't Give it the Chance."[13]

When guests overflowed into the bungalow next to the shop, May Bent became "manageress" of the first Stanley Hotel.[14] In 1904, after fire broke out, May Bent moved fifteen lodgers to a structure under construction. At completion, this building became the first purpose-built Stanley Hotel. Because May was interested in community needs, she established Nairobi's first circulating library at the Stanley. In 1907, when she left her husband and married her new business partner, Fred Tate, the couple built the Stanley into Kenya's premier hotel.[15]

Never willing to rest on her successes, May, with Fred's help, in 1912 started to build a new Stanley Hotel, with sixty rooms. When it opened in 1913, the Tates called it, logically enough, the *New* Stanley Hotel. Although World War I and the soldier-settlement scheme of the 1920s swelled business, the Tates ran the hotel from England, where they had semiretired due to poor health. In 1932, the Tates returned to Nairobi to oversee the opening of the renowned New Stanley Long Bar. In 1937, Fred Tate died in England, but May held on to the New Stanley until 1947, when she sold out to another Nairobi hotelier, Abraham Block.[16]

The New Stanley Hotel became a Nairobi legend, as did May Bent Tate. She was undoubtedly the most dogged of Kenya's female entrepreneurs, yet she was far from alone. One of the most colorful and well known of these was Beryl Markham, who trained racehorses and flew airplanes. Markham was the first woman in Africa to receive a license to train racehorses. As a trainer, she garnered public acclaim, prizes, and Kenya Derby wins. In 1931, she added flying airplanes to her accomplishments. Markham carried mail and spotted game from the air for safaris. On the international scene, she set world records. Most notably, in 1936, Markham became the first person to fly alone across the Atlantic Ocean, east to west.[17]

Another notable public woman from the 1920s and 1930s was widow Florence Kerr Wilson, who founded the country's first commercial air line, Wilson Airways. When she began operations in 1929, Florence Wilson owned one airplane, a tiny Gypsy Moth, and employed one pilot, Tom Campbell Black, who later taught Beryl Markham to fly. By 1931, Wilson had seven planes, employed three pilots, and occasionally piloted planes herself. Although Wilson died in 1966, the facility still operates as Wilson Airport.[18]

Kenya's white women also practiced a variety of professions. Unlike the American West, trained nurses were numerous in Kenya. One district nurse who came to Eldoret in 1911 traveled on a mule over the surrounding countryside tending to sick people and delivering babies.[19] Because male doctors went to the front during World War I, female nurses were more in demand than ever. This need continued through the 1920s and 1930s, when the British Colonial Service signed on nearly twenty times as many nursing sisters as female teachers and doctors.[20] One of these was Australian Vera Marie Mordaunt who, after completing nurses' training in England in 1926, joined the Colonial Nursing Staff in Kenya. In 1931 she established Kenya's first leper colony, where she personally trained her all-black staff in such matters as use of instruments, proper dressings, and dietary care.[21] Much like Mordaunt, Margaret Gillon, a nurse who came to Kenya from New Zealand during the late 1920s, spent her first years in a white European hospital, then took over Kisumu Hospital for black Kenyans.[22]

As in the West, women living in rural Kenya also took economic chances, notably hotel-keeping. During the 1910s, the "manageress" of an Eldoret hotel gained the designation "holy terror" because she reportedly used a whip to restrain rowdy guests. At nearby Nanyuki, the widowed female manager of the Sportsman's Arms and her daughter, both hunters and horse riders, were equally strict. Of drunks and other annoying clients, the mother said, "We learned to cope."[23] Other rural women acted as silent partners with men. As early as 1905, Lily Block ran a number of farms for her famous brother, hotelier Abraham Block. By providing capital for his hotel and real-estate ventures, she underwrote the expansion of Kenya's hotel industry.[24] Later in Kenya's colonial period, Elly Gramaticas recalled her mother living through the failure of the family sisal farm in Tanzania and suggesting to her husband that they try producing cigarettes. Due to her urging, the Gramaticas family developed the East African Tobacco Company, which it eventually traded for coffee and sisal farms in Kenya.[25]

As in the American West, numerous rural women turned directly to the land for their livelihoods. At Whispers Farm outside Nairobi, Olga Watkins sold *sanji* grass to get cash to build a house for her family. She then advertised that she would take on any "building job" others rejected. She contracted mostly for "long drops," or earth latrines. For herself, Olga plowed one hundred acres of land and planted coffee trees. In between, Olga fulfilled her official duties as wife of the provincial commissioner.[26]

During the years that followed, as white women gained increased autonomy and freedom, female farmers became commonplace in Kenya. In 1913, Cara Buxton took up farmland, specializing in coffee and maize. More than two decades later, Grace T. McKenzie bought a farm in Kenya, near Karen Blixen's plantation. When her sister arrived for a visit, Grace became aware that a neighbor, Major Gardiner, disapproved "of two girls living alone on a farm, without a man." McKenzie's reply: "I have settled here . . . This is my home."[27]

Married women also farmed, either while their husbands pursued careers, especially in government or politics, or as partners with brothers, husbands, sons, or others. In 1912, Mary Layard Mitford-Barber of Capetown, South Africa, came to Kenya with her husband Henry to take up farming. Mary never seemed to regret her action: "We are always at a straining point with hard work but it doesn't kill us, we get up in the morning and go on, and that is how things that were shadows become visible facts."[28]

Farming also appealed to upper-class white women. In England, farming would have been beneath elite women, but in Kenya, a woman who could manage a farm or ranch was respected. After Florence Cole, sister of Rift Valley ranchers Galbraith and Berkley Cole and the daughter of the Irish Earl of Enniskillen, married Lord Delamere, she acted as manager of Delamere's farm. This phenomenon continued throughout the colonial period. In 1929, after Galbraith Cole's death, his wife, the former Eleanor Balfour, daughter of the second Earl of Balfour, personally managed Cole's two huge ranches, which included numerous Maasai workers. In 1934, Pamela Scott took over the family estate for her politically involved father, transforming a fledgling farm of nearly four thousand acres, seventeen cows, and thirty families of untrained black workers into one of the Rift Valley's most prosperous ranches.[29]

Because they made decisions, supervised workers, and marketed crops, these women thought of themselves as full-time farmers. When the Naivasha and District Farmers Association organized in 1925, women joined, many listing themselves as farmers. They spoke in policy discussions relating to fluctuating prices, pending legislation, and labor problems. Furthermore, during the locust plague of the early 1930s, Lady Cole stood at the forefront of farmers willing to undertake locust-prevention measures. Later in the decade, Lady Farrar ran for the post of representative to the Rift Valley Constituency.[30]

Besides farming, Kenya's white women found additional ways to utilize Kenya's landscapes to support themselves. Some became professional travelers who published their accounts, especially during the 1920s and 1930s. Like other white women, female travelers believed they had a proprietary right to journey wherever they wished in Kenya and to critique the sights they saw. Although they would not have described themselves as colonizers of landscapes and exploiters of wildlife, more than one white female traveler noted her part in stripping Kenya of its game. With glee, women described the first lion or elephant they brought down. One woman said that she hunted with the "dainty rifle" her husband had given her.[31]

Other women became journalists, collectors, and photographers, especially during the 1920s and 1930s. On the one hand, such women's work spread around the world awareness of Kenya's natural beauty and abundance of wild game. In 1924, for example, the Kansan Osa Johnson traveled with her husband Martin to collect specimens for the African Hall of the American Museum of Natural History in New York City. On the other hand, a subsequent increase in settlers, tourists, and travelers that resulted from increased information about Kenya helped deplete its landscapes and resources.[32]

Women of Color and the Economy in the West and in Kenya

In the American West, women of color usually filled poorly paid jobs, including black women working as domestics and washwomen, Hispanics in fields and canneries, and Asians in shops, fields, and fisheries. A number of women of color not only expanded their skills, but achieved prominence in the public arena. The names of Clara Brown and Bridget "Biddy" Mason spring to mind. Brown accompanied a western-bound party as its cook, took in washing in Colorado, and parleyed her hard-earned income into mine claims and land purchases, which provided sufficient income to bring other family members west. Although Mason went west to California as a slave, she obtained her freedom in a 1856 lawsuit. Mason also worked as a nurse and midwife, as well as giving generously of her time and expertise to the sick and insane.[33]

The West's most well-known black woman entrepreneur was Mary Ellen "Mammy" Pleasant, who came to San Francisco as a free black in 1852. By the 1870s, Pleasant had invested in mining stock, urban lots in San Francisco and Oakland, and one of San Francisco's successful accounting firms. Despite discriminatory laws and codes, Pleasant owned boardinghouses and laundries, where she employed black women and men. Pleasant also used her wealth to challenge, especially in court, the unequal legal status of California's African Americans.[34]

American Indian women also adapted to changing conditions. From the beginning of the reservation period in 1870, they found themselves not only physically isolated from markets and from long-distance trade, but excluded from agriculture. Sioux women responded by selling garden produce to nearby whites and by producing textiles, beadwork, and other crafts for off-reservation shops. Although profits were small, Sioux women controlled them fully. A similar scenario occurred on reservations in the Southwest where Navajo women shifted their roles to retain some of their autonomy and importance in Navajo society. During the precolonial era, these women had freed men to go on raids by growing crops and tending the sheep the men brought back. After the Navajo were confined to reservations—notably the Bosque Redondo near Fort Sumner in New Mexico—raiding had to stop. In addition, white officials ordered men to farm, rather than women. Women acted quickly, taking over sheepherding and setting up looms, on which they produced sturdy and decorative blankets for sale to the tourist trade. Nor were Sioux and Navajo women exceptions. On the West Coast, Pomo women in California learned to do domestic labor for white families, which brought them a small income and gained them respect as women who could speak English and had knowledge of Anglo society. Pomo women also became expert pickers of grapes, prunes, and hops, and gradually learned to be basket makers.[35] In these three cases, as well as many more, Indian women continued to have a certain amount of income and influence, which confounded white male officials who intended Indian women to become domestic, poor, and powerless—and thus innocuous to white hegemony.

Years later in Kenya, women settlers of color faced a highly stratified situation. In towns and cities, only the most menial jobs were open to them. Asian Indian women usually took jobs inside their own communities, especially in family businesses, which offered some degree of purdah, or separation, from men. Although purdah was flexible, other women preferred female-dominated professions, notably teaching and nursing. When settler Kashiben Amin arrived in 1922, she found that she could put her education to good use by teaching and doing so in a largely female environment. Asian Indian women also formed parts of family teams who ran dukas and other family businesses. One woman described her work with her husband by saying "we really were partners."[36] For black Kenyan women, the white colonial economy was especially demanding. In the case of Kikuyu and Kamba women, British agricultural imperialism under-cut women's production of beans by mandating the large-scale grow-ing of maize as the primary food crop. The Agriculture Department, established in 1903, intervened in the market in many ways, including introducing new varieties of seeds. At the same time, the pressure on black Kenyans to pay hut taxes and school fees meant that they had to grow and sell cash crops. Gradually, the emphasis shifted away from producing filling and nutritional foods, such as mixed beans, and away from the precolonial practice of intercropping beans, millet, and maize to replenish the soil, reduce weeds, and curtail insects. Instead, the goal became to increase outputs of more marketable single-variety crops to feed urban dwellers, including white Europeans.

As in the West, where Buffalo Bird Woman wondered why white farmers grew huge fields of corn inferior to her own limited but quality yield, black Kenyan women failed to see logic in the changes. Even though many saw their roles as farmers as equal to those of wife and mother, they adapted by becoming traders. Particularly in the Nairobi area, black women farmers became "hawkers," meaning market traders. Renting stalls, especially in the Indian Bazaar, women sold produce and other products for cash, rather than supplying their families firsthand. One woman named Wangeri not only marketed produce, but made beer that she sold to Nairobians on weekends. Many of these women funded school fees for brothers and sisters so that they could obtain better jobs. Although the attempts of white and black men to control them pushed these women into an urban under-class, they did achieve a modicum of independence.[37] Like white "pioneer" May Bent and other entrepreneurs, black women participated in the frontier by taking what advantage they could of the colonial market economy.

White Women's Rights in the West and in Kenya

In the American West, thousands of women entered the public realm by way of women's clubs. Sometimes on a subtle level, other times explicitly, women's clubs were women's rights organizations, which intended to enlarge the prerogatives of white women while helping those in need. Members acted as municipal housekeepers, meaning they promoted the same order and civility outside their homes as they did inside them. White women, who had internalized the message that it was their job to protect families and communities, participated in a huge variety of organizations. Large numbers of rural women joined the Patrons of Husbandry (the Grange), the Farmers' Alliance, and the Populist Party, all of which had "female" planks in their platforms.

So many Populist women spoke from the backs of wagons and public platforms, marched and carried banners, or ran for local offices that the political humorist Joseph (Josh) Billings wrote in mock horror, "Wimmen is everywhere."[38]

Women also widened their traditional female sphere and increased their influence by participating in church-related charities, especially aid societies that helped destitute and ill people. Church women supported the work of foreign missionaries by holding such events as bazaars, box suppers, and "socials" to raise much-needed funds. Additional women joined secular organizations, including hospital and veterans' auxiliaries, Women's Relief Corps chapters, Society of the Daughters of the American Revolution units, and Red Cross groups. These helped provide Civil War relief, child welfare, schools and libraries, and orphanages.[39]

Women's clubs and their individual members also advocated the emerging cause of conserving the West's physical environment. In 1877, the Wisconsinite Jeanne Carr and her husband bought land north of Pasadena, California. As mentor of the renowned western conservationist John Muir, Carr hoped to prove herself as dedicated an environmentalist as her protégée. In that same year, Mary Ann Dyer Goodnight of west Texas began to rescue bison, especially orphaned calves.[40] Women became increasingly proactive. By 1890, the Carrs' ranch included more than two hundred types of trees and shrubs, most of them native to the West. Goodnight's bison herd grew to two-hundred head, which became a bison reserve. In the meantime, clubwoman Virginia Donaghe McClug explored Colorado's Mesa Verde cliff dwellings and lectured about them. She eventually headed a committee of the Colorado Federation of Women's Clubs that unsuccessfully lobbied for the creation of Mesa Verde National Park.[41]

Because women felt driven to accomplish as much as they could, many participated in fifteen or twenty clubs at one time, usually a mix of church-related and secular organizations. Reportedly, one Oklahoma club woman founded or led over forty groups during her lifetime. By the 1880s, so many organizations existed in the West that one Wyoming observer called the era "the golden age of women's clubs."[42] As a result of their numerous club activities, women became more aware than ever of their lack of power, especially in the political sphere. White women began to call for an enlargement of their prerogatives. In the American West between 1840 and 1890, an overt women's rights movement developed. Issues included married women's property rights, divorce laws, and woman suffrage. Western women were fortunate in having the impetus of a national women's rights movement and enthusiastically joined national activities. At the same time, even though they may have paid lip service to the ideal of proper womanhood, they expanded their spheres and demanded additional rights and responsibilities.

After the first U.S. national women's rights convention convened in Seneca Falls, New York, in 1848, western women showed increasing interest in women's rights. An early frontier, Iowa, showed great promise. In 1851, the state legislature revised Iowa's legal code, allowing married women to control their own property and permitting divorce if a couple could not live in "peace and happiness."[43] In addition, such women's rights groups as the Iowa Suffrage Memorial Association escalated the cry for woman suffrage, but it was not granted until 1920, when the Nineteenth Amendment to the U.S. Constitution gave the vote to all women in the nation. Although observers had predicted that Iowa would be one of the first states in the suffrage column, it was among the last.[44]

Suffragists had great hopes for other western jurisdictions. Shortly after the establishment of the National Woman Suffrage Association in 1869, eastern suffrage leaders Elizabeth Cady Stanton and Susan B. Anthony toured western states advocating the suffrage cause. In 1871, the pair visited Wyoming Territory, which had granted its women the right to vote two years earlier.[45] Wyoming's action had failed to animate other Plains states. Colorado was the most cooperaive. In 1868 and again in 1869, territorial legislators discussed woman suffrage inconclusively. In 1870, Governor Edward M. McCook recommended adoption, but the legislature again rejected it. Debate rose and fell until 1893, when the male voters of Colorado passed a suffrage amendment with a margin of approximately six thousand votes.[46]

Kansas was slower in allowing its women to vote. The first constitution, adopted in 1861, insured women an equal share with husbands in controlling their children and property, as well as granting them a vote in school elections. In 1887, the provision was broadened to include city and bond elections. Still, despite the seeming liberal attitudes of lawmakers and the arguments of such energetic woman-suffrage leaders as Clarinda I. H. Nichols, women did not vote in Kansas until 1912, when a state constitutional amendment provided universal suffrage.[47]

In Montana, the demand for suffrage did not even begin until after 1890, the widely accepted date for the "closing" of the frontier. In 1895, the first state suffrage association organized in Helena. In 1897, the Populist attorney Ella Knowles carried a petition bearing three thousand pro-suffrage names to the state legislature. Although a suffrage resolution was introduced in the house, it failed by five votes. In 1913 another proposal came to the legislature, shepherded by the Montana suffragist Jeannette Rankin. It too failed. Not until 1914 did Montana become the eleventh state to bestow on its women the right to vote.[48]

Woman suffrage came even later in Dakota Territory. Although local women organized rallies and presented petitions, when South Dakota became a state in 1889, voters declined to eliminate the word *male* in their constitution. In 1905, a petition thirty-six yards in length was carried up the aisle of the chamber. Yet South Dakota's women did not receive the vote until 1918, two years before the ratification of the Nineteenth Amendment.[49]

Of the Plains states, Nebraska brought up the rear. The fight had begun in 1855, when the suffragist Amelia Bloomer spoke to the territorial legislature in Omaha. In 1867, Nebraska granted the vote to its female citizens in school elections, yet in 1871 the Nebraska Constitutional Convention debated, and denied, woman suffrage. A long, drawn-out campaign followed, spearheaded by the Nebraska Woman Suffrage Association, which applied pressure through rallies, open meetings, state conventions, literature, and petitions. Despite these well-orchestrated efforts, Nebraska did not approve woman suffrage until 1919, when it became the fourteenth state to ratify the national suffrage amendment.[50]

Despite this checkered history of woman suffrage in the Plains West, western states generally comported themselves better than their eastern and southern counterparts. In spite of opposition from those who feared political participation would "soil" women's virtuous influence in society and from liquor manufacturers who believed women would vote for the prohibition of alcohol, western women continued to fight for the right to vote. In 1890, the western jurisdictions that allowed women to vote were Wyoming Territory, Utah, and Washington Territory, but by the time of the ratification of the Nineteenth Amendment to the U.S. Constitution in 1920, sixteen western states permitted women to vote. The only non-western state to do so was New York.[51]

In the meantime, other assertive women tackled western politics by running for office. Although women could not vote in most jurisdictions, many places allowed them to hold office. Thus, female politicians, who saw a close connection between societal reform and political power, entered virtually every level of local government. The West even had an early woman mayor. When Meodra Salter won election as the mayor of Argonia, Kansas, in 1887, she allegedly was the first woman in the world to hold such an office.[52] Hundreds, or perhaps thousands, of other western women held lesser elective positions, especially as members of school boards and superintendents of school systems. For several years during the late 1800s, Olive Rankin, mother of noted suffragist Jeannette Rankin, served on the Missoula, Montana, school board.[53]

Women combined political action with societal good in a number of other ways as well. For instance, Nebraskan Luna E. Kellie remembered that when the first Farmers' Alliance group organized in her area during the 1870s, it was inevitable that beleaguered farm families would join. In Kellie's view, such people eventually discovered that "they had to resort to politics to get any needed reform." Although Kellie had been taught that "it was unwomanly to concern oneself with politics," she realized that political activity was a necessary tool in women's campaigns to maintain order and morality in their homes and communities. By the time Kellie had borne eleven children and helped her husband develop the family farm, she had also served as editor, secretary, bookkeeper, and speaker for the Alliance.[54]

Later, in Kenya between 1890 and 1940, the situation was different in that little evidence exists of a Kenyan women's rights movement as such. In Britain, married women had gained the ability to divorce in 1857 and the right to hold property in 1870 and 1882. Women first had an opportunity to vote in 1918. Also, Victorian women could hold paid employment, enter the professions, and travel abroad. In British colonies, however, women were more restricted in some ways than women at home. After all, white women had gone to the colonies to transplant a stable English society, not to disrupt it by speaking in public and campaigning. In other areas, however, white women were less restricted; for example, women could travel more and by any means they chose. In 1910, Edith Maturin journeyed—partly by foot and partly by riding in a litter carried by African men—across parts of Africa, especially Kenya, before taking up a Kenyan farm in 1912. She said that had she been a man she would have been an explorer and traveler, "but being that imprisoned thing, a woman" she could indulge herself only occasionally.[55] Despite her disclaimer, Maturin seems to have thrown off successfully whatever shackles bound her as a woman.

In following decades, other women enlarged on Maturin's feat. In 1929, Frenchwoman Giselle Bunau-Varilla traveled by foot across Kenya with her lover, Mario Rocco. After two months of walking, Giselle wrote that "our skins and feet are hardened by the sun and the rough terrain that we have crossed." After six months, Mario wrote to his mother, "Giselle is pregnant but she does not let her condition interfere with our adventure." After eight months, Giselle and Mario reached Kenya, married, and bought a farm in the Highlands where she bore their first child, Dorian.[56]

No matter how exciting and free their arrival in Kenya, white women soon learned that they held a secondary position in the colonization of British East Africa. Women continued to sit at the right hand of power—their fathers, brothers, husbands, and even sons. Women did not make direct decisions concerning the empire, nor did they devise laws or set public policy. Certainly, women tried to convince men to grant them more privileges. Like their counterparts in England, they hoped for change, including stronger married women's property laws, more liberal divorce provisions, and woman suffrage. Even at home, the battle was a prolonged one. Suffragists did not gain the parliamentary vote on the same basis as men until 1928.[57]

In Kenya, women's rights issues were ill defined and frequently overwhelmed by imperial discourse and the pressing need to develop a new colony. It was late in the era of 1890 to 1940 before the attorney general's office resolved unclear policies regarding married women's property. Women had held property de facto. Also, during the 1920s women who had served in the military claimed farms under the Soldier Settlement Act. In 1935, the attorney general's office finally ruled that a revised Married Women's Property Act applied to white women, who could hold property, contract loans, be sued, or go bankrupt.[58]

Meanwhile, Kenyan courts heard a growing number of cases of white women applying for divorce, which many women's rights leaders perceived as a protective device and liberating force for women. One such divorce went in 1927 to the mother of Dorothy Vaughn, who explained her parents' split by saying that her mother "was not the sort of pioneering woman at all." So many women chose divorce that by the late 1920s and early 1930s Kenya's supreme court complained of overloads of divorce cases and the inability to render judgments in reasonable time. Although judges and attorneys agreed that the rules of civil procedures needed immediate revision, they could not decide how to proceed.[59] As a result, divorce cases remained in litigation far longer than necessary, or people with financial means returned to Britain to settle matters.

In this rather conservative colonial setting, Kenya's white women often found themselves fighting for expanded rights at the most elementary levels. One controversial issue, especially for wives of British colonial officials, was being shut out of aspects of white social life. When a woman found herself ejected from her husband's club by 6 P.M. and allowed to dine there only one night a week, that was an issue that needed resolving. Although it may sound like a superficial concern, use of the local club had far-reaching consequences. In Mombasa, for example, the club served as the social center for the white community, mostly made up of British colonial officials. By disallowing women to be present except at certain times, men controlled social life, a prerogative usually held by women. Perhaps more importantly, restrictions on women made it seem that men alone directed imperial undertakings. In 1928, after a series of arguments and requests, the Mombasa Club finally "allowed" white women to become members, provided that their husbands paid their dues. Married women and their daughters could use the club's facilities only at the sufferance of men; thus, even with their elevated status as members, women held an inferior position to men. Because white men's clubs did not encourage women to express their wills and talents, they had to look elsewhere for opportunities than in their husbands' spheres.[60]

Gradually, Kenya's white women founded women's clubs, which were sometimes social and sometimes service oriented. Through them, white women expressed their resolve to enlarge their influence and prerogatives. Like their counterparts in the American West, Kenya's white women believed that women had a gender-related mission to regulate their communities and help those in need. According to one enthusiast, members could achieve goals that men could not, for women found ways of "making contact with the people, through the women and children in the homes, which a man can never hope to make."[61]

Kenya's white women joined a variety of organizations. A number contributed their services on a volunteer basis to everything from the Red Cross to the League of Mercy. Others led troops of Brownies, Girl Guides, and Girl Scouts. During World War I, members of the Women's War Work League volunteered to fill such jobs as telegraphers, bookkeepers, and drivers, thus releasing men to serve at the front. In addition, the wives of colonial officials were active, spending untold hours in various forms of social work. They gave their time to everything from charitable activities benefiting black Kenyans to holding memberships in women's clubs.[62]

Clubwomen also threw themselves heavily into penal reform, especially for women prisoners who were usually black Kenyans convicted of such crimes as petty theft, vagrancy, or prostitution. A problem had been developing since the early 1900s, when prisons fell under the supervision of the Inspector-General of Police. In 1906, prisons shifted to the control of British governors. By 1910, twenty-five jails existed with 6,559 prisoners and 319 staff, of which seven were white, nine Asian Indian, and 303 black Kenyan.[63] The following year, the British government overhauled the system. In 1911, the Prisons Service Board came into being, so that newly autonomous facilities came under the purview of a central board in Nairobi. By 1916, there were thirty prisons with 9,530 committals and 378 staff, of which eight were white, twelve Asian Indian, and 358 black Kenyan.[64] Although statistics for prisoners do not include breakdowns by race or gender, anecdotal evidence indicates that white people were few or nonexistent, and women were in the numerical minority.

Kenya's white women favored a strict penal strategy, but they also had ideas of their own. In their view, Kenya's prisons were to be more than a sinecure for staff members and their families, who in 1916, were finally ordered to limit personal visitors and get permission for large gatherings of friends. Nor were jails to provide a relative life of ease for criminals. In 1925, detention camps were created to separate the "hardened" criminals from the lesser ones, and to provide harsher punishment for the former.[65]

In particular, white women expressed concern regarding the treatment of female prisoners. They regularly visited women's sections of prisons where they taught incarcerated women basic reading, writing, and arithmetic. They also tried to alleviate overcrowding, poor nutrition, and sexual abuse at the hands of male jailers. White women visitors reported that the situation in most of Kenya's jails was volatile, with female prisoners kept inside tiny bamboo compounds with bare plank beds. As one women held in Mombasa's old Fort Jesus prison said, "we are shut up here like food in a cooking pot with the lid on."[66]

During the 1930s, work programs in prisons became an issue. Many reformers believed that prisoners did not have enough work to keep them busy.[67] Consequently, women supported work programs that would teach prisoners some skills. White women especially argued for teaching female prisoners sewing and baking, which might lead to employment after they had served their terms. It was a losing battle, however. As white settlement disrupted rural villages and forced black women to move into inadequate housing in overcrowded urban areas where they worked largely as domestics, so did drinking, brawling, prostitution, and family abuse increase.[68] Although white women could help relieve the suffering of individual prisoners, there was little they could do to solve underlying problems.

Health reform was another issue for white clubwomen, who struggled to vaccinate native children, treat accident victims, and teach basic principles of nutrition and sanitation. Gradually, many white women became interested in improving the health of black mothers and their infants. Notably, Lady Joan Grigg, wife of Governor Sir Edward Grigg, initiated a campaign during the mid-1920s to establish rudimentary maternity hospitals and basic pediatric clinics for black children. When she discovered that government support was not forthcoming, Grigg raised money through such events as the Child Welfare Festival. The proceeds funded hospitals in Mombasa and Nairobi for Asian Indians and black Kenyan women and children, respectively.[69]

Clubwomen also initiated programs to save Kenya's landscapes for future generations. By the 1930s, growing numbers of people recognized that Kenya's land and animals demanded preservation. Otherwise, Kenya's aesthetic riches would be lost forever. Because white women thought of themselves as conservators of home and communities, they felt responsible for the environment as well. Clubwomen defined any issue that affected families as within their purview, and landscapes affected families. Clubwomen spoke, wrote, and lobbied on behalf of Kenya's land and animals. Gradually, a small number of shooting safaris became photographic safaris instead. Some people recognized that wholesale killing of wild game posed a threat to Kenya's physical environment. For example, Osa Johnson, who was an accomplished nature photographer, turned from collecting specimens to photographing them instead, even climbing to the top of formidable Mt. Kenya to get the shots she wanted.[70]

Also during the 1930s, white clubwomen tried to improve the situation for black Kenyans. Lady Eleanor Cole represented the East Africa Women's League to the Associated Countrywomen of the World, where she lobbied for funds and other aid for black Kenyans. At home in Kenya, Cole became a patron of the Nyanza Musical

Society, which not only introduced Africans to European music, but encouraged the performance and composition of what she termed "purely African music."[71] Although Cole and other women decided— from the perspective of white standards—what constituted "African" craftwork and music, they did create interest in black culture among whites.

Because so many individual women's groups existed and sometimes overlapped in their efforts, in 1917 an all-encompassing association, the East Africa Women's League (EAWL), formed in Nairobi. Its goal was far-reaching: "to study and take action on any subject of interest to white women and children in the Colony." The EAWL objectives stated that members would take "part in the social, economic, educational, and political (namely, concerning the public and civic) life of women," but would avoid "party politics." An editorial in the *East African Standard* stated that "we are convinced that the organised intelligence of women will render valuable assistance to the solution to some of our most urgent problems."[72] Within five years, the EAWL had 130 members, largely wives and daughters of public officials and farmers. Although members tended to be from the official, middle, and upper classes, other white women (but not those of color) were welcome to join.[73]

The EAWL was not explicitly a women's rights organization. On the contrary, its members dedicated themselves more to municipal housekeeping than to women's rights reform. Yet the two were closely related. By attacking problems that men ignored, spurned, or had not gotten around to, women established their own part in public life. Under the umbrella of "doing good," women led meetings, raised money, suggested programs and projects to male-dominated agencies, and lobbied legislators and other holders of public office. They also queried public officials about such political issues as the balloting system and the constitution.[74] Most women, however, saw the EAWL as providing necessary services, first to white women and eventually to women of all races. According to Mairo Hopcraft of Naivasha, women living on farms had little time to give, especially to what she called "purely social" activities, but they "were always very willing to work hard towards any EAWL projects."[75]

By the 1930s, a few assertive white women even eyed the political scene. Although white men had kept a tight lock on leadership positions, some women successfully challenged male dominance. In Nairobi, the second Lady Delamere, Gladys, who had a keen interest in good works and local politics, believed the former might be helped by the latter. During the early 1930s, she campaigned for a seat on Nairobi's Municipal Council. These jobs had recently become elective, for whites only. The council included a few Asian Indian members specially appointed by the governor, but no black Kenyan representatives. In 1934, Gladys Delamere gained election to the council, where she did such an outstanding job that four years later she became mayor, an office she held for three terms. As mayor, she especially initiated anti-poverty programs in Nairobi's ghettos and helped Europeans left financially stranded by the depression. Because Gladys helped both blacks and whites, some people criticized her unmercifully.[76]

Overall, white women who entered the public realm were more effective in boosting and liberating themselves than in helping women of color.[77] Decades later, the descendants of these white women would hail their predecessors as heroines in bringing "a new way of life to the primitive peoples they found" in Kenya, but the situation was not that simple. These commentators could only see the white side, not the damage done to black Kenyans through white women's interference.[78]

White women themselves gained through their efforts. By initiating reform, as well as speaking and writing on its behalf, white women vitalized their image as caring, active people. As they spoke, lobbied, and visited prisons they did things and went places that were previously off limits to women. On a more subtle level, white women marginalized white men from their wives' and daughters' endeavors. By forming their own "club," white women created a center of female activity in which women made the decisions. Men were now the "allowed" guests at charity balls and other EAWL functions. At the same time, women learned such "male" skills as public speaking and administering budgets. EAWL members also learned from men how to aggrandize and expand. In 1925, the Machakos, Thika, Naivasha, and Nakuru branches of the EAWL formed, followed by others in places like Nakuru and Nanyuki. These groups undertook such projects as establishing schools and libraries, cooperating with churches and agencies like the Salvation Army and Red Cross, and helping white female migrants adjust to life in Kenya. Some men could not help but notice. As the Kenyan journalist Edward Rodwell later put it, the "corporate body" of the EAWL "spread like a giant cobweb throughout Kenya." This is a perfect analogy to what women today call "networking," the slow and subtle building of connections among women until a widespread pattern is in place.[79]

Still, not all women favored such "progress." During the mid-1930s, one woman explained that although she endorsed women setting their own pace, in Kenya they had to remember that they served as models to black Kenyans and white children. Thus, "liberated" women needed to remain moral and "disciplined."[80] She approved, as did so many of Kenya's white women, of expanding women's rights, while, at the same time, remembering to take seriously their responsibilities as women and as colonizers.

Women of Color and "Rights" in the West and in Kenya

In the American West, a dynamic black woman's-club movement emerged, which provided a great deal of welfare assistance. Although women of color are usually stereotyped as the recipients of philanthropy, this is inaccurate and unfair. Until the recent advent of black and women's history, scholars paid little attention to altruistic black women, yet women of color were extremely active in dispensing relief to others. For African American women in the United States, the concept of beneficence had its roots in African cultures, which encouraged women to participate heavily in charitable efforts. In America, slave women established aid networks, while free black women organized a plethora of mutual-aid societies, many associated with black churches. As early as 1838, 119 relief associations existed in Philadelphia; more than half were female-only groups. After the Civil War ended in 1865, the number of black societies increased rapidly, fulfilling the functions of banks, insurance companies, schools, hospitals, houses, and government agencies.[81]

In the Pacific Northwest, black women's groups centered in Portland, Oregon, which had a black community as early as 1870, and in Seattle, Washington, which had one by 1890. In 1890, a widowed clubwoman, Elizabeth Thorne, offered her restaurant for the first service of the Seattle African Methodist Episcopal (A.M.E.) church. Even though women of the church subsequently formed the Ladies Social Circle, which raised money to buy land for a church building, church records list only "fathers" as the church's founders. Women's groups in Portland and Seattle also formed social clubs, organizing everything from dances to fund-raising events.[82]

These organizations of African American women focused on goals of immediate interest to black communities, including job training, control of childhood diseases, education for children and adults, and giving aid to poor black women and children. At first, black women's clubs attracted primarily educated, urban women from Kansas City and Topeka to Denver and Los Angeles. Gradually, their appeal extended to women of other social classes and to rural women. These women emphasized such issues as improved education, jobs, health care, and sanitation. As with white women's clubs, members learned how to create organizations and programs, manage money, and speak in public.[83]

Still, despite women's activism, personal and public rights seldom accrued to women of color in the American West. For one thing, much of the West was segregated by race so that black women's clubs labored without help from more powerful white women. For another, white suffrage leaders discouraged black women's participation fearing that conflating woman suffrage with black suffrage would lead to defeat. As a result, black women worked more for social justice than for suffrage. In mid- to late-nineteenth-century San Francisco, for example, black entrepreneur and reformer Mary Ellen Pleasant did not list woman suffrage as one of her primary goals. Instead, she put first better employment, fair wages, and civil rights for black Americans.[84]

In turning to Asian Indian women in Kenya between 1890 and 1940, a bit more speculation is required. Far less is known about the benevolent practices of Asian Indian women in Kenya than about women of color in the American West. This ignorance resulted, at least in part, because Asian Indians were widely thought of as "clannish," so few outsiders tried to learn how Indian communities operated. For Indians, this was just as well, for they believed in being in a state of ritual purity to enter religious buildings or attend religious ceremonies. Because so many differences existed among Indians themselves, practices varied tremendously. Purity might include removing shoes, covering the head, and bathing either parts of the body, such as the feet, or the entire self if one had recently engaged in sexual relations. Obviously, some of these restrictions were easier than others to explain to outsiders.[85]

Clearly, as in India, every community established its own clubs and organizations, as well as mosques and temples. Even small settlements had halls or centers where groups could meet. Some organizations were male-only, whereas some accepted women as members or as affiliate members. Because Asian Indians preferred to be as independent as possible, these organizations provided welfare and other services rather than relying on white government-aid programs. Women, encouraged by Muslim and Hindu beliefs to make commitments to the welfare of their families and communities, were especially active in the informal education of young children and in helping the poor and the ill.[86]

These and other Asian Indian women who exhibited a spirit of benevolence were far from passive, as they were so often portrayed. One example was the wife of Nairobi entrepreneur and political leader Alibhai Mulla Jeevanjee. During the early 1930s, Dayambai Adamjee dedicated herself to helping others by assisting in childbirth, collecting money for the poor, and raising funds for a school bus.[87] Little of this activity was visible from the outside, however. Dayambai Adamjee was known within her family and her neighborhood for her altruistic acts.

Heartened by women's activities in India, Kenya's Asian Indian women increasingly thought about their own list of "wants." More specifically, as early as 1899 in India, women representatives had participated in the fourth Indian National Congress. In 1905, they supported a boycott and, in 1914, strongly supported the war effort. In Kenya, Asian Indian women's issues appeared to relate more to their immediate situations. During the 1890s and early 1900s, these included such basic needs as being free to immigrate to Kenya, protection from enslavement, and the right to practice their beliefs and customs. Much like women of color in the American West, Kenya's Asian Indian women expanded their roles and agency by acting on individual and family levels. They worked through already established institutions, especially schools and religious institutions. Also, women recognized, and acted upon, the need to establish charitable institutions, notably boardinghouses to help new arrivals, the ill, and the indigent. Although some women expressed a desire to own property and businesses, or to enter such professions as teaching and medicine, little evidence exists of an organized "movement" among Asian Indian women to acquire these rights.[88]

Because colonialism had cost black Kenyan women so much in terms of status and prerogatives, they had the most to gain in the area from women's reform. A Mombasa woman, Shamsha Muhamad Muhashamy, explained that she had grown up watching her mother create all types of organizations. One of these was to help black women see that they were being exploited and were "at the bottom," and needed to organize to resist high prices charged by Indian merchants. Other groups campaigned to simplify weddings and funerals and bring down their costs. Shamsha Muhjamad Muhashamy did not want to leave the "customs and beliefs of our grandfathers" behind, she said "we cannot just follow the Europeans."[89]

Drawing Racial Boundaries

As white women entered the public realm, they and their men worried more about their safety. They primarily feared "others," meaning peoples of color, especially men. Thus, throughout the American West between 1840 and 1890, dividing lines based on race multiplied. These color bars were in addition to the ones established in the domestic realm; they purported to protect white women who ventured forth into the larger world. White men played an important role in establishing color bars, in part because they feared what they imagined men of color might do to white women, and in part because they suspected men of color of having a heightened sexuality that might attract white women. Enough cases existed in the West of white women freely marrying Indian men or choosing to stay with Indian husbands after captivity to suggest that Indian men might not be as inferior as white men asserted.[90] White men could either deny the possibility of white women having relationships with Indian men, or they could build walls of protective legislation around white women. When white men did the latter, they exacerbated women's anxieties so that white women helped negotiate and maintain race-based laws.

In the West, some color bars were codified, but many were informal. Because the Fourteenth Amendment (ratified 1868) to the U.S. Constitution stated that African Americans were citizens, restrictions based on race had to circumvent the Constitution. It would be 1896 before the U.S. Supreme Court ruled that segregation laws did *not* violate the Fourteenth Amendment. As a result, during the 1870s, 1880s, and early 1890s, a duality of formal and informal restrictions was everywhere. In housing, for example, people of color were sometimes kept separate by restrictive provisions, at other times by social pressure.[91] The historian Robin Higham has called this phenomenon a "quiet encroachment," a powerful force in crushing the pride and overt resistance of indigenes on virtually every frontier of the world.[92]

Because white settlers in the West were so numerous, they got away with these actions. Whites easily overwhelmed peoples of color with their physical presence, as well as their unceasing insistence on a general observance of white customs. Although numerous white westerners claimed that the region was democratic, in truth democracy existed more for them than for westerners of color. Even in gold-rush California, reputed to be the land of opportunity and riches, African Americans were at risk of everything from exclusion to personal attack. In 1850, California's constitutional convention narrowly defeated a provision that would exclude all black persons, whether free or slave, from the new state. After California was admitted to the union as a free state in that year, vestiges of slavery remained. In the state capital of Sacramento in 1850, a white man advertised the sale of an eighteen-year-old female slave "of amiable disposition," who also was a "good" washer, ironer, and cook." In 1852, the capital's newspaper, the *Democratic State Journal*, included an advertisement for a slave man for three hundred dollars. That same year, the state legislature adopted a fugitive slave law that put blacks in constant fear of arrest.[93]

Throughout the West similar policies applied. Keeping Native Americans on reservations, Hispanics in urban barrios, whites in "better" residential urban areas, African Americans in slave quarters or urban ghettos, and Asians in Chinatowns, Little Tokyos, and Little Koreas insured that each group would have separate schools, stores, and recreation venues. Generally, most white women believed that segregation would provide protection as they pursued activities away from home, including paid employment, volunteer work, and leisure time.

In the area of leisure, women's tourism provides an enlightening example of the intersection of white women and racially based color bars. During the years following the Civil War, white women increasingly endured a bit of physical discomfort to gain a sense of liberation and autonomy through travel, which they believed freed them from female "rules." In reality, these women roamed well protected by cumbersome Victorian clothing, elaborate codes of etiquette, and membership in the dominant white culture, all of which allowed them to ramble across the West without any real threat of humiliation or physical harm.[94] Consequently, white women usually found it relatively easy and safe to travel, even in the country's new system of undeveloped national parks. In 1878, when the famous Nelson Miles and Colgate Hoyt party made a late summer journey through Yellowstone, the group included several women who, laced into corsets and wearing long skirts, sought what one called "adventure."[95]

Because the increase in white women travelers constituted an opportunity for tourist-related industries, everything from park policies to commercial advertising appealed to women. From officials of railroad companies to such entrepreneurs as Fred Harvey, leaders of western tourism modified travel and altered images of the West to fit white women's wants and needs. During the 1880s, the Chicago and Northwestern Railroad advertised Minnesota as an "enchanted summer land," full of resorts that women would enjoy. On another level, the tourist's West became female, offering such attractions as the "queen" of mineral waters, the "queen" of resorts, the "queen" of lakes.[96] Hoteliers also joined the trend. Soon a growing number of resorts and tourist destinations catered to white women. In 1888, a widow who homesteaded in Kansas joined a friend for a railroad trip to Manitou Springs, Colorado. The women stayed at the Sunny Side Hotel, where they looked from their window into what one described as "streets gay with pleasure seekers, those in quest of health, and the money makers."[97]

Whether intended or not, these women made it clear that western travel was primarily for whites. For one thing, their numbers indicated that the expense of travel allowed only reasonably well-off whites to enjoy it, whereas poorly paid Indians and Hispanics hung at the fringes of tourism as workers. For another, white women tourists increasingly wanted to "visit" native peoples, preferably in their "natural" settings. Although white women had once been afraid of Indians and scornful of Hispanics, they now hoped to "observe" these peoples. In the process, women encouraged native peoples to become public spectacles. Travel-company brochures became social statements, picturing and describing Indians and Hispanics as the western "other."

By reshaping the human landscape of the West and encouraging the commodification of cultural practices, women's tourism became a kind of double colonization. White settlers had first colonized natives by taking their land and pushing them into marginal economic positions. Now, white travelers again colonized such peoples by making them into tourist sights. Because travelers were awestruck by blanket-covered Native Americans, destitute Indians who badly needed income bedecked themselves in garish beaded outfits and staged performances of "war" and "rain" dances.[98] Hispanics also made themselves, or found themselves made into, caricatures to attract the tourist dollar. Hispanic men wore exaggerated vaquero and gaucho apparel, while "señoritas" donned dramatic mantillas and petticoated skirts, and, of course, tucked flowers behind their ears. The Southwest gradually became something of a caricature as well, viewed by most Americans through what the literary scholar Krista Comer terms a "romantic frame."[99]

White women discovered that not all natives welcomed such intrusive, patronizing attention. During the 1870s, Indians attacked tourists in Yellowstone National Park. Native Americans apparently believed the land belonged to them, even though whites claimed it as their own.[100] Indians also held their own views of whites, which were frequently uncomplimentary.[101] White women did little to reassure Native Americans that their intentions were benign. In 1871, one female traveler recalled that when she found poles from an "Indian wigwam" a friend suggested she take them home as "relics." Because the woman decided the poles would make better firewood, she burned them. On another occasion, she ripped deer horns and strips of buffalo skin from a deserted dwelling as souvenirs that she called a "wigwam memento."[102]

Eventually, growing numbers of tourists and the economic benefits they brought to western areas curtailed Indians' overt resistance to tourism. On a subterranean level, however, indigenes made themselves into such parodies of white beliefs that they seemed to mock whites. Like Indians along the westward trail who shot down with arrows (and kept) coins that gullible white travelers threw into the air, tourists' Indians showed their disdain for whites by charging them to see the stereotypes they had created. During the 1870s, Northern Paiutes of Nevada enacted a battle charge during Virginia City's Fourth of July parades, a burlesque that institutionalized Native Americans as part of Virginia City's history but was melodramatic enough for whites to accept and even applaud. On non-parade days, Paiutes lived in their own separate neighborhoods and kept largely to themselves.[103]

Also, growing numbers of white female tourists encouraged indigenous peoples to produce goods for the tourist market. Some of these items were souvenirs that reinforced stereotypes, whereas others were more authentic. For instance, the Hopi potter Nam-pey-o first marketed her distinctive wares through reservation trading posts, but by 1880 increasingly sold directly to tourists and visiting collectors.[104] Artisans like Nam-pey-o surrendered to tourism because sales brought income into their impoverished villages and led to some awareness of Indian arts among whites. Similarly, Hispanic folk artists produced souvenirs for the white tourist market. As the geographer Daniel D. Arreola notes, "Curios are folk art that has become reinvented for mass cultural consumption." He adds that interest in things Hispanic left a persistent image in American minds, one of an idyllic world of siestas and sunshine.[105]

The ramifications of color barriers were not always advantageous for white women, who found themselves segregated on their own side of the color line, limited in the range of experiences a female tourist might encounter. Because they had to wear, see, say, and do what was expected of them, white women who hoped to see the "real" West experienced the region as one-dimensional. This was not true, however, for every woman who journeyed throughout the West. Some who sketched, photographed, or wrote about Indians and Hispanics disputed stereotypes and asked new questions concerning family, children, kin, and the harmony that appeared to exist between native peoples and the physical environment. These women portrayed people of character and grace. By the 1880s, some women's favorable renditions of Indians enjoyed wide circulation. Near the end of the decade, Californian Grace Carpenter produced sensitive portraits of Mendocino County's Pomo Indians that found a place in the National Gallery in Washington, D.C., and the Royal Gallery in London.[106] This alternative perspective suggests that neither racial prejudice nor the barriers it inspired were irrefutable in the American West of the late nineteenth century.

Decades later, a comparable yet more rigorous color line appeared in Kenya. Race-based strict regulations appeared first in nearby India during the mid-1850s. After the Sepoy Rebellion of 1857–1859, also known as the Indian War of Independence, British officials became mistrustful of its subjects in Asia and Africa.[107] As the first attempt to bring down the British empire in South Asia, the Sepoy Rebellion alerted British leaders that revolution was possible. As a result, rules multiplied and doors slammed shut. This attitude transferred to Kenya where whites doubted everyone of color. As a body of colonial law developed, white colonists encouraged the codification of restrictions based on race. At the same time, indigenes discovered loopholes, often using them to their advantage. A similar pattern occurred in virtually all colonial settings, including India, Africa, and Latin America.[108]

During the 1890s, early whites in Kenya established a two-sided perception of colonial society, whites on one side and peoples of color on the other. To avoid confrontation and conflict, whites wanted racial groups as isolated from each other as possible. On political matters, white field administrators served as go-betweens for black Kenyans and white policymakers. In the social realm, whites imposed a complicated set of formal and informal rules on themselves and others. White Kenyans typically believed that this segregation policy, which remained strongly in force until the 1930s, had two major purposes. In white eyes, one of these was social distancing, not only to keep whites separate, but to give them the sense of community they claimed they must have to endure in a black country. The second was to establish an invisible safety wall around white women and children—supposedly to protect them by making them invulnerable. Because whites feared resistance and revolt from "underlings," they felt compelled to protect their most susceptible members.[109] According to this logic, even though a certain amount of precaution was necessary at home, it became crucial in public settings where white males might be absent or preoccupied and thus unable to defend women and children.

From Christian missionaries to the mayor of Nairobi, white women who entered public life depended on this invisible barrier to shield them as they ventured out on their own, spoke in public, urged reforms, or traveled, activities that potentially exposed women to insult or attack by resentful Asian Indians and black Kenyans. White men frequently responded with annoyance that assertive white women put themselves in harm's way by leaving their domestic sphere. They also characterized men of color as being lascivious. White men feared, and sometimes even seemed to envy, the sexual powers they imputed to men of color. White men's paranoia reinforced women's anxieties, sometime to the point of frenzy. Once unnerved, white women accepted—and even welcomed—the laws, policies, and customs that men created to keep people away from them and clearly spelled "hands off."[110]

Of course, establishing and administering racial lines was a clear expression of power: who had it and who did not; who made decisions and who did not; and who capitulated and who did not. This struggle came up on a variety of fronts, many of which involved women as enforcers. Although some women denied the central role they played in separating themselves from peoples of color, others admitted it, stating that such separation was sensible and necessary. Others simply acknowledged color bars as part of the "burden" of belonging to a "superior race."

As in the American West, Kenya's racial barriers regulated many aspects of life. Protection of white women was to occur not only during work hours, but during leisure time as well. In Kenya, however, the color bar was higher and stronger than in the American West. Beryl Markham was one who observed it. Beryl, who had first came out to Kenya in 1905 at age three, had grown up playing with children of the Nandi Murani and speaking Swahili. As an adult, Markham regarded several black Kenyans as "friends," yet she remained very much a white Kenyan.[111] Markham was pleased that Kenya was rapidly becoming, in her words, "white" and "civilized." She commented that although white Kenyans had "a frontier cut" to their clothes and wore "broad-brimmed hats," they were still Europeans. The proof she offered? White Kenyans dressed for dinner, passed their port wine clockwise, and loved horse races. Also, white colonists dedicated their lives to nurturing "shoots of custom grafted from the old tree." To Markham, Nairobi's Muthaiga Club was the bastion of "custom." She recalled that she enjoyed talking and laughing "hour after hour" with people who "made the Africa" she knew.[112]

Sporting events were also largely segregated. Although audiences sometimes included people of mixed backgrounds and races, participants were usually homogeneous. This was true of black Kenyans' football games. Whites had taught black Kenyans a game they called football, but was more like soccer, in the hope that blacks would absorb what the British called the "moral tonic" found in sporting attitudes. One white religious leader even maintained that "Christianity and football" would solve many of Kenya's problems, meaning, at least in part, that black Kenyans would learn such values as playing by the rules, respecting time, and giving their all to a task.[113] Once deconstructed, these goals signal whites' persistence in replacing black values with white ones. At the same time, sports events that took place at white country, polo, golf, or jockey clubs were limited to white Europeans as observers and participants. White Kenyans argued that to find release in leisure activities, they needed to relax and not have to worry about keeping up appearances. They believed they could do that best with peers rather than underlings and inferiors. In other words, racist practices, especially social distancing through leisure pastimes, drew and kept white Kenyans together.[114] Black Kenyans were present only as employees. Similarly, safaris included black Kenyans as guides, servants, and porters. Because someone had to do the work, whites accepted the presence of black Kenyans. To most whites, the humble positions of black workers held made them nearly invisible, as well as nonthreatening.

The color bar restricted white women as well, establishing a host of restrictions on where they could go, what they could say, what they could eat, and how they could stand, sit, or dance. Officials' wives especially felt the limitations, for they had to exercise extreme care in their relations with various types of people. Because these women came largely from middle- and lower-middle-class backgrounds, they were not accustomed to this degree of restrictiveness. Although segregation might offer white women protection, it also created isolation. In addition, white women experienced frustration regarding white men who disregarded standards of propriety and socialized with blacks, patronized "mixed" drinking establishments, or formed liaisons with women of color. They had a never-ending task in creating additional social sanctions to keep whites, especially white men, in the fold.

Meanwhile, black women figured out ways to circumvent white-imposed barriers. Some obviously established relationships with white men. But many found ways to get around agricultural and economic restrictions as well. A woman trader named Njoki remembered that she learned to trade from her mother, a widow who had to trade to survive. Njoki said that as a girl she would "sell along the road" beans and porridge her mother made. Other women who lived along a

European boundary with white-owned coffee farms on the other side privately sold maize and other produce over the line.[115]

Also, not all white women supported racial separation and the meanness of spirit it entailed. A Swahili woman, Mishi wa Abdala, recalled that one of Mombasa's white women, "out of her own kindness," gave her a part-time job at a good wage, as well as teaching her how to sew, knit, and crochet. Other white women took a public stance, speaking out against segregation. One of these was Edel Quinn, who in 1926 left an Irish tuberculosis sanitarium to spend the final years of her life as a Legion of Mary envoy to Africa. Once in Nairobi, Quinn expressed dismay that the "races" refused to work together. Perhaps because Quinn had experienced ethnic and racial enmity at home, she understood the damage it could do. In Kenya, Quinn lamented that white Europeans disparaged Asian Indians, and that these two groups looked down on black Kenyans, who they called "the natives." Despite pleas and even official orders to return to Ireland, Quinn continued her efforts to bring Kenya's Catholics together.[116]

In spite of the positive examples, conflicted relations between whites and blacks were a hallmark of Kenya Colony. The political scholar Bruce Berman argues that as a result, Kenya created more turmoil in British politics than any other single colony.[117] Even after the reforms of the 1930s, the East Africa Women's League argued for the privileging of white women over indigenes. In 1938, the League issued a statement to the British government on behalf of the "European Women of this Country," emphasizing "native crime" as a threat to white Kenyans. This suggests that the policy of segregation was not totally effective as a protective device. Some women blamed the British government and public for the situation, charging that pressures from "home" to relax racial restrictions created chaos, disrespect for whites, and resulting attacks.[118] Unlike Edel Quinn, they did not believe that Kenya's disparate peoples could be brought together in even an approximation of harmony.

Conclusion

On the American and Kenyan frontiers, white women who entered the public realm, either through economic or benevolent activities, not only participated in frontier process, but helped shape it. For instance, white female entrepreneurs assisted the establishment of a white economy in Kenya and made it clear that they would be part of it. White women decreed the curricula of many mission and public schools for black and white children, teaching both groups white subjects, including European history with attendant white values. White women holding political positions forced patriarchal black men to accord women deference, which was tantamount to admitting they had been conquered, at least in part, by women. Perhaps most importantly, white women helped negotiate and maintain color bars. In the American West and in Kenya, even women dedicated to helping others usually imposed distance between themselves and peoples of color.

White women who gathered at white-only restaurants and clubs felt that they needed to find escape and white comradeship—to experience a brief sense of freedom from the ongoing clash between their own ways and local resistance to them. These women derived a sense of security from looking around and concluding that whites had triumphed in a country once controlled by indigenous peoples. Some would live long enough to discover that the days of triumph were, after all, just fleeting ones.

SIX
Women's Larger Agendas

ENTERING the public realm and shaping frontier process was not enough for most white women. They had in mind a list of what they defined as "social ills" to be attacked. In the American West and on the Kenyan frontier, such programs varied between women and between eras. What they shared was what might today be called a feminist undertone; a motif more subtle and pervasive than demands for particular women's rights. Although specific rights were indeed important, this theme created a larger context in which rights would become entitlements. Whether white women articulated their goals or not, their actions indicated that they wanted nothing less than to be the moral arbiters of their societies, which they hoped would lead to a sweeping elevation of women's status and stature.

Hidden in white frontierswomen's larger agendas, then, were tactics that would prove them competent mothers of their race, willing and able to educate and refine groups of people ranging from indigenes to white men. Gradually, white women's crusades to improve their own positions took on moral and religious shades. Women's discourse repeatedly invoked Providence as a force on the side of women. As an American woman said in 1836, "woman . . . forms a part in God's created intelligent instrumentality to reform the world."

She added that women were also to keep men on the right path: "when man proves recreant to his duty and faithless to his Maker, woman, with her feeling heart, should rouse him."[1]

In both the West and Kenya, determined white women developed numerous programs, which fell into two broad categories: to improve the welfare of indigenes, and to stabilize frontier institutions. This thinking meshed well with Manifest Destiny and British imperialism; through "moral guardianship" and "domestic imperialism" women could further the patriotic goals of their countries, as well as proving themselves in male-dominated realms of expansionist frontiers. Women's sense of divine empowerment helps explain why white women often trod where no sensible or rational person would—into such intimate areas as marriage, sexuality, and the nurture of children.

The result of women's exertions varied. The moral-guardian ideology in the West and domestic imperialism in Kenya did not always serve white women—or those of color—well. Despite Herculean efforts, white women frequently discovered that they had accomplished far less than they had hoped for peoples of color and not as much as they wanted for themselves. In the meantime, women of color formulated their own specific goals and reforms. Also, women of color spent time and energy counteracting the effects of white women's projects on them. In their eyes, white women not only achieved less than they expected, but created negative results as well.

White Women "Uplifting" Indigenes in the West and in Kenya

In adopting philanthropic goals, virtually no white woman would have said that she condoned hurting others. Promoting altruistic-looking programs by means of colonial expansion did hurt others, however. Not only were soldiers, forts, death, and destruction crucial to imposing new regimes on indigenous peoples, but the process of settlement disrupted existing economies, political systems, and societies. This is not meant to suggest that white women were unaware of the needs of indigenes or were ineffective spokespeople for them. In the West, numerous women became sympathetic to Native Americans and were anxious to remedy their situations.[2] White women especially hoped to help Indian women, whom white women misperceived as little more than beasts of burden for their menfolk.

White women's goals for Indians revolved around the issues of education, government policies, and land. While at Fort Laramie during the 1860s, army wife Frances Carrington sharply criticized government land policies: "At the time of my arrival it had become apparent to any sensible observer that the Indians of that country would fight to the death for home and native land, with spirit akin to that of the American soldier of our early history, and who could say that their spirit was not commendable and to be respected." Other women called for more humane and empathetic views of Indians.[3] Some urged friends and family members to spread the "truth" about the government's mistreatment of Indians. Others signed petitions or went to Washington, D.C., to lobby on the Indians' behalf. Yet others became teachers or missionaries, while a number helped organize, or participated in, the emerging Indian reform movement.

One of these was writer Helen Hunt Jackson, who migrated from Massachusetts to Colorado during the late 1860s. There she became sympathetic to Indians and in 1879 visited Boston, where she heard Standing Bear, a Ponca leader, speak. In 1881, Jackson's book, *Century of Dishonor,* exposed the U.S. government's harsh treatment of American Indians.[4] Shortly thereafter, Elaine Goodale, who taught on the Great Sioux Reservation in Dakota Territory between 1886 and 1891, felt a similar "call" to help the Indians. Because she came to realize that cultural difference did not mean inferiority, she opposed the government's directive to destroy "everything characteristically native without regard to intrinsic values."[5]

White women's effectiveness regarding Indian reform was mixed. On the public front, they had some success in changing people's minds regarding American Indians. Female speakers and writers launched attacks on existing policies and suggested different ways of handling Indians that would give them more self-rule and dignity. On a less overt level, however, white women created upset, and even chaos, among Indians. Because many white women espoused the usual frontier philosophy that white beliefs were superior, they recommended that

Indian children dress in white-style clothing, speak only English, and attend boarding schools. In 1887, even though one New Mexico field matron admitted that Indians were "learning fast," she still advocated removing young Indian children from their families and placing them in far-away boarding schools.[6]

Nor did white women hesitate to delve into the most personal Indian affairs and customs. White women told Indian women that only marriages and divorces by white law were valid. When Native Americans continued to wed and part by their own customs, white women urged the Bureau of Indian Affairs (BIA) to intervene. The BIA created a new classification—Indian "custom" marriages and divorces—that put Indians in an ambiguous position. Although they were wed or divorced in their own world, their marriages and divorces were not legal in the eyes of white society, which also considered their children illegitimate. According to one anthropologist, such tensions weakened "the stability of Indian marital and family life."[7]

White women, then, left the subjects of their reform efforts in turmoil. For themselves, white women realized some gains, including a public voice and presence, as well as societal acceptance of careers. Helen Hunt Jackson and Elaine Goodale Eastman are good examples of women who made careers of being moral figures. Moreover, throughout the American West white women's benevolence helped white women more than women of color. For instance, female missionaries who characterized American Indians as primitive peoples in desperate need of "civilizing" established a rationale for expanding their own influence and prerogatives. If Indians were deprived and pathetic, almost any step a white woman might take was justified.

As a case in point, women missionaries, who came from a variety of backgrounds, countries, and religious sects, were distraught when they learned that they were expected to perform limited duties, including domestic tasks, and to act as teachers' assistants, which put them much lower in the church hierarchy than clergy and other male leaders. Once in the field, however, they capitalized on their distance from governing bodies and the lack of accountability by insinuating themselves into policy-making and decision-making. As early as the 1850s, women in trans-Mississippi West missions had enlarged their mandate to "civilize," to nurse, and to teach so that it included establishing and managing hospitals and schools. As a result, the mission field attracted more single women, who regarded missionary work as a career and themselves as paid professionals.[8]

A salient example of assertive women was Roman Catholic Women Religious, also called nuns or sisters. In Los Angeles, the Daughters for Charity of St. Vincent de Paul arrived in 1856, thus becoming the first Women Religious in the city after the Spanish colonial period. The Daughters of Charity founded institutions to care for orphans, educate girls, care for the sick, and to help the poverty stricken. In Virginia City, Nevada, in 1867, the Sisters of Charity established the Nevada Orphan Asylum in 1867. In the Dakota Territory, the Grey Nuns arrived in 1874, the Presentation Sisters followed in 1880, and the Sisters of St. Francis migrated in 1885. Given the patriarchal nature of the church, male supervisors expected sisters to limit their activities to fit prevailing stereotypes of women's work. In far-flung mission fields, Women Religious turned to their advantage distance from supervisors back home, the lack of workers, and the need for facilities to enlarge their own roles. They not only founded their own schools and hospitals, they sometimes helped with the actual construction of walls and fireplaces. They also raised money, administered budgets, and acted as executive officers, all without advice from male clergy.[9]

One of the most outspoken Women Religious was Mary Katherine Drexel. Beginning in the late 1880s, Drexel used her family's fortune to build Indian schools on Dakota reservations and to found a religious community, the Sisters of the Blessed Sacrament for Indians and Colored People. Along the way, Drexel occasionally defied male authority. When in 1889 a bishop opposed some of Drexel's plans, she replied: "It appears to me . . . that I am not obliged to submit my judgment to yours."[10] Drexel had found a way to help impoverished westerners, as well as creating autonomy for Women Religious. She was not to be dissuaded by a mere bishop who, as a man, lacked the moral authority Drexel felt she held as a woman.

Meanwhile, another group of altruistic white women in the American West appeared—female abolitionists. Back east, women were active in abolitionist groups, notably in Boston and Philadelphia, and believed they had a gendered mission. Members of the Boston Anti-Slavery Society declared that "as wives and mothers, as daughters and sisters, we are deeply responsible for the influence we have on the human race."[11] These women also set themselves up as moral beacons for white men. The Boston Female Anti-Slavery Society stated: "We are bound to urge men to cease to do evil and learn how to do good."

When female abolitionists were criticized for writing abolitionist tracts and speaking in public, they decided that they had to campaign for their own rights as well. To help liberate black slaves, the argument went, women had to liberate themselves. At the nation's first women's rights convention at Seneca Falls, New York, in 1848, the attendees further criticized men in a Declaration of Sentiments: "The history of mankind is a history of repeated injuries and usurpations on the part of man toward woman, having in direct object the establishment of an absolute tyranny over her."[12]

During the 1840s and 1850s, white women spread these tenets throughout the American West. They took an active part in the Underground Railroad, a network of "safe-houses" that helped slaves flee the United States for Canada, formed antislavery groups, and made known their abolitionist attitudes. They soon learned that not everyone supported their cause. Iowa pioneer Joanna Harris Haines recalled that in 1852, in a county populated and controlled by slavery sympathizers, "the intense abolitionism of my parents tended to alienate us." According to Haines, "Grinnell had a number of New Englanders who were idealists and friends of humanity when thinking of far-away China, Africa, or South Carolina, but their zeal in good works cooled when the actualities came into town and next door."[13]

Unfortunately, abolitionists made other white settlers anxious, thus solidifying anti-black sentiment. In the Pacific Northwest, for example, a large proportion of Oregon's Willamette Valley settlers were white southerners with pro-slavery attitudes. In 1844, an antislavery act went into effect, but five years later the territorial legislature adopted a measure excluding blacks from Oregon. In 1857, the constitutional convention reaffirmed this measure. After Oregon became a state in 1859, racial issues continued to arise. During the Civil War, the Knights of the Golden Circle fought Union troops and supported slavery. Also during the war, calls came from white Oregonians for the settlement of black Oregonians in a new and exclusively black state, which would free Oregon from blacks.[14]

With the end of the Civil War, white female reformers were certain that not only would black slaves obtain freedom and political rights, but women would be rewarded with legal emancipation for their abolitionist efforts. But women had not gained many fans by appearing publicly and joining men in forcing the most controversial issue the young United States had ever faced. When women failed to win political rights, many became avowed suffragists who believed that women had to vote to correct other wrongs. Eastern suffrage leaders, in particular Anthony and Stanton, toured the West, lecturing wherever they could. The West had its own speakers and leaders as well, notably Oregonian Abigail Scott Duniway, known as the "mother" of woman suffrage in the Pacific Northwest.[15]

During the 1890s and first three decades of the twentieth century, analogous developments occurred in Kenya, where white women seemed determined to uplift black Kenyans. Of course, cases existed of thoughtless or negligent women who came to Kenya to help, but were of little assistance. In the words of a colonial service official, these women were not the "right sort" to take advantage of "the vast scope which exists for social work" by women.[16] They dropped out, perhaps chose another type of endeavor, or left Kenya.

White women who remained in Kenya hoped to alleviate what they labeled the "suffering" of indigenes. Although white women occasionally recognized that colonialism had caused problems, most assumed that what they called the "barbaric" state in which black Kenyans lived before the arrival of white people accounted for their woes. As with the contrasting images of the romanticized Indian and the primitive savage in the American West, white people imputed to black Kenyans two shifting personas.[17] On the one hand, blacks were supposedly heathens standing in the way of the expansion of empire. On the other hand, whites saw black Kenyans as exotic pagans who needed saving spiritually and physically. This was frequently the outlook adopted by women, who preferred a program of "civilizing" rather than genocide.

In contrast to the American West, female abolitionists often appeared first. Abolitionism in Kenya was like that in the West in other ways, however. Just as American women's interpretations of antislavery issues dispersed from East to West, British women's reform ideas spread from middle-class white women in England to white women throughout the empire.[18] Like their counterparts in the American West, white English women considered African slave women as victimized sisters they must rescue. Also like western women, white Kenyan women not only saw the abolition of slavery as a gendered moral responsibility, but labeled men as the progenitors of the slave system. In shouldering what came to be known as the "white woman's burden," Kenya's white female reformers established themselves as moral specialists not only for peoples of color, but for white men.[19]

White women's campaign to uplift black Kenyans dated back to at least the mid-nineteenth century when reform discourse convinced white women that their first step must be freeing black Africans from slavery. Unlike the American West, where slavery was limited, British East Africa had long experienced the slave trade and exported innumerable slaves to many nations. One of the earliest women to support abolitionism in East Africa was Helen Cooke Kirk, who in 1867 married Sir John Kirk, a colonial officer based in Zanzibar. At that time, Zanzibar was the administrative center for British activities in East Africa; thus, it offered Helen Kirk an opportunity to set a pattern for white women who later settled along the coast of the mainland.

As chief medical officer of the British consular office there, Dr. Kirk had long opposed the slave trade, notably by issuing an antislavery edict in 1866. He soon learned that, unlike Christian slaves, Muslim slaves had some rights and protection, as well as a promise of eventual manumission; thus it was a difficult matter to end the slave trade. Also, Muslims resisted abolitionism, arguing that slavery was condoned by the Prophet.[20] At least in part, the stench and inhumanity of the Zanzibar slave market, where slaves were kept in a stifling underground chamber until they went on the auction block, drove Kirk onward.[21]

In 1867, Helen joined John in Zanzibar. By 1872, through such deeds as undertaking massive entertaining, Lady Kirk helped her husband achieve the even more influential position of counsel-general. The historian Richard D. Wolff credits Counsel-General Kirk with making most of the on-site decisions that activated British intervention in the slave trade, whereas the historians Zoë Marsh and G. S. Kingsnorth state that Kirk was "the greatest influence in the suppression of the east coast slave trade."[22] Helen tirelessly encouraged and aided her husband in enforcing regulations against the slave trade, especially those of the 1873 Frere Treaty between the sultan of Zanzibar and Great Britain, which would halt the export of slaves from East Africa and close the slave market in Zanzibar.

There is no evidence that Helen Kirk understood that British officials used the antislave crusade to gain economic and political power in British East Africa, as well as to garner support at home for imperial expansion. Helen always referred to abolitionism as a moral issue of the first rank. Even when she undercut the Sultanate by helping Princess Selme escape from Zanzibar so that she could marry a white man of her choice, Helen seemed more concerned with the romantic and humanitarian aspects of the situation than its potential impact on the Sultan's waning power in Zanzibar.[23] Helen Kirk continued her crusade until 1883, when she left Zanzibar and returned to England for her children's schooling.

John Kirk was left to pursue abolitionism without Helen's assistance. Although John Kirk often spoke of abolitionism as a "moral" cause, he did recognize the potential for political and economic gain for Britain if local power collapsed. In 1884, when a group of Germans showed signs of gaining influence in East Africa, John Kirk redoubled his efforts to stop the slave trade, as well as abolishing slavery altogether, in hopes of destroying the Arab government in Zanzibar. In 1885, the Berlin Conference issued the Berlin Act, which strengthened Kirk's hand, in that Britain and other countries condemned the slave trade and promised to end it in their own areas of Africa. Helen Kirk was comfortably back in England when Britain's attack on slavery caused the collapse of the slave trade and the Sultanate, bringing in its wake social disruption and economic deterioration among black Africans.[24]

Besides opposing slavery, Helen Kirk and a few others like her unwittingly demonstrated that white women could exist in East African climates, thus opening the way for female missionaries. As early as the 1840s and 1850s, representatives of some sects had already seized the initiative by setting up missions in the region that would later become Kenya. Roman Catholics and Methodists were among the first to realize that Africa presented an auspicious opportunity for white missionaries, including women. Other Protestant leaders added that missionary couples would model monogamy for black men and women.[25]

Consequently, during the 1880s and 1890s a few women went to rudimentary mission stations along Kenya's coast. They fought rain and mud, fed crowds of people, and did their best to help the ill and injured. In these missions, women attempted to establish white-style homes and families as examples. Some even took in black Kenyans who had been ousted from their villages after they converted to Christianity. By serving others, these women effectively used domestic practices and beliefs to convince indigenes of the rightness of empire.[26]

One of the most well known of such women was Mary Bazett, who with two sisters came to British East Africa in 1891, representing the Church Missionary Society. Mary taught black Kenyan women at Kabete mission. In 1899, Mary married Canon Harry Leakey, after which she continued her work at Kabete. In 1903, Mary bore a boy named Louis, who would become Kenya's most well-known archeologist.[27]

Yet the total number of female missionaries in Kenya remained relatively small, largely due to horrible living conditions. Women's discomfort becomes readily apparent if one spends a few days in Mombasa, a steaming port city on Kenya's southern coast, or on the island of Zanzibar, the governmental center of the British East Africa Protectorate between 1895 and 1904. At midnight during the height of the hot, muggy season, a person perspires just sitting still. In this climate, white women wore long skirts, petticoats, and corsets, in part to set a model of "civilized" attire and in part to avoid offending the sensibilities of the many Muslims in the area. Somehow, women, ranging from the British counsel's wife to female missionaries of various religious sects, not only endured, but usually survived, enervating heat. At the same time, diseases unknown to them stalked women and their children. Also, female missionaries lived every day of their lives awash in a sea of faces and languages unfamiliar to them. Yet, despite the drawbacks, a growing number of married and single white women accepted the call. At the time, some missions preferred single women who would not become pregnant, thus inconveniencing the mission staff and perhaps endangering their own health.

Ignoring this policy, married women also went to Kenya. As early as 1878, Anne Katherine Ferrar Binns accompanied her husband, the Reverend Harry K. Binns, to Freretown, a center for freed slaves. Here Anne Binns made dresses for Kenyan women and children, taught women to sew, and protected slaves from former owners who tried to repossess them.[28] Mary Binns's journal lists such other activities as holding religion classes and prayer meetings, translating the litany into Kinyika, teaching night school, reading Scripture to children, running her household, overseeing her house help, caring for her children, and gardening. Although she watched for mail deliveries and pined for absent family members, she seemed content and pleased with her successes—one of the most important, in her words, was "rescuing a little child from slavery."[29]

Mary Binns's photograph collection further reveals the daily life and interests of a female missionary to Kenya during the late nineteenth century. Photographs of black Kenyans are numerous— black women grinding maize, wearing calf-length skirts reflecting missionary values regarding clothing, and a group of young men labeled "our boys" playing what Binns called football. Mary's parlor is very European, filled with books, an ample coffee table, and a Regulator clock. A wedding she attends features a white bride in a traditional white gown, a flower girl, and women guests wearing large fashionable hats.[30] Clearly, the Binns did not intend to leave England behind. Instead, they transplanted it for black Kenyans to emulate.

Besides Mary Binns, other early women missionaries came to Kenya. Because of what white women perceived as "turmoil" among black Kenyan women, they concentrated their efforts on black females of all ages. Like white women in the American West who saw Indian women as deprived, white women in Kenya judged the lives of black women as "deplorable." On the coast, where the slave trade had been prevalent, one mission program involved rehabilitation of female slaves. Although slaves who had lived with European families or married into local groups had a relatively easy time adapting, others found themselves caught between their societies' beliefs and white notions of freedom.[31]

White women often ran into opposition, however. Adherents of Islam frequently refused, on legal and religious grounds, to recognize the abolition of slavery and found ways to circumvent antislave provisions. Rather than selling a female slave, Muslim men "gave" young women in marriage, often demanding financial compensation. In other words, these men continued to buy and sell women as slaves.[32] Although white women harbored runaway women and petitioned courts for their freedom, they were unable to disperse antislave sentiment. Especially in places like Lamu and Takaungu, local traditions and jurisdictional complexities defeated them.

Resistance appeared to increase white women's determination, but, in their zeal, they usually failed to confront their own imposition of inferior status on black Kenyans. Although Christ called for equality, missionaries treated black Christians as inferiors.[33] When challenged, some women saw the dilemma, while others answered that "Christianizing" would take a long time before black Kenyans would stand on their own. At least in part, this attitude reflected female missionaries' well-bred but modest backgrounds. They had not grown up wielding wealth and power that might produce immediate changes. Instead, they relied on religious indoctrination and education, both long-term projects. In 1892, when Mary Bazett (later Leakey) came with her sisters Louise and Sybil from a middling English family to Mombasa, they hoped to offer "Christian education" to black women, an undertaking that would consume their entire lifetimes.[34]

Female missionaries also made health and nutrition a high priority for black Kenyans. Of course, male missionaries did so as well, and both female and male missionaries used medical treatment and medicines in evangelizing, but females especially concentrated on often ignored women and children. They were steeped in the medical discourse of the 1890s and early 1900s that characterized Africa as a hotbed of disease and its people as superstitious and ignorant, much in need of white help. In too many cases, however, "white help" actually introduced new diseases, created conditions favorable to disease, spread epidemics, and objectified black Africans through mass treatment that took no account of an individual.[35]

Altered food supplies provide an example. Although food was abundant in early periods of Kenya's history, inadequate food supplies or outright famine became common under colonial rule, thus causing black Kenyans frequently to suffer malnutrition and hunger. In late 1918 and early 1919, for example, mission teacher Elizabeth Chadwick wrote to a friend describing black children who cried "in hunger" and others who died "by the roadside" as a result of a famine in the Kavirondo District. Although government-sponsored relief committees sent maize and other foodstuffs to afflicted groups, these supplies only stemmed the current crisis. Between 1917 and 1924, Chadwick recorded an outbreak of plague, followed by smallpox, malaria, and dysentery. Meanwhile, natural disasters, including torrential rains, floods, gale-force winds, and fires ignited by lightning exacerbated already harsh conditions. As a result, Chadwick often found herself torn between her desire to teach and a more immediate need to administer medical treatment.[36]

Even though colonialism introduced problems, some black Africans noted that "white" medicine sometimes allowed people to live who might not have otherwise survived childhood or recovered from an illness or accident. Lepers also received care and treatment from whites, usually at mission stations. Consequently, a Kikuyu woman named Wanjiku, who lived in Mutira Location, said that some of the changes that white people brought with them were beneficial, especially alternative medical practices.[37]

Despite its difficulties, mission work attracted growing numbers of women. Missions increasingly accepted women, whether married or single. Three years after Mary Bazett and her sisters came to Africa, two single women, M. E. Conway and D. Mayor, joined the Binns at Freetown, where they received a warm reception. In that year, 1895, *The Taveta Chronicle,* published quarterly by the Church Missionary

Society, reported that the arrival of Conway and Mayor caused "general rejoicing," especially among "the female portion of the community attached to the Missions."[38] Called "lady missionaries," women increasingly came from such faraway countries as the United States. In 1911, Quaker Alta Howard Hoyt journeyed with her husband from Kansas to Kenya. Some years later, in 1923, Ruth T. Shaffer of the Africa Inland Mission traveled from Chicago, Illinois, to Maasai territory in interior Kenya.[39]

In Kenya, as in the American West, female evangelists occupied a lesser position than men, thus taking orders from the church's male hierarchy, including ministers, priests, and bishops. Also, they were limited to customary "women's" jobs, ranging from teaching to nursing. Because female missionaries operated in a system that conflated Christianity with civilization, progress, and technology, they too often served as pawns for superiors who lacked sensitivity to black issues, or for male mission leaders who acted as advisors, ambassadors, and informers for colonial officials. Consequently, some women moved from mission to mission, doing whatever jobs were assigned to them. Others resisted by building and managing their own hospitals, chapels, schools, and mission stations.

Much like Women Religious in the American West, an example of women who worked within the system was the Roman Catholic White Sisters. After 1878, when the White Fathers established a mission at Zanzibar, White Sisters began to arrive in small groups. Despite the resistance of White Fathers, these women carved out a niche, especially by training black women and girls in the production of saleable handicrafts so that they could achieve a degree of self-sufficiency. They also distilled medicines with which they treated black Kenyans.[40] A case of an individual woman who challenged male domination was Sister Irene Stephani, a Consolata missionary, who arrived in Mombasa in 1924. Aged twenty-four, Sister Irene traveled to Nyeri, where she supervised workers on the bishop's coffee plantation and taught them to pray. In 1923, Sister Irene Stephani became a controversial but adamant mother superior of the Women Religious at the Nyeri mission. Among other programs, she implemented a widely criticized program to help the indigent and aged.

Like the West's Katherine Drexel, Mother Stephani brooked no male resistance to her plans.[41]

Despite the efforts of these and other missionaries, at the beginning of World War I mission stations in Kenya suffered isolation and poverty. With men called to the front, women rescued the mission effort, but they received little thanks for their efforts. During the 1920s, female evangelists had to plead with home churches for continued support.[42] By the late 1920s, women were again making progress, especially in establishing "grass-hut" schools for black women and girls. They also helped found small mission printing presses and supplied them with songbooks, readers, and workbooks in Kenya's twenty-four major languages.[43]

When in 1929 a worldwide depression struck, Kenyan missions again suffered setbacks. By the mid- to late-1930s, missionary work resumed its intensity. In 1937, the Salvation Army held a congress of African Salvationists to revitalize the "love and power" of Christianity. During the following years, groups like the Methodist Missionary Society and training institutions like the Moody Bible Institute sent growing numbers of teachers and evangelists, many women among them.[44]

By the late 1930s, Kenya's missionary movement came of age. Among many others, the Quaker missionaries from Kansas, Alta and Fred Hoyt, had spent thirty years founding an industrial school, starting music classes, and teaching the principles of Quakerism, including pacifism and the equality of peoples. From Wichita, Kansas, the Hoyts and their two young sons first came to Kenya in 1911. When the Hoyt's sponsoring American institution failed to send funds, they joined in 1912 the Friends Africa Industrial Mission near Kisumu. Alta, who was seven months pregnant, traveled in a hammock carried by black Kenyans. At the new mission station, Alta supervised the education of black children. She was delighted when teachers Roxie Reeve and a Mrs. Conover arrived in 1913, also to help black women and children. Later, as Alta neared retirement, she declared that black Kenyans had "come a long way . . . spiritually, educationally, medicinally and industrially." Hoyt said she would leave Kenya satisfied that she had helped black Kenyans take their place in what she called an international community of Christian nations.[45]

Did Alta Hoyt vastly overestimate the value of her efforts? Not entirely. Even critics of the Christian mission movement admit that people like Alta Hoyt achieved many humanitarian goals, including helping enforce the government's prohibition of slavery in Kenya. Missionaries also pioneered the establishment of schools. They actively opposed such policies as black land reserves and the exploitation of black labor. And because missionaries held a supranational perspective, they attacked such aspects of colonialism as racialism. Instead, they supported social justice and the eventual independence of black Kenya.[46]

Still, in the final analysis, missionaries were imperialists who developed their own slice of the Kenya frontier. As one career colonial administrator remarked, "although the missionary was a different kind of colonist," he or she still shared the colonialist perspective: a colonial administrator thought in terms of "my colony," a settler "my farm," and a missionary "my mission," and thus they all made decisions as landed proprietors.[47] As a case in point, the White Fathers and White Sisters owned property, grew crops, and hired black workers. In 1908, the White Sisters barred Kikuyu women from cutting wood on lands that the sisters insisted now belonged to them. This was a blow to these Kikuyu women, who were the sole providers of fuel wood for their families. Apparently, "doing good" did not prevent white women from declaring ownership of black Kenyans' land and other resources.[48]

Unsurprisingly, black Kenyans had difficulty distinguishing between officials, settler-farmers, and missionaries, all of whom wanted their land. According to an oft-repeated story, a black Kenyan rebuked an early missionary, "When you arrived, we had the land and you had the Bible. Now you have the land and we have the Bible."

Another Side of the Story: Women of Color in the West and in Kenya

Native Americans developed their own responses to white women's projects; they neutralized white women's actions by subtle and not-so-subtle resistance. Some refused to let their children leave home, or continued to speak their own languages and prepare traditional foods for children living at home. Others quietly took from white teachers what they found meaningful and ignored the rest.[49]

Coping techniques appeared among other women of color as well. Although they saw the benefits of assimilation, they were unwilling to give up their own cultures entirely. Also, they feared that their children would suffer as pseudo-whites. A Chinese father in Carson City, Nevada, lamented that he had let his son "grow up" with white boys and thus desire material goods and freedoms he could not have. The father said that he and his wife hoped to "do better" with their younger son and not let him acquire what the father termed "a taste for the life of the superior race."[50]

Later, between 1890 and 1940, Asian Indian women settlers in Kenya developed their own accommodations. Generally, Asian Indian women showed little interest in imperial feminism, meaning white women expanding their own spheres by adopting the British empire's goal of helping others. To them, these ideas lacked meaning because they neither recognized what white women had gained at the expense of women of color nor considered racism a high-priority problem. Instead, Asian Indian women had in mind their own reforms resulting from living with prohibitions against female education, singing in public, playing sports, or sometimes even teaching. Thus, like women of color in the American West, Asian Indian women concentrated on improved education and employment opportunities for themselves rather than white women's goals.[51]

For black Kenyan women, the situation differed. As a result of colonialism, numerous black women had moved into urban areas, where they generally lived in poverty. Those who stayed in villages had to feed themselves and produce a surplus to make up for agricultural workers who were now urban dwellers. Kikuyu women especially contributed to the political economy of their people by conducting long-distance trade. To create time for trade, innovative women developed labor-saving devices, notably improved hoe blades. Still, black Kenyan women found themselves laboring faster and harder just to stay in place.[52]

In addition, black women often lost ground as a result of white women's programs. Tragically, white women who hoped to free black women from what they saw as a subservient position ended up undermining their status. In numerous hunting and gathering societies, the division of labor was flexible, and women had more rights and less restrictions than women in industrial societies. These assertions would have been anathema to Kenya's white women, who judged the situation of black women through late nineteenth- and early twentieth-century eyes. One white woman stated inaccurately that black Kenyan women were "practically slaves of the men."[53] Because white women misunderstood black women's roles, they created harmful schemes. For instance, by helping move black Kenyans onto land reserves, white women caused black women to lose their access to communal lands. Also, by supporting the idea that indigenes should raise maize instead of beans, white women committed an act of economic imperialism—they devalued black women's production, which rested on beans. Gradually, black women's ability to hold property, trade, and manage forms of wealth separately from their husbands either withered or took on new forms.[54]

Far from being hapless victims, black Kenyan women demonstrated agency by resisting ideas they found useless, including some Christian teachings and white conceptions of "progress." Black women also drew on long-established coping strategies, ranging from joining women's organizations to forming new family structures in time of famine. For instance, Meru women belonged to secret women's societies, which had secret rituals and barred black Kenyan men. Meru women also successfully withstood attempts of white government officials to investigate their ceremonies.[55]

In other instances, resistance came from black families and communities. Families and entire villages split asunder over the question of whether to follow their own ways or to accept missionaries' teachings, as some villagers did wholeheartedly. Opponents employed formidable tactics. Charity Waciuma recalled that her grandfather— a powerful figure in Kikuyu society—banned his granddaughters from his home because they had not been circumcised. Although he eventually relented, others insulted Charity and her sisters so that "there were frequent fights between my brothers and some of the young men who taunted us." In other cases, fathers forbid daughters to attend classes at local missions, whereas villagers reviled "mission" boys and girls. Black Kenyans who opposed Christian values found small, daily ways to ignore them or to minimize their impact. In extreme situations, black Kenyans even attacked or killed white colonialists.[56] For black women living in these conflicted situations, women's rights and social reform were not nearly as important as survival.

White Women Stabilizing Society in the West and in Kenya

In the American West, white women also hoped to create what they thought of as a stable society. One obstacle was widespread—and usually male—drinking of alcoholic beverages, which threatened public safety, as well as the family. Thus, the crusade that attracted the most women was temperance. Women targeted what they thought of as at-risk groups: Native Americans, African Americans, and white men, thus setting themselves up as moral guides and leaders of these people.[57]

After the Civil War, women's temperance activities intensified, becoming a major national cause. In 1874, the Iowan Annie Turner Wittenmyer founded the Women's Christian Temperance Union (WCTU). Under Frances Willard's aggressive presidency between 1879 and 1898, the WCTU became by 1890 the largest women's organization in the United States, with numerous groups in western locales.[58] In Montana, for example, a state temperance union formed in Butte and local units in Butte, Helena, and Missoula. In Butte, Reverend Alice Barnes became a WCTU leader, touring as an evangelist and holding the offices of state treasurer, editor, and president of the Montana WCTU. The women of Butte dubbed Barnes "Saint Courageous" for standing up to westerners who opposed temperance reform by verbally abusing Barnes, throwing paint on her clothing, and lodging complaints with the police.[59]

Women reformers like Barnes persevered because they believed they had a Providential duty. During the mid-1870s, a female founder of the Nebraska WCTU put it this way: "In all ages since the creation, woman at critical times has come to the front and with her quick discernment and her great moral courage has so changed the on-sweeping tide of sentiment for revenge and cruelty, that the Moral and the Spiritual have taken the throne and the nation has been saved."[60]

White women also wanted to "stabilize" the frontier family, especially by eliminating racial intermarriage. During early days of settlement, intermarriage had seemed inevitable in the West. Wide-spread migration and wars, ranging from Indian conflicts to the Civil War, caused people to meet, mix, and sometimes marry. Also, Native Americans tolerated and even approved of whites, who were primarily male. Hoping to assimilate Spanish newcomers through marriage, Indian women often married explorers and conquisatadors. Spain encouraged cross-cultural unions, hoping to gain control of Christian-ized Indian women married to Spanish men. Such intermarriages created a new group of mixed-heritage people called mestizos, who married French-Canadians and Americans.

In addition, some Hispanas married Anglos, particularly in New Mexico's Rio Arriba Valley, located between the eastern Sangre de Cristo Mountains and western San Juan and Jemez Mountains.[61] Farther west, such elite Californio families as the Bandinis, Picos, and Yorbas also reportedly allowed their daughters to marry Anglo newcomers, probably to tie Anglo men to the Hispanic ruling class. In Los Angeles, Spanish-speaking people not only married Anglos, but sometimes Native Americans, Asians, and African Americans.[62]

Members of the Hispanic elite were the first to rethink the situation. As more whites arrived, Spanish-heritage people increasingly viewed white newcomers as threats to their culture. Thus, many stopped their daughters from marrying white men and producing children who were only part Hispanic. Well-to-do Hispanics hoped to protect their influence and rights by preventing white men from marrying into the established power structure. By the 1840s, resistance to intermarriage was common and the number of Hispanic-white intermarriages declined.[63]

These anti-intermarriage sentiments jibed well with the beliefs of incoming migrants, especially white women, who made certain that male explorers and traders married to native women realized that their situations had changed. As the numbers of white female settlers increased, the need for white men to wed spouses of other races declined. At the same time, negative attitudes, restrictive policies, and legal prohibitions against intermarriages increased. As early as the 1840s, for example, female missionaries and settlers at Fort Vancouver on the West Coast warned that such unions would lead to a lowering of "white" standards and the increase of social problems, especially prostitution, alcoholism, and theft. They also blamed men, declaring that white male "barbarism" had led to the degradation of native women.[64]

To enforce their ideas, white women at Fort Vancouver used techniques like public disdain and rumors. They also criticized the morals of Indian wives and attributed to them everything from poor housekeeping to infidelity. White women added that intermarried couples produced mixed-breed children who constituted a burden to white society. These harsh tactics often proved effective. By making marriages between Indian women and white men "by custom of the country" appear licentious and immoral, white women generated a climate of opinion that caused a decline in the number of interracial unions and encouraged white men to leave their wives and children. When Indian wives found themselves unable to support their mixed-heritage children, white women offered to raise abandoned children, thus meeting a need they had helped create.[65]

Throughout the mid-nineteenth-century West, white women settlers reacted in similar ways to interracial unions. In Arizona of the 1860s, white women belittled native Spanish-speaking women who cohabited with white miners, especially if their children had several different fathers.[66] Although white women settlers approved of inter-ethnic unions that demanded little adjustment, such as a German man marrying an Irish woman, they opposed interracial marriages. A significant number of white men also supported these views. For instance, one white male traveler of the early 1850s disparaged the "confusion of races" found in the West, especially deprecating "half-breeds" in the coarsest of terms.[67]

In this milieu, anti-intermarriage laws flourished. At some time in their history, the trans-Mississippi states of Arizona, Arkansas, California, Colorado, Idaho, Iowa, Montana, Nebraska, Nevada, North Dakota, Oklahoma, Oregon, Utah, and Wyoming prohibited marriage between whites and blacks. In addition, Arizona, California, Idaho, Louisiana, Montana, Nebraska, Nevada, Oregon, South Dakota, Utah, and Wyoming forbid whites and Asians to marry, and sometimes whites and Indians as well.[68] The enforcement of these rules necessitated a definition of race. Because whites constructed race to be immutable, they categorized how much Indian or other type of "blood" flowed in a person's body, classifying individuals as "one-half" Indian or "one-fourth" Asian. In response, people of mixed heritages often manifested shame and refused to acknowledge their ancestry. One Oklahoma man's "one-half Cherokee blood" humiliated him to the point that he refused to apply for land allotments and government payments due him because he was part Cherokee. As a result, he left his "one-fourth" Cherokee daughters without land or other means of support.[69]

Like their predecessors in the American West, Kenyan frontierswomen also hoped to improve the quality of their daily lives by stabilizing institutions. White women who came to Kenya between 1890 and 1940 wanted a wide range of reforms: lower taxes, better housing, additional schools and hospitals, self-rule for Kenya colony, and a prosperous economy. If necessary, these would come at the expense of the same black Kenyans whom white women wanted to elevate.[70] For example, in 1934, the Naivasha and District Farmers' Association, which included women as members, considered a proposal of questionable morality: to "teach or induce" black Kenyans to eat meat. This would create local markets for white farmer's meat products and would justify putting white-owned butcher shops on black reserves.[71]

White women living in a black country had other concerns as well. They supported tighter immigration controls, so that white people with criminal records, who were impoverished, or were mentally ill could not enter Kenya and create problems for its white community. In addition, women endorsed land laws favoring white farmers and prohibiting peoples of color from claiming land in white areas.[72] In

1930, a women's protest session held in Nairobi only days after white men held a similar meeting, clearly revealed the nature of white women's self-interests. At the caucus, seventy white women opposed a British government proposal to expand political representation for Asian Indians and to consider the interests of black Kenyans paramount. Women believed that such provisions would undermine white "authority" and lead to "the loss of our homes, our rights to govern, our hopes to continue to help in consolidating White Civilisation [sic] in Africa." Female delegates further argued that because the British government had asked them to come to Kenya, it owed them "stability and safety."[73]

Obviously, white women mistrusted the very people they hoped to "civilize." Although they admitted that in the future Asian Indians and black Kenyans would have gained enough "political fitness" to share in ruling Kenya, it would not be soon. To them, Asian Indians had to prove their "ability in this respect firstly in their own country," whereas black Kenyans were not "sufficiently advanced to be yet capable of self Government in their own Mother land." White women believed that extending power to either group in 1930 would create havoc, especially for white women and children.[74]

Another important challenge, at least from the perspective of white women, was preventing women and men of different races from forming affectional and sexual relationships. Despite a 1909 edict, the Crewe Circular, in which the secretary of state for the colonies prohibited liaisons between white men and indigenous women, a number of these relationships occurred. Most importantly, white women wanted to keep white men from marrying women of color. The frontier might symbolize a place of "freedom" for white men, but white women saw it as constituting a need for curbing men of "bestial instincts." By pursuing these issues, white women believed they fulfilled their responsibility in regulating the family and sexual life of both whites and blacks. By way of comparison, white women in French, Dutch, and Spanish colonies of the era also supported familial and sexual exclusion.[75]

Several popular contentions of the era rationalized white women's actions and drove them onward. Women translated their belief in white superiority into keeping the white race as "pure" as possible. They maintained that because each racial group constituted a unit of its own, sexual affiliations that crossed lines were not only "unnatural," but produced flawed children. During the early twentieth century, a racial purity campaign back home in Britain gave added impetus to these ideas. Reform discourse quickly proceeded from whites in the metropole, especially centers like London and Manchester, to those in the colonies. Reformers' concepts of racial degeneracy and their philosophy of eugenics (the control of human breeding to produce superior children) spurred white Kenyan women to oppose interracial marriages and the birth of "inferior" children. White women, who viewed cultural progress as moving along a continuum from primitive to modern, explained that approving racial mixing would be nothing less than a white slide backward.[76]

Both white women at home and in the colonies thought of white male sexuality as a significant cause of "mixed" relationships. Because white men were easily tempted, women claimed, they needed female moral guidance to keep them on the "right" path. White Kenyan women argued that the lure to "mix" in Kenya was far greater because of a highly diverse population than back in Britain, with its relatively homogenous population. White women especially expressed their disdain of white men, including government officials, who took black Kenyan women as mistresses. Even though these interracial alliances were not well documented or often mentioned in colonial discourse, they did exist. In 1924, white farm manager Llewelyn Powys admitted that he had once become enamored of a young Kikuyu woman. "Other white men had deliberately abandoned civilized life and taken to living with black people," he wrote. "Why not I?"[77]

White women were even more outraged when a white woman established a connection with a man of color. In 1911, a group of white Kenyan women obtained a charge of prostitution against a Swedish woman because she lived with an Asian Indian man. Although the female protestors asked for an ordinance making it a crime for any white woman to allow an Asian Indian or black Kenyan man to have "carnal knowledge" of her, they were unsuccessful.[78] In 1924, the East Africa Women's League (EAWL) again protested, this time to the

Crown Advocates Department. Because league members had learned that the number of marriages between white women and Asian Indian men was on the rise, EAWL representatives asked for "earnest consideration of the problem of 'mixed marriages.'" They suggested that the government place obstacles in the way of such marriages, including a three-month waiting period to give the couple time to reconsider. Within a few days, the attorney general brushed off the complaint by saying that he could find such a law only in Belgium and that in his knowledge intermarriages were "common everywhere."[79]

Underlying these complaints was a deep and noxious issue: the need of whites to control the sexuality of "others," notably black Kenyans. In an insightful analysis of Michel Foucalt's controversial *History of Sexuality,* the scholar Laura Ann Stoler demonstrates that nineteenth-century concepts of sexuality were closely tied to the imposition of power on indigenous peoples. According to Stoler, "the discursive management of the sexual practices of colonizer and colonized was fundamental to the colonial order of things." As European thinkers and writers defined the qualities of whites and of colonial "others"—in this case, black Kenyans—they imputed to whites such superior qualities as "character" and "good breeding," whereas peoples of color were "dangerous" and "carnal." In rapidly proliferating colonial discourses concerning servants, racial purity, and personal hygiene, white writers characterized members of their own race as "controlled," but they portrayed indigenes as "promiscuous." These depictions were one more way for whites to hold sway over black Kenyans and to rationalize white interference in the most personal of matters.[80]

Despite white women, whites and peoples of color found each other and formed attachments. By the 1930s, white women openly lamented the relaxation of racial segregation that led to such connections, particularly targeting Nairobi, which increasingly included inhabitants of many backgrounds. In the eyes of white women, Nairobi was supposed to be a symbol for white people who strove to maintain racial and other principles. Although they wanted Nairobi to grow as a transport point and a market, they did not want the city to lose its white iconography. Rather than bringing people together, white women felt that Nairobi's function was to keep people in their racial and social-class "places." Nairobi failed to comply. Frequently, separation of the races fell victim to a diverse population, overcrowding, and the need for workers. One woman protested young English men working alongside Africans in garages, and young English women serving in Asian Indian shops. Such integration in employment made white women fear a moral and economic "decline" among Kenya's whites.[81]

Further, white women worried about the collapse of the entire "system" of categorizing and separating people according to race. To them, dark skin denoted difference, which equated with deviance and pathology. White women especially perceived Asian Indian men as oversexed and depraved. During the 1930s, a number of white mothers lodged complaints against black and Asian Indian men for "enticing" or defiling girls as young as six or seven years old. Whether these men were guilty is difficult to know; white courts convicted them.[82] White women also mistrusted black men, especially male servants who had access to their homes and even their bedrooms. To make white women feel in control, they used sexual stereotypes in a reductionist manner.[83] Asian Indian men became patriarchal oppressors of women but cowards underneath, whereas black male servants became dull-witted "boys," both less likely to inflict damage on white women than if they had been full-witted, virile men. For white women, then, stereotyping male "others" was a survival skill.

Another Side of the Story, Part 2: Women of Color in the West and in Kenya

Frontierswomen of color had their own ideas about matters like interracial marriage and, like human beings in any historical setting, their own stereotypes. Whites were not the only ones to identify "we" and "them"; they simply left far more evidence of their classifications.[84] Just as whites feared people of color, people of color feared whites. Women found white men frightening because they were white—because they were the "other." Given the fact that some invading white men did rape and otherwise sexually exploit women of color, these worries had some basis in fact.

During the early years of settlement in the American West, however, a number of American Indian women perceived advantages in cohabiting with or marrying white men. During the 1840s, 1850s, and 1860s, Plains Indian women who wed white fur traders gained status in their communities and were better off economically.[85] During the same era, Indians living in Indian Territory (later, Oklahoma) also married incoming whites, often through "Indian custom" or common-law marriages. As they watched growing numbers of whites migrate in, however, Indians worried that whites would someday outnumber them. Some even predicted that Indian Territory would eventually become an American state. As they feared, in 1890 the U.S. Congress declared Indian Territory to be Oklahoma Territory and allowed white claimants to seize former Indian lands.

Indian leaders realized they could not prevent incoming whites from courting and marrying Indians, who held land and other government benefits. Instead of prohibiting native-white marriages, which would have created an enforcement nightmare, Indian officials tried to protect Indian spouses from exploitation. In 1890, a Cherokee Indian could marry another Indian simply by registering with a court clerk, but, according to Article XV, Section 68 of Cherokee regulations, whites who hoped to marry Cherokees had to apply for a license and present a certificate of "good moral character" signed by ten "respectable Cherokee citizens by blood." White applicants also had to swear allegiance to the Cherokee nation. To avoid desertion of Indian spouses, whites had to participate in legal wedding ceremonies conducted by authorized clerks or ordained ministers. In turn, white spouses gained Indian citizenship, which gave them the right to apply for land allotments and other government programs.[86]

Indians living in Indian Territory developed a similar dislike of Indians marrying African Americans. During the 1820s, the U.S. government's relocation policy had forced Indians and their African American slaves to settle in Indian Territory. As early as 1839, Cherokee law forbid an Indian to marry a black slave. After the Emancipation Proclamation of 1863 liberated black slaves and recognized them as persons, Indians and blacks occasionally married. For instance, Lena Barnett, the daughter of a former slave mother and a Cherokee father, attended an Indian school and sometime during the 1870s married a Creek Indian.[87]

During the 1880s, the situation altered. As more types of people settled in the West, ethnic and racial groups became protective of their own cultures. American Indians viewed intermarriage as dangerous to their cultural and racial "purity." For instance, Choctaws not only prohibited Indian-black marriages, but in 1885 made such unions a felony. In 1888, the Chickasaw National Party opposed "the adoption of the Negro in any way, shape, or form."[88]

In addition to Native Americans, Asian groups, notably Chinese and Japanese immigrants to the West, preferred their children to marry people of their own groups. When all else failed, Asian parents resorted to matchmakers and the custom of picture brides. At least among the early generations of Asian migrants, mothers especially worked to keep their families unsullied and their cultural heritage intact.[89]

In Kenya, peoples of color held comparable attitudes. Black women often distrusted white men. White farm manager Llewelyn Powys, mentioned above, thought a Kikuyu girl charming until she learned that he was serious about the flirtation. After Powys approached the young woman's father, he said that "a new scared look came into" the girl's eyes. Apparently, she had been, in Powys's words, "willing to laugh and play" until she understood that she might end up in a white man's bed.[90]

Black Kenyan women more readily agreed to marry Asian Indian men, who seemed more like them than white men. Yet these alliances were often troubled. During the early colonial period, Indian men who took African wives did so without ritual or license. As a result, their children were known by the Indian word *jotawa,* meaning "bastard," or *chotara* in Swahili. Sometimes a black Kenyan husband appeared, claiming that he had let his wife "marry" an Indian man so she would have food, and he now wanted her back. Other situations could be equally distressing. In one instance, a black Kavirondo woman married an Asian Indian man, but when the man's community excommunicated and shunned him; it created such an impossible situation for him that he returned his wife to her father. In other cases of black Kenyan women marrying Asian Indian men, the man's family accepted the deed or disowned the couple.[91]

Gradually, the number of these marriages appeared to decrease. Formal statistics may be somewhat inaccurate, however. At least in part, because black women took Muslim names upon marriage, much like Hispanic women took their husbands' Anglo names in the American West, they and their children were recorded as Asian Indians rather than as black Kenyans. Asian-white unions also appeared to be minimal. During the mid-1830s, an Asian Indian man and a European woman who married had to start a multiracial school for their children, who did not fit into the segregated schools—African, Asian Indian, and European—existing at the time.

Conclusion

How times changed on frontiers. In Kenya, for example, during the 1890s and early 1900s the first Mary Leakey wanted to give black Kenyans the gift of white culture. She became a mainstay of the Kabete mission, beloved by all. Later, a second Mary Leakey appeared. She was Mary Douglas Nicol, an archeological illustrator who in 1935 came to Kenya, collaborated with Louis Leakey in revising archeological theory, and in 1936 married him. The second Mary Leakey, more properly known as Dr. Mary Leakey because of four honorary doctorates, also wanted to help black Africans—by discovering their origins and illuminating the complexities of their culture. In a sense, she wanted to give back what the first Mary Leakey and her colleagues had taken away. Other white women working with Mary included Nellie Grant, who located a cave full of bones and artifacts for Mary, and later, Joy Adamson, who helped Mary excavate the Ngorongoro crater in Tanzania.[92]

Clearly, white frontierswomen knew what they wanted and were willing to help each other achieve it. At the same time, in both the American West and in Kenya, white women often accomplished less than they had hoped and saw other ideas dashed to the ground. Too often, the moral-guardian argument backfired, as did domestic imperialism. In exercising their supposed moral superiority, white women created more problems for indigenes than they solved. Praise for white women soon turned into criticism, replacing the "pioneer mother" image with one of white women as exploiters. Also, by presenting themselves as needing protection—from such ills as spouse abuse and alcoholism—women placed themselves in a different category from men. Although some women argued that it was a superior category, men tended to see women who needed protection as inferior. Thus, women's techniques turned out to be largely ineffective.

For women of color, the situation was even more complicated. White women's "good" created much of their "bad." At the same time, deteriorating political and economic conditions placed additional burdens on their shoulders. Undoubtedly, both Mary Leakeys would be mortified if they knew that white women's efforts helped create a new and disadvantaged hegemonic group lumped together under the term "third world" women.

A Frontier as Product

SEVEN
Image Is Everything

OF the four elements of a frontier—philosophy, place, process, and product—white women felt they had the least control over product, which developed even as a frontier developed. Although product continued to have consequences after the formal ending of any frontier, it was already a force in the lives of the very people who created it. Women soon learned that frontiers always had products, positive and negative, and they had to endure both. Even the most successful or highly placed white women had to live with the disorder inherent in a colonial system.

From the white perspective, "good" product was easily identified. White colonialists would have listed additional territory, increased trade, and enlarged world power. Also, frontiers were attractive to whites in that they were supposedly rich and romantic. White hyperbole characterized the American West as a golden land, with enough resources—agricultural and mineral—to go around. Also in white eyes, Kenya was remote and exotic, full of economic opportunity, as well as offering chances to do something for others. At the same time, "bad" product existed. Looking back, it is easy to see that in the West, for example, massive exploitation of mineral resources resulted in erosion and damage to crop land. In Kenya, white farming undercut peasant agriculture, thus creating an impoverished class of wageworkers. For white colonialists, however, bad product would have meant something closer to their own lives, including escalating criticism of their conduct and scandals involving a few that smeared the names of all. Additional bad product was white women's disillusionment and a subsequent need to justify their actions, as well as alienation from the indigenous peoples who were supposed to have gained better and healthier lives as a result of white expansion.

Identifying the dark underside of colonialism is not a recent trend; white colonialists experienced the sting of disapproval in their own time. Typically, expansionist ventures started out on a high note—colonial discourse declared that pioneers were courageous and civilized, whereas indigenes were hostile and primitive. Gradually, however, social philosophies changed at home and problems became apparent in colonies. Soon, colonial discourse split into two camps, one clinging to the image of brave pioneers, the other mistrusting expansionism and those who carried it out. The onus for colonial mistakes and predicaments fell on many people, including home governments, officials on the ground, missionaries, and settlers. White women were especially vulnerable. If women migrated to frontiers to civilize them, the thinking went, why was the task so far from finished? If women were inherently moral and virtuous, why were frontiers so wild and uncivilized? There were no clear answers to these queries.

Also, despite the presence of growing numbers of "moral" women, matters seemed to get worse. During the 1880s and 1890s, Americans shuddered as they learned about licentious "divorce mills" located in the American West. Later, during the 1920s and 1930s, Kenya's licentious Happy Valley became a scandal of worldwide proportions. As a result, anti-colonial discourse reevaluated the role of white women, frequently transforming them from "pioneer mothers" and "mothers of empire" into progenitors of a racist hell.[1]

Between 1840 and 1940, hyperbole, myth, and scandal helped create at least three ways of looking at white female colonialists: an increasingly harsh critique, an indignant white response, and an indigenous perspective. Primarily, the *white critique* derived in large part from people reading books and articles, as well as reading or hearing exaggerated stories. The *white defense* emerged from white women's resentment of what they felt were inaccurate reports, as well as what they called unfulfilled promises that they believed home governments had made to them. The *indigenes' point of view* resulted largely from being in white employ and resenting white incursion into one's country.

The White Critique

Even though the American West had many parts—including California, Texas, the Southwest, the Pacific Northwest, the Rocky Mountain area, the prairie and deserts, and the Great Plains—the region assumed a monolithic image in the eastern United States and in Europe.[2] As a symbol, the West became a kind of shorthand for the qualities that white Americans held dear. Between 1840 and 1890, the West received some criticism, however, and western white women came in for their share of blame, especially concerning western landscapes, American Indians, and the western family.

Many voices participated in the debate regarding white women, but inquisitive female travel writers were among the most influential. These authors, who were largely British, traveled, wrote, and criticized countries and continents all over the world. Through their books, these Victorian lady travelers conveyed their accumulated knowledge—and their white prejudices—to women, and to a lesser extent to men, unable to travel themselves. The ways in which travel writers saw peoples and landscapes was the way their readers saw them. Women's travel writings not only helped objectify countries and their cultures, but reinforced women's belief in white superiority.[3]

Postmodern deconstructionist scholars offer critical and fascinating insights into the views of white female travel writers showing how they contributed to the creation of a white mythology that portrayed white people as rational and well motivated. These authors further elevated whites by defining indigenes as "others," who had unattractive qualities ranging from barbarism to irrationality. These disparate representations served to rationalize, at least for whites, conquest, settlement, and control. Although this syndrome is present in the women's travel writings considered here, the primary concern is the authors' opinions of white frontierswomen during their own eras.[4] The focus is on trying to hear kudos and criticism much as white women of the time would have heard them.

In the American West during the fifty years preceding 1890, a contradictory view of the West's white female settlers emerged. White women travelers, who were mostly European, arrived in the West with definite preconceptions. At the same time, sensational and epic images of the West—including "marauding" Indians, millions of bison, "hardy" white pioneers, and fabulous gold strikes—fed into white discourse. White European women highly romanticized the West as the very essence of the New World that seemed to hold out so much hope to the Old World, especially Europe. As Englishwoman Isabella Bird approached Rock Island on the Mississippi River during the mid-1850s, she rhapsodized, "On we flew to the West, the land of Wild Indians and Buffaloes." Meanwhile, Swedish visitor Fredrika Bremer similarly characterized the West as a "garden where the rivers carry along with them gold."[5]

Westerners grew used to the fact that visitors wanted to hear the stirring and colorful. According to Bird, so many travel writers traversed the West that by 1856, an English person who asked questions, notebook in hand, heard the same stock answers again and again.[6] Yet European women travel writers persisted in finding answers, which often refuted their own biases. The health and vigor of white women in the West startled them. Fredrika Bremer said that she seemed "to meet nothing but handsome faces, scarcely a countenance . . . may be called ugly." The elegance of dress further surprised female travel writers. English woman Frances Trollope claimed that women attended church in "full costume."[7] Evidently, these travelers expected to see female drudges, their complexions leathered by sun and wind, wearing clothing made of animal skins or faded gingham. They seemed pleasantly surprised when they discovered western women had no intention of letting themselves become "barbarized" or "primitive" just because they lived on a frontier.

Female travel writers were also amazed at the respect that western women received from men. They complimented western women for wringing courtesy and chivalrous attention from what they regarded as crude frontiersmen. They were further astonished that white women could appear in public or even travel unescorted without fear of insult or physical injury. Lady Duffus Hardy gave an especially idealized picture of a western man's reaction to encountering a woman traveling alone: "To her the manly heart yields his interest in [railroad] car or stage, gives her the best seat, that she might be screened and curtained, while he broils in the sun; for her he fights a way to the front ranks of refreshment rooms, skirmishes with the coffee pot, and bears triumphant ices aloft."[8]

European women travel writers were not nearly as impressed by "women's rights" in the West, which they found more illusory than real. As early as 1838, English traveler Harriet Martineau derided male chivalry as a poor substitute for justice. Fredricka Bremer was even more vitriolic. Visiting St. Louis in 1850, she decried the "effeminate education" that restricted women's lives and consciousness, and fitted them for little more than early marriage.[9] Other European women bemoaned western women's tendency to marry at an early age, choose a mate without consulting their parents, and ignore the tradition of a dowry.[10]

In addition, European women judged their American counterparts to be poor conservators of the West's landscapes. In 1853, Bremer urged white women to spend more time outdoors, arguing that an appreciation of nature would enhance the ability of American women to function as civilizers.[11] After the end of the American Civil War, when concern for the western environment increased, English women travelers grew even more critical. During the mid-1870s, British traveler and artist Marianne North decried the destruction of California's giant redwood trees, usually for building or for firewood. Although North wrote that "it broke one's heart to think of man, the civiliser, wasting treasures," she judged western women "barbaric" for not halting the carnage.[12]

Travel writers gave the West's white women the lowest score regarding their stewardship of Native Americans. One female observer condemned white settlers, including women, for being great colonizers but ineffective civilizers, who cared little for the fate of American Indians as settlement swept across the West.[13] Travel writers also seemed unable to understand why the West's white women had not done more to improve the lives of impoverished Indians. And, they asked, why had white civilization not taken better hold? In 1853, an Austrian woman was dismayed by California coastal Indians who, she said, had "a very low grade of civilization."[14]

Unsurprisingly, western white women did not appreciate such criticism, especially from outsiders who usually made hasty journeys and hastier assessments. Neither did western women care for the ways in which newspapers and other print media exaggerated western scandals, making western women appear spoiled or even dissolute. One of the longest and most sensational of these scandals concerned westerners' proclivity to divorce. Although settlers took established values and institutions westward with them, they revised custom when it suited their purposes. Moreover, western settlers often acted in haste, skipping time-consuming deliberations. In this setting, permissive divorce statutes and short residency requirements flourished. Perhaps most shocking of all, even though men made divorce laws, it seems that women took advantage of them. Western women obtained at least two-thirds of the divorces granted in the West; in California, women received more than two-thirds of all divorces.[15]

How could this happen, outsiders asked, if western women exercised their guardianship of home and family? As early as 1867, one commentator stated that "liberal" western divorce laws were at fault, for they "seldom compelled men or women to remain in marriages which they wished severed."[16] Whatever the cause, divorce flourished in the West. When the U.S. Bureau of the Census tracked the American divorce rate from 1867 onward, it confirmed that the divorce rate not only increased as one went west, but the ratio of divorces to population grew at a faster rate in the West than in any other region of the United States.[17] Further, census figures indicated that desertion by husbands and wives supplied the most common grounds for divorces, with cruelty a close second. More women than men pled cruelty, which included verbal abuse and "mental suffering."[18]

The image of western women was becoming tarnished around the edges. Critics in the United States and in Europe further accused westerners of frequently liberalizing their divorce codes. This charge had some truth to it. In 1862, members of the House of the Dakota territorial legislature first made divorce possible when they granted two legislative divorces. Three years later, the legislature shifted divorce to the courts. By 1877 the number of grounds stood at six and the residency requirement at a brief ninety days.

Americans became even more panicky when they learned about western divorce mills. They feared that divorce mills would lure divorce seekers to flee strict provisions in their home states and seek divorces in western jurisdictions. One of the first was in Dakota Territory. During the 1880s, the area experienced an economic boom and increased immigration, which led to the formation of North and South Dakota in 1889. South Dakota, which retained territorial divorce provisions, granted a growing number of divorces, especially in the bustling city of Sioux Falls. As a commercial center, Sioux Falls had railroads, attorneys, and courtrooms, as well as hotel and recreational facilities, all necessary prerequisites to a developing divorce industry.[19] Although public outcry eventually led to reform in South Dakota, in the meantime so-called divorce mills cropped up by 1890 in Fargo, North Dakota, and Guthrie, Oklahoma, adding even more dishonor to the reputation of the West and its women.

Later, in Kenya, white women's image underwent a comparable yet even more intense and destructive process. As in the American West, travel narratives and media stories were especially influential in people's thinking about white colonial women. These travel writers included a number of independent, recently "emancipated" women who did not hesitate to make known their own biases and opinions. Their discourse of image affected public sentiment, which in turn helped shape policy. Besides publishing books, they gave lectures and wrote popular articles; the sort of thing that stimulated widespread interest in Africa, but also slanted audiences' views of Kenya and its white inhabitants.[20]

Deconstructionist scholars have demonstrated that such themes as white superiority and imperialism lay just below the surface of travel writings. Travel writers often used figurative language, or tropes, which barely concealed the prejudices they had learned growing up in Europe in the late nineteenth century. Virtually all of them carried the cultural baggage of proper childhoods, which did not desert them when they went abroad.[21] These travel writers also visited countries for relatively short times, thus seeing things superficially. Representatives of a growing travel industry, ranging from tour guides to hoteliers, took travelers on safari, introduced them to some local people, and sent them on their way with a head full of jumbled impressions. Or perhaps tourists set off on their own, driving automobiles over Kenya's rapidly improving network of roads, and relying on the Royal East Africa Automobile Association for maps and guidance to the "must-see" attractions.[22]

Female travel writers who came to Kenya were usually from England, and often turned into botanical collectors as well, bringing back specimens of insects and plants to share with their home-bound readers. With white impudence, women travelers interpreted information and specimens in ways that suited them and their readers. Most well known was the English naturalist Mary Kingsley, who toured West Africa in the mid-1890s and collected specimens of fish for her patron institution, the British Museum. Wearing a correct Victorian skirt and shirtwaist, Kingsley employed her equally correct umbrella to jab a hippopotamus or to determine water depth. In addition, Kingsley produced quasi-anthropological studies of African tribes. Although Kingsley's writings gave readers a sense of Africa, it was definitely from a white and imperialist perspective.[23]

Travel writers in Kenya also wrote from Eurocentric points of view. The rhetoric of travel writing claimed to be scientific, educational, or informational. Readers of this literature wanted to learn about the land, flora and fauna, and peoples of Kenya. Although they sought a certain amount of escapism that would carry them into what one author termed "happier realms of thought," they also hoped to gain insight into the burning issues of the age.[24] This was especially true when it came to things colonial and African. For this study, however, the emphasis is less on authors' subliminal viewpoints than with the way their writings affected white women in Kenya.

Of the numerous female travel writers who described British East Africa and its peoples, one of the earliest was Mary French-Sheldon, who traveled on her own during the early 1890s to Zanzibar and parts of what later became Kenya Colony. Her subsequent book, *Sultan to Sultan: Adventures among the Maasai and other Tribes of East Africa,* was gracefully written and profusely illustrated, but manifested white prejudices throughout. When the author reached Mombasa, she quickly dismissed it as "an unfit place for a lady" because there were no hotel accommodations that suited her. She commented that, because "there are no white women, apart from the few women missionaries," white men drank far too much. She concluded that in Africa white people must possess "health, and endurance, as well as strong mentality, in order to get and hold control over the natives."[25]

During the 1900s and 1910s, white female travel writers were less ill-natured and more patriotic. In 1913, Charlotte Cameron's *A Woman's Winter in Africa: A 20,000 Mile Journey,* indicated that although she had traveled great distances, from Zanibar to the Cape, she had gained only a cursory understanding of the countries she visited. In typical female travel-writer fashion, she began with a demurrer: "this book is in no way historical, statistical, or political, simply the impressions of a woman traveler." She offered escapism; in Kenya, she stated, there is "beauty everywhere." She also included such racially inspired "hints" for tourists as "Don't give the natives whatever they demand, for they are never satisfied." Cameron revealed her own attitude toward colonialism when she complimented the English bungalows with pretty gardens that covered the hillsides in Mombasa; this "Anglicization" of Mombasa was a certain sign that British culture was taking hold in British East Africa. Cameron seemed satisfied with what she saw in Kenya, and offered no real critique.[26] Also in 1913, Edith Maturin, who had spent her girlhood reading travel and adventure books and in 1910 had journeyed through parts of Africa, published *Adventures Beyond the Zambesi*. As readers expected, she described the charms of Kenya. Maturin also extended a common judgment of her era to white female settlers. According to her, white women teachers who endured ants, huts, heat, and inadequate pay from the educational department were "heroic."[27]

A decade later, the format of travel writers had not altered much. Even in the relatively informed 1920s, female travel writers seemed unable to shake the long-standing influence of imperialism and racial prejudice. During the early 1920s, a single woman, Etta Close, traveled in Kenya, Uganda, and the Belgian Congo. In a 1924 book, Close described Kenya's white women as a veritable "jumble" of different types, ranging from admirable figures to jaded playgirls of the so-called smart set. She also observed black Kenyans. In a condescending way, Close wrote that at first "all native boys looked alike" to her, but that she soon learned to see them as individuals. Similarly, she came to regard some of the black girls as "exceedingly pretty." Close initially accepted other current stereotypes as well, including the belief that men bought brides rather than offering parents bridewealth, usually in the form of goats, to make up for the loss of their daughter's labor and to establish the lineage of the couple's children.[28]

Yet times were changing. Since the end of World War I, colonialism had gradually fallen into disfavor around the world. Countries like Russia waged revolutions to gain independence from control by royals. At the same time, the development of the social sciences, notably anthropology, created interest in world cultures. Meanwhile, citizens of Great Britain found themselves bedeviled by high taxes, frequent military engagements, and other woes, for which they blamed the "out-dated" racial attitudes of colonial settlers living in far-flung places like India and Kenya. As a result, self-doubt and criticism crept into colonial discourse. In this climate of opinion, definitions of the imperial mission and colonialism turned upside down. Missionaries who were once lauded as good-hearted and self-sacrificing people became paternalistic, wrong-headed reformers. Formerly courageous settlers were colonialist oppressors and land crooks. Forward-thinking government officials were exploitive imperialists. At the same time, the British empire's slogan, "Wider still and wider, Shall they bounds be set," changed from a cause for pride to a shame-inducing statement of arrogance.[29]

This shift in thinking was more than the usual stabilization phase of colonization regulating natural and human resources, trade, and labor. Instead, the three principles of colonialism women had been taught to rely upon—construction of "otherness," a firm belief in the white guardianship of black Kenyans, and the goal of a final stage of trusteeship—were eroding under their feet.[30] White women found themselves caught in changing times—and changing discourse. One British woman, Evelyn Brodhurst-Hill, who migrated to Kenya during the early 1920s, explained that settlers once known as "heroes" and "pioneers" who braved "the terror of the unknown" now appeared as wily rascals exploiting black Kenyans.[31]

At least in part because of such writings, throughout Great Britain disapproval grew concerning the way white settlers conducted themselves. London became a center of protest and activism, much of it aimed at white colonialists, yet pro-colonialism continued as well. In 1929, a Mrs. Patrick Ness claimed to cover ten thousand miles by taking the railroad and driving an automobile. After seeing parts of Kenya, she remarked that a white woman was a "familiar object" in the "new-style Kenya." On visiting a farm, she remarked that she had learned what it meant to be a "woman pioneer"; isolation and hard work were her lot. She patriotically concluded that, despite the hardships, many white women "lived and worked thus, cheerfully helping to make our great empire what it is!" Turning her attention to black Kenyans, she could not break free of the white imperialist viewpoint. Assuming that white culture was the best culture, she stated that Kenya's greatest problem to be solved was "the way the awakening native is to be led." She laid the responsibility for the future of black Kenyans squarely at the feet of the white women and men who had "uprooted" them.[32] On this point, female pioneers did not receive her admiration.

During the lean years of the 1930s, criticism became harsh. In 1931, May Mott-Smith claimed to travel across Africa from "port-to-port" and offered the usual disclaimer that her book was not a "profound treatise." She then launched into an attack on what she called "overrated Kenya." Mombasa had too many automobiles and the Uganda Railroad was "uncomfortable." Nairobi looked like "a frontier mining camp." The stores were expensive, hotels dirty, and the roads impossible. In addition, much in Kenya struck Mott-Smith as "slovenly." In her eyes, white men dressed carelessly. She thought that white women acted "clannish" and "uppity." When a Nyanza coffee planter invited her to visit, she declined because travel in Kenya was "exceedingly expensive." Rather than learning more about Kenya, Mott-Smith returned to Mombasa and took passage to Europe, where she wrote her self-revelatory book.[33]

Four years later, Lady Evelyn Cobbold, who excused her book as "an elaborated diary" written for her own "amusement," raised similar issues and passed similar judgments. She termed Kenya a "land of illusion," meaning that Kenya had natural beauty, but also included what Cobbold called "deplorable settlements." Nairobi was an "unworthy capital" of such a scenic land. Cobbold agreed with Mott-Smith that white women fought a "grim battle" against endless difficulties. They were, she said, "pioneers of whom the Mother Country can indeed be proud." Unlike Mott-Smith, Cobbold accepted an invitation to a coffee plantation, but not a typical one. After visiting Lady MacMillan's coffee estate, Cobbold lavished praise on its rhinoceros and water buffalo preserves. Still, Cobbold fell back on imperialist rhetoric. To her, white settlers had made little progress in "civilizing" Kenya. Assuming that white women were responsible for "improving" black Kenyans, Cobbold wrote that they had a long way to go.[34]

In 1940, traveler Margaret Wrong's book *Across Africa* revealed changing attitudes. Wrong was unusually forthright in describing Kenya as "troubled." Rather than saying that white Kenyan women were "brave" and black Kenyans "backward," Wrong stated that "racial tensions" divided Kenyans. According to Wrong, discontent came especially from diverging ideas between white and black Kenyans. Wrong blamed white settlers for giving black Kenyans glimpses of higher standards of living, yet failing to provide the skills and salaries necessary to attain them. Wrong also cited as a divisive force the segregation of many different communities—white, black, Asian Indian, Muslim, and others—that met but did not blend.[35]

As in the American West, such criticism stunned Kenyan women. They responded that unsolicited advice came largely from non-Kenyans who did not interview white Kenyans. They also felt cheated and mistreated. Although they had done what the British government told them to, they had come out on the wrong end. As moral guardians, women seem to have failed. On top of this came the development of Happy Valley and its attendant scandals, often blamed on women who, as society's moral forces, should have known better.

The Happy Valley way of life emerged in part from the mentality of the 1920s, including a nihilist outlook, excessive drinking, and drug use. Happy Valley also evolved from developments within Kenya. Because the decade marked the beginnings of long-awaited prosperity and government stability, white settlers replaced wattle-and-daub huts with real English-style houses. At the same time, Kenya attracted new types of settlers, including "verandah" farmers who had money and need not worry about making a profit. Among these were women and men seeking a hedonistic lifestyle, as well as adventurers who came on safari and stayed. They settled in the white highlands between the Aberdares and the town of Gilgil, especially in the Wanjohi Valley, which became the notorious Happy Valley. Their lives focused—or so it seemed to onlookers—on eating, drinking, and sex. During race weeks in Nairobi after Christmas and during midsummer, they thronged to the Norfolk Hotel and the Muthaiga Club, from which they shocked Nairobians.[36]

When British author Evelyn Waugh visited Kenya in 1930, he remarked that an "extensive body of abusive literature" had already grown up around the colony. Although Waugh had prepared himself to dislike Kenya, he fell in love with it. "There is a quality about it which I have found nowhere else but in Ireland, of warm loveliness and breadth and generosity." Waugh corroborated the tales of wild parties and the consumption of alcohol and drugs, but could not understand why people believed that the Happy Valley crowd represented white Kenyans as a whole.[37]

During the 1930s, Happy Valley's reputation worsened. While other nations suffered from the depression, Kenya's settlers apparently played. In many minds, "Happy Valley" no longer meant an elite few in the Wanjohi Valley, but cast suspicion on all white Kenyans. From this, a contradictory situation developed. Either observers idealized Kenya's early settlers and called for various reforms among its white citizens or they denigrated the entire colonial experiment in Kenya.

As a result, white Europeans in Kenya found themselves alternately praised or, more frequently, castigated for their sins, which many felt they had not committed.

In the meantime, Josslyn Hay, who had first arrived in Kenya in 1924, contributed disproportionately to the legend of Happy Valley. Only recently out of Eton and just married to a twice-divorced woman eight years his senior, Hay found an escape in Kenya from wagging tongues.[38] It was Hay's wife, Lady Idina Sackville Hay, who coalesced the Happy Valley crowd and implemented the legend that made Kenya look like a refuge for the dissipated and sex crazed, as well as for other outcasts of proper British society. At the Hays' home, Clouds, Idina staged house parties that bordered on orgies and where the favored drugs of the 1920s, cocaine and morphine, were standard among guests.[39]

Happy Valley came to represent Kenya, being emblematic of everything that outsiders thought wrong with colonialism. People back home identified Kenya as part of the newly defined "colonial problem." At the time, the 1920s and 1930s, racial awareness was rising in Britain, while black nationalism was developing in Kenya. As the British government attempted to create racial and other reforms, imperialism came in for reassessment. At first, Joss Hay spent his days racing horses and playing polo, paying little attention to his farm near Nakuru. By 1925, he had begun a series of extramarital affairs. In 1930, Hay divorced Idina and married Mary (Molly) Ramsay-Hill, who left her husband for Hay. The couple moved into Oserian, the Moroccan-style estate on the edge of Lake Naivasha that Major Cyril Ramsay-Hill had recently built for his wife. With a comfortable inherited income on Molly's side, the Hays had little to fear from the stock-market crash of 1929 and the ensuing depression. To make Oserian, meaning the place of peace, suitable for lavish parties, the Hays redecorated the house. Already known as the "Djinn Palace," Oserian soon picked up an additional name, the "Pink Gin Palace."[40]

The beautiful and once-serene estate of Oserian soon symbolized, within Kenya and without, hedonism and gluttony of all sorts. There were, of course, others besides Hay and his wives and lovers involved in the Happy Valley saga. During the early 1930s, the American heiress

Laura Corrigan reportedly hired the best chef in London to cook for her guests; after dinner she gave them expensive gifts, including gold cigarette cases and diamond wristwatches.[41] At various times, other notable women like Karen Blixen and Beryl Markham caroused with Happy Valley's members, at their homes and at Nairobi's Muthaiga Club.

Yet it was at Oserian that champagne, heroin, and partner swapping continued uninterrupted, at least until 1940, when Jock Broughton brought his young bride, Diana, to Kenya. It was Diana Broughton's and Joss Hay's subsequent love affair that apparently led to Hay's murder, if not by Broughton then perhaps by a disappointed mistress of Hay's.[42] Happy Valley's good times had finally gotten out of hand and resulted in a slaying. The gunshot that ended Hay's philandering also catapulted stories about Kenya's Happy Valley into the international media. Who had killed Josslyn Hay, the Earl of Erroll and the unparalleled playboy of Kenya's Happy Valley set? In January 1941, this question flashed across newspaper front pages and punctuated radio broadcasts. Sir John Henry (Jock) Delves Broughton was arrested and incarcerated with six other Europeans among twelve thousand prisoners of color in Nairobi's prison.[43] Due to contradictory evidence, Jock Broughton was released by the Nairobi court, free of all charges. No one else was arraigned, nor was the murder ever solved. These many years later, authors still write books full of speculation and offering different candidates as the culprit.[44]

Some blame the media for Kenya's sagging image because it exaggerated Happy Valley. One man, the son of white settlers, said that Happy Valley involved only a dozen elite families. The most telling comment was that of Doreen Field, who remarked that Happy Valley brought Kenya "unfortunate notoriety." In her view, a single episode in Kenya's development distorted the colony's entire history.[45] In addition, only a few people besmirched the image of white Kenyans worldwide. One white woman who had grown up in Kenya during the Happy Valley era remembered its devotees as "elegant, idle, and often outrageous." Similarly, the Kenyan author Elspeth Huxley dismissed the men of Happy Valley as "playboy pseudo-settlers" who wore silk shirts, corduroy trousers, and wide-brimmed hats, and drove boxy cars equipped with rifle racks. Huxley saw the women, especially Lady Idina Hay, as little more than flighty birds of paradise.[46] Yet these loud, outrageous people were enough to trivialize the Kenya Colony and its frontier across the world.

The White Response

In the American West, white women developed sharp answers to their critics. White women were exasperated with travel writers' accounts, feeling them to be largely inaccurate. In addition, white women in the American West felt victimized by hasty judgments and embellished reporting. To make matters worse, white western women were disillusioned with the hopes that Manifest Destiny had raised. Moreover, western women resented European women's commentaries and criticisms, especially regarding Native Americans whose situation they claimed they had tried to improve. How could European women, they asked, understand white-Indian relations in the faraway American West? Why did European women think they had all the answers after one or two brief sojourns in the West?

White western women also castigated travel writers and journalists, charging that they were more interested in attracting readers than in accurate reporting. In 1876, for example, Nebraskan Caroline Winne denigrated what she called the growing tendency of reporters to invent "massacres." Worse yet, she said, the U.S. Cavalry always emerged victorious. After one cavalry raid of local Indians, Winne wrote to her family, saying that inflammatory newspaper reports were far-fetched indeed. "Come to get down to the facts," Winne wrote, "the one hundred Indians killed amounted to just 4 killed." In apparent disgust, she added, "As there were four soldiers killed and light wounded, we failed to see the success."[47]

Western women's sense of betrayal added to their growing angst. Although U.S. government propaganda and the popular press had assured women that westward migration would result in "civilization" and improved lives for Indians, American Indians were worse off than ever. Women pointed out that they had been led to believe that by seizing and civilizing, they would bring to Indians education, medical care, and peace, none of which had come to pass. The kind of media appeals that women so harshly indicted had occurred everywhere. In 1880, for example, William Fowler's *Woman on the Frontier* told women that as "pioneer and colonizer" they would be the "great educators of the frontier." Fowler also assured women that they would soften the "fierce temper of the pagan tribes."[48]

White women felt that they had responded fully to their country's call. As exhorted, they had exerted their moral and "civilizing" energies. Yet Indians remained exploited and misused, while women received much of the blame. In response, women asked themselves if they were somehow failing in their gender-associated responsibilities. Unsurprisingly, many answered no. Rather than holding themselves responsible, women fell back on a gendered defense. Because they lacked political power and participation in decision-making, western women lashed out at the people who did wield political power and make decisions—white men.

Women indicted men, including their own husbands and sons. Women migrants censured men who created rancor by cheating or otherwise mistreating Native Americans. Other women complained about men who, firmly convinced of their right to invade native land, refused to pay tolls to use bridges that Indians had built and rejected the idea of compensating Indians for depleted grazing land, game reserves, and water supplies. White men even captured Indians whom they forced to serve as guides.[49] Further, women explained that white men often devised a variety of schemes and scams to amuse or profit themselves. A typical trick involved fleecing an Indian in a trade or paying with counterfeit money. Other men physically abused or assaulted Native American women. Women noted that white men were not above taking scalps, captives, and hostages; nor did men refrain from torturing and killing natives.

According to women's construction of the situation, white men in power were most at fault, especially "petty" bureaucrats and "untrustworthy" generals. After an Indian "war" during the mid-1850s, Oregon settler Elizabeth Lord claimed that the conflict had occurred because local authorities—white men—allowed other white men to conduct "wholesale seizures of native lands." Later, during the Indian wars of the 1870s, white settler Caroline Winne accused General Philip H. Sheridan of being "drunk all the time in Chicago in his fine house" and alleged that General William T. Sherman had never fought an Indian and "knew nothing about them."[50]

White women also berated other men in roles of authority, including government and military leaders, Union and Confederate soldiers, and Catholic priests and Protestant missionaries. Disgusted by the Indians' worsening situation, some women even questioned Manifest Destiny. Women pointed fingers at men who purposely slaughtered buffalo so that Indians, robbed of subsistence, would become dependent on whites and thus vulnerable to accepting white "civilization." Was it right, many asked, for Indians to suffer to meet white goals and aspirations?[51] According to army wife Margaret Carrington in 1868, the idea of Manifest Destiny left Native Americans only destructive alternatives: "abandon his home, fight himself to death, or yield to the white man's mercy."[52]

Underneath, of course, white women were scared. They believed that revengeful Indians might attack. Surely, women said, Indians had a long list of grievances. Also, Indians were hunters and warriors. Many pointed out, as did white settler Agnes Cleaveland, that "from time immemorial, American Indians had lived by raiding, whether of the natural bounty of the land or the garnered resources of their neighbors." Women thought that such Indians could easily turn on white women, their families, and their neighbors.[53] Those women who had observed violent confrontations felt especially helpless; they realized they were incapable of quelling a clash once it got started. In their panic, white women failed to come to terms with the responsibility they shared with men for the tragic situation.

In Kenya, white women experienced a parallel situation. As colonialism came under increasing fire during the 1920s and 1930s, criticism of white women colonialists intensified. In a sense, Kenya's white women increasingly lived in a borderland. Physically, they were no longer part of Britain, yet black Kenya did not want them either. Psychologically, they were undergoing transition from moral forces to callous racists. White women found it impossible to live happily in this borderland, yet they had nowhere to go, either geographically or emotionally. With reproach raining down upon their heads, white women settlers grew skittish and defensive. As in the American West, white women lambasted the press. In 1935, white settler E. J. F. Knowles wrote to a friend complaining about a purported "battle" between natives and whites. "The British press have let themselves go over," she complained. According to her, the rumored "uprising" of three hundred workers involved a handful and was a "mixture of tragedy and farce," followed by "handshaking and beaming smiles."[54]

Travelers also came in for their share of blame. In 1934, settler Eve Bache acerbically commented that travelers, many of whom were writers and journalists, did not even know where they were, much less understand events transpiring around them. Bache claimed that she had met travelers who called Kenya Colony by the name of Nairobi and thought Mombasa was in India. Bache despaired of other inaccuracies as well. She attacked one writer who said she had to wear mud boots during her entire stay in Nairobi. The same woman contended that only one car at a time could use Nairobi streets. Bache scoffed at both ideas as false, inapplicable to what she called the "real Nairobi." Equally absurd to Bache were travelers' accounts that described the highlands as either humid or unpleasantly cool. Bache felt personally insulted by claims that the white inhabitants of the highlands, including women, seldom attended church and drank far too much alcohol. Bache said she was unsure whether such assertions came from ignorance or "a fixed determination" to misrepresent Kenya and its peoples.[55]

Evelyn Brodhurst-Hill shared Bache's views. In 1936, she complained that she felt bullied and "just a little weary of interference" from home. What she termed "uninformed criticism" more than annoyed her, and when young white women came to Kenya to promote racial fusion by marrying black men she threw up her hands in disgust at the lack of understanding of what these marriages entailed for white brides thrust into black cultures.[56]

White Kenyan women questioned where their female detractors got their information. One said she had tired of hearing theories "masquerading as facts." She was especially weary of hearing "scholarly beliefs" regarding "so-called Africans." She was outraged that the British public had drawn the conclusion that "Africans" were happier before white settlers arrived. If that were true, she scoffed, black Kenyans "must have had peculiar ideas of enjoyment."[57]

As had white women in the West, Kenya's white women blamed men. Many resented what they saw as myopia or outright chicanery on the part of British officials, who had established and supported in Kenya some of the strictest color bars known in colonial history. In addition, throughout the 1920s and 1930s the British government continued to promote settlement schemes, describing Kenya as in a pioneer stage of development and full of opportunities for white settlers. White Kenyans protested that although the government encouraged settlers to participate in imperialist expansion, it refused to support many aspects of settlers' endeavors and denounced them for making race-related mistakes.

Again like white women in the American West, white women in Kenya felt betrayed. Kenya was not what they had been led to expect. During the 1930s, white settler Alyse Simpson called Kenya Colony "the land that never was," meaning that Kenya's image was more hyperbole than truth.[58] White women believed that they had responded to British promises of glory only to find themselves more often damned than not. They reacted to criticism in the worst possible way—with a spirited, and sometimes sarcastic, defense. White women responded especially emotionally to the widespread charge that Kenya's white settlers dominated the vast majority of arable land in the highlands, leaving only poorly producing segments for black Kenyans. Some women even cited Kenyan officials who estimated that white settlers controlled closer to 20 percent of Kenya's high potential soil, or about 8,460 square miles out of 32,300 square miles of tillable land. Apparently, these women believed such statistics. In 1927, white settler M. Aline Buxton threw out a challenge: let the "people at home" come to Kenya "in an amiable spirit" and they would discover their idea of settlers as land grabbers was mistaken.[59]

White women also felt threatened by new policy decisions, particularly the dismantling of color bars. Many believed that because they lived in a potentially explosive situation they would be safer if color bars were kept in place. At the same time, white women, like their counterparts in the American West, wondered if they should assume guilt for doing a slow, or perhaps ineffective, job of civilizing. Imperial philosophies now seemed to repudiate women, suggesting that they had not carried out their mission. Some women went so far as to ask British authorities if they had failed as "civilizers." Were they being punished by having land returned to black Kenyans?[60]

Some white women wondered what more they could do to improve relations between white settlers and black Kenyans. They agreed that such goals as equality were admirable and even necessary, but must come slowly. They gave the long-standing argument that black Kenyans should be trained, educated, and schooled in democracy rather than being expected to make a sudden leap. One woman judged impossible the "meteoric rise" advocated in "certain quarters," meaning reformers, missionaries, and government officials.[61]

Clearly, Kenya's white women held a different view than did outsiders. Because they had invested themselves in the colonization of Kenya, they felt compelled to justify their actions. In addition, white women believed that the British Empire had guaranteed them benefits if they uprooted their families and went to Kenya. These included a white-dominance policy and unending glory in the annals of empire, the very things women felt were being taken from them.

Kenya's white women pointed out that they had even received kudos and implied promises from American men. When Theodore Roosevelt visited Kenya in 1909, he gave a speech lauding white pioneers:

> You have brought freedom where there was slavery. You are bringing health where there was disease. You are bringing food where there was famine. You are bringing peace where there was continual war. Be proud of yourselves, for the time is coming when the world will be proud of you.[62]

Roosevelt was wrong. In 1909, he still operated under the influence of Manifest Destiny. The American West had yet to face the maelstrom of segregation versus newer antisegregation ideas.

Even as Roosevelt's depiction turned sour, the British government continued to assure settlers of prosperity and permanence. Unwilling to let imperialism die a natural death, government authorities leased Kenya land to white settlers for 999 years, a provision that had a sound of continuity about it. In the meantime, British government agencies and companies had constructed buildings that suggested stability. As early as 1913, the ambitious and remarkable provincial commissioner's office had appeared, the first in a square of fine public buildings, which eventually included the imposing treasury building. The following year, the Standard Bank erected its first branch in Nairobi. In 1919, the Imperial British East Africa Company headquarters stood as square and stolid as Britain represented itself. When Kenya Railway headquarters went up in 1929, it bespoke the power of big business in Kenya Colony. During the 1930s, British officials announced a grand design for Nairobi, which included City Hall, built during the mid-1930s and still one of the most impressive structures in Nairobi.[63]

Like Roosevelt's prophecy, British promises and the buildings that reinforced them stood on shifting sands. During the early 1930s, cracks appeared in the imperial structure. A series of British government reports recommended that policies regarding black Kenyans be revised. White settlers felt that they would not only lose land, but would be in danger. Representatives of the white Naivasha Settlers' Association argued that black Kenyans no longer had any claim to Kenya land. Moreover, they maintained that the people who could make the land the most productive should be the ones to occupy and utilize it.[64]

At first, white Kenyans refused to dismantle segregation policies. When forced to comply, some white settlers became antagonistic. For women, protecting oneself had become such an important part of life that they turned acrimonious when British public opinion declared the principle of segregation outdated. Like western women, they were afraid for their safety. In addition, white women believed racial segregation protected everything in which they believed, including "purity" of the white race. In other words, racial prejudice remained strong among Kenya's white women. During the early 1930s, one revealed her prejudices when she objected to riding in a railway compartment next to people she described as being of "alien races" with equally "alien ideas as to cleanliness." She was upset that despite her efforts to live up to "certain standards" she was put on a level "with those who have none or next to none." Rather than uplifting "backward races," she perceived racial integration as a step toward lowering European values and practices.[65] She clearly could not surrender her lifelong indoctrination.

At home, some British observers suggested a compromise. Perhaps the government could "repatriate" Kenya's white settlers to other holdings in the British empire. At least, reformers argued, the government should immediately halt its own efforts to increase white expansion in Kenya. In Kenya itself, the debate over such ideas grew fevered. Most whites felt that because British officials had invited white settlers to Kenya, the British government must take responsibility for them. They did not want to be repatriated from Kenya. Ian Hardy, the son of a white settler who migrated during the 1920s, remembered that his father came to Kenya with staying as his goal. During the 1930s, Hardy's father and mother never discussed the possibility of leaving Kenya. According to Hardy, his parents had made Kenya their home.[66]

In spite of the outcry, during the 1930s the British government continued to encourage immigration to Kenya. It also relocated teachers and other professionals to Kenya from other parts of the British empire. Marjorie Hood, the wife of a transferred teacher, recalled her migration to Kenya during the mid-1930s as "no hardship." Before her departure, her friends in the West Indies assured Hood that she was "lucky" to be going to Kenya. After her arrival, Hood found Kenya "very pleasant." She soon grew committed to Kenya. Years later, she said she never regretted coming, and never thought about leaving. Even in retirement, Hood remained in Kenya, her adopted homeland.[67]

Indigenes' Perspective

During such heated interchanges, most indigenous peoples stood as silent observers. Because they kept their own counsel and left few written documents that have reached archives, their opinions are difficult to recapture. As early as 1972, the historian Philip D. Curtin noted that retrieving the voice of average people was a difficult task, especially for historians who rely heavily on documentary evidence.[68] An additional caution comes from the postmodern scholar Gayatri Chakravorty Spivak who notes that there is more than one subaltern voice; that the subaltern point of view has many origins and varieties.[69] Although modern-day historians have tried to devise alternate methodology, the subaltern voice is still muffled. From recent anthropological studies, however, it becomes clear that indigenous women, like white women, experienced frontier product as two-sided. On the "good" side, some were able to draw strength from white women, such as missionaries or teachers, learning how to educate themselves and organize for reform. On the "bad," colonial migration damaged these women culturally and economically, forcing them to live in poverty or turn to prostitution.[70]

In the American West between 1840 and 1890, Native Americans had responses—they were obviously displeased that whites had taken their lands and disrupted their lives. They also had ideas about white female settlers. During the 1980s scholars began retrieving Native American history, and destroying the stock images that had so long shrouded Indian women.[71] Other subsequent historians moved ahead, developing new theories and concepts.[72] Out of these changes has come the realization that Indian women exercised personal agency, both through overt action and through relatively silent resistance as well. Native American women did not need to speak or use assertive techniques; they exerted their will by picking and choosing among missionaries' offerings and inducements; taking what suited them and rejecting what threatened their position, status, and culture.[73] These insights have at once clarified and clouded scholars' understandings of Native American viewpoints. On the one hand, it is clear that American Indians, especially women, expressed their feelings in subtle actions as well as words. On the other, how can such subtleties be identified and demonstrated?

Some evidence regarding Indian women's attitudes appears in white women's sources. Army wife Alice Baldwin recalled an incident during which she agreed to partially disrobe so that native women could inspect her corset, hoopskirts, and crinolines. Although Baldwin sat among them, "listening to their chatter and laughter" and thinking they might be offering "uncomplimentary comments," she decided that "it all meant sincerity."[74] In another case, Oklahoma settler Leola Lehman described how Native American women and she befriended each other. Lehman came to understand that Indians' hesitation toward whites stemmed from the terrifying stories they had heard and apparent eccentricities in behavior they had observed.[75]

According to such white reports, a number of Native American women overcame their fears and established friendly relations with white women. Yet, in Indian sources, some women discounted such happenings. One Native American woman, a Yavapai who was born and reared on the San Carlos reservation in Arizona, believed that Anglo-Indian relationships were impossible because white people did not like Indians, and Indians did not like whites. In her eyes, dislike was inevitable because the two groups were "different tribes." She personally believed Native Americans were "better off" staying away from whites and living their own way.[76] Other Indian women said they had so often witnessed whites' brutality to their people that they could never overcome their bitterness. In their view, Indians might stage stomp dances for white women, create mock battles, or invite them to beef issues, but the gap between the two peoples remained unbridgeable.[77]

In the American West, it is likely that both motifs appeared, one of friendship and one of hate. Certainly, villages frequently split over the issue of accepting or rejecting white ideas. Although some villagers adopted the teachings of female missionaries, others rejected them. Some viewed white female teachers as benevolent, but others charged them with just wanting a job. Some Indians trusted Indian agents and their wives, whereas others despised them for cheating Indians at clothing and food issues.[78]

In Kenya, indigenes were also divided, a pattern typical of other colonies or world-systems. Early in Kenya's colonial period, black Africans showed more acceptance of white ways than they did in later years. As they observed white people, black Africans frequently developed doubts, which led to resistance and neo-traditionalism. With time, black Africans also recognized the vast differences between their thought-systems and those of whites. On the one hand, prescientific black Africans tended to view nature as irregular and easily provoked. On the other, technologically developed whites, who had some control over physical events, were more likely to perceive nature as regular and orderly, manageable through scientific methodology and technical devices. Because so much room existed for misunderstanding, blacks were often disappointed and disillusioned with whites. Moreover, black Africans increasingly questioned whether they had received any benefits at all from whites.[79]

Little wonder, then, that black Kenyans found it impossible to fathom the demands of their white female employers. A wide range of opinions regarding white women existed among black Kenyans. Those who liked and respected white women balanced women's foibles with their virtues, whereas those who disliked and feared white women could find little good in them. As in the West, groups of black Kenyans were often so polarized regarding white women that they split villages in two. Although one segment leaned toward, and worked for, whites, the other rejected everything white they possibly could. The latter group looked on whites, especially white women missionaries and teachers, as spoilers. Occasionally, a leader emerged who attempted to reconcile the two ways, but the white and black cultures stood far apart and both sides were stubborn. Cultural barriers were too massive to allow real empathy to develop between white women and black Kenyans.[80]

Perhaps the people who best knew the strengths and weaknesses of the average white woman were the black Kenyans who served white women and thus observed them on a daily basis. Unfortunately, such opinions are not easy to recapture. As in the American West, partial insight into black Kenyans' relations with whites is found in the writings of whites. In 1923, white settler Marguerite Mallett spent some time among the Maasai. Like westerner Alice Baldwin had done so many years before, Mallett offered her rings, wristwatch, dress, shoes, and stockings for the examination of black Kenyan women. Mallett said that many exclamations of wonder followed. On other occasions, black women's curiosity carried them into Mallett's house to admire her treasures or to watch silently as she starched and ironed her white dresses.[81]

Reconstructing black Kenyans' reactions from dominant sources leaves much to be desired. It is far more revealing to find direct evidence of the subaltern voice itself. Creative anthropological studies have begun filling this void, but historians lack the documentation they need.[82] Only a few black Kenyans generated written accounts in English regarding their white employers. Most notably, Karen Blixen's devoted cook, Kamande Gatura, left recollections that include his feelings about Blixen. He remembered that after he came to Blixen's farm with his father and four of his wives, Blixen treated his father's leg wound, then sent him to the Scotland Mission Hospital for surgery. Blixen hired Kamande to feed her dogs, a demeaning job in modern eyes. Still, given his new rootlessness, Kamade was grateful; he soon called Blixen "Mama."[83]

After Blixen gave Kamande Gathura lessons from the *Sultan Cook Book*, he became a cook. He claimed that white guests came from a distance away to enjoy what he called his "excellent meals." In return, Kamande received four shillings a month and a plot of land to cultivate. Kamande's most unhappy recollection of Blixen was that she once hit Kamande on the head for a breach of service, causing him to cry. Kamande was quick to point out that Blixen also complimented him daily for his excellent service. Also, every Friday she slaughtered five cattle to feed her workers. He concluded that Blixen was "indeed an excellent woman, because she never hated anybody or doctrines, even Mohammedans."[84] Was Kamande Gathura simply writing pleasant sentiments that would not offend? It is hard to know. Charles Waithaka, who worked for Karen Blixen tending coffee on land that his family had once controlled, also remembered Blixen as a generous woman who involved herself in her workers' problems and contributed to their solutions.[85]

In another diary and collection of family papers, located and translated for this study, black workers had a less sanguine opinion of whites than Kamade Gathura and Charles Waithaka. During the 1920s and 1930s, members of the Ngugi family stood with one foot in black culture and the other in white. The Ngugis were black Kenyans who had converted to Christianity and were educated at mission schools, yet continued to live in their village, to buy land with goats, and to give bridewealth in goats, cows, beer, sugarcane, and blankets. When it came to such items as books, shorts, shirts, and foodstuffs they could not grow, the Ngugis had to pay cents and shillings, even though it took one day for a woman to earn twenty cents and a man twenty-five.[86] During the late 1920s and early 1930s, a kilogram of sugar cost ten cents and a calico dress fifty cents. Because a goat cost twenty shillings it took about two months to make enough to purchase one.[87] As black Kenyans learned from whites to measure life in terms of material goods and a cash economy, they soon begrudged the low wages that held them to a standard of living far below that of white settlers. Still, black Kenyans had little choice but to work for whites at poverty-level wages. Ngugi family rate-receipts indicate that poll and hut taxes had to be paid regularly in cash in the amount the white government dictated. The Ngugis surely recognized that such taxes were a method of getting cheap labor, for Kenyans had to work for whites so they could pay their taxes.[88]

Oral evidence is also difficult to come by and challenging to interpret. Quite rightly, Spivak points out that written and oral materials are two different forms of discourse, in that speaking leaves little time for forethought and word choice.[89] In oral interviews conducted for this study, black Kenyans revealed mixed views of white colonists. Muigua Ngunjiri, born in 1904 in Kenya's central province, went to work at age fourteen on a coffee plantation near Thika for ten cents a day. He found white people conceited and unwilling to adjust their ways to accommodate black customs. He felt, however, that white women were less rigid and demanding than white men. Although he pointed out that white settlers grossly underpaid black Kenyan workers, Muigua Ngunjiri added that he eventually procured a small piece of land and permission to grow a little coffee. In most cases, black Kenyans, especially in the "white" highlands, were not allowed to plant coffee or other crops that would compete with white settlers' output. If they defied this ruling, black Kenyans could find themselves involved in court suits and liable for monetary fines.

Because Muigua Ngunjiri received special permission to raise coffee, however, he said that he was able to raise his family's standard of living slightly and send his children to school.[90]

Esther Njoki proved a bit more vocal than Muigua Ngunjiri. Her experience with white employers began after World War I, when black Kenyans had grown more critical. Esther Njoki probably came to plantation labor sometime during the late 1920s or early 1930s. Even though she had some mission education at Kambui, she labored on a plantation near Thika for about twenty cents per day. When she worked as a "digger" she was assigned many rows of coffee trees, which sometimes took from 8 A.M. to 7 P.M. to complete. When she picked coffee, she began at 6 A.M. Workers received five cents for each twenty-liter can, or "debbi," that they filled and carried to the nearby rail station before 6 P.M. Although champion pickers could fill ten containers, typical workers averaged four to six debbis a day.[91]

Esther explained that women, who worked at separate sites from men, were more exploited by whites than were black men. During the early years, women were paid in kind, such as sugar or salt, and later made less cash per day than men. The only exception came at coffee-picking time, when black women earned as much or more than men by filling more debbis. Esther said that supervisors sometimes physically abused women workers, and refused to let women return to their villages to plant food crops until the plantation work was done. Esther remembered more than one occasion when she and her mother planted fields by moonlight.[92]

Esther Njoki had little contact with white women, who seldom hired black women for house duties. Njoki explained that white women considered black women dirty, ignorant, and slow to carry out instructions. It seems, however, that prejudice was far from one-sided. Esther remarked that black women had little desire to enter white houses; they feared white women because they were so "different" and "strange," and were not circumcised (discussed in chapter 8) like most black Kenyan women. According to Esther, black women were also extremely suspicious of white men, and thought it would be an arch disgrace to bear a white man's child.[93]

Workers who daily scrutinized women and thus had more to say about them were male domestic servants. One of these was a male Kikuyu cook. With pride, he stated that he earned six shillings a month and got along quite well with his white mistress, largely because he spoke English. He liked to work alongside the household's white women, but felt demeaned by working with what he called black "girls." Even though these young women usually served in limited capacities as "ayahs" or nursemaids, he felt uncomfortable in their presence. He explained that men considered such women whores, akin to what he called "barmaids," because they worked and sometimes slept in white peoples' houses.[94]

Another male houseworker, Njonge Kimana, also liked his mistress, but had serious reservations regarding whites in general. When he was a teenager, he started as a kitchen "toto," meaning a young helper in "Kisettla," or settler bastardization of Swahili. Njonge assisted the cook, polished silver, and waited tables. Because he wanted to avoid the slaps and blows with a stick that white employers inflicted when a servant brought tea late or did something wrong, he worked hard to avoid physical punishment. Like other black servants, he wore a long white caftan. According to him, white women preferred not to see black skin or the black male body. He also recalled that white women feared "filth." If a letter came to the house, he had to go out and fetch it, then deliver it wearing white gloves. In Njonge Kimana's view, white women were demanding and "tough."[95]

Over the years, Njonge Kimana developed tremendous affection for his mistress, Emma Hopcraft, whom he described as "special." He remembered that Emma learned to speak some Swahili and Kikuyu so she could communicate with him and other servants. He praised Emma as a hard worker who tended a vegetable garden, from which she sold turnips and other produce. Although Njonge Kimana feared Emma's husband whom he said was "hard" on black workers, he respected Emma "like his mother." Tears welled in his eyes when he recalled that Emma had given him his first watch. When Emma died, he said, he refused to take payment for digging her grave, thus showing agency in a system that offered little opportunity for black Kenyans to express their emotions or say no to white men.[96]

Conclusion

Arriving at a definitive, or even a fair, assessment of frontier product is impossible. On frontiers themselves, there were many opinions, even among people of the same race or social class. Meanwhile, rumor, myth, and inaccurate reporting further muddled the situation. These circumstances are a reminder that people, including historians, can never know the actual past. In fact, historical writings are simply one more form of discourse revealing the issues and sentiments of an era.

Historians can, however, easily recognize the product of the past because it continues to cause bitter feelings, as well as extended policy debates. In the American West, frontier product marginalizes groups of people economically and socially, while keeping white elitism alive. In Kenya, product casts the shadow of colonialism, which is virtually recreated in financial-aid packages with definite "requirements," worldwide discussions of the "black" problem, and in the continuing tendency to look down on African countries, calling them the "third" world. In the American West and in Kenya, frontier product lingers on.

EIGHT
A Legacy of Violence

VIOLENCE was always a frontier product, emerging from an ideology that accepted its omnipresence and condoned its use. Thus, whatever the frontier, all its women had to endure the threat of physical brutality, including rape, as well as the strife associated with racism. White women, who had helped create a divisive society, had no choice but to live with it. Female migrants of color, who had little responsibility for frontier product, also had to face the risk of barbarity. Indigenous women, however, bore the brunt of colonialist-inspired violence.

Violence on the American and Kenyan Frontiers

Physical violence of various sorts was a given on any of the world's frontiers, including the American West. People grew accustomed to it, expected it, and used it themselves on occasion. After all, the West's very environment could be brutal. One of the most difficult adjustments that pioneers had to make was to new and often hostile surroundings. Even in southwestern New Mexico of the 1880s, a reputedly healthful climate made life tenuous. In 1889, snowfall in the

Mimbres Valley reportedly measured "hip deep." In that year, three American cowboys perished in a blizzard; their frozen bodies were found lying in the snow, all life gone from them. In the spring, the snow melted, causing floodwaters to gush out of the mountains and cut a fourteen-foot-wide path of destruction that claimed additional lives.[1]

On the American frontier, violence also came from other people. In a society created and maintained by bodily force, it is unsurprising that crime and other forms of belligerence were also widespread. In response, westerners developed a legal and personal belief in protecting themselves, as well as family members and friends. The western historian Richard Maxwell Brown couches the growing notion of self-defense in terms of "no duty to retreat," that is, that an individual had a right to stand his or her ground in the face of attack or atrocity.[2]

For women, two types of corporeal aggression existed. *Public* violence might include an attack or rape away from home, whereas *personal* violence involved offenses originating within a woman's home and family. In western towns and cities, for example, women feared public crime, especially murder and rape. They stayed home in the evening, went out only in the company of friends, or carried small "ladies" pistols in their muffs, umbrellas, and reticules (purses).[3] In western forts, a "town" where the possibility of military action hung over women's heads, army wives also mastered the use of weapons. Army wife Ada Vogdes, who, in her words, was "frightened to death" when she first arrived at Fort Laramie and Fort Fetterman during the late 1860s, came to enjoy armed horseback rides outside sheltering walls.[4]

Even during daylight hours, the West's urban women lived with tension. In early towns, everything from shootouts to public executions were common. Executions drew huge, unruly crowds whose members sometimes paid entrance fees to see a person hanged. It was common for parents to take their children to hangings as a moral lesson—so they could see the results of breaking the law. During the 1860s, a Denver, Colorado, mother of three, who lived near a hanging tree, had different worries. In a forerunner of today's drive-by shootings, bullets fired by rowdy and inebriated onlookers sometimes penetrated her house. During hangings of especially notorious people, she created protective cocoons for her children by wrapping them in buffalo robes and putting them in the attic, far from random bullets.[5]

Western mining towns were especially tumultuous. A woman who lived in California gold camps during the 1840s and early 1850s remembered an infusion of "gun men, gamblers, blacklegs, and all the new class of the sporting element (men and women)" to the gold-rush state. She added that "men wore guns and shot to kill." In 1856, when her father was shot to death in a settlement known as French Bar, she called the shooting "another cold-blooded murder."[6]

Later, during New Mexico's silver and gold rushes of the 1880s, the mining town of Kingston, New Mexico, proved tempestuous. Early in the 1880s, the silver town of Kingston had twenty-two saloons but only one church. Although no one seemed to count the madams, pimps, and brothels—such as Sadie Orchard's "house" on Virtue Street—they were abundant and were frequently the center of disturbance. When Kingston's population reached twenty-five hundred, a fair number were what one observer called "gamblers and their friends in the demi-monde." When Kingstonites engaged in "shooting scrapes" in the streets, people inside buildings plunged to the floor in case stray bullets came through canvas or whipsaw walls. The townspeople also had regular clashes with Apache Indians, led before his death in 1880 by the daring Chief Victorio.[7]

In addition, in surrounding towns like Hillsboro, Silver City, and Chloride Flats, men and women regularly accosted one another. Reports of murder, along with the lesser crimes of stealing and rustling, appeared in Hillsboro's *Sierra County Advocate*. Perpetrators and victims included Anglos, Hispanics, African Americans, and Asians. South of Hillsboro, Silver City's *Enterprise,* and to the north, Chloride's *Black Range,* astonished readers with stories of knife fights and shootings. Men shot each other in saloons, brothels, homes, and on the streets. At Fort Bayard in 1889, two African American soldiers, engaged in an altercation concerning a woman, shot at each other. Women wielded pistols as well. Also in 1889, a Pinos Altos woman fired on her lover after a quarrel, killing him.[8]

Additional reports of violent episodes reminded people that life could expire at any moment. In Espaneta, New Mexico, in 1889, a bear killed and ate most of an aged Hispanic woman, leaving behind only some torn clothing, bones, and hair. Also, accidents were endemic in mines, where premature explosions of dynamite or cave-ins claimed numerous lives. Revenge seemed to lie at the bottom of other altercations. In Doña Ana County, a dying gunman confessed that he had been hired to kill the deputy sheriff. Other revengeful people used widely accessible "giant powder"—dynamite—to blow up an enemy's home or office, or simply resorted to setting easily ignited wood buildings on fire.[9]

Another disruptive element was the "red-light" or "tenderloin" districts of western towns and cities. Because urban areas had high proportions of men in their populations, prostitution was common and full of hazards of its own. Although Native American and African American women were sometimes prostitutes, white women dominated the profession in most western areas. In Helena, Montana, for example, between 1865 and 1886, prostitution provided the greatest source of paid employment for white women. To avoid being run out of business, prostitutes paid regular "fines" to the Helena authorities. In 1883, however, the Northern Pacific Railroad reached Helena, bringing in families with wives and mothers who saw prostitution as a moral issue rather than wage labor. They made life extremely unpleasant for prostitutes, pressuring local government to abolish prostitution, or at least move its practitioners to another part of town. Unwilling to forego the income from prostitution, Helena's politicians enacted codes segregating prostitutes in "red light" or "tenderloin" districts.[10]

In other parts of the West, "good" women also felt it was their moral responsibility to campaign against prostitution. Thus, local officials contained prostitution in out-of-the-way and unsafe areas, frequently near stockyards or railroad tracks. Authorities also criminalized prostitutes by adopting regulations "concerning offenses against good morals and decency." In 1885, the mining town of Silver City, New Mexico, adopted an ordinance making it unlawful "for any bawdy house or house of ill fame, house of assignation, or place for the practice of fornication, or common ill-governed or disorderly house" to exist within corporate limits. The provision further prohibited "any lewd or indecent act of behavior," with the punishment being a fine, up to thirty days in jail, or agreeing to leave the area.[11] Although city officials intended such codes to protect the "good" people who lived inside town, they created areas near a city's borders that became magnets for everyone from drunks and petty thieves to drug dealers and murderers.

Besides defining prostitution as a moral issue, white female reformers argued that prostitution often brought physical harm and brutality to those around it. No one knew that better than prostitutes, who found customers in a variety of situations, including streets, saloons, and hotels. Others waited for clients to come to them, either in small houses called cribs or in brothels. Each situation had its own hazards. In a crib, a patron might abuse a woman who had no one to call for help. In brothels, madams and prostitutes sustained frequent injuries and sometimes death, often at the hands of their own associates. In New Mexico in 1888, prostitute Bessie Harper assaulted another prostitute, Millie Forest, beating her senseless with a stone tied up in a towel and inflicting multiple lacerations of the face and scalp. In 1889, a Miss Cordelia languished in a Pinos Altos jail after she "shot up" and wounded some of the girls who worked in a house run by a Miss Williams. The following year, a French woman who managed a brothel called "Nettie's Place" was found dead with a Colt .41-caliber bullet through her forehead. The newspaper account made the scene clear: the woman "had bled terribly as the bed clothes were saturated and there was a large pool of blood on the floor," while the man lay "with the brains oozing from his skull."[12]

In addition, prostitutes' customers were frequently unstable and reckless. Some used drugs, including opium, which was available "under the counter" from some apothecaries, merchants, and laundry-men, or so-called "hop joints" or "opium dens." Many men routinely drank until they were drunk and dangerous. One inebriated cowboy shot a clean hole through his own ear. In another case, a shotgun exploded accidentally; the mishap blew off the side of a man's head, exposing his brains. And, in what a journalist described as a "little shooting scrape," a card dealer in a Silver City saloon drew a pistol on a customer and shot him through the hand. The madams and prostitutes who witnessed such mayhem knew that the next blow might fall on them, that the next bullet might take them down permanently.[13]

In a very different venue, one seldom discussed during the 1800s, women who were legal wives also got hurt by personal abuse in their own homes from their own husbands. During the 1870s, the wife of a Montana sheriff admitted that her relationship was characterized by "beating and everything else." Many people believed that drunken husbands fell into rages and beat their wives and children. "A wife he thrashes, children lashes," was a common saying regarding alcoholic husbands. The Minnesota feminist Jane Swisshelm recommended that abusive, drunken husbands be whipped. Herself a disillusioned wife who had left a drunken husband, Swisshelm added that women who remained married to alcoholics should be committed to insane asylums.[14]

At the time, however, custom and law gave men the right to control their wives. Husbands could physically or verbally chastise wives. In most jurisdictions, husbands could also force sex on wives without such action being considered rape. During the mid-nineteenth century, however, a growing outcry protesting such legalities encouraged western states to adopt cruelty, including sexual and sometimes verbal abuse, as a ground for divorce. Texas added cruelty as early as 1841 and Kansas in 1855.[15] Adultery also appeared to be widespread and frequently led to impassioned encounters. During the mid-nineteenth century, California became infamous for rampant adultery and the armed imbroglios that resulted. In 1853, a Massachusetts man in California commented that he was amazed "to notice the frequency of family difficulties resulting from the infidelity of husband or wife or both."[16]

Of course, white women were not the only ones to fear physical violence in the American West. Because of the additional factor of racial prejudice, women of color lived even closer to the threat of harm. No matter what a woman's race or ethnicity, she could not escape violence. Neither the law nor social pressure protected women of color from rape. If potential rape was a nagging thought at the back of white women's minds, it was more of a real possibility for women of color. If raped, these women would most likely remain silent because no police investigation would result from their complaints.[17] Even murders of women of color often went unreported and unpunished.

In addition, women suffered racially inspired brutality. Among Native Americans tales of cruelty are legion. A Cheyenne woman explained that she was afraid of white soldiers because white troops had attacked her "peaceable" village near the Mexican border, leaving death and destruction in their wake. She remembered that she watched, without being able to help, a woman of her tribe "crawling along on the ground, shot, scalped, crazy, but not yet dead." She added that every time she saw a white soldier she thought of that woman.[18] Also during the 1860s, the Yavapai Indians of Arizona experienced ruthlessness during the course of their removal to the San Carlos reservation. One Yavapai woman related that her father, who was a young boy at the time, watched as soldiers killed his mother and his aunt. He remembered the scene as one of dead bodies "everywhere." Later, the same soldiers killed so many Yavapai that they piled corpses on top of each other. According to him, that place came to be known as Skull Valley.[19]

Hispanics bore their share of assaults as well. A Hispanic woman who worked as a matron at the Mission of San Diego during the 1840s and 1850s described what she called Indian "uprisings," one of which led to the death of two boys and one man, a vaquero.[20] On other occasions, Hispanics received abuse at the hands of Anglos. Hispana Antonia de Soza of Tucson, Arizona, recalled that during the 1880s men she called "Texans" drank at a saloon near her family's ranch. When inebriated, they donned masks and attacked Spanish-speaking families in the area. De Soza also remembered that local Anglos and Hispanics harassed Apache and Chinese families who lived in Tucson, even to the point of ejecting them from public parks and dance platforms. She said that later her brother was fatally shot and robbed. The family, who searched for him everywhere, did not find his body until two months later.[21]

Even the ruthlessness of slavery tainted the supposedly egalitarian West. Emma, a black slave woman born in Mississippi and sold to a Texas planter, probably during the early 1840s, explained that her master expected slaves to rise at 4 A.M. and labor in the fields until dusk settled. During the evening, he set male slaves to chopping wood and building fences, and female slaves to carding cotton, weaving cloth, and knitting stockings. According to Emma, her master used threats to keep the slaves working, sometimes until midnight: "Marse give each one a chore to do at night and iffen it warn't did when we went to bed, we's whipped."[22]

When Texas entered the United States on December 29, 1845, it did so as a slave state. A woman who was a slave during the 1850s recalled that her master's black "driver" (overseer) instilled fear in slaves to keep them working. She said he would tie men to trees and "cowhide 'em till the blood run down onto the ground." Pregnant women received similar treatment. When they became "slothful and not able to do their part," the man had holes dug in the ground to accommodate their bellies while he beat them "nearly to death." Even black slave women's bodies were at their owners' command. A woman named Rose stated that she was forced to produce future laborers. When Rose reached age sixteen, sometime around 1860, her master ordered her to fix a cabin for herself and Rufus, whom she regarded as a bully. She failed to understand the full implications of her master's order until Rufus climbed into the bunk with her. She began to holler, then put her feet against Rufus and pushed him out onto the floor. Rufus tried again, but Rose warded him off with a heavy, three-foot-long poker. When the master informed Rose that she would bear Rufus's children or be whipped at the stake, she bent to his will.[23]

Even after slavery formally ended in 1863, life-threatening actions continued. A Washington state woman recalled that her family migrated to the Pacific Northwest in 1888. The North Western Improvement Company transported black workers and their families from Illinois to Roslyn in Washington state as, unbeknownst to them, strikebreakers. Striking miners warned that they would blow up the train carrying the African Americans and, indeed, sticks of dynamite were found between the tracks. The black workers had to be protected by armed guards when they went to work in the mines and even when they bought groceries.[24]

Whites were not the only ones to act out their bitterness and aggression. In New Mexico, Anglos and Hispanics had similar conflicts. Hispanics objected to Anglos pushing them off their land and obtaining legal titles through unfair means. They also opposed the practice of white American settlers hiring native New Mexicans as field-workers, usually for long hours and low wages. By the time Colonel Stephen Watts Kearney and his troops planted the American flag in Santa Fe at the beginning of the Mexican War in 1846 and declared New Mexico an American possession, most Mexicans viewed Americans with suspicion and mistrust. Rather than welcoming the conquerors, numerous New Mexicans whispered of rebellion.

When the Mexican War ended in 1848, conditions worsened for Mexicans in New Mexico Territory. Although the Treaty of Guadalupe Hidalgo assured protection of existing land claims, many Americans demanded that *ricos*—landowners—show documents or other proof of ownership, which seldom existed under the old system of Spanish land grants. Anglos also urged ricos to sell their lands to pay debts, taxes, or legal fees. During the mid-1870s, a member of a religious order, Sister Blandina Segale, gave the New Mexicans' side of the story: "Deceit and dishonesty will rob the poor natives of everything. . . . Nothing too bad for the natives—nothing too good for the land-grabbers." She added that "the land-grabbers are not representative Americans, but ruthless characters who wish to get away from law and order." In 1888, a number of Hispanic ranchers organized as *Las Gorras Blancas* (The White Caps), which unsuccessfully attacked Anglo ranchers who fenced land used as public grazing areas.[25]

In neighboring Texas, Hispanics also forcibly resisted their exploitation, thus causing another type of viciousness. In 1848, when Hispanics in Texas became American citizens, they protested against white American-Texans seizing their land, taking over communal grazing sites, offering them lower-than-standard wages, and generally mistreating and reviling them. During the 1850s, a Mexican patriot, Juan Nepmuceno Cortina, tried to protect Mexican-Texans living along the Rio Grande. From the perspective of American-Texans, Cortina was little more than a bandit and outlaw. Cortina returned the insults. From his base at the Rancho del Carmen in Cameron County, in 1859 Cortina labeled the American conquerors "flocks of vampires" who robbed, imprisoned, and murdered Mexicans, burned their houses, and seized their lands, all with "a smile on their faces." Out of this and other similar interchanges came the "Cortina War," which lasted well into 1860, when Texas Rangers and U.S. soldiers succeeded in quelling it.[26]

As Asians arrived in the American West, they too found life much harder than they had expected on what they called "Gold Mountain." In Nevada, a significant number of Chinese women were prostitutes. These women were obtained through purchase from relatives or through kidnaping. Others had no other way to support themselves. One brothel in Virginia City that operated next to a Chinese saloon included opium smoking on its list of attractions. Its owner, known only as China Mary, welcomed men of all racial groups and social classes. Women who worked in these establishments endured a chaotic lifestyle. During the 1860s, groups of white men attacked Chinese areas of town, both to demonstrate white superiority and because they were afraid of economic competition from Chinese workers. Later, in New Mexico, Mexicans repeatedly crossed the border to rob Chinese workers. One journalist commented that "it would appear that these renegades from Mexico consider the Chinamen their especial prey." Often, Chinese men and women had to pick up everything they owned and make a quick move to another location.[27]

In Kenya, women also lived with the threat of physical harm on a daily basis. As in the American West, the physical environment could be punishing. An Asian Indian woman remembered that Kisumu of the 1910s had "many wild animals around." She added that there was "a lot of malaria and blackwater fever and plague because of the rats and mice." Later, during the mid-1930s, the nature photographer Vivienne DeWatterville pointed out that the very sparseness of Kenya's landscape was another sort of violence. DeWatterville called Kenya's plains a "primitive vastness."[28] Women found themselves caught between extremes of gorgeous sunsets marred by voracious mosquitoes, or of rich farmland swept by rampaging floods that carried away topsoil and crops. Women fought all the brutal adversities to which African farmers had fallen victim for centuries. They dealt with fires, windstorms, and floods. They also learned to fall asleep despite the sound of hyenas and leopards prowling in the darkness.[29]

When compared to the American West, Kenya's other forms of violence appear quite modern. Certainly, in early twentieth-century settings, improved assault technology was employed. Also, customary English law, which for centuries had shown little tolerance for violent crime and urged victims to retreat or to flee the scene altogether, was called into question. Passivity was seldom realistic in a frontier setting, especially during the increasingly fractious twentieth century. Consequently, on the Kenya frontier, many types of crime were prevalent and victims often resisted. In Kenyan cities, notably Nairobi, Kenya's urban women faced street crime, including the possibility of personal attack. Moreover, theft was commonplace. In 1910 alone, Nairobi's police blotter listed twenty-four hundred arrests and nineteen hundred convictions. The understaffed police force was able to retrieve less than half of the stolen money, watches, jewelry, and clothing. Much of it turned up in Nairobi's red-light district near the railway station on Victoria Street, where prostitutes informed the police about what one officer called "bad characters" with stolen goods. During this era, murder was punished by execution at the hands of a firing squad; later, murderers died by hanging.[30]

In addition, the ways in which white Kenyans amused themselves could create danger. In any specific locality, the ongoing hub of white social life usually focused on the local hotel's bar, dining room, billiard room, and verandah. White men drank heavily and brawls often occurred. Men who routinely carried guns did not hesitate to use them. In Nairobi, the exclusive Norfolk Hotel, which opened on Christmas day in 1904, was frequently a trouble spot. The Norfolk went out of its way to attract the more elite Europeans. It boasted a dining room that seated one hundred people and offered varied cuisines, including French.[31] As early as 1905, the Norfolk's owners promoted the hotel as "a fashionable rendezvous of the Highlands." Soon, the Norfolk's guest book included the names of Kenya's "best" white families, ladies and lords among them. These people sometimes acted more like rabble than aristocracy. While the ladies dined with friends or played bridge, many of the lords, and sometimes a few of the women as well, sat on the Norfolk's verandah shooting pistols at the streetlight that stood next to the police station across the street. One of these men was Lord

Delamere, who liked to drink heavily at the Norfolk, organize Rugby games in its public rooms, and take occasional potshots at various streetlights.[32]

Annual race weeks in Nairobi were even worse. The writer Charles Miller compared Nairobi during race week to "Dodge City at the end of a cattle drive." According to Miller, men on horseback galloped through town, shooting out streetlights with pistols and rifles. Others engaged in fistfights, which often resulted in someone being thrown out a window, even from upper floors. Miller also invokes the wild West when he writes, "customers at any bar could be scattered two or three times a night when some horseman cantered through the doors, peppered the ceiling with birdshot and helped himself to the nearest whisky bottle without dismounting."[33]

Unarguably, Nairobi was risky, especially at night. It was not only during annual race week, however, that drunken men on horseback careened through the streets, shooting at the gas streetlamps. On any given evening, the River Road area and the Indian bazaar were for only the most self-confident or the very foolish. Around Victoria Street, the red-light district, whites and Asian Indians stood out from the largely black Kenyan population. For such men, a simple misstep, like intervening on behalf of a woman being hassled, could result in a fatal stab wound.[34]

Even though judges were overwhelmed by assault cases, they preferred to have altercations settled in their courtrooms rather than on the streets. In early Nairobi, for example, "Pioneer Mary" Walsh reportedly protected herself by carrying a sheathed stick, which she employed in a brash and ugly practice, hitting black Kenyans she found bothersome. Later, in 1907, when several white women accused three Nairobi rickshaw drivers of acting insolently, a group of white men seized the drivers and publicly flogged them in front of the courthouse. Apparently, it was not uncommon for white settlers, even those as prominent as Ewart Grogan, to publicly punish black Kenyans for what whites defined as acts of disrespect.[35] White women in similar situations went to the police, whose primary duty was to protect white settlers and their belongings. White women charged black Kenyan or Asian Indian men with verbal disrespect or physical assault. There is no way to tell if these were instances of white women's fears or real incidents of dangerous aggression. In the cases that made it to court, white judges upheld white women accusers and endorsed whatever actions white women took to defend themselves. During the 1930s, when white nursing sister Vera Mordaunt killed a black man with her golf clubs after he entered her window, a white court ruled Mordaunt's action "quite justifiable."[36] Another way of assessing accountability might have been to argue that defendants of color were blameless because they had been pushed too far by whites, suffered too much poverty and exploitation, and endured the erosion of their cultures. Because Kenya's white legal system was designed to protect whites rather than giving the benefit of the doubt to black Kenyans, it assigned to whites the right to determine criminal acts.

Women suffering spouse abuse or other marital violence sometimes resorted to the courts as well. During the early 1900s, cases came to court or otherwise entered official records involving white women enduring abuse. Some women in unhappy situations tried to abort themselves of babies. At the same time, cruelty and adultery became common causes for divorces among white couples in colonial Kenya. By the 1920s and 1930s these causes were used by white Kenyans, both from the Happy Valley set and from other quarters as well.[37]

Court rulings did not stop white women from agonizing about what could happen to them. Nor did women take much reassurance from the welter of permit laws, vagrancy and loitering prohibitions, and social behavior codes that existed in each of Kenya's five "white" towns: Eldoret, Kisumu, Mombasa, Nairobi, and Nakuru. Although everything from the existence of police officers to spatial separation of urban peoples by race was supposed to convince white women they were safe, women did not feel safe.[38] With huge numbers of men— both white and of color—around them at all times, white women especially worried about rape. At times, both urban and rural women approached the point of near panic. As a result, a number of Kenya's white women, like their western counterparts, learned to use and bear weapons ranging from pistols to shotguns. During the 1920s and 1930s,

British officials in Kenya exacerbated white women's fears by discouraging women from taking up their own farms or staying on farms alone during a husband's absence.[39]

White courts were a source of fear both for urban black Kenyans and Asian Indians. Women worried about husbands, sons, fathers, and brothers who were arrested, often on exaggerated or false charges. In a few cases, men who pled guilty received one or more years of "hard labor" and as many as "twenty strokes" of a rawhide lash. In other instances, male defendants pled innocent, but had little chance of successfully defending themselves in white courts.[40]

Nor could rural women protect men who worked for white women. Although wives and mothers-in-law occasionally sent husbands and sons and sons-in-law to work with scratched faces and swollen lips, they resented white women's mistreatment of their men.[41] It was common, however, for white female employers, who disparaged black male workers as uneducable and shiftless, to speak of the need to whip houseboys regularly. As one very opinionated woman thoughtlessly said in the mid-1930s, "it is only fair to say that a well-trained African houseboy takes a lot of beating."[42]

The practice of whipping domestic servants was in harmony with punishments used back in Britain, where masters regularly caned schoolboys and mistresses brutalized domestic servants. Whipping also imitated the action of white male planters in Kenya who frequently set up their own "police" forces led by "boss boys" or "head-men" to patrol a farm's boundaries, as well as keeping workers in line. White men also used physical discipline. In an extreme case, one planter took potshots with a rifle at black workers he thought were malingering. Unsurprisingly, he eventually hit one, wounding the man seriously. Llewelyn Powys, brother of a white settler, described another more typical scene. When he found Kikuyu and Swahili workers in a bloody altercation, he fired a warning shot over their heads. Just as the Kikuyu men swarmed toward Powys, his brother, Willie, arrived on the scene, swearing at them "roundly in their own language, calling them the sons of bastard-snakes and then, treating them as if they were a lot of naughty children, and sending them back to their houses." When a black Kenyan, whom Llewelyn called a "big leader," approached his brother brandishing a spear, Powys said that "a well-directed blow" toppled the man, upon which the others left the scene.[43]

For their own part, women of color were also endangered. Especially in urban areas, they were even more at risk for rape, kidnapping, and murder than white women. They not only lived in dangerous neighborhoods, but, as women of color, received little regard or respect. Yet because black women had to make do with the dregs of the economy, they often took employment with white families as domestics and nursemaids, which made them vulnerable to sexual harassment by white men. Women of color also found that one of the few jobs open to them was working as prostitutes. Unlike the American West, white women seldom worked as prostitutes. Because Kenya was a long, expensive trip for white women interested in working as prostitutes, few made the journey. In addition, the British Colonial Office tried to eliminate the "poorer sort" of white people from Kenya settlers by imposing financial and other immigration restrictions. Prostitutes were definitely considered the poorer sort in England, where battles against prostitution had been waged for decades. One group called puritans wanted the practice of prostitution repressed, while people known as regulators argued for only enough control to stop the spread of venereal disease.[44]

In Kenya, women of color from Kenya and from many other nations supplied men's sexual needs. Like towns and cities in the American West, Nairobi had a thriving tenderloin district around the railway station on Victoria Street. The most well-known house was "The Japanese Legation," so-called because a number of the prostitutes were Japanese women, who came to Nairobi via Zanzibar. At another area on Athi River Road were Syrian women who had been brought to Nairobi to work as prostitutes. Many more bordellos could be found in the Indian Bazaar, but these were reputedly shabby and unclean. Some black women practiced prostitution more informally. One explained that she would go to pick beans by the river, taking with her a gunnysack that she used as a blanket. When she lay on the sack, men understood that she was offering her body for sale. She would "motion for him to lie down with her," after which a man would pay her in coins. White male officials were hesitant to crack down on prostitution or run the women out of town because they wanted Nairobi to attract great numbers of male workers, who were either unmarried or had left their families at home. In that situation, whites felt that, despite its attendant ills, prostitution was a necessary service industry.[45]

Yet as in the American West, some prostitutes found subtle ways to fight the system. Black women in Nairobi's Pumwani District, set aside for only black Kenyans, practiced prostitution, yet demonstrated that they need not be total victims of the colonial system. Rather than live in abject poverty, these women *chose* to work as prostitutes, either for occasional periods of time or as a steady undertaking. As Kayaya Thababu, a Meri woman who arrived in Pumwani around 1925, put it, "At home, What could I do? Grow crops for my husband or my father? In Nairobi I can earn my own money, for myself." Some of these women solicited customers on the streets, in bars, or hotels, while others operated in small houses akin to cribs in the West. A number of women had rooms or owned houses in which they provided ritualized comforts. Kayaya Thababu explained that local customers "knew that [her] house belonged to a woman who never had a husband." She added that "I didn't go openly looking for men, and men came to my room with respect," so that no one would identify them as customers. She and other women would cook dinner, draw a bath, and engage in sex. Another Pumwani woman, Amina Hall, said, "If you spoke to these men, and told them about yourself, and kept your house clean, and gave them bath water after sex, he would give you a few more pennies." If a man was a regular client, the woman would allow him to stay the night and would give him breakfast the next morning. These women counted white men among their racially mixed clientele, while others served as full-time mistresses to white soldiers and government employees. In addition to prostitution, some women brewed and sold beer, the proceeds of which they often invested in trade, houses, and property. In that sense at least, they profited from the colonial economy.[46]

During the 1920s and 1930s, prostitutes in Nairobi, especially in the Pumwani area, continued to be entrepreneurs who earned enough money to buy houses and function as heads of their own households, or subsidized natal families by sending money back to their villages. In essence, daughters who contributed to their families' economies supported the continuance of the very peasant agrarian society that British policy destroyed. Also, women created a degree of autonomy and freedom for themselves, which they had not had in their villages. Although British officials took various steps to halt these women's incipient power, they were unable to stop what was technically illegal property ownership by women or the distribution of profits to rural families. British officials imposed the English "regulator" philosophy, in that they claimed they were trying to control the spread of venereal and other diseases by segregating residential areas and enforcing health provisions that separated blacks, whites, and Asian Indians from each other. Still, rather than forcing these women to bend to its will, British policy had to bend to theirs.[47]

Bigotry and Its Repercussions in the American West and in Kenya

Bigotry was another form of frontier violence. It wove together threads of physical and psychological harm into one fabric. Although intolerance frequently led to actual physical turbulence, including attacks, riots, even murder, it also constituted an indirect kind of molestation that demeaned people and barred them from taking advantage of a wide range of opportunities. In some cases, it led to a quiet tug-of-war over cultural practices. Like other forms of brutality, insults and disdain often elicited like behavior in return.

In the American West, for example, white women often expressed harsh and unthinking criticism of Indians' scanty clothing. Coming from a society that advocated covering the body with layers and complex types of apparel, white women thought Native Americans to be nearly nude. One of the first white women to enter the Pacific Northwest during the 1840s expressed surprise that the West's "barbaric" people, unlike the more "civilized" whites, wore little or no clothing.[48] This kind of thinking continued throughout the era. Regarding one of her first encounters with an Indian man, Colorado migrant Harriet Smith recorded in her diary in 1862 that she was "a little streaked for he had nothing on but a blanket and great earrings and bracelet, all brass."[49] The only way that Native Americans could elicit approval from white women was by wearing clothing similar to whites. If Indians looked something like whites, women passed judgments that were more positive, including "clean and wholesome in appearance" and "the most respectable that we have seen." If Indians emulated whites too closely, however, white women thought them audacious and pretentious."[50]

At the same time, white women frequently dismissed as ostentatious and excessive Indian quill work, beading, and jewelry, ignoring the intricate craftwork involved. White women, who wore such distinctive nineteenth-century sartorial trends as hoopskirts, bustles, and leg-o'-mutton sleeves, called Indians' appearance "peculiar." These women, who envisioned themselves as the carriers of white customs to aboriginal peoples, thought their own styles quite becoming, whereas they condemned Indian fashions as absurd.[51]

Western women's attitudes toward language were equally prejudicial. As molders of children, white women, especially those who had some education themselves, had an interest in hearing English well spoken. When they got close enough to Native Americans to hold a conversation, these women were astonished to learn that Indians spoke little or no English. Apparently, women had assumed that all people who lived in North America spoke English. In 1863, westward-bound Ellen Adams commented, with obvious dismay, "Some of the Indians could not understand a single word of English." Another woman thought Indians "stupid" because they did not "understand French any better than they did English."[52] In this situation, western women rejected the use of native languages as a means of communication. Rather, they assumed that English should and would become the dominant tongue for all western peoples. When Indians did manage to speak a few words of English, women derided their lack of fluency. "They do not understand any of our language," one woman declared, "and when they can speak a word of it they seem to think that they have done something very smart."[53]

Clearly, a power struggle underlay the issue of language in the West. Whites imposed English on inhabitants of the American West, yet held them to such a high standard that they could never be thought of as anything but slow and inferior. At the same time, whites refused to learn local languages, thus protecting themselves from charges of ineptness. In addition, the fact that everything from newspapers to legislation were in English prevented non-English speakers from understanding or behaving in accordance with the white system.

Later, in Kenya, inter-group relations appeared even more fraught with ill-feeling and emotion than in the West. As in the American West, clothing was a highly contested area between Kenya's white and black women. The question of what constituted acceptable dress was an issue for white women who believed that their style of clothing, like the rest of white culture, was the best in the world. White women assumed that black Kenyans would willingly give up their usual outfits, so appropriate for a tropical climate, in favor of long-skirted cotton dresses for women and shirts and trousers for men. White people even imposed their sartorial values on black brides and grooms. At a mission-sponsored wedding of a black Kenyan couple in 1921, the bride wore a white dress and veil, while the groom sported a western-style suit and tie.[54]

To allow black Kenyans to wear their customary dress would be tantamount to admitting that black ways were valid, a concession white women could not afford to make. If they gave in on the matter of clothing, women would dilute their authority. They would also forfeit a powerful tool of socialization. Although black Kenyan women also refused to surrender, some gradually compromised by donning baggy dresses, but wearing brightly colored bandanas on their heads.

White women's insistence on "proper" clothing not only hampered black Kenyans, but white women as well. If they were to act as models, white women had to wear "civilized" clothing at all times. Although female missionaries' clothing was highly unsuitable, these women believed they had a duty to set an example. Clothed during the 1890s in such accouterments of white civilization as corsets and floor-length skirts and during later decades in nylon hosiery, hats, and gloves, these women could not have been comfortable, especially in the tropical areas of Kenya. Later, during the 1920s and 1930s, when codes of dress and behavior for women relaxed, some women continued to follow the usual code. For example, white female teachers, who thought of themselves as ideals for black women, wore skirts, blouses, jackets, and shoes with nylon stockings in the classroom and added broad-brimmed hats when in public.[55]

Besides the issue of what constituted appropriate clothing, the language to be spoken on a routine basis provided another point of conflict. In general, frontier conquerors usually assumed that their "superior" language would become, as it had in the earlier American West, the standard for politics, business, and education. English also was the language of choice (by whites) for daily transactions and most relationships. Unlike white women in the West, many white Kenyans made an effort to learn Kenyans' languages, especially Swahili. Whites' willingness to learn local languages may have been something of a reverse power play. In a sense, whites made Swahili the language of oppression; black Kenyans had to learn it in addition to their local and tribal languages. For another, whites, who assumed that "inferior" black Kenyans would have difficulty learning English, could treat them as stupid and incapable by talking to them in hackneyed, bastardized versions of their "own" language, Swahili. The situation was even more difficult for black women, who were often barred from English-speaking schools by what one termed "discrimination" because of gender.[56]

Whatever the psychological underpinnings, most of Kenya's white women looked upon learning a bit of Swahili as a necessity. It was common for white women to study Swahili before and after migration to Kenya. Settler Marjorie Hood, who journeyed from her home in the West Indies to Kenya during the mid-1930s, remembered that what she called her "biggest adjustment" was having to learn Swahili. Apparently, thousands of others found themselves in the same situation, for the *East African Standard* carried advertisements for phrase books, while the *Kenya Settlers' Cookery Book and Household Guide* (1928) included a list of household terms and instructions in both languages.[57]

For women, learning Swahili had its negative sides. Having to study a new tongue was certainly one difficulty. Another was far more subtle. Because whites believed they had an exclusive hold on English, many a white woman conversed with her family and friends in English, secure in the false belief that her servants could not understand her. Far brighter than whites thought them to be, black Kenyans picked up English quickly and thus knew more about family members and the workings of the household than their employers would have believed possible.

Unlike the earlier American West, Kenya's white women primarily related to indigenes through the difficult connection of mistress and servant. White women, who lacked sufficient language skills to give clear directions and relay their high expectations, tried to teach black men to clean, cook, and wash clothes according to European customs and standards. Men, who were unaccustomed to such work, found white women's domestic ways strange, amusing, and even unfathomable. The result was a relationship fraught with misunderstanding, frustration, and angst on both sides.

Another way that white women tried to protect themselves was by urging white men to keep in force the system known as *kipande*, or worker registration. Every black male worker was required to enroll with the proper authorities and receive a small booklet. As early as 1903, each worker had a service book that included his or her name, approximate age, tribal designation, physical description, and thumb print. Kipande was legally enacted in 1915 and formalized in 1921 as the Native Registration Ordinance No. 56. A worker's "book" was key to the plan's effectiveness. After leaving a position or after being dismissed, the worker had to present the book so that the employer could give the reason for severing employment and add his or her opinion of the book's holder. When seeking another job, the book's bearer would present it as identification, as well as his or her employment record.[58] Although service books were originally intended to protect white employers from convicts and other undesirables, it put black laborers at the mercy of the whites who wrote in their books. Kipande was also used during World War I to discourage black Kenyans from deserting.

Even though a few black Kenyans were proud of their books, most felt demeaned by the practice of registration and fearful of the power that kipande gave whites. Black workers resisted by having reports in their books forged or using another person's book to get a job. Workers not only showed agency by these rebellious acts, but defeated the purpose of kipande. During the early 1930s, the registration system came under increasing attack. Some white and many black Kenyans argued that kipande insulted black workers, who had to register and carry cards in order to get jobs. White women asked that kipande be kept in place as it allowed them to gain some measure of the character and capacity of house workers.[59] For white women, a key issue was the possibility of assault. For white men overseeing field laborers, a fugitive could be annoying and even troublesome, but white women believed that being alone in a house with several black male workers could lead to a man attacking, raping, or even killing them. Although kipande was a matter of efficiency in hiring to white men, white women saw it as one of protection.

Frequently, black men recognized—and resented—white women's distrust of them. Because a few white women let their qualms turn into hysteria, their black servants could hardly fail to notice. In some cases, proud Kikuyu men, who constituted much of the domestic labor force for white women, were not only offended, but felt dishonored as well.[60] Male servants also feared that white women would spitefully write negative reports in their books. Thus, kipande worsened relations between white women employers and their black male employees.

These white women and black men seemed locked in a tragic pantomime. White women employers exercised power over their black employees through daily confrontations, which included white women's obvious disdain for blacks, the refusal of a white woman to validate a black man through eye contact, and the forced superimpositions of white values and culture. The weight of domestic routines and the "correct" use of British products bore down on black servants unaccustomed to such things. Although black Kenyans had their routines and ceremonies, they made sense to them; white women's routines and ceremonies did not. Black Kenyans played their own role in the struggle by "misbehaving." Today, psychologists might call such a relationship co-dependent, in which an insubordinate black allowed a white mistress to rant and condemn all blacks. In turn, black workers justified their resistance on the basis of white women's prejudice and pettiness. This interplay created a situation that was hardly effective, profitable, or pleasant for either side.

Not all white women held such harsh views. A few even developed sympathy for the indigenes' point of view. Although one woman agreed that most black servants were basically ignorant and lazy, she (patronizingly) found them loyal, efficient, and willing to try new tasks. After years in Kenya, she finally realized that servants had no reason to make a distinction between an aluminum teapot and one of Queen Anne silver. Neither should they understand why a damask table napkin was not as equally suitable as a dishcloth for cleaning knives. She recognized that her household help saw her as "tiresome and unreasonable" when she objected to them packing a silver cream and sugar set and teapot in a picnic basket.[61]

Less enlightened white women who held onto their prejudices toward black Kenyans also suffered another abuse—verbal and psychological. Acrimonious pressure from folks back home let white women know that attitudes were changing. As early as the 1910s, a spate of books appeared that predicted doom for white settlers in black countries. Authors warned that divisions among whites would cause the "loss" of black countries for the British empire. Some writers specifically indicted white settlers, branding them as little more than economic opportunists.[62] In reaction, white women perceived black Kenyans as enemies. In a very real sense, black Kenyans were the enemy, perhaps not of individual white people, but of imperialism and colonialism. Often black "arrogance" or "stupidity," as whites called it, was in reality resistance to white domination. More than one white woman noted that her servants looked at her with eyes filled with hatred.

White people even had high-placed opponents, ranging from members of Parliament and Church of Scotland spokesperson Eleanor Rathbone. Although Rathbone obtained most of her information secondhand and, in her own way, wanted to control black Kenyans, she accused Kenya's white women of knowing and caring little about black women. Rathbone and her allies worked with the Committee for the Protection of Coloured Women in the Colonies to stop customs to which they objected, including what whites called "bride prices" and the highly controversial and widespread practice of female circumcision, meaning female genital cutting of the clitoris and sometimes the labia as well. As Rathbone and others created their own discourse in reports, letters, and pamphlets they wrote and distributed throughout Great Britain, they further alienated white settlers by advocating during the middle to late 1920s immediate "compulsory education of all classes" of black Kenyans. Although they represented themselves as proponents of black Kenyans, they wanted heightened white control in Kenya, but not under the leadership of white Kenyans.[63]

Increasingly, casual visitors to Kenya were also disdainful of white settlers. One Briton, Anne McDonald, who came "to see for herself" during the 1930s, wrote in her journal that she agreed with critics like Rathbone. McDonald concluded that the majority of white people in Kenya were "content with a distant view which makes it difficult to recognise the Africans as people and impossible to distinguish individual characteristics." Because whites were the interlopers, McDonald continued, it was up to them to bridge the great gulf they had created between the two races.[64]

On hearing such criticism, a number of white women in Kenya stiffened their backs. As white women had done in defense of Kenya's worsening image, they once again spoke out—often acerbically—on their own behalf. One woman who had lived in Kenya during the 1920s and early 1930s asserted that the "answer" to colonial problems was not to be found in high-flown, romanticized colonial rhetoric, which proposed to educate all indigenes according to Western standards and force them to adopt Western civilization, much as Rathbone had proposed. In her self-serving view, teaching people to use their hands had to come before reading and writing. Black Kenyans could then support themselves by following trades, while the talented ones could rise to other well-paid endeavors. As far as she was concerned, forcing black Kenyans to live in poverty and flinging a smattering of book knowledge at them only created further chaos, for which settlers were in turn blamed.[65]

White women were also culpable regarding their attitudes toward Asian Indians, in which they showed little interest. In fact, white women were as biased against migrants of color as they were against indigenes. In general, whites feared Indians' growing share of trade. When crime increased during the early 1900s and Indian shops or dukas became a target of black thieves and looters, the white and understaffed police force gave them little help. Although police officers were charged with protecting the forces of capitalism, white capitalism came first.[66] In fact, beginning in 1911 and lasting into the 1940s, police authority extended only to white sections: white urban areas and white plantations, farms, and estates.

Regarding Asian Indians, white women held on to the prejudices they had brought with them to Kenya. Whites especially urged the British government to ban the immigration of Indians and opposed equality for Indians. White women complained that the presence of Indians complicated their lives and their mission—how could they, white women asked, bring civilization to Kenya when Indians constituted a corrupting force?[67] When young Winston Churchill, who in 1905 became colonial under-secretary, visited Kenya during the early 1900s he expressed an opposite view. From an outsider's—and more objective—viewpoint, he pointed out that from Sikh soldiers who fought in "conquest and pacification" to traders, laborers, and bankers, Asian Indians had played crucial roles in Kenya."[68] Churchill's opinions meant little to Kenya's white farmers and entrepreneurs.

Landownership became the primary issue. The so-called "Indian Question," meaning whether Asian Indian migrants to Kenya had the right to take up farm land in the "white" highlands, caused much bitterness and debate. The official policy of barring Indians from landowning in the highlands began in 1906 and raised the issue of how to regulate the Indian population of Kenya. The "Indian Question" came to a head in 1921 and 1922 when the Indian Association in Nairobi escalated long-standing demands for an end to segregation, for equal representation on the heavily white legislative council, and for the right to purchase land in the "white" highlands.[69]

In the middle of this contretemps, a group of white women met late in 1921 at the New Stanley Hotel in Nairobi. After heated deliberations, they sent a plea to the secretary of state for the colonies to consider the vulnerable position of white women and children if segregation was abolished and equality granted. Women added their voices, especially opposing what they called child marriage (many Asian Indian women married at thirteen or fourteen years of age) and the reported lack of sanitation among Asian Indians. They further cited "the danger of Indian influences on the natives destroying among millions the prestige of a handful of whites." They even sent a cable to Queen Mary: "We the women of Kenya humbly implore your assistance to protect us and our children from the terrible Asiatic menace that threatens to overwhelm us."[70]

In the "white" highlands of the Mt. Kenya area, tempers ran high as well. One woman remembered that talk of armed revolt flowed freely in the Gilgil area and that white settlers boycotted Indian businesses. She added that with approximately 20,000 whites in the country and 120,000 Indians, the settlers were "duly worried."[71] Although settlers met in Nakuru early in 1923 and prepared for armed rebellion, the issue was soon settled to the disadvantage of the Indians. An observer sympathetic to the Asian Indian side explained that the split between Asian Indians and whites came about because white settlers wanted to impose white ways that "had little relevance to the Asian way of life." He added that "even more damaging to Asian sensibilities was the initial assumption of race superiority" and "benevolent paternalism" that created a "soul-killing atmosphere" during the 1920s and 1930s. In his portrayal of whites as the "other," white men and women were less than attractive or noble.[72]

In the meantime, relationships between white and black Kenyans worsened. Because British leaders vacillated regarding policy, white settlers held out hope for a future in a white-dominated Kenya. Unfortunately for Kenya's white settlers, times had altered, pinning them between the old and the new. Changes had begun during World War I, when black Kenyan men were sent to the front. Although whites ranked blacks as inferior to themselves, they did not hesitate to appropriate them as porters, hospital personnel, and fighters. Also, blacks saw something of the world beyond their homes and lived with people of different racial and ethnic backgrounds. In the process, black

Kenyans lost a good deal of the respect and awe they had held for early white settlers. When blacks fought alongside whites, they saw whites reduced to powerlessness and, on occasion, outright cowardice. Back home, black Kenyans felt they were assessed unfairly, including paying higher taxes, giving their livestock for military rations, and serving as porters for military supplies. The white war had interrupted their usual lives and forced upon them commitments they did not want or understand. In addition, they resented the maiming and death of fathers, husbands, sons, and brothers in a war was not theirs. One Swahili woman whose brother was "taken" as a servant to a European office remembered the war with quiet anguish: "They went; those who died, died, those who returned, returned." She was among the fortunate: her brother returned.[73]

The upheaval of the war years brought other developments as well. During the 1920s, socialists criticized private enterprise, the very system on which the British empire was based. By the late 1920s and early 1930s, psychologists and social scientists analyzed white moral codes and suggested revised value systems.[74] At the same time, archeologists and anthropologists enlarged cultural understanding and sparked an interest in comparative perspectives. All of these developments put white colonialism in question.

Denunciations of white colonialism stirred up black Kenyans, who had never been quiescent. Nandi villagers once sent back the head of a black clerk who had requested the payment of delinquent taxes to the district office with a message: "Here is the hut tax of the Nandi." Other less militant black Kenyans bore their resentment and suspicion in silence, resisting whenever an opportunity presented itself. During the 1920s and 1930s, the growing disharmony between Whitehall and Nairobi encouraged black Kenyans to think of a future independent, black-dominated nation called Kenya. They not only stepped up their resistance, but became more sophisticated in their tactics. During the early 1920s, Kikuyu-inspired political parties organized; their platforms supported the abolition of worker registration, lower taxes, unrestricted use of forests, better education, and the return of stolen land. Subsequent quarrels between black and white Kenyans led, in 1922, to the arrest of several Kikuyu leaders, including the outspoken

Harry Thuku, and a riot in Nairobi that left twenty people dead. The previous year, Kikuyu leader Harry Thuku had sent a list of grievances to the British colonial secretary. Thuku had written: "When we went to do war work we were told by His Excellency the governor that we should be rewarded, but it is our reward to have our tax raised . . . our ownership of land called into question." In return, Thuku received promises from the British government—empty promises that were never fulfilled.

In the meantime, the Kikuyu Central Association (KCA) kept black Kenyans' demands in front of the public. In response, the British government sent the Ormsby-Gore commission to Kenya in 1922 to assess the situation. Black Kenyans who testified emphasized three needs: the return of their land, schools for their children, and the right to participate in the cash-crop economy. When the Ormsby-Gore commission returned a report favorable to white settlers, black Kenyans were incensed. In 1927 and 1928, the British tried again, sending the Hilton-Young commission to interview white and black Kenyans. The Hilton-Young report recommended that at some future date a collaborative government between black Kenyans and migrants to Kenya should be put in place. This time white settlers were outraged, especially when black political parties increased in strength. The late 1920s and 1930s witnessed a series of struggles over long-standing issues, including land, education for black Kenyans, and the continuing practice by some black Kenyans of female circumcision.[75]

Of these, circumcision proved emotional and thus crucial. White women's concern for their black counterparts had carried many of them into the sacred domain of black Kenyans' customs. Typically, white women regarded as disgusting and barbaric those black Kenyans who continued to circumcise young women as a mark of their entry into adulthood. More moderate critics saw female genital cutting as a serious menace to female health. In fact, some girls did die from unclean conditions or botched surgery. Also, some mothers died in childbirth due to a constricted and scarred birth passage, and infant mortality was high.[76]

Many black Kenyans held a very different view. They resented white interference in their long-standing rituals. To them, female circumcision was far more than a physical operation. Rather, it constituted a critical spiritual experience for a young woman, providing her with a religious stepping-stone to a wholesome and fulfilling life. As far as black Kenyans, including women, could see, white people offered them no comparable rite as a replacement. In addition, some black leaders argued that by depriving women of sexual pleasure, the procedure reduced the danger of immorality in their communities.[77]

For these people, the specific practice of female circumcision was entwined with the larger question of black identity. In their eyes, whites typically stamped out black dance, music, art, literature, and language. All things that had defined black Kenyans were disappearing—turned into useless, barbarous practices by white sanctions and edicts. Were they, black Kenyans asked themselves, to become pseudo-whites, or perhaps left to float, indigent and lacking cultural moorings, in limbo between their tribal pasts and the white colonial present? To many black Kenyans, white restrictions on black spiritual ceremonies suggested that one or the other of these terrible alternatives was about to occur. Without their cultural and religious values, black Kenyans feared they would lose not only their identities, but their consciousness of themselves. They would cease to exist in either this world or the next. What would become of their children, they wondered, the boys and girls that whites had wrenched away from black tradition but had not taken to their bosoms as their own?[78]

At the same time, other black Kenyans supported reforms aimed at female genital cutting, or at least continued to support Protestant missionaries who increasingly opposed female circumcision. Like other white-inspired controversies, female circumcision split families, communities, and tribal groups; the Kikuyu, for example, found themselves sharply divided. Kikuyu leaders especially saw the practice as symbolic of black people resisting colonialism.[79] The Kikuyu Central Association argued that white opposition to black customs was an additional plank in the white platform of cultural hegemony. Even Christian Kikuyu men and women failed to see the Biblical proscription for ending female circumcision.[80] The matter came to a crisis in 1929. When the Church of Scotland Mission attempted to abolish female circumcision among the Kikuyu, the reaction from many was swift and explicit. Numerous Kikuyu children stopped attending mission schools and families absented themselves from church services. Finally, a sixty-three-year-old woman missionary was forcibly circumcised and left to bleed to death. During the next few years, white religious leaders, as well as government officials, energetically backpedaled.[81]

By the end of the 1930s, something of a truce existed. The British government "accepted" a "minor" operation—the removal of the clitoris—by an authorized practitioner. The "major" operation of a cliteridectomy and labiadectomy combined was outlawed. Although officials realized that both procedures continued in secret and under unsanitary conditions, they also recognized that an onslaught against these practices would reap more loss of lives than allowing them to continue.[82] These and other rifts and disruptions pointed to a bad end for the colony, yet neither British officials nor Kenya's white settlers were ready to accept the situation and make the necessary adjustments. In Kenya, white migrants still envisioned themselves as hardy pioneers. The Australian Christine McFarland, who migrated with her husband in 1935, was initially "a bit scared of conditions and of wild animals," but she set to work, helping her husband "dig out" the land and planting a large English-style garden. Later, McFarland's daughter dubbed her mother a "true pioneer."

Despite temporary "peace" in Kenya, continuing frontier violence would eventually lead to the Mau Mau Emergency or Mau Mau Rebellion, terms that became only too familiar to people living in Western nations. Americans soon understood that the term *Mau Mau* meant an anti-white resistance movement with nationalist overtones. The roots of Mau Mau were deep in frontier Kenya's history. Had white Kenyans been listening during the 1920s and 1930s, rather than pushing Britain for independence under white rule, they would have known even then that black resistance was growing. Many types of black Kenyans had what Charity Waciuma later called a "deep sense of grievance" in their hearts.[83] Revolutionaries included black male and female squatters farming white land that had once been under the control of their kin or tribes;[84] male and female laborers paid about one-fifth of British laborers; even young, mission-educated black men and women who had a variety of reasons. One educated women who became a soldier, Wambui Waiyaki Otieno, remembered that members of her family had long resisted the British. In 1892, her great-grandfather, who was arrested, mistreated, and exiled, enjoined his people: "You must never surrender one inch of our soil to foreigners, for if you do so, future children will die of starvation." She planned to follow their lead.[85]

In addition, it would take escalating violence—revolution and Mau Maus—to convince white settlers and white authorities that black Kenyans were fed up with white pioneers, that they wanted their lands back as well as the right to rule themselves. In 1952, freedom fighters—including women combatants, spies, smugglers, and suppliers—attacked whites, bringing the harsh reprisal of European troops on themselves.[86] The calamitous and bloody state of emergency was not resolved until 1960, when the British government agreed that Kenya would have its independence as a black African nation, rather than a multiracial one. Black Kenyans' dream turned into reality in 1963 when Kenya proclaimed its status as an independent nation.

Conclusion

Clearly, frontiers were not quiet and peaceful, nor were they good places for people seeking calm lifestyles. Altercations of one kind or another existed throughout frontier periods. Rancor and violent outbursts were common. Today, the American West and free Kenya in the early twenty-first century continue to cope with the legacy of American Manifest Destiny or of British imperialism. Two momentous aspects of colonialism were outright violence and more subtle bigotry, both of which cast a long shadow over the contemporary American West and Kenya. These features of colonial society cling tenaciously, causing disruption and ill-feeling years after the collapse of formal colonialism. It is one thing to reclaim a region or a country; quite another to erase the negative "product" of colonialism from them. Although the American West and Kenya may be post-colonial in spirit and law, they are not yet post-colonial in form.

CONCLUSION

WHAT, then, does this comparison of women settlers in the mid- to late-nineteenth-century American West and in early twentieth-century Kenya reveal? Are these women's experiences and the frontiers on which they lived too disparate to be worthy of comparison, or do the similarities outweigh the differences, thus demonstrating something useful regarding frontier growth and the colonialist ideas that underwrote it? The answer is that the parallels between women in the two regions were not only numerous, but the occurrence of so many similarities in diverse situations makes the resemblances even more remarkable.

Rather than emerging as exceptional and even unique, the West, at least with regard to its women, was analogous to the Kenyan frontier. Perhaps most importantly, comparisons demonstrate that white peoples' social constructions of gender and race stayed largely the same over a one-hundred-year period, and remained consistent in frontier regions lying thousands of miles away from each other. Ideas of gender and race often determined women's opportunities and influenced their responses. As a result, contemporary problems that hark back to Manifest Destiny in the American West or imperialism in Kenya are not peculiar to either region.

Contrasting women on two frontiers also has demonstrated that race and gender, and to a lesser degree social class, influenced the way women behaved in more matters than did a frontier's location, its indigenous peoples, or its time period. Contrasts and comparisons have also supplied data concerning women's lives on the American and Kenyan frontiers, and have begun to answer larger questions, including the degree to which white women supported and spread imperialist doctrines and policies. Both regions also underwent certain changes over time. Notably, slavery was prohibited and migrants of color increased in number.

More specifically, looking first at *philosophy*, it is clear that the American West and colonial Kenya became frontiers because of white expansionist beliefs, called Manifest Destiny in the West and imperialism in Kenya. This ideology preached that Providence intended white people to emigrate to lands already inhabited by others, carrying with them their "superior" ways. Even if women migrated to help themselves rather than to help others, they still brought "enlightenment" and served as models of Western civilization. Because white society of the time charged women in particular with maintaining virtue and supporting the spread of churches and schools, white women settlers felt uniquely prepared for the task of colonizing. Thus, white women migrated to the West and to Kenya bearing with them a "genteel conceit," a belief that they could bring superior civilization to the residents of these regions.

Clearly, white women judged indigenous peoples inferior to themselves and very much in need of "uplifting." Consequently, rather than using their journeys to learn more about the people among whom they would live, most women clung to their original prejudices. White women migrating to the American West had more contact with indigenous peoples, which led to more conflict than on Kenya-bound routes. At the same time, white women's racial attitudes biased them against all peoples of color. White female migrants thought little of women settlers of color, even though they were also frontier newcomers. Rather than getting to know these women, white women helped segregate and internally colonize them.

Female settlers of color also harbored prejudice against white women. This may have been well deserved, for white women appear to be the only group who attempted to force their ways on others. Women of color, who relocated largely seeking economic and other opportunities, found themselves in an amorphous position between white and indigenous women. Discriminatory policies and segregation made it difficult for them to maximize the possibilities that had attracted them to a particular frontier.

Many, but not all, indigenous women also appear to have disliked or feared white women. Some of them got close to female missionaries, teachers, and nurses, for whom they expressed respect or even affection, and some converted to Christianity joyfully, but others resisted learning about white religion and culture. In the American West, a Yankton Sioux woman, ZitkalaŜa, remembered her white teacher as a "well-meaning, ignorant woman who was inculcating in our hearts her superstitious ideas." ZitkalaŜa also came to understand her mother's seeming ambivalence. For instance, the mother allowed her daughter to attend a white-run Indian school, but "sent a curse" upon the whites who had disrupted her family, her life, and her culture. ZitkalaŜa explained that although her mother "meant always to give up her own customs," she ended up making "only compromises."[1]

A similar split existed among black Kenyan women. Some sided with whites, learning what they could from them, whereas others resented the impact of white colonization. Many of those who saw their family members scattered, their cultures disrupted, and their people demeaned usually held a view of white women that was tinged with bitterness. A Kikuyu woman, Charity Waciuma, got to the core of the matter: "But worse than the stealing of the land, worse than the failure of communication, was the lack of human respect."[2]

In turning to the second element of a frontier—*place*—important variations become noticeable between the American West and Kenya as physical regions. The two frontiers lay in different hemispheres, peaked in different centuries, and involved racially different indigenous peoples. In addition, the West was more accessible to farm families and the working classes. Because Kenya demanded a substantial capital investment it was more attractive, at least during the early years, to the middle and upper classes. As a result, the American

West drew far more settlers than did Kenya. In 1870, approximately halfway through the period examined here, the Plains state of Nebraska alone counted over 122,000 white settlers and nearly 800 black settlers. In 1931, at about the same point in the migration to Kenya, slightly over 14,000 Europeans, or whites, as well as over 26,000 Asian Indians born outside the colony resided in Kenya.[3]

Despite these differences, significant physical resemblances between the two places existed. The American West and Kenya were vast tracts of land with varied climatic zones, including plains, desert, and rainy areas. Eras—meaning time periods of frontiers—were not as important as they might have been, given that indigenous peoples in the West and in Kenya were in preindustrial phases of development when settlers began to arrive in force. Also, migrants to both frontiers spoke primarily English and included a large proportion of women. A sizeable number of people of color also migrated to the American West and to Kenya. In addition, both regions had indigenous populations who resisted encroachment by settlers. This created frontier conditions, that is, a geographical area where two or more groups of people confronted each other and fought for dominance of the area.

Comparing only white women settlers in relation to place, clear parallels emerge regarding the way these women adapted. Largely because of prescribed roles and societal constructions of gender, white women viewed frontiers through different lenses than did men. Yet women, whether in the nineteenth-century American West or twentieth-century Kenya, seemed to have remarkably similar perspectives. One of their maxims was to live crudely when they had to and rely on cultural borrowing when necessary, but to return to their known ways as soon as possible. As a result, white women settlers in the West and in Kenya were alike in the manner in which they approached frontier process. Although they were half a world and half a century away from each other, women migrated for similar reasons, undertook equivalent preparations, and on arrival coped with comparable situations. All of these were true of Susan Magoffin, the wife of an army officer in Santa Fe, New Mexico, during the mid-1840s, and of Helen Kirk, the wife of the governor in the far-flung British outpost of Zanzibar during the 1890s. Moreover, whether regarding towns and cities, housing, social class, or land and labor systems, white women thought much alike.

Two additional white precepts concern frontier place. White people expected very different behavior from indigenes than they did from themselves. Inhabitants of a frontier were supposed to give up their ways entirely and adopt the new, whether they found them useful or not. ZitkalaŜa doubted that many whites ever "paused to question whether real life or long-lasting death lies beneath this semblance of civilization."[4] The other principle was to change a frontier place in a physical way. No matter how scenic or unyielding it was, white women wanted to bring physical landscapes in harmony with their own values and aesthetic standards. If their frontier was not already a "white man's country" when they arrived, they intended to make it one as soon as possible.

Meanwhile, female migrants of color made their own adaptations to the frontier. In this endeavor, the methods that women of color used were very close to those of white women. They, too, initially lived in a rough manner and borrowed what they needed, but gradually reestablished their own forms—such as housing and religious practices—as soon as they could. Also like white women, those of color accepted the realities of place, drew on those around them for support, and tried to maintain and preserve their own cultures.

In the third phase of a frontier, *process*, white women participated actively, proving themselves effective colonizers. Working in missions, schoolrooms, and kitchens, white women colonized the minds of indigenes. Although individual men also appeared in missions and schoolrooms, men as a group contributed more in the way of military might and enforcement to keep inhabitants in line physically and legally. The female talent was that of subtle subversion, of almost casually instilling white ideas among black men, women, and children.

Female migrants of color tended to be on the receiving end of frontier process. In rural and urban areas, they lived in separate areas from whites. In paid employment, they found themselves limited to restricted endeavors; for example, domestic work for African American women in the American West and shopkeeping for Asian Indian women in Kenya. Although some women of color were hurt by the white structure, others showed themselves to be people of creativity in developing resistance techniques. Rather than being passive recipients, women of color wielded a considerable amount of personal agency.

Regarding the fourth element of a frontier—*product*—white women were not satisfied with what they helped create. For one thing, they soon discovered that the outside world increasingly criticized them. For another, indigenous peoples often had little respect for them. In addition, white women settlers had to live on a daily basis with violence and racist practices that not only restricted indigenes, but white women as well. Some white women gradually saw connections between the colonization by gender that they experienced and the colonization by race that they imposed on indigenes. When dissatisfied, women often blamed white men, citing them for selfishness and hunger for power.

Additionally, calls for reform came from settlers of color and indigenes. An understanding of product also helps explain why American Indians and Hispanics continued fighting for rights and recognition, whereas black Kenyans were able to reconquer their country. Besides the will and determination of black Kenyans, several other factors explain the disparity. Despite the efforts of white women, white society never took permanent root in Kenya as it did in the American West. In Kenya, white culture remained uneasily layered on top of black culture, whereas in the West, whites took over the region and its peoples, purposely trying to destroy indigenous culture and to establish themselves as the "native" society. In Kenya, numbers of whites were far less than those of blacks, but in the West whites were so numerous that they broke up and scattered groups of Indians and Hispanics, often isolating them on reservations or in barrios where they quietly resisted by clinging to their beliefs and cultures. As a consequence, despite white women's efforts in Kenya, cultural persistence was found throughout the country. Although white women worked hard to colonize indigenous Kenyans, large pockets of black Kenyan culture and society continued to exist, even in supposedly white Nairobi. As intrusive and disruptive as white women were, black women continued to live their own lives and maintain numerous aspects of their culture, including polygymy, female circumcision, wives' separate huts, and control of women-grown crops or other products.[5]

Other larger forces interfered with white women's colonizing efforts in Kenya. White settlers became more dependent than western-ers on indigenous labor, partly because of the widespread myth that white people could not labor as hard or long in hot climates as could black Kenyans. Kenya lay far from Great Britain and had its own sub-form of government, whereas the West's boundaries were contiguous to the United States and its government was the same. Kenyan settlers had far less voice in their own governance than did western settlers, who eventually became full-fledged American citizens and voters. Although westerners felt somewhat alienated from the federal government in Washington, D.C., they had more clout than Kenyan settlers in local matters that immediately affected them.

In 1963, black Kenyans took a huge stride by declaring Kenya's independence, yet peoples in both the American West and in Kenya continue to endure the effects of Manifest Destiny and imperialism. Because the frontier structure, especially racism, permeated all aspects of life, dismantling it is proving to be an enormous undertaking. Even in the twenty-first century, aspects of white behavior and values suffuse daily life so that whites and peoples of color, in the American West and in Kenya, act in ways that propagate colonial systems and attitudes. Because colonialism had the goal of one culture for all peoples, its policies blurred racial and ethnic lines at the same time that these groups were kept institutionally in their "place."[6] For example, in the American West members of such groups as American Indians, Hispanics, and Asians still tend to rank near the bottom of the white-generated social scale. Also, they are often marginalized geographic-ally in urban areas; culturally in such activities such as sports, the symphony, and local celebrations; and economically in jobs and profes-sions. On a more positive note, however, many westerners hold up harmonious pluralism as an ideal at the same time that peoples of color demand fuller rights and responsibilities.

In Kenya, remnants of colonialism are also seen. Many Africans speak with an English accent and use English slang. These practices seem innocuous enough, but they indicate that black Kenyans watch a great deal of English television and read English-style newspapers. Also, perusing the shelves in any Nairobi bookstore reveals that black urban Kenyans purchase a great many "white" books and magazines, meaning that whites still shape numerous texts and discourses in Kenya. In these everyday matters, black Kenyans perpetuate their historical connection to what was the British empire. The alternative appears to be American culture, especially television serials, sports figures and teams, and popular music. This is not meant to denigrate such interests, only to note that they help keep the African or black Kenyan culture submerged. Looking closer, however, it becomes apparent that important exceptions to this submersion also exist. In Kenya, black people still consciously resist Westernization. Another exception is seen in rural villages where black Kenyans maintain their own customs and clothing. Still another is found in tourism, where a black Kenyan identity and history surfaces, although not always in unadulterated form.

Because frontier product persists in the American West and Kenya in these and other significant ways, it seems premature to call these areas postcolonial societies. They are postcolonial only in the sense that formal colonial systems are defunct. As the literary scholar Edward Said puts it, "the people who were oppressed before are often still oppressed, though perhaps in different ways."[7]

In addition to the above, three methodological issues deserve discussion. The first concerns postmodernism. Deconstructionists have brilliantly analyzed colonial discourse, giving researchers and lay-persons alike an enlarged understanding of the implications of colonial rhetoric for colonial reality. These scholars have demonstrated ways in which white colonialists constructed images of the "other," then employed them as rationalizations for racist policies and programs. Still, these scholars are studying white history and casting whites in the role of actors. If one shifts sides and takes another point of view, it becomes clear that for peoples of color, whites were the "other."

What did black Kenyans say and feel about white colonialism and about themselves? The deconstructionist scholar Gayatri Chakravorty Spivak has noted the difficulties involved in finding the subaltern voice and challenged scholars to be creative in identifying sources.[8] In this case, it is useful to consider modern black writers, such as Ngũgĩ Wa Thiong'o, who draw on the past and present to give a black Kenyan perspective on colonization. Also, black Kenyans, including W. R. Ochieng' and B. A. Ogot, have written textbooks and other works that indicate what black Kenyans are being taught about their colonial past. In addition, a wealth of material, much of it oral, exists regarding black Kenyans and other Kenyans of color, more of which can be collected. However it is to come about, the black construction of whites as "others" must occur to round out the colonialist picture and its interpretation.

This leads to the second methodological point, that *all* peoples of color, whether migrants or indigenes, must be taken into account. As new scholarship multiplies, this approach will become increasingly possible. Even now, scholars are beginning to envision colonial history as far more than the flat figures of white colonizers pitted against indigenous colonizees. Rather, in the West and in Kenya, numerous groups interacted and shaped historical developments. Enlarged insight comes, for example, from discovering that American Indians were prejudiced against African Americans, even adopting anti-miscegenation policies to discourage members of the two groups from marrying. Knowing that black Kenyan fathers usually disliked the idea of their daughters marrying Asian Indian men opens additional ways of thinking about discrimination in Kenya.

The third concern is the potential contributions of other approaches, notably world-systems theory and bio-history, or ethological history. According to the first of these outlooks, the colonial "worlds" of the American West and of Kenya experienced parallel trends and cycles, including commodification (exchange based on currency), state formation, and the establishment of hegemonic power largely through political and economic power.[9] During the time periods considered by this study, the West and Kenya experienced like stages: migration from outside, conflict, colonization, and continuing resistance on overt and covert levels. These systems appeared to have a coherent pattern, despite location, time period, and types of peoples involved. Similarly, by drawing on bio-history, it might be suggested that genes play a role in the evolution of culture, that human beings have certain biologically defined characteristics. World-systems theory reinforces bio-history, demonstrating that people come to similar conclusions in different times and situations, which indicates that people, horses, and other complicated beings have some similar qualities. For instance, it appears that people of any group—defined by race, class, or other features—prefer to dominate others.[10] Certainly, striving for true equality has not characterized human history, even in the supposedly democratic American West or in the multiculturally oriented world of the twenty-first century. Rather, people are much like horses. Due to characteristics such as age or assertiveness, certain horses rule others. Although a human caretaker can temporarily disrupt a horse hierarchy by adding or subtracting members of a herd, the horses will rapidly reestablish what they consider to be an appropriate rank order. Herds of horses at boarding stables become adept at this, either quickly letting a new arrival know his or her place, or efficiently rearranging themselves after a horse's departure.[11]

Colonialism is much the same. Colonizers arrive (including peoples of color), inhabitants protest, and a struggle ensues for rank in the new order. Over time, the pecking order makes constant adjustments; some of this occurs as people arrive or vie for power, others as people leave or die. The important point is that horses and humans both respond to an inner need to dominate, or, if they happen to be on the lower end, to resist such domination.[12] In other words, a history of colonialism is a history of opposition to colonial rule.

But why, as noted in the introduction and throughout, were colonizers so often white and the colonized so often peoples of color? In Kenya, an Akamba woman, Berida Ndambuki, explains the situation in terms of education rather than race: "I really wish I had gone to school so I could read and speak English, be as smart as those who have. White people have become so clever, but it's not that they are white, just that they have education."[13] Of course, she is largely correct. The biologist Jared Diamond, who studies history from the perspective of science, agrees with Berida that color was not the determining factor in colonial dominance, any more than color influences horse hierarchies. Nor was white colonialism underwritten by unusual ability and intelligence. Instead, Diamond describes something of a circle. Ancient peoples of color, notably in Africa, devised basic principles and elements of culture that made their way to Eurasia. Over time, those principles and elements developed into the technology that Europeans eventually turned against their very inventors to conquer them. Far from celebrating the achievements of Europeans and their domination over others, Diamond views the benefits of "modern civilization" as mixed. He stresses instead that different environments allowed some people to develop at a rapid rate and others at a slower pace.[14]

For Diamond, the ability to produce food led to population density, technology, literacy, political systems, and germs to which others were vulnerable. He explains that sub-Saharan Africa had a deficit of domesticated plants and animals, as well as having a smaller land area than Europe. Finally, Diamond says, "the remaining factor behind Africa's slower rate of post-Pleistocene development compared with Eurasia's is the different orientation of the main axes of these continents," which controlled the rate of movement of plants, animals, and people from one area to another. Thus, Diamond believes that what he calls "real estate" rather than race underwrote white colonization. Instead of arguing for biologically defined roles for human beings, Diamond maintains that, despite unnecessary repeated mistakes, humans are able to learn from their pasts to improve their futures.[15]

Additionally, it must be remembered that white people colonized not just peoples of color, but other whites as well. The Asia scholar Benedict Anderson comments that the British empire included the countries of Australia, Canada, Ireland, New Zealand, and South Africa; in some cases, they remained colonies even after their population became largely white. Anderson contends that colonialism originated in "ideologies of *class*, rather than those of nation." From rulers claiming divinity to aristocrats threatened by "democracy," upper-class people supported the concept of innate superiority: theirs over lesser white people and that of all white people over those of color. In Anderson's view, colonial empires reinforced "domestic aristocratic bastions, since they appeared to confirm on a global, modern stage antique conceptions of power and privilege." Although racism was an active element of empire, colonialism had more to do with social class than is usually recognized.

What do Diamond's and Anderson's controversial theories demonstrate? And where do horses fit in? It seems fair to say that all the evidence is not yet in regarding colonialism in general and women in particular. In addition, the skill of synthesizing expanded types of evidence, including the oral and anthropological, is still developing. In these days of globalization, there is much to be gained by considering different sources, theories, and methodological approaches when looking beyond national boundaries and attempting to recognize historical similarities to redirect the course of history.[16]

There are still questions raised or implied that must be left for twenty-first century people to confront. For instance, it is highly significant that a number of white women settlers in Kenya and the American West criticized colonialist programs and policies at the very same time they effectively colonized the minds of indigenous peoples. Are people of the twenty-first century doing the same thing by designing policies that aim for one goal yet achieve another? Are people who believe themselves to be well meaning critiquing racial and gender prejudice, yet putting in place policies that separate types of people in new ways and perhaps more widely than ever before? Are women of color discontent with the very reforms that are intended to help them?

Certainly, the New York World Trade Center tragedy of September 11, 2001, and the ensuing war against terrorism gives these issues a new immediacy, for the world is growing more volatile and dangerous at the same time that its peoples are becoming more divided. If twenty-first-century leaders and their nations choose to pursue it, comparative history gives them the ability to answer the above and other related questions. It also offers a way of understanding—and perhaps of altering—the historical conditions that underlie the rage that pervades the modern world.

Notes

Introduction

1. Ian Tyrrell, "American Exceptionalism in an Age of International History," *American Historical Review* 96 (October 1991): 1031–55; and Michael Kammen, "The Problem of American Exceptionalism: A Reconsideration," *American Quarterly* 45 (March 1993): 1–43.

2. John Harmon McElroy, *Finding Freedom: America's Distinctive Cultural Formation* (Carbondale: Southern Illinois University Press, 1989), xii–xiii. See also Byron E. Shafer, ed., *Is America Different? A New Look at American Exceptionalism* (New York: Oxford, 1991). That western women are similar to those in other countries is demonstrated in Janet L. Finn, *Tracing the Veins: Of Copper, Culture, and Community from Butte to Chuquicamata* (Berkeley: University of California Press, 1998).

3. E. A. Hammel, "The Comparative Method in Anthropological Perspective," *CSSH* 22 (April 1980): 145–55; Bernard S. Cohn, "History and Anthropology: The State of Play," *Comparative Studies in Science and History* (April 1980): 198–221; Kathryn Kish Sklar, "A Call for Comparisons," *American Historical Review* 95 (October 1990): 1109–14; and Carl J. Guarneri, "Reconsidering C. Vann Woodward's *The Comparative Approach to American History*," *Reviews in American History* 23 (September 1995): 552–63. Guarani states on p. 5 that "comparing American history internationally is an idea whose time has returned."

4. Peter Kolchin, "Comparing American History," *Reviews in American History* 10 (December 1982): 64–81.

5. Robert F. Berkhofer, Jr. *A Behavioral Approach to Historical Analysis* (New York: Free Press, 1969); David Harry Miller and Jerome O. Steffen, eds., *The Frontier: Comparative Studies* (Norman: University of Oklahoma Press, 1977); George M. Frederickson, "Giving a Comparative Dimension to American History: Problems and Opportunities," *Journal of Interdisciplinary History* 40 (Summer 1985): 108–110; Richard Hogan, "Carnival and Caucus: A Typology for Comparative Frontier History," *Social Science History* 11 (Summer 1987): 139–67; and A. A. Van Den Braembussche, "Historical Explanation and Comparative Method: Towards a Theory of the Society," *History and Theory* 28 (February 1989): 1–24.

6. For discussion, see George M. Fredrickson, "Comparative History," 457–73, in Michael Kammen, ed., *The Past Before Us: Contemporary Historical Writing in the United States* (Ithaca, NY: Cornell University Press, 1980), and Frederickson, "Giving a Comparative Dimension to American History," 107–10; Maurice Mandelbaum, "Some Forms and Uses of Comparative History," *American Studies International* 18 (Winter 1980): 19–34; Raymond Grew, "The Case for Comparing Histories," *American Historical Review* 85 (October 1980): 763–78, and Grew, "The Comparative Weakness of American History," *Journal of Interdisciplinary History* 16 (Summer 1985): 87–101; and Michael P. Malone, "Beyond the Last Frontier: Toward a New Approach to Western American History," *Western Historical Quarterly* 20 (November 1989): 409–27.

7. Theda Skocpol and Margaret Somers, "The Uses of Comparative History in Macrosocial Inquiry," *Comparative Studies in Science and History* 22 (April 1980): 174–97; and David Thelen, "Of Audiences, Borderlands, and Comparisons: Toward the Internationalization of American History," *Journal of American History* 79 (September 1992): 444–45.

8. Stanton W. Green, "The Agricultural Colonization of Temperate Forest Habitats: An Ecological Model," in William W. Savage, Jr. and Stephen I. Thompson, eds., *The Frontier: Comparative Studies* (Norman: University of Oklahoma Press, 1979), 69–103; and Thomas D. Hall, "World-Systems Analysis: A Small Sample from a Large Universe," in Thomas D. Hall, ed., *A World-Systems Reader* (Lanham, MD: Rowman and Littlefield, 2000), 3–28. For further discussion, see Christopher Chase-Dunn and Thomas D. Hall, *Rise and Demise: Comparing World-Systems* (Boulder, CO: Westview, 1997); and Thomas D. Hall, "Frontiers, and Ethnogenesis, and World-Systems: Rethinking the Theories," 271–88, in Hall, *World Systems Reader*. Also helpful are Jerry H. Bentley, *Old World Encounters: Cross-Cultural Exchanges in Pre-Modern Times* (Oxford, England: Oxford University Press, 1995), and Richard J. Perry, *From Time Immemorial: Indigenous Peoples and State Systems*. (Austin: University of Texas Press, 1996).

9. An excellent discussion of different types of world-systems and their comparison is found in Chase-Dunn and Hall, *Rise and Demise*, 27–58, 200–31. For display and rituals as methods of separating groups of people, see Richard E. Leakey and Roger Lewin, *Origins* (New York: E. P. Dutton, 1977). That apes act in a similar fashion to humans can be seen in Jane Goodall, *The Chimpanzees*

of Gombe: Patterns of Behavior (Cambridge, MA: Belknap Press of Harvard University Press, 1986); and Blake Edgar, Ancestor: In Search of Human Origins (New York: Villard Books, 1994).

10. Walter Burkert, Creation of the Sacred: Tracks of Biology in Early Religions (Cambridge, MA: Harvard University Press, 1996), 2–3.

11. Abel A. Alves, Brutality and Benevolence: Human Ethology, Culture, and the Birth of Mexico (Westport, CT: Greenwood, 1996), 1–16, 233–37. Quote is on 235.

12. Dianne Hales, Just Like a Woman: How Gender Science is Redefining What Makes Us Female (New York: Bantam, 2000), 239–58.

13. See Erik H. Erikson, Young Man Luther: A Study in Psychoanalysis and History (New York: Norton, 1958).

14. Three excellent examples are Mary Poovey, Uneven Development: The Ideological Work of Gender in Mid-Victorian England (Chicago, IL: University of Chicago Press, 1988); Gayatri Chakravorty Spivak, In Other Worlds: Essays in Cultural Politics (NY: Metheun, 1987); and Barbara Maria Stafford, Voyage into Substance: Art, Science, Nature, and the Illustrated Travel Account, 1760–1840 (Cambridge, MA: MIT University Press, 1987).

15. For understanding bio-history, see Richard Leakey and Roger Lewin, Origins Reconsidered: In Search of What Makes Us Human (New York: Doubleday, 1992), esp. 203–36.

16. Paola Cavalieri and Peter Singer, eds., The Great Ape Project: Equality beyond Humanity (New York: St. Martin's, 1993).

17. Richard Dawkins, River Out of Eden: A Darwinian View of Life (New York: Basic Books, 1995), 43.

18. Robert M. Miller, Understanding the Ancient Secrets of the Horse's Mind (Neenah, WI: Russell Meerdinck, 1999), 16–18, 41–43; Jackie Budd, Reading the Horse's Mind (London: Howell Book House, 1996), 46–47; and Léonie Marshall, Your Horse's Mind (Wiltshire, England: Crowood, 1996), 45–54.

19. Miller, Understanding the Ancient Secrets of the Horse's Mind, 18, 48. See also Stephen Budiansky, The Nature of Horses (New York: Free Press, 1997), 63–65, 91–101.

20. Tom Ainslie and Bonnie Ledbetter, The Body Language of Horses (New York: William Morrow, 1980), 85; Henry Blake, Thinking With Horses (North Pomfret, VT: Trafalgar Square, 1993), 61–63; and Budiansky, Nature of Horses, 89–91.

21. Budd, Reading the Horse's Mind, 58–62, and Blake, Thinking With Horses, 128–43.

22. Moyra Williams, Horse Psychology (London: J. A. Allen, 1976), 143–44; Budd, Reading the Horse's Mind, 102–19; and Marshall, Your Horse's Mind, 55–57.

23. Author's observations of Dandi Bar Junior (a.k.a. Goldy) and Mac the Star, 1995 to 2002, Muncie, Indiana. For horses' emotions, see Blake, Thinking With Horses, 144–58. A discussion of bonding is in Budiansky, Nature of Horses, 81–89.

24. James C. Scott, Domination and the Arts of Resistance: Hidden Transcripts (New Haven, CT: Yale University Press, 1990), 58.

25. Ibid., xii, 109.

26. Klaus Immelmann and Colin Beer, *A Dictionary of Ethology* (Cambridge, MA: Harvard University Press, 1989), 13–14, 133–34.

27. Marjorie R. Dilley, *British Policy in Kenya Colony* (New York: Thomas Nelson, 1966), v; Jürgen Osterhammel, *Colonialism: A Theoretical Overview* (Princeton: Markus Wiener, 1997), 22; Gregory H. Nobles, *American Frontiers: Cultural Encounters and Continental Conquest* (New York: Hill and Wang, 1997), 14; Walter Nugent, "Frontiers and Empires in the Late Nineteenth Century," in Walter Nugent and Martin Ridge, eds., *The American West: The Reader* (Bloomington: Indiana University Press, 1999), 40; and Patricia Nelson Limerick, "Going West and Ending Up Global," *WHQ* 32 (Spring 2001), 17.

28. One definition is in Gus Deveneaux, "The Frontier in Recent African History," *The International Journal of African Historical Studies* 11 (1978): 68. For the importance of women, see A. J. Christopher, "Northern Africa and the United States: Comparison of Pastoral Frontiers," *Journal of the West* 20 (January 1981): 52–59.

29. Benedict Anderson, *Imagined Communities,* 2d ed. (London: Verso, 1991), 144. In his book *The Spectre of Comparisons: Nationalism, Southeast Asia and the World* (London: Verso, 2000), Benedict discusses the relation of nationalism to imperial ventures.

30. Ngũgĩ Wa Thiong'o, *Decolonising the Mind: The Politics of Language in African Literature* (Nairobi: East African Educational Publisher, 1981).

31. Margaret Strobel, *European Women and the Second British Empire* (Bloomington: Indiana University Press, 1991), 1–10. That white women did not lose imperial holdings is in Helen Callaway, *Gender, Culture and Empire: European Women in Colonial Nigeria* (Urbana: University of Illinois Press, 1987), 3–29.

32. The historian Walter Nugent dates the high period of western development as 1848 to 1889, in Walter Nugent, *Into the West: The Story of Its People* (New York: Knopf, 1999), 54–55.

33. E. S. Atieno-Odhiambo, "The Formative Years: 1945–1955," in B. A. Ogot and W. R. Ochieng', *Decolonization and Independence in Kenya, 1940–1993* (London: James Currey, 1995), 25–47; and Strobel, *European Women and the Second British Empire*, xii.

34. William G. Robbins, *Colony and Empire: The Capitalist Transformation of the American West* (Lawrence: University Press of Kansas, 1994), 145–47.

35. Walter Nugent, "Frontiers and Empires in the Late Nineteenth Century," 161–63, in Patricia Nelson Limerick, Clyde A. Milner II, and Charles E. Rankin, eds., *Trails: Toward a New Western History* (Lawrence: University Press of Kansas, 1991). Also helpful is Robin W. Winks, "Australia, the Frontier, and the Tyranny of Distance," 135–63, in Philip Wayne Powell, W. J. Eccles, Warren Dean, Leonard Thompson, and Robin W. Winks, *Essays on Frontiers in World History* (College Station: Texas A & M University Press, 1983).

36. Dietrich Gerhard, "The Frontier in Comparative View," *Comparative Studies in Science and History* 1 (March 1959): 205–29.

37. Richard White, "A Commentary," in Robert Borofsky, ed., *Remembrance of Pacific Pasts: An Invitation to Remake History* (Honolulu: University of Hawaii Press, 2000), 170.

38. Frederick Cooper and Ann Laura Stoler, eds., *Tensions of Empire: Colonial Cultures in a Bourgeois World* (Berkeley: University of California Press, 1997), 8–9.

39. Gayatri Chakravorty Spivak, *A Critique of Postcolonial Reason: Toward a History of the Vanishing Present* (Cambridge, MA: Harvard University Press, 1999), 269–75, 281–83.

40. Especially useful is Cynthia Salvadori, *Through Open Doors: A View of Asian Cultures in Kenya*, (Nairobi: Paperchase, 1996).

41. "Introduction," in Joan Wallach Scott, ed., *Feminism in History* (Oxford, England: Oxford University Press, 1996), 7–9.

42. Michael G. Kenny, "A Place for Memory: The Interface between Individual and Collective History," *Comparative Studies in Science and History* 41 (July 1999): 420–21.

43. Berida Ndambuki and Claire C. Robertson, *"We Only Come Here to Struggle": Stories from Berida's Life* (Bloomington: Indiana University Press, 2000), xi–xv.

44. Thomas R. Trautman, "Editorial Foreword," *Comparative Studies in Science and History* 41 (July 1999): 417.

45. For folktales, see Eric Hobsbawm and Terence Ranger, *The Invention of Tradition* (Cambridge: Cambridge University Press, 1992).

46. For global trade systems, see Andre Gunder Frank, *ReORIENT: Global Economy in the African Age* (Berkeley: University of California Press, 1998). Quote is in W. R. Ochieng', *A History of Kenya* (Nairobi: Macmillan Kenya, 1992), 71.

47. Igor Kopytoff, *The African Frontier: The Reproduction of Traditional African Societies* (Bloomington: Indiana University Press, 1987), 7–12.

48. Richard W. Etulain, *Re-Imaging the Modern American West: A Century of Fiction, History, and Art* (Tucson: University of Arizona Press, 1996); Richard W. Slatta, *Comparing Cowboys and Frontiers* (Norman: University of Oklahoma Press, 1997), and Nugent, *Into the West*.

49. *Random House Webster's Dictionary* (New York: Random House, 1999), 266. See also Ladis K. D. Kristof, "The Nature of Frontiers and Boundaries," *Annals of the Association of American Geographers* 49 (September 1959): 269–82; and Fred M. Shelley and Colin Flint, "Geography, Place and World-Systems Analysis," 69–82, in Thomas D. Hall, ed., *A World-Systems Reader* (Lanham, MD: Rowman and Littlefield, 2000).

50. Robin W. Winks, "Region in Comparative Perspective," 13–35, in William G. Robbins, Robert J. Frank, and Richard E. Ross, eds., *Regionalism and the Pacific Northwest* (Corvallis: Oregon State University Press, 1983).

51. Walter Nugent, "Comparing Wests and Frontiers," 807–08, in Clyde A. Milner II, Carol A. O'Connor, and Martha A. Sandweiss, eds., *The Oxford History of the American West* (New York: Oxford University Press, 1994).

52. Ochieng', *History of Kenya*, 87.

Chapter 1

1. Margaret Strobel, *European Women and the Second British Empire* (Bloomington: Indiana University Press, 1991), viii–ix. For postcolonial theory, refer to Donna Landry and Gerald Maclean, eds., *The Spivak Reader: Selected Works of Gayatri Chakravorty Spivak* (New York: Routledge, 1996). A critique is Russell Jacoby, "Marginal Returns: The Trouble With Post-Colonial Theory," *Lingua Franca* 5 (September-October 1995): 30–37. Empires as historical realities are in Edward Ingram, *Empire Building and Empire-Builders* (London: Frank Cass, 1995), xiii–xvi.

2. Gideon S. Were and Derek A. Wilson, *East Africa Through a Thousand Years* (repr., Nairobi: Evans Brothers, 1996), 132; and W. R. Ochieng', *A History of Kenya* (repr., London: Macmillan Kenya, 1992), 87–100. Useful for details is Gordon H. Mungeam, *British Rule in Kenya, 1895–1912* (Oxford: Clarendon Press, 1966).

3. Elizabeth Furniss, *The Burden of History: Colonialism and the Frontier Myth in a Rural Canadian Community* (Vancouver, Canada: University of British Columbia Press, 1999), 63.

4. Benjamin F. Gue, "Early Iowa Reminiscences," *Iowa Historical Records* 16 (July 1900): 110; Leonard F. Parker, "Teachers in Iowa before 1858," *Lectures upon Early Leaders in the Professions in the Territory of Iowa, Delivered at Iowa City, 1894* (Iowa City: Iowa State Historical Society, 1894), 30; and Suzanne H. Schrems, "Teaching School on the Western Frontier: An Acceptable Occupation for Nineteenth-Century Women," *Montana* 37 (Summer 1987): 53–63.

5. Barbara Melosh, *"The Physician's Hand": Work, Culture, and Conflict in American Nursing* (Philadelphia: Temple University Press, 1982), 3–7; and Jean Todd, in Pioneer Daughters Collection, c. 1850 to 1955, South Dakota State Historical Research Center, Pierre (hereafter citied as SDSHRC).

6. Friede Van Dalsem, in Pioneer Daughters Collection, c. 1850 to 1955, SDSHRC, Pierre; and "Lavinia Goodyear Waterhouse," Pacific Grove (California) Heritage Society *Newsletter* (February/March 1989), unpaged.

7. Richard D. Wolff, *The Economics of Colonialism: Britain and Kenya, 1870–1930* (New Haven, CT: Yale University Press, 1974), 1–2; and John R. Godard, *Racial Supremacy being Studies in Imperialism* (Edinburgh, Scotland: Morton, 1905), 11, 216.

8. George M. Fredrickson, *White Supremacy: A Comparative Study in American and South African History* (New York: Oxford University Press, 1981), 7–13; and V. Y. Mudimbe, *The Idea of Africa* (Bloomington: Indiana University Press, 1994), 212–13.

9. Catherine Hall, *White, Male and Middle-Class: Explorations in Feminism and History* (New York: Routledge, 1992), 75–93; and Mary Poovey, *Uneven Development: The Ideological Work of Gender in Mid-Victorian England* (Chicago, IL: University of Chicago Press, 1988), 3–4, 164–201.

10. Frederick Freeman, *A Plea for Africa* (Philadelphia: Whetham, 1836), 69.

11. R. Coupland, *The British Antislavery Movement* (London: Butterworth, 1933), 22, 189, 201, 222.

12. Paul Tingay, *Seychelles* (London: New Holland, 1995), 19–20; and James Walvin, *Black Ivory: A History of British Slavery* (London: Harper Collins, 1992), 44–45, 306–7.

13. Andre Gunder Frank, *ReORIENT: Global Economy in the African Age* (Berkeley: University of California Press, 1998), 6–12.

14. Ronald Robinson and John Gallagher, *Africa and the Victorians: The Official Mind of Imperialism* (London: Macmillan, 1961), 1–3. See also R. Coupland, *The Exploitation of East Africa, 1856–1890* (London: Faber and Faber, 1939).

15. Rev. Oliver Prescott Hiller, *A Chapter on Slavery* (London: Hodson, 1860), 12.

16. M. P. K. Sorrenson, *Origins of European Settlement in Kenya* (Nairobi: Oxford University Press, 1968), 31; and Charles Miller, *The Lunatic Express* (London: Macmillan, 1971), 84–85.

17. Miller, *Lunatic Express*, 327–444.

18. Ochieng', *History of Kenya*, 91.

19. *The Taveta Chronicle*, No. 15, March 1899, 144.

20. Medical Department, "Miss M. Leonard inquires re medical work for a lady doctor in Kenya Colony," MOH/1/8056,1922, Kenya National Archives, Nairobi (hereafter cited as KNA, Nairobi).

21. Medical Department, "Application for a Post as a [Nursing] Sister," 1923, MOH/1/10081, KNA, Nairobi.

22. "Mrs. Andrew Odegaard," undated, Pioneer Daughter Collection, c. 1850 to 1955, SDSHRC, Pierre.

23. *Waterloo (Iowa) Courier*, 3 April 1860.

24. Mari Sandoz, *Old Jules Country* (New York: Hastings House, 1965), 300–301.

25. Quoted in H. Arnold Barton, *Letters from the Promised Land* (Minneapolis: University of Minnesota Press, 1975), 291.

26. *Ninth Census*, vol. 1: *Population and Social Statistics* (Washington, D.C.: Government Printing Office, 1872), 606, 686.

27. Bertha Josephson Anderson, "Autobiography," c. 1940, Montana Historical Society, Archives (hereafter cited as MHS).

28. Frieda Knobloch, *The Culture of Wilderness: Agriculture as Colonization in the American West* (Chapel Hill: University of North Carolina Press, 1–2, 18, 150–54.

29. Quoted in, Mary Baillie and George Baillie, "Recollections in the Form of a Duet," 1939, Wyoming State Archives, Museum, and Historical Department, Cheyenne (hereafter cited as WSAMHD).

30. Mark I. West, ed., *Westward to a High Mountain: The Colorado Writings of Helen Hunt Jackson* (Denver: Colorado Historical Society, 1994), 1–5.

31. Quote is in Richard D. Wolff, *The Economics of Colonialism: Britain and Kenya, 1870–1930* (New Haven, CT: Yale University Press, 1974), 134–35.

32. Lord and Lady Francis Scott, "Papers," 1919–1976, unnumbered microfilm, KNA, Nairobi.

33. For Blixen's story, see Judith Thurman, *Isak Dinesen: The Life of Karen Blixen* (New York: Penguin, 1982).

34. Miller, *Lunatic Express*, 336–37, 439.

35. For examples, see Charles Allen, ed., *Tales From the Dark Continent* (New York: St. Martin's Press, 1979); Elizabeth Watkins, *Oscar From Africa: The Biography of Oscar Ferris Watlins* (London: Radcliffe, 1995); and Scott, "Papers."

36. G. R. Morrison, *Mixed Farming in East Africa* (London: East Africa, 1935), 102, 108.

37. Provincial Commissioner, Ukamba Province, Land File, "Miss Plowman applies for land," 24 August 1908, DC/MKS.10S/1/5, KNA, Nairobi.

38. Examples are *The Kenya Annual and Directory, 1922* (Nairobi: Caxton, 1922); *Kenya* (Nairobi: Kenya Land Settlement Advisory Committee, 1924); *Kenya* (Nairobi: Kenya Empire Exhibition Council, 1924); and *New Homes, New Hopes in Kenya Colony* (Nairobi: Kenya Association, 1932).

39. Quote is from Etta C. Close, *A Woman Alone in Kenya, Uganda and the Belgian Congo* (London: Constable, 1924), 179–80. For Happy Valley, consult Nicholas Best, *Happy Valley: The Story of the English in Kenya* (Great Britain: Marlborough, 1996).

40. Examples are Anne McDonald, "African Roundabout, 1932–35," undated, Rhodes House Library, Oxford (hereafter cited as RHL); and Lady Evelyn C. Cobbold, *Kenya, The Land of Illusion* (London: Murray, 1935). Quoted in Daisy M. Chown, *Wayfaring in Africa: A Woman's Wandering from the Cape to Cairo* (London: Heath Cranton, 1927), 17.

41. Emma Pérez. *The Decolonial Imaginary: Writing Chicanas into History* (Bloomington: Indiana University Press, 1999), 4–7, 22–27. Also helpful is Leticia M. Garza-Falcón, *Gente Decente: A Borderlands Response to the Rhetoric of Dominance* (Austin: University of Texas Press, 1998).

42. See Erlinda Gonzalez-Berry and David R. Maciel, eds., *The Contested Homeland: A Chicano History of New Mexico* (Albuquerque: University of New Mexico Press, 2000).

43. Virginia M. Bouvier, *Women and the Conquest of California, 1542–1840: Codes of Silence* (Tucson: University of Arizona Press, 2001), 82–83. Also helpful are Erlinda Gonzales-Berry and David R. Maciel, eds., *Contested Homeland*.

44. Apolinaria Lorenzana, "Reminiscences," 1878, Bancroft Library, University of California, Berkeley (hereafter cited as BL). Also helpful are Salomé Hernández, "*Nueva Mexicanas* as Refugees and Reconquest Settlers, 1680–1696," and Janet Lecompte, "The Independent Women of Hispanic New Mexico, 1821–1846," both in Joan M. Jensen and Darlis A. Miller, eds., *New Mexico Women: Intercultural Perspectives* (Albuquerque: University of New Mexico Press, 1986), 41–70; Glenda Riley, *Building and Breaking Families in the American West* (Albuquerque: University of New Mexico Press, 1996), 18–19; and Albert L. Hurtado, *Intimate Frontiers: Sex, Gender, and Culture in Old California* (Albuquerque: University of New Mexico Press, 1999), 7–11. Spanish influence on Indians is in Charles C. Colley, "The Desert Shall Blossom: North African Influence on the American Southwest," *Western Historical Quarterly* 54 (July 1983): 277–90. For Mexican women during the twentieth century see Vicki Ruiz, *Out of the Shadows: Mexican Women in Twentieth Century America* (New

York: Oxford University Press, 1998), and Deena J. González, *Refusing the Favor: The Spanish-American Women of Santa Fe, 1820–1880* (New York: Oxford University Press).

45. For the legal system in *El Norte,* see Charles R. Cutter, *The Legal Culture of Northern New Spain, 1700–1810* (Albuquerque: University of New Mexico Press, 2001).

46. Eliza Byer Price, "Recollections of My Father, Samuel Dyer," 1905, University of Missouri Western History Manuscript Collection and State Historical Society of Missouri Manuscripts (hereafter cited as UMWHMC and SHSMM), Columbia; and interview with Esther Easter, in George P. Rawick, ed., *The American Slave* (Westport, CT: Greenwood, 1972), 7:90–91. For blacks, see William Loren Katz, *The Black West* (New York: Simon and Schuster, 1987) and *Black Pioneers: An Untold Story* (New York: Atheneum, 1999); and Quintard Taylor, *In Search of the Racial Frontier: African Americans in the American West, 1528–1990* (New York: Norton, 1998). Others sources can be found in Bruce Glasrud, *African Americans in the West: A Bibliography of Secondary Sources* (Alpine, TX: Center for Big Bend Studies, 1998).

47. Glen Schwendermann, "Nicodemus: Negro Haven on the Soloman," *Kansas Historical Quarterly* 34 (Spring 1968): 26. For Exodusters, see Nell Irvin Painter, *Exodusters: Black Migration to Kansas after Reconstruction* (New York: Knopf, 1977). Also useful is Taylor, *In Search of the Racial Frontier*, 136–138, 141–43, 213.

48. Delilah L. Beasley, *The Negro Trail Blazers of California* (Los Angeles: Times Mirror, 1919), 123, 173–78; "California Colored Women Trail Blazers," in Hallie Q. Brown, ed., *Homespun Heroines and Other Women of Distinction* (Xenia, OH: Aldine, 1926), 241–42; and Rudolph M. Lapp, *Blacks in Gold Rush California* (New Haven, CT: Yale University Press, 1977), 184. For other black women, see William Loren Katz, *Black Women of the Old West* (New York: Atheneum, 1995).

49. Kenneth W. Porter, "Negro Labor in the Western Cattle Industry," *Labor History* 10 (1969), 327; and Erwin N. Thompson, "The Negro Soldier and His Officers," in John M. Carroll, ed., *The Black Military Experience in the American West* (New York: Liveright, 1971), 182.

50. Madeline Yuan-yin Hsu, *Dreaming of Gold, Dreaming of Home: Transnationalism and Migration between the United States and South China, 1882–1943* (Stanford, CA: Stanford University Press, 2002). For specific examples, see Mary Paik Lee, *Quiet Odyssey: A Pioneer Korean Woman in America* (Seattle: University of Washington Press, 1990); and Barbara Yasui, "The Nissei in Oregon, 1834–1940," *Oregon Historical Quarterly* 76 (1975): 225–57. Also helpful is Ronald Takaki, *Strangers from a Different Shore: A History of Asian Americans* (New York: Penguin, 1989); Sucheng Chan, Douglas Henry Daniels, Mario T. García, and Terry P. Wilson, eds., *Peoples of Color in the American West* (Lexington, MA: D. C. Heath, 1994); and Benson Tong, *Unsubmissive Women: Chinese Prostitutes in Nineteenth-Century San Francisco* (Norman: University of Oklahoma Press, 1996).

51. Cynthia Salvadori, *We Came in Dhows,* 3 vols. (Nairobi: Paperchase, 1996), 1:140; and Andrew Fedders and Cynthia Salvadori, *Peoples and Cultures of Kenya*

(repr., Nairobi: Transafrica, 1994), 153. Quote is in Sarah Mirza and Margaret Strobel, eds., *Three Swahili Women: Life Histories from Mombasa, Kenya* (Bloomington: Indiana University Press, 1989), 46.

52. Antoinette Burton, *Burdens of History: British Feminists, Indian Women, and Imperial Culture, 1865–1915* (Chapel Hill: University of North Carolina Press, 1994), 19–25, 41–52.

53. Sitara Kahn, *A Glimpse Through Purdah: Asian Women—The Myth and the Reality* (Staffordshire, England: Trentham, 1999), 3–6, 12–15; and Padama Anagol, "Indian Christian Women and Indigenous Feminism, c. 1850–c. 1920," in Clare Midgley, ed., *Gender and Imperialism* (Manchester, England: Manchester University Press, 1998), 79–103. For *sati,* consult L. Mani, "Continous Traditions: The Debate on *Sati* in Colonial India," in K. Sangari and S. Vaid, eds., *Recasting Women in Indian Colonial History* (New Brunswick, NJ: Rutgers University Press, 1989), 88–126. British interference with Indian women's sexuality is in Himani Bannerji, "Age of Consent and Hegemonic Social Reform," in Midgley, *Gender and Imperialism*, 21–44.

54. Salvadori, *We Came in Dhows*, 1:54.

55. Ibid., 1:170.

56. Ibid., 1:190, 3:70; 2:24, 150, 160, and 3:164–65.

57. Ibid., 3:43.

58. Quintard Taylor, "Mary Ellen Pleasant: Entrepreneur and Civil Rights Activist in the Far West," in Glenda Riley and Richard W. Etulain, eds., *By Grit and Grace: Eleven Women Who Shaped the American West* (Golden, CO: Fulcrum, 1997), 119.

59. J. S. Mangat, *A History of the Asian in East Africa, c. 1886 to 1945* (Oxford: Clarendon Press, 1969), 1–9, 27–29, 80–85; John H. A. Jewell, *Mombasa: The Friendly Town* (Nairobi: East African Publishing, 1976), 23–26; Fedders and Salvadori, *Peoples and Cultures of Kenya*, 155, and Cynthia Salvadori, *Through Open Doors: A View of Asian Cultures in Kenya,* rev. ed. (Nairobi: Kenway, 1989), 9–10, and Salvadori, *We Came in Dhows* (Nairobi: Paperchase, 1996), 1:12.

60. Robert J. Hind, "The Internal Colonial Concept," *Comparative Studies of Society* 26 (July 1984): 543–68; and Deena J. González, *Refusing the Favor: The Spanish-Mexican Women of Santa Fe, 1820–1880* (New York: Oxford University Press, 1999), 3–9.

Chapter 2

1. Quoted in Sarah Mirza and Margaret Strobel, eds., *Three Swahili Women: Life Histories from Mombases, Kenya* (Bloomington: Indiana University Press, 1989), 28.

2. Quoted in, Bruce E. Mahan, "By Boat and Covered Wagon," *Pal* 49 (July 1968): 247–48.

3. *Eddyville (Iowa) Free Press*, 16 April 1855.

4. W. Kirkland, "The West, the Paradise of the Poor," *United States Magazine* 15 (August 1844): 182–90.

5. *Iowa: The Home For Immigrants* (Des Moines: Iowa Board of Immigration, 1870), 63–65.

6. For examples, see Isaac Galland, *Galland's Iowa Emigrant: Containing a Map, and General Descriptions of Iowa Territory* (Chillicothe, OH: n.p., 1840); and John B. Newhall, *A Glimpse of Iowa in 1846* (Iowa City: Iowa State Historical Society, 1957). For farther west, see George Alexander Thompson, *Handbook to the Pacific and California* (London: Simpkin and Marshall, 1849); and Joseph E. Ware, *The Emigrant's Guide to California*, ed. John W. Caughey (repr., Princeton, NJ: Princeton University Press, 1932).

7. Candy Moulton, *Writer's Guide to Everyday Life in the Wild West: From 1800–1900* (Cincinnati, OH: Writers' Digest, 1999), 307.

8. E. May Lacey Crowder, "Pioneer Life in Palo Alto Country," *Iowa Journal of History and Politics* 46 (April 1948): 156.

9. Kitturah Belknap, "Reminiscences," 1975, Lane County Pioneer Historical Society, Eugene (hereafter cited as LCPHS). For food, see Jacqueline Williams, *Wagon Wheel Kitchens: Food on the Oregon Trail* (Lawrence: University Press of Kansas, 1993); and Glenda Riley and N. Jill Howard, "Thus You See I Have Not Much Rest," *Idaho Yesterdays* 37 (Fall 1993): 27–35.

10. Mary Ann Hafen, "Memoir," 1938, published as *Recollections of a Handcart Pioneer of 1860: A Woman's Life on the Mormon Frontier* (Lincoln: University of Nebraska Press, 1983), 23–26.

11. Edith H. Hurlbutt, "Pioneer Experiences in Keokuk County, 1858–1874," *Iowa Journal of History* 52 (October 1954): 327–28.

12. Moulton, *Writer's Guide to Everyday Life in the Wild West*, 293–94.

13. David M. Emmons, *Garden in the Grasslands: Boomer Literature of the Central Great Plains* (Lincoln: University of Nebraska Press, 1971), 25–46; and Pauline Neher Diede, *Homesteading on the Knife River Prairies* (Bismarck, ND: Germans from Russia Heritage Society, 1983), 14–25.

14. "Seventy Years in Iowa," *Annals of Iowa*, 27 (October 1945): 98.

15. Jessie Benton Frémont, *A Year of American Travel: Narrative of Personal Experience* (San Francisco: Book Club, 1960), 14, 26–28, 30, 32–34, 39.

16. Angelina Harvey to Mary Ann Wheaton, November 19, 1863, "Harvey File," BL, Berkeley.

17. Jo Ann Levy, *They Saw the Elephant: Women in the California Gold Rush* (Norman: University of Oklahoma Press, 1992), 136–39. 178–87.

18. Interview with Esther Easter, in George P. Rawick, ed., *The American Slave* (Westport, CT: Greenwood, 1972), 7:90–91. See also, Joan E. Cashin, "Black Families in the Old Northwest," *Journal of the Early Republic* 15 (Fall 1995): 450–53.

19. Interview with Jenny Proctor in, Rawick, *American Slave*, 7:216–17.

20. David Beesley, "From Chinese to Chinese American: Chinese Women and Families in a Sierra Nevada Town," *California History* 67 (September 1988): 170–73.

21. *British Parliamentary Papers: Kenya/Malawi, 1890–99* (Shannon: Irish University Press, 1971), 116.

22. Quoted in W. R. Ochieng', *A History of Kenya* (London: Macmillan, 1985), 105.
23. Charles Miller, *The Lunatic Express* (London: Macmillan, 1971), 570–71.
24. Judith Thurman, *Isak Dinesen: The Life of Karen Blixen* (London: Penguin, 1982), 141–43; and Linda Donelson, *Out of Isak Dinesen in Africa: The Untold Story* (Iowa City: Coulsong, 1995), 7–8.
25. East African Protectorate, Mombasa, "White Settlement in B.E.A. Protectorate," 1918, PC/Coast/1/11/301, KNA, Nairobi; Etta C. Close, *A Woman Alone in Kenya, Uganda and the Belgian Congo* (London: Constable, 1924); and Anne McDonald, "African Roundabout, 1932–35," undated, RHL, Oxford. Also, see H. F. Ward and J. W. Mulligan, *Handbook of British East Africa* (Nairobi: Caxton, 1912), 258–74.
26. Harry H. Johnston, *British Central Africa* (London: Metheun, 1897), 185–88.
27. Lord Cranworth, *A Colony in the Making, Or, Sport and Profit in British East Africa* (London: Macmillan, 1912), 86–87.
28. Lord Cranworth, *Profit and Sport in East Africa* (London: Macmillan, 1919), 113–14.
29. Cranworth, *Colony in the Making*, 87–91.
30. *A Handbook of Kenya Colony* (London: His Majesty's Stationery Office, 1920), 322–23; and Eve Bache, *The Youngest Lion: Early Farming Days in Kenya* (London: Hutchinson, 1934), 14.
31. *Kenya* (Nairobi: Kenya Association, 1930), unpaged; and *Railways and Harbours Travel Guide to Kenya and Uganda* (London: Royal Mail, 1931), 11, 34.
32. Ibid., 35, 60, 97.
33. *New Homes, New Hopes in Kenya Colony* (Nairobi: Kenya Association, 1932), 4–6; and *The Travellers' Guide to Kenya and Uganda* (Nairobi: Kenya and Uganda Railways, 1939), 205–9.
34. Bache, *Youngest Lion*, 19.
35. Isak Dinesen, *Letters from Africa, 1914–1931* (Chicago, IL: University of Chicago Press, 1981), xlii.
36. Elspeth Huxley, *Nine Faces of Kenya* (London: Harvill, 1990), 85.
37. Ibid., 86.
38. Ibid.
39. Bache, *Youngest Lion*, 21–22.
40. Ibid., 23–24.
41. Esther E. Hopcraft, *Esther's Story* (Victoria, B.C.: Baharini, 1996), 58.
42. Mary Mitford Barberton, "Journal," 1914, in Raymond Mitford-Barberton, "Papers," 1912–1923, Mss. Box 236, KNA, Nairobi.
43. Dorothy Vaughan, "Reminiscences of 1909–1950s," undated, RHL, Oxford.
44. McDonald, "African Roundabout, 1932–35"; and Bache, *Youngest Lion*, 15–16.
45. Errol Trzebinski, *The Kenya Pioneers* (London: Heinemann, 1985), 9–10.
46. Daphne Moore, "Diary," 1929–34, RHL, Oxford.
47. M. H. Hamilton, *Turn the Hour: A Tale of Life in Colonial Kenya* (Sussex, England: Book Guild, 1991), 19.
48. Bache, *Youngest Lion*, 14.

49. Moore, "Diary."
50. Hopcraft, *Esther's Story*, 53, 55–56.
51. Bache, *Youngest Lion*, 15.
52. Moore, "Diary."
53. Ibid.
54. Kevin M. D. Patience, *Steam in East Africa: A Pictorial History of the Railways in East Africa, 1893–1876* (Nairobi: Heinemann, 1976), 19.
55. Cynthia Salvadori, *We Came in Dhows*, 3 vols. (Nairobi: Paperchase, 1996), 1:12.
56. Ibid., 1:13.
57. Ibid., 3: 78.
58. F. Rowling, *Kenya and Its Peoples* (London: Sheldon, 1938), 29, 31.
59. Septima M. Collis, *A Woman's Trip to Alaska* (New York: Cassell, 1890), i, 194.
60. Lloyd E. Hudman, "Tourism and the American West," *Journal of the West* (July 1994), 67–76.
61. Margaret Long, "Our Summering of 1890, Yellowstone Journal," 1890, University of Colorado at Boulder, University Libraries, Archives.
62. Patience, *Steam in East Africa*, 18.
63. Close, *Woman Alone*, 1–3.
64. Examples are in Monty Brown, *Where Giants Trod: The Saga of Kenya's Desert Lake* (London: Quiller, 1989). Quote is from *Travellers Guide to Kenya and Uganda* (Nairobi: Kenya and Uganda Railways, 1939), 92, 113.
65. Katharine Haun, "A Woman's Trip across the Plains, from Clinton, Iowa, to Sacramento, California, by way of Salt Lake City," 1849, Huntington Library, San Marino (subsequently cited as HL).
66. Ward G. DeWitt and Florence Stark DeWitt, eds., *Prairie Schoolner Lady: The Journal of Harriet Sherrill Ward, 1853* (Los Angeles: Westernlore, 1959), 46.
67. Glenda Riley, "The Specter of a Savage: Rumors and Alarmism on the Overland Trail," *Western Historical Quarterly* 15 (October 1984): 427–44.
68. British East Africa Protectorate, 1895–97, Miscellaneous Inward File, August 1895, "Mombasa re forts," PC/Coast/1/1/16, KNA, Nairobi.
69. Ochieng', *History of Kenya*, 93–94.
70. Ibid., 100.
71. Ibid., 88–100.
72. For early railroads and autos, see "The Early Days at Lake Naivasha," Broadside, undated, Elsamere Conservation Centre, Naivasha.

Chapter 3

1. Susanna Brown Bergh, Montana American Mothers Biography Project, 1975–76, Montana Historical Society, Helena (hereafter cited as MHS).
2. Jesse Minard, 1975, in Pioneer Daughters Collection, c. 1850–1955, SDSHRC, Pierre; Clara Field McCarthy, "Clara's Episodes: A Reflection of Early Wyoming, 1901–1911," 1964, WSAMHD, Cheyenne; Stella [no last name given], "letter to My Dear Little Sister," 28 January 1866, Nebraska State

Historical Society, Lincoln (hereafter cited as NSHS); and Mrs. Lee A. Jones, "Reminiscences of Early Days in Havre," undated, MHS, Helena.

3. Amelia C. Glecker, 1975, in Pioneer Daughters Collection, c. 1850–1955, SDSHRC, Pierre.

4. Little Tokyos are found in Barbara Yasui, "The Nissei in Oregon, 1834–1940," *Oregon Historical Quarterly* 76 (1975): 225–57; and Yuji Ichioka, "*Amerika Nadeshiko*: Japanese Immigrant Women in the United States, 1900–1924," *Pacific Historical Review* 46 (1980): 339–58.

5. Quoted in Ronald Takaki, *Strangers from a Different Shore: A History of Asian Americans* (New York: Penguin, 1989), 117.

6. Mary Lowman, "letter to Respected Bro (Joseph C. Foster)," 14 May 1861, NSHS, Lincoln; Mrs. Joe C. Horton, "Diary," 1874, Kansas State Historical Society, Topeka (hereafter cited as KSHS); Ellen Payne Paullin, ed., "Etta's Journal," January 2, 1874–July 25, 1875," Part 2, *Kansas History* 3 (Winter 1980): 275; Anonymous, "Household Account Book," January–July 1880, SDSHRC, Pierre: Ida McPherren, "Sheridan Market Report," 1890, *Sheridan* (Wyoming) *Post*, 8 May 1890, WSAMHD, Cheyenne; and Anna Gillespie, "Coxville, Nebraska, to Fay, Oklahoma, by Wagon (1899): The Journal of Anna Gillespie," *Nebraska History* 63 (Fall 1984): 361.

7. Dennis Porter, "Orientalism and Its Problems," in Francis Barker et al., eds., *The Politics of Theory* (Colchester: University of Essex, 1983), 179–93.

8. Errol Trzebinski, *The Kenya Pioneers* (London: Heinemann, 1985), 39.

9. Elspeth Huxley, *White Man's Country: Lord Delamere and the Making of Kenya*, 2 vols. (London: Macmillan, 1935).

10. James H. E. Smart, *Nairobi: A Jubilee History, 1900–1950* (Nairobi: East African Standard, 1950), 7.

11. Megan Vaughan, *Curing Their Ills: Colonial Power and African Illness* (Stanford, CA: Stanford University Press, 1991), 129–54; Luis White, *The Comforts of Home: Prostitution in Colonial Nairobi* (Chicago, IL: University of Chicago Press, 1990), 23, 47–48; and Trevor Fisher, *Prostitution and the Victorians* (New York: St. Martin's Press, 1997), 137–45.

12. Smart, *Nairobi*, xxix.

13. Ibid., 2:18, 21, 26; and Elspeth Huxley, *Nine Faces of Kenya* (London: Collins Harvill, 1991), 72.

14. Daisy M. Chown, *Wayfaring in Africa: A Woman's Wanderings from the Cape to Cairo* (London: Heath Cranton, 1927), 100; and Lady Daphne Moore, "Diary," 1929–34, RHL, Oxford.

15. Alyse Simpson, *The Land That Never Was* (Lincoln: University of Nebraska Press, 1937), 35.

16. Nora K. Strange, *Kenya To-Day* (London: Stanley Paul, 1934), 29–30; *New Homes, New Hopes in Kenya Colony* (Nairobi: Kenya Association, 1932), 6; and quoted in Grace Crile, *Skyways to a Jungle Laboratory: An African Adventure* (London: Heinemann, 1937), 48.

17. Nupur Chaudhuri, "Shawls, Jewelry, Curry, and Rice in Victorian Britain," in Nupur Chaudhuri and Margaret Strobel, eds., *Western Women and Imperialism:*

Complicity and Resistance (Bloomington: Indiana University Press, 1992), 231–46.

18. "Nyeri" in East Africa Women's League, *They Made It Their Home* (Nairobi: East African Standard, 1962), unpaged.

19. M. H. Hamilton, *Turn the Hour: A Tale of Life in Colonial Kenya* (Sussex, England: Book Guild, 1991), 23–24; and quoted in Huxley, *Nine Faces of Kenya*, 204–5.

20. Heidi I. Hartmann, "The Family as the Locus of Gender, Class, and Political Struggle: The Example of Housework," *Signs* 6 (1981): 366–94.

21. Abbie Mott Benedict, "My Early Days in Iowa," *Annals of Iowa* 17 (July 1930): 341; and Bessie L. Lyon, "Grandmother's Story," *Pal* 5 (January 1924): 6. For regions, see Glenda Riley, *The Female Frontier: A Comparative View of Women on the Prairie and Plains* (Lawrence: University of Press of Kansas, 1988), 76–101.

22. Lucie Dickinson Lott, in Pioneer Daughters Collection, c. 1850–1955, SDSHRC, Pierre; Mrs. George W. Snow, "Memoirs," undated, WSAMHD, Cheyenne; and John C. Hudson, "Frontier Housing in North Dakota," *North Dakota History* 42 (Fall 1975): 4–15.

23. Ava Day, "Letters to Nebraska Historical Society," 28 March and 23 May 1964, NSHS, Lincoln; and Polly Bemis, "Papers," undated, Idaho State Historical Society, Boise (hereafter cited as IDSHS).

24. Anna Ramsey, "Letters to My Darling Children," 31 March 1876; to My Dear Daughter, 17 June 1875 and 8 December 1875, Minnesota Historical Society, St. Paul (hereafter cited as MHS, St. Paul).

25. Madeleine Platts, "Diary," 1912–13, RHL, Oxford.

26. Mrs. K. Armstrong, "Recollections of Kenya, 1919–1930," undated, RHL, Oxford.

27. Pamela Scott, *A Nice Place to Live* (Norwich, England: Russell, 1991), 18.

28. Hamilton, *Turn the Hour*, 25; and Mrs. V. M. Carnegie, *A Kenyan Farm Diary* (London: Blackwood, 1931), 56.

29. Scott, *Nice Place to Live*, 59, 62.

30. *Kenya* (Nairobi: Kenya Association, 1930), unpaged; and Carnegie, *Kenyan Farm Diary*, 2, 3, 11, 14.

31. Esther E. Hopcraft, *Esther's Story* (Victoria, B.C.: Baharini, 1996), 67–68, 70–72, 77.

32. Cynthia Salvadori, *We Came in Dhows*, 3 vols. (Nairobi: Paperchase, 1996), 3: 41.

33. Ibid., 1: 32, 64, and 2: 44–45.

34. Ibid., 2:17.

35. "Introduction," 2–3, in Clyde A. Milner II, Carol A. O'Connor, and Martha A. Sandweiss, eds., *The Oxford History of the American West* (New York: Oxford University Press, 1994).

36. Quote from W. Kirkland, "The West, the Paradise of the Poor," *United States Magazine and Democratic Review* 15 (August 1844): 182–90. For social classes, see Riley, *Female Frontier*, 23–25.

37. Dorothy St. Arnold, "Reminiscences," c. 1926, MHS, St. Paul.

38. Benedict, "My Early Days in Iowa," 323–55.

39. Kathie Ryckman Anderson, "Era Bell Thompson: A North Dakota Daughter," *North Dakota History* 49 (Fall 1982): 12.
40. Mathilda E. Engstad, "The White Kid Glove Era," undated, SHSND, Bismarck; Alice Richards McCreary, "Various Happenings in the Life of Alice Richards McCreary," undated, WSAMHD, Cheyenne; Homer E. Socolofsky, ed., "The Private Journals of Florence Crawford and Arthur Capper, 1891–92, *Kansas Historical Quarterly*, 2 parts, 30 (Spring and Summer 1964): 15–61, 163–208; and Sarah Wood Ward, in Pioneer Daughters Collection, c. 1850–1955, SDSHRC, Pierre. Also helpful is Scott G. McNall and Salley Allen McNall, *Plains Families: Exploring Sociology through Social History* (New York: St. Martin's Press, 1983), 246–77.
41. Thomas B. Marquis, trans., "Red Ripe's Squaw: Recollections of a Long Life," *Century Magazine* 118 (June 1929), 201. See also Glenda Riley, "Writing, Teaching, and Recreating Western History through Intersections and Viewpoints," *Pacific Historical Review* 42 (August 1993): 339–57; and Riley, *Women and Indians on the Frontier, 1825–1915* (Albuquerque: University of New Mexico Press, 1984).
42. Stella M. Drumm, ed., *Down the Santa Fe Trail and into Mexico: The Diary of Susan Shelby Magoffin, 1846–47* (New Haven: Yale University Press, 1926), 120–21; and Fray Angelico Chávez, "Doña Tules, Her Fame and Her Funeral," *El Palacio* 62 (1957): 230–32.
43. Drumm, *Down the Santa Fe Trail*, 68, and Leola Lehman, "Life in the Territories," *Chronicles of Oklahoma* 41 (Fall 1963): 373–75. See also Riley, *Women and Indians*, 176–78.
44. Rosalia Leese, "History of the Bear Party," 27 June 1874, BL, University of California, Berkeley.
45. A. Walter, *Report on the Non-Native Census Enumeration made in the Colony and Protectorate of Kenya, 6 March 1931* (Nairobi: Government Printer, 1932), 24.
46. *Kenya* (Nairobi: Kenya Association, 1930), unpaged.
47. Lord and Lady Francis Scott of the Deloraine Estate, "Papers," 1919–76, Microfilm, no number, KNA, Nairobi.
48. Etta Close, *A Woman Alone in Kenya, Uganda, and the Belgian Congo* (London: Constable, 1924), 180. For officials and settlers, see M. Aline Buxton, *My Kenya Days* (London: Arnold, 1927), 6–7, 11.
49. J. M. Coetzee, *White Writing: On the Culture of Letters in South Africa* (New Haven, CT: Yale University Press, 1988), 2–3; and quoted in Huxley, *Nine Faces of Kenya*, 205.
50. Homi K. Bhabha, "Difference, Discrimination and the Discourse of Colonialism," in Francis Barker et al., eds., *The Politics of Theory* (Colchester: University of Essex, 1983), 195, 199.
51. Sarah Mirza and Margaret Strobel, eds., *Three Swahili Women: Life Histories from Mombasa, Kenya* (Bloomington: Indiana University Press, 1989), 43, 47, 69, 76.
52. Walter, *Report on the Non-Native Census*, 5, 7.
53. Salvadori, *We Came in Dhows*, 3:78; and Cynthia Salvadori, *Through Open Doors: A View of Asian Cultures in Kenya* (Nairobi: Paperchase, 1996, 1983), 7. For white

women's views, consult Janaki Nair, "Uncovering the Zenana: Visions of Indian Womanhood in Englishwomen's Writings, 1813–1940," *Journal of Women's History* 2 (1990): 195–403.

54. Provincial Commissioner, Office of Nyanza Province, "Population," 1928, PC/NZA/3/6/2/2, KNA, Nairobi; and Walter, *Report on the Non-Native Population*, 18. For census, see J. B. Blacker, "Demography," in W. T. W. Morgan, ed., *East Africa: Its Peoples and Resources* (Nairobi: Oxford University Press, 1969), 41–58.

55. Ministry of Information and Broadcasting, *Kenya: An Official Handbook* (Nairobi: Colourprint, 1988), 8–10, 19–21; and Andrew Fedders and Cynthia Salvadori, *Peoples and Cultures of Kenya* (repr., Nairobi: Transafrica, 1994), 6.

56. Ieuan Griffiths, *The African Inheritance* (London: Routledge, 1995). Also useful is Roland Oliver and Gervase Mathew, *History of East Africa: The Early Period* (Nairobi: Oxford University Press, 1967).

57. Donald Featherstone, *Khaki and Red: Soldiers of the Queen in India and Africa* (London: Arms and Armour, 1997), 9–12, 17–18.

58. Homi Bhabha, "Of Mimicry and Man: The Ambivalence of Colonial Discourse," *October* (1983): 125–34.

59. Anne McDonald, "African Roundabout, 1932–35," undated, RHL, Oxford; Buxton, *My Kenya Days*, 4; and Eve Bache, *The Youngest Lion: Early Farming Days in Kenya* (London: Hutchinson, 1934), 37.

60. Genesta Hamilton, *A Stone's Throw: Travels from Africa in Six Decades* (London: Hutchinson, 1986), 84; and Carnegie, *Kenyan Farm Diary*, 15–16.

61. Stanton W. Green, "The Agricultural Colonization of Temperate Forest Habitats: An Ecological Model," in William W. Savage, Jr. and Stephen I. Thompson, eds., *The Frontier: Comparative Studies* (Norman: University of Oklahoma Press, 1979), 80–83.

62. Sister Blandina Segale, *At the End of the Santa Fe Trail* (Columbus, OH: N.p., 1932), 161. An excellent coverage is Howard R. Lamar, *The Far Southwest: 1846–1912* (New Haven, CT: Yale University Press, 1955).

63. Gilbert L. Wilson, transcriber, *Buffalo Bird Woman's Garden* (St. Paul: Minnesota Historical Society, 1987), 119–20.

64. Nellie Quail, "Interview," Ft. McDowell Indian Reservation, 31 July–1 August 1967, Prescott College Yavapai Oral Tradition Project, Arizona State Museum, University of Arizona, Tucson.

65. Albert L. Hurtado, "Indian Labor in California in the 1850s," 144–50; Sucheng Chan, "Asian Americans: Resisting Oppression, 1860s–1920s," 366–75; and Mario G. García, "Mexican Women Workers in Texas, 1880–1920," 173–79, all in Sucheng Chan, Douglas Henry Daniels, and Mario T. García, eds., *Peoples of Color in the American West* (Lexington, MA: D. C. Heath, 1994).

66. Caroline Phelps, "Diary," 1840, Iowa State Historical Society, Iowa City (hereafter cited as ISHS). For the West Coast, see Albert L. Hurtado, "'Hardly a Farm House—A Kitchen without Them': Indian and White Households on the California Borderland Frontier in 1860," *Western Historical Quarterly* 14 (July 1983): 245–70.

67. Sandra L. Myres, ed., "Evy Alexander: The Colonel's Lady at Ft. McDowell," *Montana* 24 (Summer 1974), 32–34.

68. Mary E. Ackley, *Crossing the Plains and Early Days in California* (San Francisco: Privately printed, 1928), 86; Caroline D. Budlong, *Memories: Pioneer Days in Oregon and Washington Territory* (Eugene, OR: Picture Press, 1949), 38; and Hurtado, "'Hardly a Farm House—A Kitchen without Them,'" 245–70.

69. Rachel Elizabeth Wright, "The Early Upper Napa Valley," 1928, BL, University of California, Berkeley.

70. Hurtado, "Indian Labor in California in the 1850s," 144–50, García, "Mexican Woman Workers," 173–79, both in Chan et al., *Peoples of Color*.

71. Stanley B. Greenberg, *Race and State in Capitalist Development: Comparative Perspectives* (New Haven: Yale University Press, 1980), 30–32; and BEA Protectorate, "Miscellaneous Inward," 1895–1897, PC/Coast/1/1/16, KNA, Nairobi; and Elspeth Huxley, *Settlers of Kenya* (Westport, CT: Greenwood, 1948), 9–10.

72. W. McGregor Ross, *Kenya from Within: A Short Political History* (London: Cass, 1968), 41–55; "Hopcraft photograph album," undated, Loldia House, Naivasha, Kenya, consulted 15 April 1998; and interview with David Hopcraft, 30 April 1998, Loldia House, Naivasha, Kenya.

73. Charity Waciuma, *Daughter of Mumbi* (Nairobi: East African Publishing, 1969), 106–7.

74. Marjorie Dilley, *British Policy in Kenya Colony* (New York: Nelson, 1966), 134–35, 239, 242–64; and Zoë Marsh and G. W. Kingsnorth, *An Introduction to the History of East Africa* (Cambridge, England: Cambridge University Press, 1965), 164–68.

75. David Read, *Barefoot Over the Serengeti* (London: Cassell, 1979), 184.

76. Wambui Waiyaki Otieno, *Mau Mau's Daughter: A Life History* (Boulder, CO: Lynne Rienner, 1998), 21.

77. Bruce Berman and John Lonsdale, "Crisis of Accumulation, Coercion and the Colonial State: The Development of the Labour Control System, 1919–29," in Bruce Berman and John Lonsdale, eds., *Unhappy Valley: Conflict in Kenya and Africa*, Book One: *State and Class* (London: Currey, 1992), 101–26; Anne Phillips, *The Enigma of Colonialism: British Policy in West Africa* (Bloomington: Indiana University Press, 1989), 156–63; Frederick Cooper, *From Slaves to Squatters: Plantation Labor and Agriculture in Zanzibar and Coastal Kenya, 1890–1925* (New Haven: Yale University Press, 1980), 1–6, 378: and Richard D. Wolff, *The Economics of Colonialism: Britain and Kenya, 1870–1930* (New Haven, CT: Yale University Press, 1974), 47–67, 89–110. For Kenya's labor, consult Anthony Clayton and Donald C. Savage, *Government and Labour in Kenya, 1895–1963* (London: Cass, 1974).

78. Regina Smith Oboler, *Women, Power, and Economic Change: The Nandi of Kenya* (Stanford, CA: Stanford University Press, 1985), 8–10, 294–96, 310–19.

79. Claire C. Robertson, *Trouble Showed the Way: Women, Men, and Trade in the Nairobi Area, 1890–1990* (Bloomington: Indiana University Press, 1997), 92.

80. Jane L. Collins and Greta R. Krippner, "Permanent Labor Contracts in

Agriculture: Flexibility and Subordination in a New Export Crop," *Comparative Studies in Science and History* 41 (July 1944): 510–15. Quote is in Wolff, *Economics of Colonialism*, 131.

81. John Lonsdale and Bruce Berman, "Coping with the Contradictions: The Development of the Colonial State in Kenya, 1895–1914," *Journal of African History* 20 (1979): 487–505; and Wolff, *Economics of Colonialism*, 140–43. For the British viewpoint, see Prosser Gifford and William R. Louis, eds., *France and Britain in Africa: Imperial Rivalry and Colonial Rule* (New Haven: Yale University Press, 1971).

82. Bache, *Youngest Lion*, 132.

83. *The Travellers' Guide to Kenya and Uganda* (Nairobi: Kenya and Uganda Railways, 1939), 205.

84. Quoted in G. H. Mungeam, *British Rule in Kenya, 1895–1912* (Oxford, England: Clarendon, 1966), 136.

85. George Bennett, *Kenya, A Political History: The Colonial Period* (London: Oxford University Press, 1963), 19–21; and Paul Mosley, *The Settler Economies: Studies in the Economic History of Kenya and Southern Rhodesia, 1900–1963* (Cambridge, England: Cambridge University Press, 1983), 172–87.

86. Bennett, *Kenya, A Political History*, 24–28.

87. Clayton and Savage, *Government and Labour in Kenya, 1895–1963*, 20.

88. Ibid., 191–92; and Scott, *Nice Place to Live*, 51.

89. Roger Van Zwanenberg, "The Political Economy of Colonialism in Kenya: The Role of Settlers in the Economy," unpublished paper, 8 October 1969, unpaged, Dept. of History, University College, Nairobi. Copy in author's possession.

90. Political Record Book, Part II, Section O, "European Settlement," 1909, DC/KBU/3/37, KNA, Nairobi.

91. From a lecture by D. M. Rocco to the Museum Society (Nairobi) on 17 March 1988, "The East African Campaign and Its Aftermath," privately held by D. M. Rocco, copy in author's possession; and Buxton, *My Kenya Days*, 20.

92. Coetzee, *White Writing*, 18–22.

93. Scott, *Nice Place to Live*, 61, 117; Ruth Nasimiyu, "Women in the Colonial Economy of Bungoma: Role of Women in Agriculture, 1902–1960," *Journal of East African Research and Development* 15 (1985): 56–73; and Carolyn M. Clark, "Land and Food, Women and Power, in Nineteenth Century Kikuyu," *Africa* 50 (1980): 357–70.

Chapter 4

1. David W. Hess, "Pioneering as Ecological Process: A Model and Test Case of Frontier Adaptation," in William W. Savage, Jr. and Stephen I. Thompson, eds., *The Frontier: Comparative Studies* 2 vols. (Norman: University of Oklahoma Press, 1979), 2: 123–52.

2. Dean L. May, *Three Frontiers: Family, Land, and Society in the American West, 1850–1900* (Cambridge, England: Cambridge University Press, 1994), 278–79.

3. Britania J. Livingston, "Notes on Pioneer Life," 22 December 1928, quoted in Meridel Le Sueur, *North Star Country* (New York: Duell, Sloan and Pearce, 1945), 118.

4. Anne E. Bingham, "Sixteen Years on a Kansas Farm, 1870–1886," Kansas State Historical Society *Collections* 15 (1919–22): 516. Also see J. A. Munro, "Grasshopper Outbreaks in North Dakota, 1808–1948," *North Dakota History* 16 (July 1949): 143–64; and Robert N. Manley, "In the Wake of the Grasshoppers: Public Relief in Nebraska, 1874–1875," *Nebraska History* 44 (December 1963): 255–75.

5. Lorna B. Herseth, ed., "A Pioneer's Letter," *South Dakota History* 6 (Summer 1976): 309; Thomas D. Clark, "Starting Life at Ground Level on a Nebraska Homestead," in Clark, ed., *The Great American Frontier* (Indianapolis: Bobbs-Merrill, 1975), 115, 175; and Fannie Forbes Russel, "My First Year in Montana, 1864–1865," 1920, MHS, Helena.

6. Kate Roberts Pelissier, "Reminiscences of a Pioneer Mother," *North Dakota History* 24 (July 1957): 132; Herseth, "A Pioneer's Letter," 310–11; Clark, "Starting Life at Ground Level on a Nebraska Homestead," 175; and Angel Kwolek-Folland, "The Elegant Dugout: Domesticity and Moveable Culture in the United States, 1870–1900," *American Studies* 25 (Fall 1984): 21–37.

7. John C. Hudson, *Plains Country Towns* (Minneapolis: University of Minnesota Press, 1985), 104–20; and Deborah J. Hoskins, "Brought, Bought, and Borrowed: Material Culture on the Oklahoma Farming Frontiers, 1889–1907," in John R. Wunder, ed., *At Home on the Range, Essays on the History of Western Social and Domestic Life* (Westport, CT: Greenwood, 1985), 121–36.

8. Mary W. M. Hargreaves, "Women in the Agricultural Settlement of the Northern Plains," *Agricultural History* 50 (January 1976): 187.

9. William D. Andrews and Deborah C. Andrews, "Technology and the Housewife in Nineteenth-Century America," *Women's Studies* 2 (1974): 309–28; Susan Strasser, *Never Done: A History of American Housework* (New York: Pantheon, 1981), 2–10; W. F. Kumlien, *Basic Trends of Social Change in South Dakota: II: Rural Life Adjustments*, S.D. Agricultural Experiment Station Bulletin 11 (Brookings: South Dakota State College, 1941), 19; and Ellen Throop, "Reminiscences of Pioneer Days," undated, NSHS, Lincoln.

10. Quoted in *Nebraska Farmer*, 8 December 1934.

11. Roger G. Barker, "The Influence of Frontier Environments on Behavior," in Jerome O. Steffen, ed., *The American West: New Perspectives, New Dimension* (Norman: University of Oklahoma Press, 1979), 61–93.

12. Glenda Riley, *A Place to Grow: Women in the American West* (Arlington Heights, IL: Harlan Davidson, 1992), 147–59, 164–76; and Riley, *The Female Frontier: A Comparative View of Women on the Prairie and Plains* (Lawrence: University Press of Kansas, 1988), 102–47. Quote is in Sarah Kenyon to relative, 11 October 1861, "John Kenyon Papers," ISHS, Iowa City.

13. Barbara B. Zimmerman and Vernon Carstensen, eds., "Pioneer Women in Southwestern Washington Territory: The Recollections of Susanna Maria Slover McFarland Price Ede," *Pacific Northwest Quarterly* 66–67 (1976): 143,

147; and Christiane Fischer, "A Profile of Women in Arizona in Frontier Days," *Journal of the West* 16 (July 1977): 43.

14. Sarah Royce, *A Frontier Lady: Recollections of the Gold Rush and Early California*, Ralph Henry Gabriel, ed., (New Haven, CT: Yale University Press, 1932), 85.

15. *Ninth Census*, Vol. I: *The Statistics of the Population of the United States* (Washington, D. C.: Government Printing Office, 1872), 4–5.

16. Anonymous, "Pilgrim Baptist Church: A Brief Resume of History," c. 1977, MHS, St. Paul; Patricia G. Harpole, ed., "The Black Community in Territorial St. Anthony: A Memoir," *Minnesota History* 49 (Summer 1984): 42–55; and Eva Neal, "Family Papers," 1881–1963, MHS, St. Paul. For a later group, see Jesse T. Moore, Jr., "Seeking a New Life: Blacks in Post–Civil War Colorado," *Journal of Nebraska History* 3 (1993): 166–87.

17. Bobette Perrone, H. Henrietta Stockel, and Victoria Kreuger, *Medicine Women, Curanderas, and Women Doctors* (Norman: University of Oklahoma Press, 1993), 85–98.

18. Doña Jesús Moreno de Soza, "Reminiscences," 1939, Antonio Soza Papers, Arizona Historical Society, Tucson (hereafter cited as AHS).

19. Glenda Riley, *Women and Nature: Saving the "Wild" West* (Lincoln: University of Nebraska Press, 1990), 18.

20. "Report of Commissioner Johnston of the First Three Years' Administration of the Eastern Portion of British Central Africa, dated 31 March 1894," in *British Parliamentary Papers, Kenya/Malawi, 1890–1899* (Shannon: Irish University Press, 1971), 117.

21. Alyse Simpson, *Red Dust of Africa* (London: Cassell, 1952), 1, 3, 35, 38; and Mrs. E. C. R. LeBreton, "Grim's Tale," 1980, RHL, Oxford.

22. Elspeth Huxley, *The Flame Trees of Thika: Memories of an African Childhood* (Middlesex, England: Penguin Books, 1962), 7; and Elspeth Huxley, *The Mottled Lizard* (Middlesex, England: Penguin Books, 1962), 286, 309.

23. Elspeth Huxley, *Nine Faces of Kenya* (London: Harvill, 1991), 109–10, and *White Man's Country*, 2: 255–58; Molly Ievers Ryan, *Over My Shoulder: Kenya Walkabout* (Dublin: Grange, 1987), 28; and interview with Mairo Low Hopcraft, by author, Loldia House, Naivasha, 15 April 1998.

24. Margaret Elkington, "Recollections of a Settler in Kenya 1905–1970," 1971, RHL, Oxford.

25. Huxley, *Nine Faces of Kenya*, 97; LeBreton, "Grim's Tale," and Helen Meyers, "Blowing My Own Trumpet 1910–31," 1978, both at RHL, Oxford.

26. LeBreton, "Grim's Tale."

27. Elspeth Huxley and Arnold Curtis, eds., *Pioneers' Scrapbook: Reminiscences of Kenya, 2890 to 1968* (London: Evans, 1980), 85.

28. Ibid., 44.

29. Peggy Frampton, *Seven Candles for My Life* (Edinburgh: Pentland, 1994), 41.

30. Huxley and Curtis, *Pioneers' Scrapbook*, 56.

31. *Mombasa Times and Uganda Argus*, 1906 and 1927, KNA, Nairobi.

32. Quote from Grace Theresa McKenzie, "Two Blades of Grass, 1935–1937," undated, and Madeleine Platts, "Diary," 1912–13, both at RHL, Oxford.

33. Cara Buxton, "Letters," 1913–1924, RHL, Oxford; and Huxley, *Nine Faces of Kenya*, 111.

34. "Cattle Ranchers Are His Customers," unidentified and undated clipping, in Peggy Forrester, "Papers," 1914–56, RHL, Oxford.

35. Nora K. Strange, *Kenya To-Day* (London: Stanley Paul, 1934), 165–67; and Mrs. K. Armstrong, "Recollections of Kenya, 1919 to 1930," undated, RHL, Oxford. For farm jobs, see R. F. Osburn, *Practical Points for Settlers* (Nairobi: East African Standard, 1941).

36. Elkington, "Recollections"; and "Cattle Ranchers Are His Customers," RHL, Oxford.

37. Interview with Peter Low by author, 6 May 1998, Naivasha, Kenya; Arnold Curtis, ed., *Memories of Kenya: Stories from the Pioneers* (London: Evans, 1986), 74; and John Overton, "War and Economic Development: Settlers in Kenya, 1914–1918," *Journal of American History* 27 (1986): 79–103.

38. Huxley and Curtis, *Pioneers' Scrapbook*, 80.

39. Interview with Mairo Low Hopcraft by author, Loldia House, Naivasha, April 15, 1998.

40. Strange, *Kenya To-Day*, 2670.25.

41. Interview with Dorian Rocco, by author, Muthaiga Club, Nairobi, April 20, 1998.

42. Cynthia Salvadori, *We Came in Dhows*, 3 vols. (Nairobi: Paperchase, 1996), 1: 32, 64; 2: 44–45.

43. Ibid., 1: 40.

44. Ibid., 1: 27, 78, 171.

45. Ibid., 2: 122, 134; and Sirpa Tenhunen, "Women's Hidden Work and Agency in Calcutta," in Karen Armstrong, ed., *Shifting Ground and Cultured Bodies: Postcolonial Gender Relations in Africa and India* (Lanham, MD: University Press of America, 1999), 102–18.

46. Jean Bacon, *Life Lines: Community, Family, and Assimilation Among Asian Indian Immigrants* (New York: Oxford University Press, 1996), x, xiii–xiv, 17, 30–31, 40, 203–4.

47. Kathryn Stoner Hicks Moody, "Territorial Days in Minnesota," 7 July 1960, and Lydia M. Sprague Scott, "Diary, 1878–1890," both at MHS, St. Paul; Clara Ann Dodge, "Letters," 1841–1849, ISHS, Iowa City; and Mor Hetteen of Roseau County, in Minnesota American Mothers Committee Biographies, 1975, MHS, St. Paul. Also, see Riley, *Female Frontier*, 62–63, 92–93.

48. Elliott West, *Growing Up With the Country: Childhood on the Far Western Frontier* (Albuquerque: University of New Mexico Press, 1984), 73–98; and Elizabeth Hampsten, *Settlers' Children: Growing Up on the Great Plains* (Norman: University of Oklahoma Press, 1991), 13–34.

49. Riley, *Female Frontier*, 52–53, 62, 84–85.

50. Matilda Peitzke Paul, "Recollections," 1938, ISHS, Iowa City. Other examples are in Glenda Riley, *Frontierswomen: The Iowa Experience* (Ames: Iowa State University Press, 1981), 21–22, 34, 38, 42, 59, 62, 65, 72–73, 83–85, 115, 121.

51. Mary B. Welch, *Mrs. Welch's Cookbook* (Des Moines, IA: Mills, 1884); Julia K. S. Hibbard, "Reminiscences, 1856–68," undated, and Arnold Fladager, "Memoir of

My Mother, Mrs. M. Fladager," 1927, both at MHS, St. Paul; and Nannie T. Alderson and Helena Huntington Smith, *A Bride Goes West* (Lincoln: University of Nebraska Press, 1969), 205–6.

52. For social events, see Alderson and Smith, *Bride Goes West*, 269; Mary Baillie and George Baillie, "Recollections in the Form of a Duet," 1939, Enid Bennetts, "Rural Pioneer Life," 1939, Lottie Holmberg, recorder, Laura Ingraham Bragg, "Recollections," undated, and Lena Carlile Hurdsman, "Mrs. Lena Hurdsman of Mountain View," 1939, all at WSAMHD, Cheyenne; Minnie Doehring, "Kansas One Room Public School," 1981, KSHS, Topeka; W. H. Elznic, in Pioneer Daughters' Collection, SDSHRC, Pierre; and Graphia Mewhirter Wilson, "Pioneer Life," 1939, University of Wyoming American Heritage Center, Laramie (hereafter cited as UWAHC).

53. For example, Bulah Liles Patterson, Interview, 27 October 1983, Institute of Oral History, University of Texas at El Paso (hereafter cited as UTEP).

54. Julia Archibald Holmes, "A Journey to Pike's Peak," *The Sibyl* (Middletown, NY) 3 (March 15, 1859), 1. A fuller discussion is in Riley, *Women and Nature*, 114–34.

55. Deena J. González, *Refusing the Favor: The Spanish-Mexican Women of Santa Fe, 1820–1880* (New York: Oxford University Press, 1999), 24, 32–33. Also useful is Alfredo Enríquez and Mirandé Evangelina, *La Chicana: The Mexican-American Woman* (Chicago: University of Chicago Press, 1979).

56. González, *Refusing the Favor*, 74–75, 98–100.

57. Sandra L. Stephens, "The Women of the Amador Family, 1860–1940," in Joan M. Jensen and Darlis A. Miller, eds., *New Mexico Women: Intercultural Perspectives* (Albuquerque: University of New Mexico Press, 1986), 258–59.

58. "The Little Flower Club," ca. 1920s, AHS, Tucson.

59. Raymond S. Brandes, transcriber, "Times Gone By in Alta California: The Recollections of Señora Doña Juana Machado Alípaz de Wrightington," *Californians* 8 (November/December 1990): 43–57.

60. Sarah Deutsch, *No Separate Refuge: Culture, Class, and Gender on an Anglo-Hispanic Frontier in the American Southwest, 1880–1940* (New York: Oxford University Press, 1989), 44.

61. González, *Refusing the Favor*, 73–74; and Glenda Riley, *Building and Breaking Families in the American West* (Albuquerque: University of New Mexico Press, 1996), 79–82, 98–100.

62. Mary Mitford-Barberton, "Journal," 1914, in Raymond Mitford-Barberton, "Papers," 1912–1923, KNA, Nairobi.

63. McKenzie, "Two Blades of Grass," RHL, Oxford; and St. Andrew's Church Woman's Guild, *The Kenya Settlers' Cookery Book and Household Guide* (Nairobi: Kenway, 1994).

64. Huxley and Curtis, *Pioneers' Scrapbook*, 30–31.

65. Ryan, *Over My Shoulder*, 15–16, 36.

66. Peggy Frampton, *Seven Candles for My Life* (Edinburgh: Pentlan, 1994), 31; K. A. Hill-Williams, "Memoirs, 1908–50s," undated, RHL, Oxford; and Interview with Mairo Hopcraft.

67. *Mombasa Times and Uganda Argus*, 23 November 1902; Lady Lucy Marguerite Thomas, "Reminiscences, 1904–1946," undated, and Lady Daphne Moore, "Diary, 1924–34," both at RHL, Oxford.

68. Jeannette A. Pierce, "Records of Thomson's Falls Country Club," 1927–1962, RHL, Oxford. For listings of clubs, see *The Kenya Annual and Directory, 1922* (Nairobi: Caxton, 1922), 84–89.

69. Genesta Hamilton, *A Stone's Throw: Travels from Africa in Six Decades* (London: Hutchinson, 1986), 89–90, 108–09; Huxley and Curtis, *Pioneers' Scrapbook*, 18–19, 126; Mirella Ricciardi, *African Saga* (London: Collins, 1981), 48; and Armstrong, "Recollections of Kenya."

70. Quote from Buxton, "Letters." See also Mrs. Maurice Martineau, "Letters from Kenya," 1904, RHL, Oxford.

71. Sitara Khan, *A Glimpse Through Purdah: Asian Women—The Myth and the Reality* (Staffordshire, England: Trentham, 1999), 47–51; and Salvadori, *We Came in Dhows,* 3: 17, 23, 25, 75.

72. Khan, *Glimpse Through Purdah*, 51–53, 89; and Salvadori, *We Came in Dhows*, 2: 134.

73. Louis Brenner, ed., *Muslim Identity and Social Change in Sub-Saharan Africa* (Bloomington: Indiana University Press, 1993), 198–99, 200–203.

74. Salvadori, *We Came in Dhows*, 3: 21 and 1: 132–33.

75. Ibid., 2: 92–93.

76. Janet L. Finn, *Tracing the Veins: Of Copper, Culture and Community from Butte to Chuquicamata* (Berkeley: University of California Press, 1998), 129.

77. Jo Ella Powell Exley, *Texas Tears and Texas Sunshine: Voices of Frontier Women* (College Station: Texas A & M University Press, 1985), 130–41.

78. Thomas D. Hall, "A Heuristic for Comparing Frontiers," unpublished paper presented at the Western History Association conference, San Antonio, Texas, October 13, 2000.

79. John W. Cell, *The Highest Stage of White Supremacy: The Origins of Segregation in South Africa and the American South* (Cambridge, England: Cambridge University Press, 1982), ix, 1–20; Nettie Sandford, *Early Sketch of Polk County* (Newton, IA: Clark, 1874), 33; and interview with Mrs. C. W. Callerman, Oklahoma City, Oklahoma, 1937, Indian-Pioneer Papers, Western History Collection, University of Oklahoma Library, Norman (hereafter cited as WHC, UOL).

80. John C. Hudson, "The Study of Western Frontier Populations," in Jerome Steffen, ed., *The American West: New Perspectives, New Dimension* (Norman: University of Oklahoma Press, 1979), 25–60.

81. Alderson and Smith, *Bride Goes West*, 132, 136.

82. For sunbonnets, see Mary Raymond, "My Experiences as a Pioneer," 1929, 1933, NSHS, Lincoln; Muriel H. Wright, "Mrs. John Williams: A Pioneer in the Indian Territory," *Chronicles of Oklahoma* 30 (Winter 1953/53): 378; and Lillian Schlissel, "Mothers and Daughters on the Western Frontier," *Frontiers* 3 (Summer 1979): 31–32. Anti-marriage is in Mollie Dorsey Sanford, *Mollie: The Journal of Mollie Dorsey Sanford in Nebraska and Colorado Territories, 1857–1866*

(Lincoln: University of Nebraska Press, 1976), 20, 39, 73; and Carrie Roberts, in Montana American Mothers' Biography Project, MHS, Helena.

83. *The "Leader" Annual and Gazetteer of British East Africa, 1914* (Nairobi: Caxton, 1914), 131; and W. MacLellan Wilson, comp., *Kenya* (Nairobi: Kenya Empire Exhibition Council, 1924), 39.

84. Quoted in Huxley and Curtis, *Pioneers' Scrapbook*, 111. For railroads, see Eve Bache, *The Youngest Lion: Early Farming Days in Kenya* (London: Hutchinson, 1934), 168; and for the mail, Lord and Lady Francis Scott, "Papers," 1919–1976, unnumbered microfilm, KNA, Nairobi.

85. M. Aline Buxton, *Kenya Days* (London: Edward Arnold, 1927), 20. For home leaves, see R. M. Maxon, *John Ainsworth and the Making of Kenya* (Lanham, MD: University Press of America, 1980), 105, 172, 207, 403.

86. Margaret Elkington, "Recollections of a Settler in Kenya, 1905–1970," 1971, RHL, Oxford.

87. K. A. Hill-Williams, "Memoirs"; and Platts, "Diary."

88. Elkington, "Recollections."

89. Wilson, *Kenya*, 34.

90. M. K. Hamilton, *Turn the Hour: A Tale of Life in Colonial Kenya* (Sussex, England: Book Guild, 1991), 66.

91. Armstrong, "Recollections of Kenya."

92. Anne McClintock, *Imperial Leather: Race, Gender and Sexuality in the Colonial Contest* (New York: Routledge, 1995), 214, 223–26.

93. John H. A. Jewell, *Mombasa: The Friendly Town* (Nairobi: East African Publishing, 1976), 33–36.

94. Errol Trzebinski, *The Kenya Pioneers* (London: Heineman, 1985), 173; H. Macnaghten, "Letters," 1906–1919, RHL, Oxford; and Majorie Murray, "Collection," Photographs, 1924–1936, Mss. 45, KNA, Nairobi.

95. Esther Hopcraft, *Esther's Story* (Victoria, BC: Baharini, 1996), 60. Similar accounts are Meyers, "Blowing My Own Trumpet"; and Huxley and Curtis, *Pioneers' Scrapbook*, 104.

96. An example is H. Macnaghten, "Selected Letters," undated, RHL, Oxford. Those who stayed were Edith Klapprott, "Papers," c. 1976; Janice Cott Kane, "Papers," 1978–1982; and Alta Howard Hoyt, "We Were Pioneers," undated, all in KNA, Nairobi.

97. *British Parliamentary Papers, Kenya/Malawi, 1890–1899* (Shannon: Irish University Press, 1971), 115; and *Kenya* (Nairobi: Kenya Land Settlement Advisory Committee, 1924), 83.

98. Ricciardi, *African Saga*, 70, 86; and Meyers, "Blowing My Own Trumpet."

99. Interview with Mairo Hopcraft. For an idealized view, see May Baldwin, *Kenya Kiddies: A Story of Settlers' Children in East Africa* (Philadelphia: Lippincott, undated). A description of white schools is in *The Kenya Annual and Directory* (Nairobi: Caxton, 1927), 69–70.

100. David Read, *Barefoot Over the Serengeti* (London: Cassell, 1979), 187.

101. Interview with Robert R. McConnel, "Mr. Bob," by author, Ngowe House, 9 April 1998, Malindi, Kenya.

102. Huxley, *Mottled Lizard*, 75, 77, 249; and Leonore Davidoff, "Class and Gender in Victorian England," in Judith L. Newton, Mary P. Ryan, and Judith R. Walkowitz, *Sex and Class in Women's History* (London: Routledge, 1983), 27.

103. G. Kerby, "The Education of European Children in Contact with Primitive Races," 1927, RHL, Oxford; and Anna Davin, "Imperialism and Motherhood," in Frederick Cooper and Ann Laura Stoler, eds., *Tensions of Empire: Colonial Cultures in a Bourgeois World* (Berkeley: University of California Press, 1997), 87–151.

104. Huxley, *White Man's Country: No Easy Way; A History of the Kenya Farmers' Association and Uganda Limited* (Nairobi: East African Standard, 1957); Huxley, *A New Earth: An Experiment in Colonialism* (London: Chatto and Windus, 1960); Huxley and Margery Perham, *Race and Politics in Kenya* (London: Faber, 1944); and Huxley and Curtis, *Pioneers' Scrapbook*.

105. Interview with Doreen Tofe Field, 9 April 1998, by author, Ngowe House, Malindi, Kenya.

106. Quote from David Anthony, producer, *Black Man's Land, White Man's Country*, London, David Anthony Productions, 1973.

Chapter 5

1. Bruce Berman, *Control and Crisis in Colonial Kenya: The Dialectic of Domination* (London: Currey, 1990), 75–83.

2. Lady Lucy Marguerite Thomas, "Reminiscences, 1904–1946," undated, RHL, Oxford.

3. "Running a Boardinghouse in the Mines," *California Emigrant Letters* 24 (December 1945): 347; and E. J. Guerin, *Mountain Charley; of the Adventures of Mrs. E. J. Guerin, Who Was Thirteen Years in Male Attire* (Norman: University of Oklahoma Press, 1986).

4. Jo Ella Powell Exley, ed., *Texas Tears and Texas Sunshine: Voices of Frontier Women* (College Station: Texas A & M University Press, 1985), 227–42; and Christie Daily, "A Woman's Concern: Milliners in Central Iowa, 1870–1880," *Journal of the West* 21 (April 1982): 26–27.

5. Rex C. Myers, "An Inning for Sin: Chicago Joe and Her Hurdy-Gurdy Girls," *Montana* 27 (April 1977): 24–33; and Jo Ann Levy, *They Saw the Elephant: Women in the California Gold Rush* (Norman: University of Oklahoma Press, 1992).

6. Glenda Riley, *Frontierswomen: The Iowa Experience* (Ames: Iowa State University Press, 1981), 143–52.

7. Bertha Martinson Sonsteby, in Minnesota American Mothers Committee, 1975, MHS, St. Paul.

8. Exley, *Texas Tears and Texas Sunshine*, 227–42.

9. Dee Garceau, "Single Women Homesteaders and the Meanings of Independence: Places on the Map, Places in the Mind," *Frontiers* 15 (1995): 1–26.

10. Abbie Bright, "Diary," 1870–71, KSHS, Topeka; and Serena J. Washburn,

"Autobiography, 1836–1904," undated, Montana State University Library, Bozeman (hereafter cited as MSUL).

11. Alice Stewart Hill, "Papers," undated, Denver Public Library (hereafter cited as DPL).

12. Ruth T. Shaffer, *Road to Kilimanjaro* (Grand Rapids, MI: Four Corners, 1985), 117.

13. *The African Standard*, Vol. 1, 3 August 1903, 8; and 15 August 1903, 6.

14. Jan Hemsing, *Old Nairobi and the New Stanley Hotel* (Nairobi: Church, Riatt, 1974), 8–10.

15. Ibid., 18, 23.

16. Ibid., 31–47.

17. Beryl Markham, *West with the Night* (London: Penguin, 1988); Mary S. Lovell, *Straight on Till Morning: The Life of Beryl Markham* (London: Arena, 1987); and Errol Trzebinski, *The Lives of Beryl Markham: Out of Africa's Hidden Seductress* (London: Mandarin, 1994).

18. Elspeth Huxley and Arnold Curtis, eds., *Pioneers' Scrapbook: Reminiscences of Kenya 1890 to 1968* (London: Evans), 27–28.

19. Ibid., 102.

20. Sir Charles Jeffries, *Partners for Progress: Men and Women of the Colonial Service* (London: George G. Harrap, 1949), 152.

21. "Interview with Velia Carn, re Vera Marie Mordaunt," 4 May 1998, by author, Elsamere Conservation Centre, Naivasha. Also helpful are Katharine Robertson Jardine, "Reminiscences of Nursing in Kenya, 1930–1951," undated, RHL, Oxford; and Medical Department, "Instructions for Nursing Sisters in East Africa Protectorate, 1918," MOH/1/8229, KNA, Nairobi.

22. Margaret J. Gillon, "The Wagon and the Star," undated, RHL, Oxford.

23. Betty Minchin, "Papers," undated, unnumbered microfilm, KNA, Nairobi; and Miss K. A. Hill-Williams, "Memoirs, 1908–1950s," undated, RHL, Oxford.

24. Errol Trzebinski, *The Kenya Pioneers* (London: Heinemann, 1985), 114, 102–03.

25. Interview with Elly Grammaticas, 2 May 1998, by author, Loldia House, Naivasha, Kenya.

26. Huxley and Curtis, *Pioneers' Scrapbook*, 23–24.

27. Cara P. Buxton, "Papers," 1913–24, unnumbered microfilm, KNA, Nairobi; and Grace Theresa McKenzie, "Two Blades of Grass 1935–37," undated, RHL, Oxford, England.

28. Centenary of Mary Layard Mitford-Barberton, in Raymond Mitford-Barberton, "Papers," 1963, Mss. Box 236, KNA, Nairobi.

29. Elspeth Huxley, *Out in the Midday Sun* (Middlesex, England: Penguin, 1987), 92–93.

30. Naivasha and District Farmers Association, "Minute Book," January 1925 to 13 August 1962, 8, 57, 59–60, 88–89, privately held by Dorian Rocco, Nairobi, Kenya. Also helpful is Elspeth Huxley, *No Easy Way: A History of the Kenya Farmers Association and Uganda Limited* (Nairobi: East African Standard, 1957).

31. Edith Maturin, *Adventures Beyond the Zambesi* (London: Eveleigh Nash, 1913), 21.

32. Osa C. Johnson, *I Married Adventure* (London: Hutchinson, 1940), 295–303.

33. Kathleen Bruyn, *"Aunt" Clara Brown: Story of a Black Pioneer* (Boulder, CO: Pruett, 1970); Bobi Jackson, "Biddy (Bridget) Mason," in Darlene Clark Hine, ed., *Black Women in America: An Historical Encyclopedia* (Brooklyn, NY: Carlson, 1993), 753–54; and Donna Mungen, *Life and Times of Biddy Mason: From Slavery to Wealthy California Laundress* (N.p.: N.p., 1976);

34. Quintard Taylor, "Mary Ellen Pleasant: Entrepreneur and Civil Rights Activist in the Far West," in Glenda Riley and Richard W. Etulain, eds., *By Grit and Grace: Eleven Women Who Shaped the American West* (Golden, CO: Fulcrum, 1999), 115–34.

35. Patricia C. Albers, "Sioux Women in Transition: A Study of Their Changing Status in Domestic and Capitalist Sectors of Production," 175–236, in Patricia Albers and Beatrice Medicine, *The Hidden Half: Studies of Plains Indian Women* (Washington, D.C.: University Press of America, 1983); Carol Douglas Sparks, "The Land Incarnate: Navajo Women and the Dialogue of Colonialism, 1821–1870," 135–56, in Nancy Shoemaker, ed., *Negotiators of Change: Historical Perspectives on Native American Women* (New York: Routledge, 1995); Mary Shepardson, "The Gender Status of Navajo Women," 159–76, in Laura F. Klein and Lillian A. Ackerman, *Women and Power in Native North America* (Norman: University of Oklahoma Press, 1995); Victoria D. Patterson, "Evolving Gender Roles in Pomo Society," 126–45, in Klein and Ackerman, *Women and Power*.

36. Cynthia Salvadori, *We Came in Dhows,* 3 vols. (Nairobi: Paperchase, 1996), 2: 56, 122, 134, 165; and Sitara Khan, *A Glimpse Through Purdah: Asian Women— The Myth and the Reality* (Staffordshire, England: Trentham, 1999), 29–35.

37. Jean Davison, *Voices from Mutira: Change in the Lives of Rural Gikuyu Women, 1910–1995* (Boulder, CO: Lynne Rienner Publishers, 1996), 71–73; and Claire C. Robertson, *Trouble Showed the Way: Women, Men, and Trade in the Nairobi Area, 1890–1990* (Bloomington: Indiana University Press, 1997), 4–7, 34–35, 38–51, 61–67, 77–85. For women's independence, see Claire C. Robertson, "Transitions in Kenyan Patriarchy: Attempts to Control Neirobi Area Traders, 1920–1963," 47–72, in Kathleen Sheldon, ed., *Courtyards, Markets, City Streets: Urban Women in Africa* (Boulder, CO: Westview, 1996).

38. Marilyn Dell Brady, "Populism and Feminism in a Newspaper by and for Women of the Kansas Farmers' Alliance, 1891–1894," *Kansas History* 7 (Winter 1984–85): 280–90; O. Gene Clanton, "Intolerant Populist? The Disaffection of Mary Elizabeth Lease," *Kansas Historical Quarterly* 34 (Summer 1968): 189–200; and Katherine B. Clinton, "What Did You Say, Mrs. Lease?" *KHQ* 1 (Fall 1969): 52–59. Also helpful is Karen Blair, *The Clubwoman as Feminist: True Womanhood Redefined, 1868–1914* (New York: Holmes and Meier, 1980).

39. Mrs. R. O. Brandt, "Social Aspects of Prairie Pioneering: The Reminiscences of a Pioneer Pastor's Wife," *Norwegian-American Studies* 7 (1933): 16–17; and Darlene Ritter, "The Faith of Pioneer Women," *Nebraska Humanist* 6 (Fall 1983): 26–30.

40. Quoted in Gloria Ricci Lothrop, "Women Pioneers and the California Landscape," *The Californians* 4 (May–June 1986): 16–23.

41. Glenda Riley, *Women and Nature: Saving the "Wild" West* (Lincoln: University of Nebraska Press, 1990), 80–96; Vera Norwood, *Made From This Earth: American Women and Nature* (Chapel Hill: University of North Carolina Press, 1993), 125–27; and Polly Welts Kaufman, *National Parks and Woman's Voice: A History* (Albuquerque: University of New Mexico Press, 1996), 28–30.

42. Mathilda C. Engstad, "The White Kid Glove Era," undated, SHSND, Bismarck; and Marilyn Hoder-Salmon, "Myrtle Archer McDougal: Leader of Oklahoma's 'Timid Sisters,'" *Chronicles of Oklahoma* 60 (Fall 1982): 32–43.

43. Ruth A. Gallaher, *Legal and Political Status of Women in Iowa, 1838–1918* (Iowa City: State Historical Society, 1918), 152–55.

44. Riley, *Frontierswomen*, 158–70.

45. Beverly Beeton and G. Thomas Edwards, "Susan B. Anthony's Woman Suffrage Crusade in the American West," *JW* 21 (April 1982): 5; Dr. Grace Raymond Hebard, "How Woman Suffrage Came to Wyoming," undated, WSAMHD, Cheyenne; Katharine A. Morton, "A Historical Review of Women's Suffrage," *Annals of Wyoming* 12 (April 1940): 23–25; and Virginia Scharff, "The Case for Domestic Feminism: Woman Suffrage in Wyoming," *Annals of Wyoming* 56 (Fall 1984): 29–37.

46. Billie Barnes Jensen, "Let the Women Vote," *Colorado Magazine* 41 (Winter 1964): 13–19; and Jensen, "Colorado Woman Suffrage Campaign of the 1870s," *Journal of the West* 12 (April 1973): 254–71.

47. Elizabeth Cochran, "Hatchets and Hoopskirts: Women in Kansas History," *Midwest Quarterly* 2 (April 1961), 230; and Martha B. Caldwell, "The Woman Suffrage Campaign of 1912," *Kansas Historical Quarterly* 39 (August 1943): 300–318.

48. Mary Long Alderson, "A Half Century of Progress for Montana Women," 1934, MHS, Helena.

49. Dorinda Riessen Reed, *The Woman Suffrage Movement in South Dakota* (Pierre: South Dakota Commission on the Status of Women, 1975), 5–7, 11–14, 18–113; Ruth B. Hipple, "History of Women Suffrage in South Dakota," 1920, Woman Suffrage Papers, SDSHRC, Pierre; and Mary Kay Jennings, "Lake County Woman Suffrage Campaign in 1890," *South Dakota History* 5 (Fall 1975): 390–401.

50. Ann L. Wiegman Wilhite, "Sixty-Five Years till Victory: A History of Woman Suffrage in Nebraska," *Nebraska History* 49 (Summer 1968): 149–68; and items in Suffrage Collection, NSHS, Lincoln.

51. Glenda Riley, *The Female Frontier: A Comparative View of Women on the Prairie and Plains* (Lawrence: University Press of Kansas, 1988), 192–93.

52. Elizabeth Cochran, "Hatchets and Hoopskirts: Women in Kansas History," *Midwest Quarterly* 2 (April 1961): 232.

53. Olive Pickering Rankin, in Montana American Mothers Bicentennial Project, 1975/76, MHS, Helena.

54. Luna E. Kellie, "Memoirs," undated, NSHS, Lincoln; and Douglas A. Bakken, ed., "Luna E. Kellie and the Farmers' Alliance," *Nebraska History* 7 (Winter 1984/85): 201–2.

55. Maturin, *Adventures Beyond the Zambesi*, 1–3.

56. Mirella Ricciardi, *African Saga* (London: Collins, 1981), 43, 48, 53.

57. Laura Ann Stoler, "Carnal Knowledge and Imperial Power, Gender, Race, and Morality in Colonial Asia," in Micaela di Leonardo, ed., *Gender at the Crossroads of Knowledge: Feminist Anthropology in the Postmodern Era* (Berkeley: University of California Press, 1991), 61–65; and Philippa Levine, *Victorian Feminism, 1850–1900* (Gainesville: University Press of Florida, 1994), 137–41.

58. Mrs. K. C. Armstrong, "Recollections of Kenya, 1919 to 1930," undated, RHL, Oxford; and Legal Department, Attorney General's Office, "The Married Women's Property Act," 1935, AG/1/609, KNA, Nairobi.

59. Dorothy Vaughan, "Reminiscences," 1909–1950s, RHL, Oxford; and Judicial Dept., "Divorce Ordinance Correspondence," 1931–1952, DC/KSM/1/15/113, KNA, Nairobi.

60. Edward Rodwell, *The Mombasa Club* (Mombasa: Rodwell, 1988), 15, 21, 30, 44, 49, 53; and Karen Tranberg Hansen, "White Women in a Changing World: Employment, Voluntary Work, and Sex in Post–World War II Northern Rhodesia," in Nupur Chaudhuri and Margaret Strobel, eds., *Western Women and Imperialism: Complicity and Resistance* (Bloomington: Indiana University Press, 1992), 247–50.

61. Quote from Charles Jeffries, *Partners for Progress: Men and Women of the Colonial Service* (London: Harrap, 1949), 156. Examples are in Daphne Moore, "Diary," 1929–1934, RHL, Oxford; and M. H. Hamilton, *Turn the Hour: A Tale of Colonial Life in Kenya* (Sussex, England: Book Guild, 1991), 26–29, 88.

62. Postmaster General's Office, "Women's War Work League," 1918, DC/Coast/1/18/13, KNA, Nairobi.

63. Rosendo P. Abrero, *Historical Review of the Kenya Prisons Service from 1911 to 1970* (Naivasha: Prison Industries, 1972), 1–2.

64. Ibid., 3–4.

65. Provincial Commissioner, Mombasa, "Visits to Gaolers and Matrons," 1916, KNA, Nairobi; and Abrero, *Historical Review of the Kenya Prisons Service*, 5.

66. Esther E. Hopcraft, *Esther's Story* (Victoria, BC: Baharini, 1996), 134; and quoted in Margaret Wrong, *Across Africa* (London: International Committee on Christian Literature, 1940), 9. Prison conditions are discussed in Hester Katherine Henn, "Papers," 1940–1962, unnumbered, KNA, Nairobi.

67. Provincial Commissioner Coast, Mombasa District, "Inspections, Prisons," 1929–1058, PC/Coast/1/17/109, KNA, Nairobi.

68. Wrong, *Across Africa*, 8.

69. Huxley, *Out in the Midday Sun*, 50–53.

70. Johnson, *I Married Adventure*, 317.

71. Lady Eleanor Cole, *Random Recollections of a Pioneer Kenya Settler* (Suffolk, England: Baron, 1975), 60, 65.

72. Quoted in Cecil Davis, comp., *The Kenya Annual and Directory* (Nairobi: Caxton, 1922), 77; and the editorial in East Africa Women's League, *Seventy Years* (Nairobi: East Africa Women's League, 1987), 3.

73. Davis, *Kenya Annual*, 77.

74. East Africa Women's League, *Seventy Years*, 5–15.

75. Quoted in ibid., 11.

76. Huxley, *Out in the Midday Sun*, 54–55.

77. Jean Haggis, "White Women and Colonialism: Towards a Non-recuperative History," 79–103, and Clare Midgley, "Anti-slavery and the Roots of 'Imperial Feminism,'" 161–79, both in Clare Midgley, ed., *Gender and Imperialism* (Manchester, England: Manchester University Press, 1998).

78. East Africa European Pioneers' Society, "Newsletters," 1954–1960, in Mrs. B. D. Hughes, Collection, 1950–1960s, Ms. 13, KNA, Nairobi.

79. Ibid., 3, 5–15.

80. Nora K. Strange, *Kenya To-Day* (London: Paul, 1934), 168–70.

81. Walter Weare, "Mutual Benefit Societies," in Darlene Clark Hine, ed., *Black Women in America* (Brooklyn, NY: Carlson, 1993), 829–31.

82. Susan H. Armitage and Deborah Gallacci Wilbert, "Black Women in the Pacific Northwest: A Survey and Research Prospectus," in Karen J. Blair, ed., *Women in Pacific Northwest History: An Anthology* (Seattle: University of Washington Press, 1988), 140–43.

83. Ibid.

84. Taylor, "Mary Ellen Pleasant," in Riley and Etulain, *By Grit and Grace*, 115–34.

85. Ibid., 1: 10–11, 1: 17.

86. Cynthia Salvadori, *Through Open Doors: A View of Asian Cultures in Kenya* (Nairobi: Kenway, 1989 rev. ed.), 1: 10.

87. Salvadori, *We Came in Dhows*, 2: 17.

88. Ibid., *We Came in Dhows*, 1: 33, 52, and 3:113, 160.

89. Sarah Mirza and Margaret Strobel, eds., *Three Swahili Women: Life Histories from Mombasa, Kenya* (Bloomington: Indiana University Press, 1989), 102–5.

90. Dawn L. Gherman, "From Parlor to Teepee: The White Squaw on the American Frontier" (Ph.D. diss., University of Massachusetts, 1975), 216–19; and Glenda Riley, *Women and Indians on the Frontier, 1825–1915* (Albuquerque: University of New Mexico Press, 1984), 180–84.

91. George M. Frederickson, *White Supremacy: A Comparative Study in American and South African History* (New York: Oxford University Press, 1981), 246–47, 268–69.

92. Robin Higham, "Frontiers—A Global View," *JW* 34 (October 1995): 49.

93. Levy, *They Saw the Elephant*, 209–13.

94. Brigitta Maria Ingemanson, "Under Cover: The Paradox of Victorian Women's Travel Costume," in Bonnie Frederick and Susan H. McLeod, eds., *Women and the Journey: The Female Travel Experience* (Pullman: Washington State University Press, 1993), 5–19.

95. James S. Brust and Lee H. Whittlesey, "'Roughing It Up the Yellowstone to Wonderland': The Nelson Miles/Colgate Hoyt Party in Yellowstone National Park, September 1878," *Montana* 46 (Spring 1986): 56–64.

96. Chicago and Northwestern Railways, "The Enchanted Summer-Land," undated, 1–5, brochure in author's possession.

97. Serena J. Washburn, "Autobiography," 1836–1904, Special Collections, MSUL, Bozeman.

98. Ella Carroll, "Pleasant Memories," undated, Norlin Library, University of Colorado at Boulder.

99. New Mexico State Tourist Bureau, "Recreational Map," 1941, brochure in author's possession; and Krista Comer, *Landscapes of the New West: Gender and Geography in Contemporary Women's Writing* (Chapel Hill: University of North Carolina Press, 1999), 124. Also enlightening is Hipólito Rafael Chacón, "Creating a Mythic Past: Spanish-style Architecture in Montana," *Montana* 51 (Autumn 2001): 46–59.

100. Attack reported in Rex C. Myers, ed., *Lizzie: The Letters of Elizabeth Chester Fish, 1864–1893* (Missoula, MT: Mountain Press, 1989), 48–49.

101. William Anthes, "The Indian's White Man," *Journal of the West* 40 (Fall 2001), 26–33.

102. Annie B. Schencks, "Journal: Camping Tour in Rocky Mountains," August, 1871, Colorado Historical Society, Denver (hereafter cited as CHS).

103. Eugene M. Hattori, "'And Some of Them Swear Like Pirates': Acculturation of American Indian Women in Nineteenth-Century Virginia City," in Ronald M. James and Elizabeth C. Raymond, eds., *Comstock Women: The Making of a Mining Community* (Reno: University of Nevada Press, 1997), 232.

104. "Nampeyo," in Arizona Women's Hall of Fame, 1986, AHS, Tucson, 85–86.

105. Daniel D. Arreola, "Curio Consumerism and Kitsch Culture in the Mexican-American Borderland," *Journal of the West* 40 (Spring 2001): 24–25.

106. Phil Kovinick, *The Woman Artist in the American West, 1860–1960* (Fullerton, CA: Muckenthaler Cultural Center, 1976), 32.

107. Recent interpretations are Seema Alavi, *Sepoys and the Company: Tradition and Transition in Northern India, 1770–1830* (New York: Oxford University Press, 1996); and Tapti Roy, *Politics of a Popular Uprising: Bundelkhand innn 1857* (New York: Oxford University Press, 1995).

108. Lauren Benton, "Colonial Law and Cultural Difference: Jurisdictional Politics and the Formation of the Colonial State," *Comparative Studies in Science and History* 41 (July 1999): 563–88.

109. Berman, *Control and Crisis*, 83–84; and Vron Ware, *Beyond the Pale: White Women, Racism, and History* (New York: Verso, 1992), 37–38.

110. A discussion of white women's fears in Africa is in Margaret Strobel, *European Women and the Second British Empire* (Bloomington: Indiana University Press, 1991), 4–5.

111. Markham, *West with the Night*, 64, 132.

112. Ibid., 138–40.

113. W. MacLellan, comp., *Kenya: Its Industries, Trade, Sports, and Climate* (Nairobi: Kenya Empire Exhibition Council, 1924), 35–36.

114. For a similar case, see Phyllis M. Martin, *Leisure and Society in Colonial Brazzaville* (Cambridge, MA: Cambridge University Press, 1995).

115. Robertson, *Trouble Showed the Way*, 83

116. Mirza and Strobel, *Three Swahili Women*, 77; and Desmond Forristal, *Edel Quinn, 1907–1944* (Dublin: Dominican, 1994), 3, 95, 108, 111.

117. Berman, *Control and Crisis*, 79.

118. Eve Bache, *The Youngest Lion: Early Farming Days in Kenya* (London: Hutchinson, 1934), 65; and Office of the Attorney General, "Indecent Assaults on Women and Children," 1935–42, AG/1/609, KNA, Nairobi.

Chapter 6

1. Elizabeth Emery and Mary P. Abbott, "Letter to *The Liberator*," *The Liberator* 6, 27 August, 1836, 138. Control of men is in Marilyn Lake, "Australian Frontier Feminism and the Marauding White Man," in Clare Midgley, ed., *Gender and Imperialism* (Manchester, England: Manchester University Press, 1998), 123–36.
2. Ronald J. Quinn, "The Modest Seduction: The Experience of Pioneer Women on the Trans-Mississippi Frontier" (Ph.D. diss., University of California at Riverside, 1977).
3. Quoted in Frances M. A. Roe, *Army Letters from an Officer's Wife, 1871–1888* (New York: Appleton, 1909), 96–97; and Lois L. Murray, *Incidents of Frontier Life* (Goshen, IN: Evangelical United Mennonite Publishing, 1990), 92.
4. Evelyn I. Banning, *Helen Hunt Jackson* (New York: Vanguard, 1973); Valerie Sherer Mathes, "Helen Hunt Jackson and the Ponca Controversy," *Montana* 39 (Winter 1989): 42–53; Mathes, "The California Mission Indian Commission of 1891: The Legacy of Helen Hunt Jackson," *CH* 72 (Winter 1993–94): 338–59; and Mathes, *Helen Hunt Jackson and Her Indian Reform Legacy* (Austin: University of Texas Press, 1990).
5. Kay Graber, ed., *Sister to the Sioux: The Memoirs of Elaine Goodale Eastman* (Lincoln: University of Nebraska Press, 1978), 29, 43–44, 64–65.
6. Quoted in "From Our Matrons," in *Ramona Days* (Santa Fe: Ramona Industrial School, 1887), 19.
7. S. F. Cook, *The Conflict Between the California Indian and White Civilization, IV: Trends in Marriage and Divorce since 1850* (Berkeley: University of California Press, 1943), 2–3, 13–14, 29.
8. Sandra L. Myres, *Westering Women and the Frontier Experience, 1880–1915* (Albuquerque: University of New Mexico Press, 1982), 252–53. See also Susan Peterson and Courtney Vaugh-Roberson, *Women With Vision: The Presentation Sisters of South Dakota, 1880–1985* (Urbana: University of Illinois Press, 1988); and Daniel C. Eddy, *Daughters of the Cross; or, Woman's Mission* (Boston, MA: Wentworth, 1856).
9. "Sister Frederica McGrath, D.C., Responds to Criticism in the Nevada Legislature, 1873," 73–74, and "The Daughters of Charity Arrive in Los Angeles, 1856," 153–55, both in Anne M. Butler, Michael E. Engh, S.J., and Thomas W. Spalding, C.F.X., eds., *The Frontiers and Catholic Identities* (Maryknoll, NY: Orbis, 1999); and Susan Peterson, "Doing 'Women's Work': The Grey Nuns at Fort Totten Indian Reservation, 1874–1900," *North Dakota History* 52 (Spring 1985): 18–25; Peterson, "Religious Communities of Women in the West: The Presentation Sisters' Adaptation to the Northern Plains Frontier," *JW* 21 (April 1982): 65–70; Peterson, "From Paradise to Prairie: The

Presentation Sisters in Dakota, 1880–1896," *SDH* 10 (Summer 1980): 210–22; and Peterson, "Challenging the Stereotypes: The Adaptation of the Sisters of St. Francis to South Dakota Indian Missions, 1885–1910," *Upper Midwest History* 4 (1984): 1–10; and Carol K. Coburn and Martha Smith, "'Pray for Your Wanderers': Women Religious on the Colorado Mining Frontier, 1877–1917," *Frontiers* 15 (1995): 27–52.

10. Anne M. Butler, "Mother Katharine Drexel: Spiritual Visionary for the West," in Glenda Riley and Richard W. Etulain, eds., *By Grit and Grace: Eleven Women Who Shaped the American West* (Golden, CO: Fulcrum, 1997), 198–99, 201–5.

11. Quoted in Glenda Riley, *Inventing the American Woman: An Inclusive History* (Wheeling, IL: Harlan Davidson, 2001), 1: 199.

12. Ibid., 1: 199.

13. "Seventy Years in Iowa," *Annals of Iowa* 27 (October 1945): 100, 144–45.

14. Karen Blair, ed., *Women in Pacific Northwest History: An Anthology* (Seattle: University of Washington Press, 1988), 138–39.

15. Ruth Barnes Moynihan, *Rebel for Rights: Abigail Scott Duniway* (New Haven, CT: Yale University Press, 1985); and Moynihan, "Abigail Scott Duniway: Mother of Woman Suffrage in the Pacific Northwest," in Riley and Etulain, *By Grit and Grace*, 174–97.

16. Quote from Sir Charles Jeffries, *Partners for Progress: Men and Women of the Colonial Service* (London: George G. Harrap, 1949), 156.

17. For a discussion of this phenomenon, see Homi Bhabha, "Of Mimicry and Man: The Ambivalence of Colonial Discourse," 85–92, in Homi Bhabha, *The Location of Culture* (London: Routledge, 1994).

18. Ann Laura Stoler and Frederick Cooper, "Between Metropole and Colony: Rethinking a Research Agenda," in Cooper and Stoler, eds., *Tensions of Empire: Colonial Cultures in a Bourgeois World* (Berkeley: University of California Press, 1997), 3–55.

19. Clare Midgley, *Women Against Slavery: The British Campaigns, 1780–1870* (London: Routledge, 1992); Midgley, "Anti-slavery and Feminism in Nineteenth-century Britain," *Gender and History* 3 (1993): 343–62; and Midgley, "Anti-slavery and the Roots of 'Imperial Feminism'" in Midgley, ed., *Gender and Imperialism*, 161–79.

20. Accounts of slavery are in Sarah Mirza and Margaret Strobel, eds., *Three Swahili Women: Life Histories from Mombasa, Kenya* (Bloomington: Indiana University Press, 1989), 19–24, 31–70.

21. Martin A. Klein, "Introduction: Modern European Expansion and Traditional Servitude in Africa and Asia," in Martin A. Klein, ed., *Breaking the Chains: Slavery, Bondage, and Emancipation in Modern Africa and Asia* (Madison: University of Wisconsin Press, 1993), 16–17; and Sir John and Lady Helen Kirk, "Papers," 1842–1920, Microfilm #34620, KNA, Nairobi. Islamic slavery is in Frederick Cooper, *Plantation Slavery on the East Coast of Africa* (New Haven, CT: Yale University Press, 1977).

22. Richard D. Wolff, *The Economics of Colonialism: Britain and Kenya, 1870–1930* (New Haven: Yale University Press, 1974), 34; and Zoë Marsh and G. W.

Kingsnorth, *An Introduction to the History of East Africa* (Cambridge: Cambridge University Press, 1965), 46.

23. Emily [Princess Selme] and Rudolph Ruete, "Papers," 1885–1994, C/A 312, Zanzibar National Archives.

24. Wolff, *Economics of Colonialism*, 31–40, 45. Kirk's career is in Reginald Coupland, *The Exploitation of East Africa, 1856–1890* (London: Faber and Faber, 1939); and the economics of slavery is in Wilhelm G. Clarence-Smith, *The Economics of the Indian Ocean Slave Trade in the Nineteenth Century* (London: Cass, 1989).

25. Lewis Gann and Peter Duignan, *White Settlers in Tropical Africa* (Baltimore: Penguin, 1962), 32–36.

26. Examples are Elizabeth Mary Matheson, *An Experience So Perilous* (London: Mellifont Press, 1963); Medical Department, "The Mother Superior of the White Sisters Appealed for Medicine, 1920, MOH/1/7995; Gladys B. (Leakey) Beecher, "Family Papers," 1850s to 1960s, unnumbered microfilm, KNA, Nairobi; and Alta Howard Hoyt, "We Were Pioneers," undated, 9a0.09HOY, all at KNA, Nairobi. Overviews include C. P. Snow, *The Planting of Christianity in Africa*, 4 vols. (London: Lutterworth, 1948–1954); Robert Delavignette, *Christianity and Colonialism* (London: Burns and Oates, 1964); and Mrs. Thomas Butler, *Missions As I Saw Them* (London: Henry Hook, 1924). For domesticity, see Anne McClintock, *Imperial Leather: Race, Gender and Sexuality in the Colonial Contest* (New York: Routledge, 1995), 35–36.

27. Beecher, "Family Papers; and Louis S. B. Leakey, *White African* (London: Hodder and Stoughton, 1937), 5–8.

28. Rev. and Mrs. H. K. Binns, Journals, 1878–1881, and Photograph Albums, 1895–1921, in Nancy Shepard, Records, 1878–1921, Mss. 2, KNA, Nairobi.

29. Ibid.

30. Ibid.

31. Margaret Strobel, "Slavery and Reproductive Labor in Mombasa," in Claire C. Robertson and Martin A. Klein, eds., *Women and Slavery in Africa* (Madison: University of Wisconsin Press, 1983), 111–29; and Allen Isaacman, "Ex-Slaves, Transfrontiersmen and the Slave Trade: The Chikunda of the Zambesi Valley, 1850–1900," in Paul E. Lovejoy, ed., *Africans in Bondage: Studies in Slavery and the Slave Trade* (Madison: University of Wisconsin Press, 1986), 273–309.

32. Provincial Commission, Seyidi, "Marriages of the Freed Slaves," 1912, PC/Coast/1/3/18, KNA, Nairobi.

33. Margaret Strobel, *European Women and the Second British Empire* (Bloomington: Indiana University Press, 1991), 52–55; and Klein, "Introduction," in Klein, *Breaking the Chains*, 14, 27.

34. Gladys S. Beecher (Leaky), "Family Papers," 1850s to 1960s, unnumbered microfilm, KNA, Nairobi.

35. Megan Vaughan, *Curing Their Ills: Colonial Power and African Illness* (Stanford, CA: Stanford University Press), 23–25, 38–39, 52, 58–59, 156–66.

36. Elizabeth Chadwick, "Papers," 1917–1923, Mss. Box 236, KNA, Nairobi.

37. Ibid.; and Jean Davison, *Voices from Mutira: Change in the Lives of Rural Gikuyu Women, 1910–1995* (Boulder, CO: Lynne Rienner, 1996), 51.

38. *The Taveta Chronicle*, No. 3, December 1895, 20; and No. 5, July 1895, 33.

39. Alta Howard Hoyt, "We Were Pioneers," undated, 910.09 Hoy, KNA, Nairobi; and Ruth T. Shaffer, *Road to Kilimanjaro* (Grand Rapids, MI: Four Corners, 1985), xi–xii.

40. Elizabeth Mary Matheson, *An Experience So Perilous* (London: Mellifont, 1963), 13, 21, 29, 108–09; and Medical Department, "The Mother Superior of the White Sisters Appealed for Medicine," 1920, MOH/1/7995, KNA, Nairobi.

41. Gian Paola Mina, *Her Life a Light: Sister Irene Stephani* (Turin, Italy: Instituto Suore Missionarie Della Consolate, 1991), 34–39, 43–45, 61, 95, 104, 119, 213–15, 261.

42. East Africa Protectorate, Mombasa, "White Settlement in B. E. A. Protectorate," 1918, PC/Coast/1/11/301, KNA, Nairobi; and Butler, *Missions As I Saw Them*, 262, 279–80, 283.

43. Shaffer, *Road to Kilimanjaro*, 19, 39, 43, 101; and Jean Kenyon MacKenzie, *Friends of Africa* (Cambridge, MA: Central Committee on the United Study of Foreign Missions, 1928), 151–61.

44. For Salvation Army, see Rosalie Trembeth, "Papers," 1937–1943, RHL, Oxford; for Methodist Missionary Society, see Grace Ovenden, "Papers," 1940–1955, unnumbered microfilm, KNA, Nairobi; and for Moody Bible Institute, see Shaffer, *Road to Kilimanjaro*.

45. Hoyt, "We Were Pioneers."

46. Snow, *Planting of Christianity in Africa*, 4: 90–107; and Delavignette, *Christianity and Colonialism*, 90.

47. Robert W. Strayer, *The Making of Mission Communities in East Africa* (London: Heinemann, 1978), 31–41; and Delavignette, *Christianity and Colonialism*, 66, 72.

48. Liz Osborn, "Women and Trees: Indigenous Relations and Agroforestry Development," in Stephen H. Arnold and Andre Nitecki, eds., *Culture and Development in Africa* (Trenton, NJ: Africa World Press, 1990), 49–58; and Provincial Commissioner, Ukamba Province, Land File, "A Miss Plowman Applies for land," 1908, DC/MKS.10A/1/5, KNA, Nairobi.

49. Carol Devens, *Countering Civilization: Native American Women and Great Lakes Missions, 1630–1900* (Berkeley: University of California Press, 1992).

50. Sue Fawn Chung, "Their Changing World: Chinese Women on the Comstock, 1860–1910," in Ronald M. James and C. Elizabeth Raymond, ed., *Comstock Women: The Making of a Mining Community* (Reno: University of Nevada Press, 1997), 215–16.

51. Valerie Amos and Pratibha Parmar, "Challenging Imperial Feminism," *Feminist Review* 17 (July 1984): 3–6. See also Pally Dhillon, *Kijabe: An African Historical Saga* (Fayetteville, NC: N.p., 2000).

52. Ruth Nasimiyu, "Women in the Colonial Economy of Bungoma: Role of Women in Agriculture, 1901–1960," *Journal of Eastern African Research and Development* 15 (1985): 56–73; Carolyn M. Clark, "Land and Food, Women and Power, in Nineteenth Century Kikuyu," *Africa* 50 (1980): 357–73; and Margaret Jean Hay, "Luo Women and Economic Change During the Colonial Period,"

in Margaret J. Hafkin and Edna G. Bay, eds., *Women in Africa: Studies in Social and Economic Change* (Stanford, CA: Stanford University Press, 1976): 87–109.

53. Strobel, *European Women and the Second British Empire*, 50–51. Quote in Daisy M. Chown, *Wayfaring in Africa: A Woman's Wanderings from the Cape to Cairo* (London: Heath Cranton, 1927), 103.

54. Achola P. Okeyo, "Daughters of the Lakes and Rivers: Colonization and the Land Rights of Luo Women," in Mona Etienne and Eleanor Leacook, eds., *Women and Colonization: Anthropological Perspectives* (New York: Praeger, 1980), 186–213; Claire C. Robertson, "Black, White, and Red All Over: Beans, Women, and Agricultural Imperialism in Twentieth-Century Kenya," *Agricultural History* 71 (Summer 1997): 259–299; M. S. Ogutu, "The Changing Role of Women in the Commercial History of Busia District in Kenya, 1900–1983," *Journal of Eastern African Research and Development* 15 (1985): 56–73; and Melissa Llewelyn-Davies, "Women, Warriors, and Patriarchs," in Sherry B. Ortner and Harriet Whitehead, eds., *Sexual Meanings: The Cultural Construction of Gender and Sexuality* (New York: Cambridge University Press, 1981), 330–58.

55. Kennell A. Jackson, Jr., "The Family Entity and Famine among the Nineteenth-Century of Kenya: Social Responses to Environmental Stress," *Journal of Family History* 1 (Winter 1976): 192–215; Kathleen A. Staudt, "Rural Women Leaders: Late Colonial and Contemporary Contexts," *Rural Africana* 3 (Winter 1978): 4–21; and Joan Harris, "Revolution or Evolution?" *Africa Report* 30 (March–April 1985): 30–32. For Meru women, see E. Mary Holding, "Anthropological Studies," 1938–1940s, KNA, Nairobi.

56. Charity Waciuma, *Daughter of Mumbi* (Nairobi: East African Publishing, 1969), 62–63; Delavignette, *Christianity and Colonialism*, 22; and Margaret Gillon, "The Wagon and the Star," undated, RHL, Oxford.

57. See Ruth Borden, *Women and Temperance: The Quest for Power and Liberty, 1873–1900* (Philadelphia: Temple University Press, 1981).

58. Jack S. Blocker, Jr., "Annie Wittenmyer and the Women's Crusade," *Ohio History* 88 (Autumn 1979): 420–21; and Mary Long Alderson, "A Half Century of Progress for Montana Women, 1934," MHS, Helena.

59. Ibid.

60. Ada M. Bittenender, "History of the Women's Christian Temperance Union in Nebraska," c. 1893, WCTU Records, NSHS, Lincoln.

61. Virginia M. Bouvier, *Women and the Conquest of California, 1542–1840: Codes of Silence* (Tucson: University of Arizona Press, 2001), 114–15; Rebecca McDowell Craver, *The Impact of Intimacy: Mexican-Anglo Intermarriage in New Mexico, 1821–1846* (El Paso: Texas Western Press, 1982), 12–13, 23–30; and Gary B. Nash, "The History of Mestizo America," in Martha Hodes, *Sex, Love, Race: Crossing Boundaries in North American History* (New York: New York University Press, 1999), 10–31.

62. Douglas Monroy, *Thrown Among Strangers: The Making of Mexican Culture in Frontier California* (Berkeley: University of California Press, 1990), 99–162.

63. A. Miller, "Cross Cultural Marriages in the Southwest: The New Mexico

Experience, 1846–1900," *New Mexico Historical Review* 57 (October 1982): 336–37; Jane Dysart, "Mexican Women in San Antonio, 1830–1860," *Western Historical Quarterly* 7 (October 1976): 365–75; Peggy Pascoe, "Race, Gender, and Intercultural Relations: The Case of Interracial Marriage," *Frontiers* 12 (Fall 1991): 5–18; and Deena J. González, *Refusing the Favor: The Spanish-Mexican Women of Santa Fe, 1820–1880* (New York: Oxford University Press, 1999).

64. John A. Hussey, "The Women of Fort Vancouver," *Oregon Historical Quarterly* 92 (Fall 1991): 266–67.

65. Ibid., 271–72.

66. Susan L. Johnson, "Sharing Bed and Board: Cohabitation and Cultural Difference in Central Arizona Mining Towns," *Frontiers* 7 (Fall 1984): 36–42.

67. Gary D. Sandefur, "American Indian Intermarriage," *Social Science Research* 15 (December 1986): 347–49.

68. Paul R. Spickard, *Mixed Blood: Intermarriage and Ethnic Identity in Twentieth-Century America* (Madison: University of Wisconsin Press, 1989), 374–75. See also Eugene H. Berwanger, *The Frontier Against Slavery: Western Anti-Negro Prejudice and the Slavery Extension Controversy* (Urbana: University of Illinois Press, 1967).

69. "Interview with B. M. Austin," 15 November 1937, #9189, vol. 3, Indian-Pioneer Papers, WHC, UOL, Norman.

70. See, for instance, Madeleine Platts, "Diary," 1912–1923, RHL, Nairobi; and Elspeth Huxley, *Settlers of Kenya* (Westport, CT: Greenwood, 1948), 56–66.

71. Naivasha and District Farmers Association, "Minutes Books," 9 January 1925–13 August 1962, privately held by Dorian Rocco, Nairobi.

72. Two examples are in Cecil Davis, comp., *The Kenya Annual and Directory, 1922* (Nairobi: Caxton Printing, 1922), 54–55, 57, 59; and Colony of Protectorate of Kenya, *Code of Laws* (Nairobi: Government Printer, 1931), 377–86.

73. East Africa Women's League, "Report on the Women's Conference," 27 June 1930, RHL, Oxford.

74. Ibid.

75. Ann Laura Stoler, "Carnal Knowledge and Imperial Power: Gender, Race, and Morality in Colonial Asia," in Micaela di Leonardo, ed., *Gender at the Crossroads of Knowledge: Feminist Anthropology in the Postmodern Era* (Berkeley: University of California Press, 1991), 52–53, 57–61.

76. Elspeth Huxley, *The Mottled Lizard* (London: Penguin, 1986), 167; Leonore Davidoff, "Class and Gender in Victorian England," in Judith L. Newton, Mary P. Ryan, and Judith R. Walkowitz, eds., *Sex and Class in Women's History* (London: Routledge, 1983), 20–21; and J. M. Coetzee, *White Writing: On the Culture of Letters in South Africa* (New Haven, CT: Yale University Press, 1988), 10; Laura Ann Stoler, "Sexual Affronts and Racial Frontiers," in Cooper and Stoler, *Tensions of Empire*, 198–237. Metropole and colony are in Stoler and Cooper, "Between Metropole and Colony," in Cooper and Stoler, *Tensions of Empire*, 3–55.

77. Davidoff, "Class and Gender in Victorian England," in Newton, Ryan, and Walkowitz, *Sex and Class in Women's History*, 20–21; R. M. Maxon, *John Ainsworth and the Making of Kenya* (Lanham, MD: University Press of America,

1980), 85; and Llewelyn Powys, *Black Laughter* (New York: Harcourt Brace, 1924), 123–24.

78. Crown Advocates Dept., "Swedish Women: Legislation re Prostitutes," 12 May 1911, AG/49/28, KNA, Nairobi.

79. Crown Advocates Dept., "Legislation to Prevent Marriages between Indian Men and White Women," 27 March 1924, AG/27/26, KNA, Nairobi.

80. Ann Laura Stoler, *Race and the Education of Desire: Foucault's History of Sexuality and the Colonial Order of Things* (Durham, NC: Duke University Press, 1995), 3–4, 11–12.

81. Anne McDonald, "African Roundabout, 1932–35," undated, RHL, Oxford.

82. Office of the Attorney General, "Indecent Assaults on Women and Children," 1935–42, AG/1/609, KNA, Nairobi.

83. Sander L. Gilman, *Difference and Pathology: Stereotypes of Sexuality, Race and Madness* (Ithaca: Cornell University Press, 1985), 24–25.

84. Ibid., 15–21.

85. Michael Lansing, "Plains Indian Women and Interracial Marriage in the Upper Missouri Trade, 1804–1868," *Western Historical Quarterly* 31 (Winter 2000): 413–33.

86. James R. Carsklowey, in J. G. Starr, "Papers," Cherokee History, Volume 19, WHA, UOL; and Wendy St. Jean, "'You Have the Land, I Have the Cattle': Intermarried Whites and the Chickasaw Range Lands," *Chronicles of Oklahoma* 78 (Summer 2000): 182–95.

87. "Interview with Lena Barnett," 15 October 1937, #7838, vol. 14, Indian-Pioneer Papers, WHA, UOL, Norman.

88. Quintard Taylor, "Slaves, Freedmen, and Native Americans in Indian Territory (Oklahoma), 1865–1907," in Sucheng Chan, Douglas Henry Daniels, Mario T. García, and Terry P. Wilson, eds., *Peoples of Color in the American West* (Lexington, MA: D. C. Heath, 1994), 288–99.

89. David Beesley, "From Chinese to Chinese American: Chinese Women and Families in a Sierra Nevada Town," *California History* 67 (September 1988): 168–79; and Sally M. Miller, "California Immigrants: Case Studies in Continuity and Change in Societal and Familial Roles," *Journal of the West* 33 (July 1993): 25–34.

90. Powys, *Black Laughter*, 123–24.

91. Salvadori, *We Came in Dhows*, 3 vols. (Nairobi: Paperchase, 1996), 3:83, 170–73.

92. Joy Adamson, *The Searching Spirit: An Autobiography* (London: Collins and Harvill, 1978), 20; and Elspeth Huxley, ed., *Nellie: Letters from Africa* (London: Weidenfeld and Nicolson, 1984), 126–27.

Chapter 7

1. See, for example, Royal Institute of International Affairs, *The Colonial Problem: A Report* (London: Oxford University Press, 1937). For during the 1930s, see Barbara Bush, "'Britain's Conscience on Africa': White Women, Race and

Imperial Politics in Inter-War Britain," in Clare Midgley, ed., *Gender and Imperialism* (Manchester, England: University of Manchester Press, 1998), 200–223.

2. For western variations, see David M. Wrobel and Michael C. Steiner, eds., *Many Wests: Place, Culture, and Regional Identity* (Lawrence: University Press of Kansas, 1997).

3. Margaret Strobel, *European Women and the Second British Empire*. (Bloomington: Indiana University Press, 1991), 39–41; Dorothy Middleton, *Victorian Lady Travellers* (New York: E. P. Dutton, 1965), 3–15; and Leo Hamalian, ed., *Ladies on the Loose: Women Travellers of the Eighteenth and Nineteenth Centuries* (South Yarmouth, MA: John Curley, 1981), xii–xvi. For types of literature, refer to Patrick Brantlinger, *Rule of Darkness: British Literature and Imperialism, 1830–1945* (Ithaca: Cornell University Press, 1988).

4. Robert Young, *White Mythologies: Writing History and the West* (London: Routledge, 1994), 7, 17, 129. Two essential works are Edward W. Said, *Orientalism* (New York: Vintage, 1979); and Donna Landry and Gerald Maclean, eds., *The Spivak Reader: Selected Works of Gayatri Chakravorty Spivak* (New York: Routledge, 1996). For feminist theory and colonialism, see Chandra Mohanty, "Under Western Eyes: Feminist Scholarship and Colonial Discourse," *Feminist Review* 39 (1988): 61–88; and Jane Haggis, "Gendering Colonialism or Colonising Gender? Recent Women's Studies Approaches to White Women and the History of British Colonialism," *Women's Studies International Forum* 13 (1990): 105–15.

5. Isabella Bird, *The Englishwoman in America* (Madison: University of Wisconsin Press, 1966), 143; and Fredrika Bremer, *The Homes of the New World; Impressions of America* (New York: Harper, 1868), 555.

6. Bird, *Englishwoman in America*, 137.

7. Fredrika Bremer, *America of the Fifties: Letters of Fredrika Bremer* (New York: American-Scandanavian Foundation, 1924), 259; and Francis Trolloppe, *Domestic Manners of the Americans* (New York: Dodd Mead, 1927), 60.

8. Quoted in Robert G. Athearn, *Westward the Briton* (New York: Charles Scribner's, 1953), 66–67.

9. Harriet Martineau, *Retrospect of Western Travel* (London: Saunders and Otley, 1838), 24; and Bremer, *America of the Fifties*, 245.

10. Frances and Theresa Pulszky, *White, Red, Black: Sketches of Society in the United States* (New York: Negro Universities Press, 1968), 234–35.

11. Vera Norwood, *Made From This Earth: American Women and Nature* (Chapel Hill: University of North Carolina Press, 1993), 5.

12. Marianne North, *A Vision of Eden: The Life and Work of Marianne North* (London: Royal Botanic Gardens, Kew, 1980), 88, 192, 193, 196.

13. Ibid., 2.

14. Sara Mills, *Discourses of Differences: An Analysis of Women's Travel Writing and Colonialism* (London: Routledge, 1991), 83–94. Quote is from "Ida Pfeiffer, 1853," 84, in Marion Tinling, ed., *With Women's Eyes: Visitors to the New World* (Hamden, CT: Archon, 1993).

15. U.S. Department of Commerce and Labor, *Marriage and Divorce, 1867–1906*, 2 vols. (repr., Westport, CT: Greenwood, 1978), 1: 24–26, 79–164.

16. Albert D. Richardson, *Beyond the Mississippi* (Hartford: CT: American, 1867), 148.

17. U.S. Department of Commerce and Labor, *Marriage and Divorce,* 1: 14–15, 70–71.

18. Ibid., 1: 24–26, 79–164.

19. Doane Robinson, "Divorce in Dakota," *South Dakota Historical Collection* (Pierre: South Dakota State Historical Society, 1924): xii, 268–72; and Harry Hazel and S. L. Lewis, *The Divorce Mill: Realistic Sketches of the South Dakota Divorce Colony* (New York: N.p., 1908); and Lois Abby Lane, "The Divorcees," undated, Old Courthouse Museum, Sioux Falls, SD.

20. Bush, "'Britain's Conscience on Africa,'" 202–5. Examples of male adventure writing are Cherry Kearton and James Barnes, *Through Central Africa from East to West* (London: Cassell, 1915); and J. H. Patterson, *In The Grip of the Nyika: Further Adventures in British East Africa* (London: Macmillan, 1910).

21. Dea Birkett, *Spinsters Abroad: Victorian Lady Explorers* (Oxford: Blackwell, 1989), 18–32.

22. Mrs. A. S. Pickford, "Maps," undated, Royal East African Automobile Association, KNA, Nairobi.

23. Mary Kingsley, "Journey into the Jungle," in Hamalian, *Ladies on the Loose*, 533, 547; and Middleton, *Victorian Lady Travellers*, 149–176. An enlightening study of Kingsley is Dea Birkett, *Mary Kingsley: Imperial Adventuress* (London: Macmillan, 1992).

24. Mary Louise Pratt, *Imperial Eyes: Travel Writing and Transculturation* (London: Routledge, 1992), 4–7; and Cherry Kearton, *Cherry Kearton's Travels* (London: Hall, 1941), v.

25. M. French-Sheldon, *Sultan to Sultan: Adventures among the Maasai and other Tribes of East Africa* (Boston: Arena, 1892), 63, 66, 77, 81.

26. Charlotte Cameron, *A Woman's Winter in Africa: A Twenty Thousand Mile Journey* (London: Paul, 1913), i, 55–59.

27. Edith Maturin, *Adventures Beyond the Zambesi* (London: Nash, 1913), 1–3, 183–85, 385.

28. Etta Close, *A Woman Alone in Kenya, Uganda and the Belgian Congo* (London: Constable, 1924), 7–8, 23–24, 179.

29. Elspeth Huxley, ed., *Nellie: Letters from Africa* (London: Weidenfeld and Nicolson, 1984), 94.

30. Jürgen Osterhammel, *Colonialism: A Theoretical Overview* (Princeton, NJ: Wiener, 1997), 72, 108–11.

31. Evelyn Brodhurst-Hill, *So This Is Kenya!* (Glasgow: Blackie, 1936), 157–159.

32. Mrs. Patrick Ness, *Ten Thousand Miles in Two Continents* (London: Metheun, 1929), 41, 46, 48, 50, 61.

33. May Mott-Smith, *Africa from Port to Port* (London: Shaylor, 1931), 404–10.

34. Lady Evelyn C. Cobbold, *Kenya, the Land of Illusion* (London: Murray, 1935), ix, 24, 27, 33, 70.

35. Margaret Wrong, *Across Africa* (London: International Committee on Christian Literature, 1940), 9–11.
36. James Fox, *White Mischief* (London: Penguin, 1982), 22–23.
37. Quoted in Charles Hayes, *Oserian: Place of Peace* (Nairobi: Rima, 1997), 227–31.
38. Fox, *White Mischief*, 30.
39. Ibid., 31.
40. Hayes, *Oserian*, 225–27.
41. Elspeth Huxley, *Out in the Midday Sun* (London: Penguin, 1987), 61.
42. Fox, *White Mischief*, 66–84.
43. Ibid., 95.
44. See for example, Leda Farrant, *Diana, Lady Delamere and the Lord Erroll Murder* (Nairobi: Publishers Distribution Services, 1997).
45. Interview with Marjorie Hood, 9 April 1998, by author, Ngowe House, Malindi; Interview with Dorian Rocco, 20 April 1998, by author, Muthaiga Club, Nairobi; and interview with Doreen Tofe Field, 9 April 1998, by author, Ngowe House, Malindi.
46. Elspeth Huxley, *The Mottled Lizard* (London: Penguin, 1986), 199; and Mirella Ricciardi, *African Saga* (London: Collins, 1991), 68.
47. Thomas R. Buecker, ed., "Letters of Caroline Frey Winne from Sidney Barracks and Fort McPherson, Nebraska, 1874–1978," *Nebraska History* 62 (Spring 1981), 20.
48. William W. Fowler, *Woman on the American Frontier* (Hartford, CT: Scranton, 1880), 3, 33, 359, 365, 502, 505.
49. Ella Bird-Dumont, "True Life Story of Ella Bird-Dumont, Earliest Settler in the East Part of Panhandle, Texas," undated, Barker Texas History Collection, Austin; and John D. Unruh, *The Plains Across: The Overland Emigrants and the Trans-Mississippi West, 1840–1860* (Urbana: University of Illinois Press, 1979), 157, 169–70, 177.
50. Elizabeth L. Lord, *Reminiscences of East Oregon* (Portland, OR: Irwin-Hodgson, 1903), 142; and Buecker, "Letters of Caroline Frey Winne," 25.
51. Mary Ann Tatum, "Diary," 1870, ISHS, Iowa City.
52. Margaret I. Carrington, *Ab-sa-ra-ka, Home of the Crows: Being the Experience of an Officer's Wife on the Plains* (Philadelphia: Lippincott, 1868), 184.
53. Agnes Morley Cleaveland, *No Life for a Lady* (Lincoln: University of Nebraska Press, 1977), 38.
54. E. J. F. Knowles, "Papers," undated, RHL, Oxford.
55. Eva Bache, *The Youngest Lion: Early Farming Days in Kenya* (London: Hutchinson, 1934), 222–47.
56. Brodhurst-Hill, *So This Is Kenya!*, 157–159.
57. Evelyn Brodhurst-Hill, "Letters and Notes," undated, RHL, Oxford.
58. Alyse Simpson, *The Land That Never Was* (Lincoln: University of Nebraska Press, 1937).
59. Elspeth Huxley, *A New Earth: An Experiment in Colonialism* (London: Chatto and Windus, 1960), 260; and M. Aline Buxton, *Kenya Days* (London: Arnold, 1927), 99.

60. East Africa Women's League, "Report on the Women's Conference," Nairobi, 27 June 1930, RHL, Oxford.

61. Elsa Pickering, *When the Windows Were Opened: Life on a Kenya Farm* (London: Geofrey Bles, 1957), 223.

62. Quoted in Errol Trzebinski, *The Kenya Pioneers* (London: Heineman, 1985), 8.

63. Katie Martin and Richard Martin, *Historic Nairobi* (Nairobi: Space Sellers, 1992), unpaged.

64. "Unidentified clipping," *East Africa Standard*, undated, KNA, Nairobi.

65. Bache, *Youngest Lion*, 65.

66. "Interview with Ian W. Hardy," 2 April 1998, by author, at The Ark, Aberdare National Park, Kenya.

67. Interview with Marjorie Hood, 9 April 1998, by the author, Ngowe House, Malindi.

68. Philip D. Curtin, ed., *Africa and the West: Intellectual Responses to European Culture* (Madison: Univesity of Wisconsin Press, 1972), vii–ix.

69. Ranajit Guha and Gayatri Chakravorty Spivak, eds., *Selected Subaltern Studies* (New York: Oxford University Press, 1988), 5–15; and Gayatri Chakravorty Spivak, *A Critique of Postcolonial Reason: Toward a History of the Vanishing Present* (Cambridge, MA: Harvard University Press, 1999), 198–311.

70. Hilde Thurnwald, "The Changes of Family Life and the Status of Women," in Richard Thurnwald, *Black and White in East Africa: The Fabric of a New Civilization* (London: Routledge, 1935), 142–203; and Bertha Jones, "Collection," 1942–1959, Manuscript 5, and Canon and Mrs. Alan Page, "Collection, miscellaneous papers," 1950s, unnumbered microfilm, both at KNA, Nairobi.

71. Maryann Oshana, "Native American Women in Westerns: Reality and Myth," *Frontiers* 6 (Fall 1981): 46–50; Rosemary and Joseph Agonito, "Resurrecting History's Forgotten Women: A Case Study from the Cheyenne Indians," *Frontiers* 6 (Fall 1981): 8–16; Patricia Albers and Beatrice Medicine, eds., *The Hidden Half: Studies of Plains Indian Women* (Washington, D.C.: University Press of America, 1983). Also helpful are Rayna Green, "Native American Women," *Signs* 6 (Winter 1980): 218–67; Margot Liberty, "Hell Came With Horses: Plains Indian Women in the Equestrian Era," *Montana* 32 (Summer 1982): 10–19; Glenda Riley, "Some European (Mis) Perceptions of American Indian Women," *New Mexico Historical Review* 59 (July 1984): 237–66; and Gretchen M. Bataille and Kathleen Mullen Sands, *American Indian Women: Telling Their Lives* (Lincoln: University of Nebraska Press, 1984).

72. Jodye Lynn Dickson, "Amazons, Witches and 'Country Wives': Plains Indian Women in Historical Perspective," *Annals of Wyoming* 59 (Spring 1987): 48–56; Rebecca Tsosie, "Changing Women: The Cross-Currents of American Indian Feminine Identity," *American Indian Culture and Research Journal* 12 (1988): 1–37; Devon I. Abbott, "Medicine for the Rosebuds: Health Care at the Cherokee Female Seminary, 1876–1909," *American Indian Culture and Research Journal* 12 (1988): 59–71; Lisa E. Emmerich, "'Right in the Midst of My Own People': Native American Women and the Field Matron Program," *American Indian Quarterly* 15 (Spring 1991): 201–16; and Gail H. Landsman, "The 'Other' as

Political Symbol: Images of Indians in the Woman Suffrage Movement," *Ethnohistory* 39 (Summer 1992): 247–84.

73. Vicki Ruiz, "Dead Ends or Gold Mines? Using Missionary Records in Mexican-American Women's History," *Frontiers* 12 (1991): 33–56; and Carol Devens, *Countering Colonization: Native American Women and Great Lakes Missions, 1630–1900* (Berkeley: University of California Press, 1992). See also Vicki L. Ruiz and Susan Tiano, eds., *Women on the U.S.-Mexico Border: Responses to Change* (Boulder, CO: Westview, 1991); and Peggy Pascoe, "Gender Systems in Conflict: The Marriages of Mission-Educated Chinese American Women, 1874–1939," *Journal of Social History* 22 (Fall/Summer 1988–1989): 631–52.

74. Robert C. and Eleanor R. Carriker, eds., *An Army Wife on the Frontier: The Memoirs of Alice Blackwood Baldwin, 1867–1877* (Salt Lake City: Tanner Trust Fund, 1975), 99–100.

75. Leola Lehman, "Life in the Territories," *Chronicles of Oklahoma* 41 (Fall 1963): 373–75.

76. "Interview with Nellie Quail," 1 August 1967, Fort McDowell Indian Reservation, held by Arizona State Museum, Tucson (hereafter cited as ASM).

77. Examples are in Eliza Spalding Warren, *Memoirs of the West: The Spaldings* (Portland, OR: Marsh Printing Co., 1916), 20–21; and Laura W. Johnson, *Eight Hundred Miles in an Ambulance* (Philadelphia: Lippincott, 1889), 61–65.

78. Sarah Winnemucca Hopkins, *Life Among the Piutes: Their Wrongs and Claims* (New York: Putnam, 1883).

79. James W. Fernandez, "Fang Representations Under Acculturation," in Curtin, *Africa and the West*, 3–48.

80. Ngũgĩ wa Thiong'o, *The River Between* (Nairobi: East African Educational Publishers, 1965), 86, 142, 147; and Lewis Gann and Peter Duignan, *White Settlers in Tropical Africa* (Baltimore: Penguin, 1962), 12.

81. Marguerite Mallett, *A White Woman Among the Maasai* (New York: Dutton, 1923), 97, 99–101.

82. Gayatri Chakravorty Spivak, "Subaltern Studies: Deconstructing Historiography," in Ranajit Guha and Spivak, eds., *Selected Subaltern Studies: Deconstructing Historiography* (New York: Oxford University Press, 1988), 3–34. Early anthropological studies are in Curtin, *Africa and the West*.

83. Peter H. Beard, collector, *Longing for Darkness: Kamante's Tales From Out of Africa* (New York: Harcourt Brace Jovanovich, 1975), unpaged.

84. Ibid.

85. "Interview with Charles Waithaka," 18 March 1998, by Edward Chegge, Central Province, Kenya.

86. Ngugi family, "Papers," 1935–1943, privately held, translated by Edward Chegge, Central Province, Kenya. Copy of translation in author's possession.

87. Interview with Esther Njoki, 20 March 1998, by Edward and Lawrence Chegge, Central Province, Kenya; in author's possession.

88. Mrs. E. Harrold, "Collection," 1936–1960s, KNA, Nairobi. The poll tax ordinance is found in Colony and Protectorate of Kenya, *Ordinances Enacted during the Year 1930* (Nairobi: Government Printer, 1931), 782–85.

89. "Introduction," in Guha and Spivak, *Selected Subaltern Studies*, 15–27. A helpful discussion is in Gayatri Chakravorty Spivak, *The Post-Colonial Critic: Interviews, Strategies, Dialogues*, ed. Sarah Harasym (New York: Routledge, 1990).

90. "Interview with Muigua Ngunjiri," 15 March 1998, by Edward Chegge, Central Province, Kenya.

91. "Interview with Esther Njoki," 16 March 1998, by Edward Chegge, Central Province, Kenya.

92. Ibid.

93. Ibid.

94. Ibid.

95. "Interview with Mjonge Kimana," 3 May 1998, by author, Loldia House, Naivasha, Kenya.

96. Ibid.

Chapter 8

1. Stephen I. Thompson, *Pioneer Colonization: A Cross-Cultural View* (New York: Addison-Wesley, 1973), 2–4; and Silver City *Enterprise*, 8 November 1889, 15 November 1889, and 20 September 1889.

2. Richard Maxwell Brown, *No Duty to Retreat: Violence and Values in American History and Society* (Norman: University of Oklahoma Press, 1991), 5–6, 155–57.

3. Margaret T. Gordon and Stephanie Riger, *The Female Fear: The Social Cost of Rape* (Urbana: University of Illinois Press, 1991), 2–3, 21.

4. Ada A. Vogdes, "Journal," 1866–1872, HL, San Marino, California.

5. Mrs. Charles A. Finding, "The Story of a Colorado Pioneer," *Colorado Magazine* 2 (1925): 52.

6. Mrs. Lee Whipple-Halsam, *Early Days in California* (N.p.: N.p., 1924), 14–16.

7. James A. McKenna, *Black Range Tales* (New York: Wilson-Erickson, 1936), 89; and Lambert Florin, *Ghost Towns of the West* (N.p.: Promontory Press, 1970), 629–30.

8. Silver City *Enterprise*, 21 June 1889, and circa July 1890.

9. Ibid., 8 November 1889, 8 November 1889, and 28 June 1889.

10. Paula Petrik, "Capitalists with Rooms: Prostitution in Helena, Montana, 1865–1900," *Montana* 31 (Spring 1981): 28–41; Petrik, "Strange Bedfellows: Prostitution, Politicians and Moral Reform in Helena, Montana, 1885–1887," *Montana* 35 (Summer 1985): 2–13; and Rex C. Myers, "An Inning for Sin: Chicago Joe and Her Hurdy-Gurdy Girls," *Montana* 27 (April 1977): 24–33. The best book on western prostitution is Anne M. Butler, *Daughters of Joy, Sisters of Misery: Prostitutes in the American West* (Urbana: University of Illinois Press, 1985).

11. Ordinance No. 98, 3 April 1885, Silver City, NM; and Silver City *Enterprise* 10 January 1890.

12. *Enterprise*, 22 September 1889, 29 November 1889, and 24 October 1890.

13. Ibid., 5 April 1889, 28 November 1890, and 1 June 1889.

14. Case is in Anne M. Butler, *Gendered Justice in the American West: Women Prisoners in Men's Penitentiaries* (Urbana: University of Illinois Press, 1997), 124–26. Doggerel quoted in Jerome Nadelhaaft, "Wife Torture: A Known Phenomenon in Nineteenth-Century America," *Journal of American Culture* 10 (Fall 1987): 42. For Swisshelm, see Elizabeth H. Pleck, *Domestic Tyranny: The Making of Social Policy Against Family Violence* (New York: Oxford University Press, 1987), 55–56. For cases of abuse, see David Peterson del Mar, "Violence against Wives by Prominent Men in Clatsop County," *Oregon Historical Quarterly* 100 (Winter 1999): 402–33.

15. Betsy Downey, "Battered Pioneers: Jules Sandoz and the Physical Abuse of Wives on the American Frontier," *Great Plains Quarterly* 12 (Winter 1992): 31–49; Melody Graulich, "Violence against Women in Literature of the Western Family," *Frontiers* 7 (1984): 14–20; and Graulich, "Every Husband's Right: Sex Roles in Mari Sandoz's *Old Jules*," *Western American Literature* 18 (Spring 1983): 3–20.

16. Daniel Duster, letter to "Dear John [Dustin]," 2 November 1853, Edward Wiltsee Collection, Wells Fargo Archives, San Francisco.

17. Gordon and Riger, *Female Fear*, 8–9,

18. Thomas B. Marquis, "Red Ripe's Squaw," *Century Magazine* 118 (June 1929), 203.

19. Interview with Nellie Quail, 31 July 1967, Fort McDowell, copy at ASM, Tucson.

20. Apolinaria Lorenzana, "Recollections," undated, San Diego Historical Society, California.

21. Doña Jesus Moreno de Soza, "Reminiscences," 1939, AHS, Tucson.

22. Interview with Emma Taylor, in George P. Rawick, ed., *The American Slave*, vol. 5, Part 4 (Westport, CT: Greenwood, 1972) 73–74.

23. Interview with Susan Merritt, in Rawick, *American Slave*, vol. 5, Part 4, 174–78.

24. Interview with Liola McClean Cravens Woffort, no date, Manuscript Collection, University of Washington Library, Seattle (hereafter cited as UWL).

25. Sister Blandina Segale, *At the End of the Santa Fe Trail* (Columbus, OH: Columbian, 1932) 161.

26. Quoted in "Difficulties on Southwestern Frontier," Thirty-Sixth Congress of the United States, Session 1, House Executive Document No. 52, 79–82.

27. Sue Fawn Chung, "Their Changing World: Chinese Women on the Comstock, 1860–1910," in Ronal M. James and C. Elizabeth Raymond, eds., *Comstock Women: The Making of a Mining Community* (Reno: University of Nevada Press, 1997), 208–14; and Silver City *Enterprise*, 15 November 1889.

28. Vivienne DeWatteville, *Speak to the Earth* (London: Metheun, 1935), 4.

29. Cynthia Salvadori, *We Came in Dhows*, 3 vols. (Nairobi: Paperchase, 1996), 2: 151; and Lady Eleanor Cole, *Random Recollections of a Pioneer Kenya Settler* (Suffolk, England: Baron, 1974), 42–43, 56.

30. Brown, *No Duty to Retreat*, 4–5; Else Pickering, *When the Windows Were Opened: Life on a Kenya Farm* (London: Geofrey Bles, 1957), 29, 140–41; and Charles Miller, *The Lunatic Express* (Nairobi: Westlands, 1971), 509.

31. Errol Trzebinski, *The Kenya Pioneers* (London: Heinemann, 1985), 101.

32. Ibid., 102, 107.

33. Miller, *Lunatic Express*, 574.

34. Ibid., 509; and Salvadori, *We Came in Dhows*, 2: 71.

35. David M. Anderson, "Policing the Settler State: Colonial Hegemony in Kenya, 1900–1952," in Dagmar Engels and Shula Marks, eds., *Contesting Colonial Hegemony: State and Society in Africa and Indian* (London: British Academic Press, 1994), 254–55.

36. Vron Ware, *Beyond the Pale: White Women, Racism, and History* (New York: Verso, 1992), 38–40; Miller, *Lunatic Express*, 536; and interview with Velia Carn, by author, Elsamere Conservation Centre, Naivasha, Kenya, May 1998.

37. East Africa Protectorate, Mombasa, "Search for Mr. Casnahan," 1914, PC/Coast/1/17/86; Legal Department, Attorney General's Office, "Criminal Procedure Ordinance: Prosecution for Causing Miscarriages by Women," 1924, AG/52/27; and Judicial Department, "Divorce Ordinance Correspondence," 1931–1952, DC/KSM/1/115/133, all in KNA, Nairobi.

38. Anderson, "Policing the Settler State," 256.

39. Dane Kennedy, *Islands of White: Settler Society and Culture in Kenya and Southern Rhodesia, 1890–1939* (Durham, NC: Duke University Press, 1987), 141.

40. Office of the Attorney General, "Indecent Assaults on Women and Children," 1935–42, AG/1/609, KNA, Nairobi.

41. Nora K. Strange, *Kenya To-Day* (London: Paul, 1934), 155, 157.

42. Ibid., 158.

43. Anderson, "Policing the Settler State," 259; Miller, *Lunatic Express*, 536; and Llewelyn Powys, *Black Laughter* (New York: Harcourt Brace, 1924), 34–38.

44. Claire C. Robertson, *Trouble Showed the Way: Women, Men, and Trade in the Nairobi Area, 1890–1990* (Bloomington: Indiana University Press, 1997), 72–73, and Trevor Fisher, *Prostitution and the Victorians* (New York: St. Martin's Press, 1997), x–xiii, 95–97, 137–40.

45. Quote in Robertson, *Trouble Showed the Way*, 93; and Janet M. Bujra, "Women 'Entrepreneurs' of Early Nairobi," 1974, unpublished paper, Dept. of Sociology, University of Dar Es Salaam, RHL, Oxford.

46. Ibid.; and Luise White, *The Comforts of Home: Prostitution in Colonial Nairobi* (Chicago, IL: University of Chicago Press, 1990), 13–17, 55–58, quotes on 51, 55, and 57.

47. Ibid., 46–48, 55–58, 68–70; and Luise S. White, "A Colonial State and an African Petty Bourgeoisie: Prostitution, Property, and Class Struggle in Nairobi, 1936–1940," in Frederick Cooper, ed., *Struggle for the City: Migrant Labour, Capital, and the State in Urban Africa* (Beverly Hills, CA: Sage, 1983), 167–94.

48. Sarah White Smith, "Diary," in Clifford Drury, ed., *First White Woman over the Rockies*, vol. 1 (Glendale, CA: Arthur H. Clark Co., 1966), 87.

49. Fleming Fraker, ed., "To Pike's Peak by Ox-Wagon: The Harriet A. Smith Day-Book," *Annals of Iowa* 35 (Fall 1959): 132.

50. Margaret M. Hecox, *California Caravan: The 1846 Overland Trail Memoir of Margaret M. Hecox* (San Jose, CA: Harlan-Young, 1966); and "Diary of a Trip across the Plains in '59," BL, Berkeley, California.

51. For clothing, see Glenda Riley, *Women and Indians on the Frontier, 1825–1915* (Albuquerque: University of New Mexico Press, 1984), 126–28, 141, 192–93.

52. Ellen Tompkins Adams, "Diary of Ellen Tompkins Adams, Wife of John Smalley Adam, M. D.," 1863, BL, Berkeley, CA.; and Sandra L. Myres, ed., *Ho for California! Women's Overland Dairies from the Huntington Library* (San Marino, CA: Huntington Library, 1980), 117.

53. See, for example, Mary Jane (Bryan) Guill, "The Overland Diary of a Journey from Livingston County, Missouri, to Butte County, California," 5 May to 5 September 1860, California State Library, Sacramento (hereafter cited as CSL); Thomas R. Buecker, ed., "Letters of Caroline Frey Winne from Sidney Barracks and Fort McPherson, Nebraska, 1874–1878," *Nebraska History* 62 (Spring 1981): 10; Esther Bell Hanna, "Journal," 1852, BL, Berkeley; Hecox, *California Caravan*, 28; and Lucy Sexton, *The Foster Family, California Pioneers* (Santa Barbara, CA: Schouer, 1925), 134. Quote is in Leo M. Kaiser and Priscilla Knuth, eds., "From Ithaca to Clatsop Plains: Miss Ketcham's Journal of Travel," *OHQ*, pt. 2, vol. 62 (December 1961); 368.

54. Marjorie Murray, "Collection," Photographs, 1924–1936, Mss. 45, KNA, Nairobi.

55. Ibid.

56. Sarah Mirza and Margaret Strobel, eds., *Three Swahili Women: Life Histories from Mombasa, Kenya* (Bloomington: Indiana University Press, 1989), 97.

57. "Interview with Marjorie Hood," 9 April 1998, by author, Negowe House, Malindi, Kenya; *East African Standard,* 6 October 1934, 11; and *The Kenya Settlers' Cookery Book and Household Guide* (Nairobi: East Africa Standard, 1958), 292–314.

58. H. M. Sub-Commissioner of Mombasa, "Outward File, Nairobi," PC/Coast/1/12/24, 1903, KNA, Nairobi.

59. Reginald Coupland, *East Africa and Its Invaders* (Oxford: Clarendon Press, 1938), 14: and Strange, *Kenya To-Day*, 165–66.

60. "Interview with Mjonge Kimana," 3 May 1998, by author, Loldia House, Naivasha, Kenya.

61. M. Aline Buxton, *Kenya Days* (London: Arnold, 1927), 42–43, 50–55.

62. B. L. Putnam Weale, *The Conflict of Colour* (London: Macmillan, 1910); Lothrop Stoddard, *The Rising Tide of Color Against White World-Supremacy* (London: Chapman & Hall, 1922); and Leonard Woolf, *Imperialism and Civilization* (London: Hogarth, 1928).

63. Eleanor Rathbone, "Papers," 1928–38, unnumbered microfilm, KNA, Nairobi.

64. Anne McDonald, "African Roundabout, 1932–35," undated, RHL, Oxford. Also helpful is Angela Woollacott, "'All This Is the Empire, I Told Myself': Australian Women's Voyages 'Home' and the Articulation of Colonial Whiteness," *American Historical Review* 102 (October 1997): 1003–29.

65. Eve Bache, *The Youngest Lion: Early Farming Days in Kenya* (London: Hutchinson, 1934), 272–73.

66. Anderson, "Policing the Settler State," in Engels and Marks, *Contesting Colonial Hegemony*, 249–52.

67. Major W. Robert Foran, *The Kenya Police, 1887–1960*, 3 vols. (London: Hale, 1962), 1:67–68; Marjorie R. Dilley, *British Policy in Kenya Colony* (New York: Nelson, 1966), 141–44; and Salvadori, *We Came in Dhows*, 3: 112–13.
68. Winston S. Churchill, *My African Journey* (New York: Hodder and Stoughten, 1908), 3: 49.
69. J. S. Mangat, *A History of the Asians in East Africa, c. 1886–1945* (Oxford: Clarendon Press, 1969), 97–131; W. R. Ochieng', *A History of Kenya* (Nairobi: Macmillan, 1985), 104–6.
70. Lawrence W. Hollingsworth, *The Asians of East Africa* (London: Macmillan, 1960), 84–89.
71. Mrs. K. Armstrong, "Recollections of Kenya, 1919 to 1930," undated, RHL, Oxford.
72. Quoted in Salvadori, *We Came in Dhows*, 3: 161.
73. Robert Young, *White Mythologies: Writing History and the West* (London: Routledge, 1990), 12–13; Trzebinski, *Kenya Pioneers*, 195; quote in Mizra and Strobel, *Three Swahili Women*, 63.
74. Lewis H. Gann and Peter Duignan, *White Settlers in Tropical Africa* (Baltimore: Penguin, 1962), 13.
75. Quote from Miller, *Lunatic Express*, 519; and Ochieng', *History of Kenya*, 113–21.
76. Jocelyn Murray, "The Church Missionary Society and the 'Female Circumcision' Issue in Kenya, 1929–1932," *Journal of Religion in Africa* 8 (1976): 92–104.
77. Ngũgĩ wa Thiong'o, *The River Between* (Nairobi: East Africa Educational Publishers, 1965), 142; and E. Mary Holding, "Anthropological Studies, 1938–1940s," Manuscript #7, KNA, Nairobi.
78. Ngũgĩ wa Thiong'o, *Moving the Centre: The Struggle for Cultural Freedoms* (Nairobi: East Africa Educational Publishers, 1993), 76–77.
79. Jean Davison, *Voices from Mutira: Change in the Lives of Rural Gikuyu Women, 1910–1995* (Boulder, CO: Lynne Rienner, 1996), 43.
80. Ibid., 40–41.
81. Murray, "The Church Missionary Society and the 'Female Circumcision' Issue," 99–100; and Elspeth Huxley, *Out in the Midday Sun* (London: Penguin, 1987), 50.
82. Holding, "Anthropological Studies."
83. Charity Waciuma, *Daughter of Mumba* (Nairobi: East African Publishing, 1969), 101. See also Robert B. Edgerton, *Mau Mau: An African Crucible* (New York: Free Press, 1989).
84. Tabitha Kanogo, *Squatters and the Roots of Mau-Mau 1905–63* (London: J. Currey, 1987); Wunyabari O. Maioba, *Mau Mau and Kenya: An Analysis of a Peasant Revolt* (Bloomington: Indiana University Press, 1993); and Greet Kershaw, *Mau Mau from Below* (Oxford: J. Currey, 1997).
85. Wambui Waiyaki Otieno, *Mau Mau's Daughter: A Life History* (Boulder, CO: Lynne Reiner, 1998), 16. Also helpful is Cora Ann Presley, *Kikuyu Women, the Mau Mau Rebellion, and Social Change in Kenya* (Boulder, CO: Westview Press, 1992).

86. Otieno, *Mau Mau's Daughter*, 4–5. See also, Muthoni Likimani, *Passbook Number F. 47927: Women and Mau Mau in Kenya* (New York: Praeger, 1985).

Conclusion

1. Zitkala-Sa, *American Indian Stories* (Lincoln: University of Nebraska Press, 1985), 67, 89, 94.
2. Charity Waciuma, *Daughter of Mumba* (Nairobi: East African Publishing, 1969), 107.
3. *Ninth Census*, Vol. 1: *The Statistic of the Population of the United States* (Washington, D.C.: Government Printing Office, 1872), 606, 608; and A. Walter, *Report of the Non-Native Enumeration Made in the Colony and Protectorate of Kenya: Sixth March 1931* (Nairobi: Government Printer, 1932), 7, 8.
4. ZitkalaŜa, *American Indian Stories*, 99.
5. See, for example, Jean Davison, *Voices from Mutira: Change in the Lives of Rural Gijuyu Women, 1910–1995* (Boulder, CO: Lynne Rienner, 1996); and Berida Ndambuki and Claire C. Robertson, *"We Only Come Here to Struggle": Stories from Berida's Life* (Bloomington: Indiana University Press, 2000).
6. For discussions of these conditions, see Raymond S. Franklin, *Shadows of Race and Class* (Minneapolis: University of Minnesota Press, 1991), 155; R. D. Grillo, *Pluralism and the Politics of Difference* (Oxford, England: Oxford University Press, 1998), 216–36; Elizabeth Furniss, *The Burden of History: Colonialism and the Frontier Myth in a Rural Canadian Community* (Vancouver, Canada: University of British Columbia Press, 1999), 11–13; Patricia Seed, *American Pentimento: The Invention of Indians and the Pursuit of Riches* (Minneapolis: University of Minnesota Press, 2001), 163–78.
7. Edward Said, "An Interview," in Robert Borofsky, *Remembrance of Pacific Pasts: An Invitation to Remake History* (Honolulu: University of Hawaii Press, 2000), 443.
8. Donna Landry and Gerald Maclean, eds., *The Spivak Reader* (New York: Routledge, 1996), 203–36.
9. For world-systems analysis, see Thomas D. Hall, ed., *A World-Systems Reader* (Lanham, MD: Rowman and Littlefield, 2000), 3–28; Christopher Chase-Dunn and Thomas D. Hall, *Rise and Demise: Comparing World-Systems* (Boulder, CO: Westview, 1997); Richard J. Perry, *From Time Immemorial: Indigenous Peoples and State Systems* (Austin: University of Texas Press, 1996).
10. Richard Dawkins, *The Blind Watchmaker: Why the Evidence of Evolution Reveals a Universe Without Design* (New York: Norton, 1986), 9–11; and Dawkins, *River Out of Eden: A Darwinian View of Life* (New York: Basic Books, 1995). Standard works include Richard E. Leakey and Roger Lewin, *Origins* (New York: E. P. Dutton, 1977); and Jane Goodall, *The Chimpanzees of Gombe: Patterns of Behavior* (Cambridge, MA: Belknap Press, 1986). More recent are Blake Edgar, *Ancestor: In Search of Human Origins* (New York: Villard, 1994); Abel A. Alves,

Brutality and Benevolence: Human Ethology, Culture, and the Birth of Mexico (Westport, CT: Greenwood, 1996); and Walter Burkert, *Creation of the Sacred: Tracks of Biology in Early Religions* (Cambridge, MA: Harvard University Press, 1996).

11. Robert M. Miller, *Understanding the Ancient Secrets of the Horse's Mind* (Neenah, WI: Meerdink, 1999), 47–55; and Stephen Budiansky, *The Nature of Horses* (New York: Free Press, 1997), 89–95.

12. Jackie Budd, *Reading the Horse's Mind* (New York: Howell, 1996), 59–63.

13. Claire Robertson, *"We Only Come Here to Struggle": Stories from Berida's Life* (Bloomington: Indiana University Press, 2000), 6.

14. Jared Diamond, *Guns, Germs, and Steel: The Fates of Human Societies* (New York: Norton, 1997), 16–17, 22–25.

15. Ibid., 386–389, 401; and Jared Diamond, *The Third Chimpanzee: The Evolution and Future of the Human Animal* (New York: Harper Collins, 1992), 368.

16. An international comparative study is Janet L. Finn, *Tracing the Veins: Of Copper, Culture, and Community from Butte to Chuquicamata* (Berkeley: University of California Press, 1998).

Index

abolitionists, 34, 203–7

adventurers: in the American West, 44; in Kenya, 46–47, 66, 177; women travel writers, 233–36, 238–42

African American women: domestic space, 124; entrepreneurs in the American West, 171; and interracial marriage, 225–26; migration to the American West, 48–49, 62; and violence, 268–69; women's club movement, 185–86

agriculture: in the American West, 43–44, 107; coffee plantations, 46, 104; in Kenya, 46, 111, 112, 169–70; and race, 172–73; women in the fields, 122–23, 128–30

Anderson, Bertha, 43

Asian Indians: and capitalism, 90–91; and class in Kenya, 102–3; and domestic space, 130–31; entrepreneurs in Kenya, 172; and the environment, 131; and interracial marriage, 226–27; migration to Kenya, 50–52, 75–77; resistance to whites, 215; social networks, 136–38; and white bigotry, 286–87; and women's clubs in Kenya, 186–88

Asian women, 49–50, 62–63

Bache, Eve, 249

bandas, 95

Barcelo, Gertrudis, 99–100

Barnes, Rev. Alice, 217–18

Bazett, Mary, 208

Belknap, Kitturah, 59

Bemis, Polly, *153*

Bent (Tate), Mayence, 91, 166–67

Binns, Anne Katherine Ferrar, 209

bio-history: comparative, 6–10, 301–2; display, 89, 117–18; and gender, 5–6

Blixen, Karen, 45, 65, 257

Block, Lily, 168

Boers, 64, 101

Brown, Clara, 171

Buffalo Bird Woman, 107

Bunau-Varilla, Giselle, 177

capitalism: in the American West, 16; and black Kenyans, 112–13; and British imperialism, 16, 44; and race, 139, 143; in urban areas, 87, 90–92

Carpenter, Grace, 193

Carr, Jeanne, 174

"Chicago Joe", 165

children, 132, 134–135, 140–41, 145–46

Cholmondeley, Hugh, 89

Civil War, 123

class: in the American West, 97–100; and British migration, 63–64, 67–68, 74; and colonization, 303–4; and frontier homes, 94, 96; in Kenya, 100–6; and race, 99–100, 102–6, 303–4; and sports, 136; subordinate group, 9–10

coffee plantations, 46, 104

Cole, Lady Eleanor, 182–83

Collis, Septima M., 77

colonialism. *See also* imperialism; and bio-history, 9–10; and black cultures, 103–4; and class, 303–4; criticism of, 232, 240–42; and education, 302–3; internal colonization, 53; and technology, 303

Colonists' Association, 64–65

Cortina, Juan Nepomuceno, 270–71

culture: and consumer goods, 139, 143; and gender, 6; holidays, 156; vs. human nature, 5

debbis, 126–27

Delamere, Lady Gladys, 184

Devi, Mathra, 52

Dinesen, Isak. *See* Blixen, Karen

domestic space. *See also* public sphere; and agriculture, 122–23; American West & Kenya, 296–97; and class, 94, 96; creation of, 119–20, 151–52, 155; and the environment, 128–29, 158; furniture, 121, 127; help, 131–32; homes, 93–97; during national crises, 123; and reforms in Kenya, 220–24; and reforms in the American West, 201–3; social networks, 132, 135–36; technology, 121–22, 127; upholding "standards" in Kenya, 141–46;

upholding "standards" in the American West, 138–41

Drexel, Mary Katherine, 203

East Africa Women's League (EAWL), 183–85, 197, 222–24

economy. *See also* agriculture; capitalism; and altered food supplies, 211, 216; labor systems, 16–17, 107–8, 110–18, 172–73; and tourism, 192–93

Eldoret, Kenya, 71

Eliot, Sir Charles, 39

employment: in the American West, 34–35, 42–44, 153–54; entrepreneurs in Kenya, 166–70, 172; entrepreneurs in the American West, 164–65, 171; in Kenya, 45–46, 153–54; labor systems, 16–17, 107–8, 110–18, 172–73; in urban areas, 123

environment: frontier ecology, 119; game in Kenya, 170; white proprietorship, 166; women's clubs in Kenya, 182; women's clubs in the American West, 174; women travel writers, 233–36, 238

Farmers' and Planters' Association, 64

Feige, Dr. Friede, 35

feminism. *See also* domestic space; and bio-history, 6; and segretation, 185–86; women's clubs in Kenya, 180–85; women's clubs in the American West, 173–77; women's rights movement, 178–85

Frémont, Jessie Benton, 61

French-Sheldon, Mary, 239

frontier(s). *See also* philosophy; imperialism, 11, 293; nature of, 21–25; place, 16, 119, 295–97; process, 297–98; product, 24–25, 231–33, 298–300; towns and cities, 150

Gathura, Kamande, 257

gender: and bio-history, 5–6; colonizing methods, 13–14; and frontier homes, 93–94; and frontier process, 297–98; and frontier product, 293–94, 298–300; and race, 3–4; and sexuality,

American West, 14, 15; and industry,
56–57; literature, 57–58, 63–64, 66–69;
and the mythology of the American
West, 233–36, 246–47; routes to
Kenya, 69–72, 73–77; routes to the
American West, 58, 61; settlement,
12, 13–14, 17, 18–19; settlers, 26, 27;
soldier-settlement in Kenya, 46,
65–66; wagons, *148*
missionaries: in the American West, 33,
100; criticism of, 240; in Kenya, 36,
39–40; and reforms in Kenya, 208–14;
and reforms in the American West,
202–3; Spanish, 47–48; White Sisters
in Kenya, 212–13
Mombasa, Kenya, 74–75, 88
morality. *See also* genteel conceit; philosophy; abolitionists in Kenya, 206–7;
abolitionists in the American West,
34, 203–5; Happy Valley scandals,
243–46; industrialization, 35; prostitution, 265–66; reforms in Kenya,
220–24; reforms in the American
West, 201–3
Mordaunt, Vera Marie, 168
Mumbo cult, 81
mythology of the American West, 2,
233–36, 246–47

Nairobi, Kenya, 88–92, 166–67, 223–24,
272–74
Nandi, 81, 112
Nash, Esther, 74
Native Americans: and class in the
American West, 99; and colonial crit-
icism, 254–55; and environment, 124;
European view of, 235–36; interracial
marriages, 219, 225–26; reservations
in the American West, 171–72; resist-
ance to whites, 192, 214–15; and
tourism, 192–93; and violence, 268;
and white settlers, 247–48; and white
women's reforms, 201–3
Ngugi family, 257–58
Ngunjiri, Muigua, 258–59
Njoki, Esther, 259
Nyeri, Kenya, 92

Odegaard, Emma, 41–42

philosophy (frontier): in the American
West, 54, 233–36, 246–48, 294–95;
domestic space, 119–20; and frontier,
22–23; and interracial marriage,
221–22; in Kenya, 54, 249–50, 294–95;
and migrants of color, 53; and Native
Americans, 201–3; and racism, 32–33;
and reforms in Kenya, 205, 209–10,
220–24; travel writers in Kenya,
238–42
place (frontier), 119, 295–97. *See also*
towns and cities
Pleasant, Mary Ellen, 53, 171, 186
politics: American West & Kenya, 16; and
Asian Indians, 286–87; government,
11, 114–15; Kikuyu Central
Association, 289; and race, 184,
189–90; women's clubs in Kenya,
180–85, 187–88; women's clubs in the
American West, 173–77; women's
rights movement, 178–80
Preston, Florence, 45
prisons, 180–82
process (frontier), 297–98
product (frontier), 24–25, 231–33, 293–94,
298–300
prostitution: in the American West, 49,
265–67, 271; in Kenya, 90, 276–78
public sphere. *See also* domestic space;
agriculture, 170; temperance movement, 217–18; women's clubs in
Kenya, 180–85; women's clubs in the
American West, 173–77; women's
rights movement, 178–80

Quail, Nellie, 107
Quinn, Edel, 197

race: abolitionists in Kenya, 206–7; abolitionists in the American West, 34,
203–5; bigotry in the American West,
278–80; child rearing, 140–41, 145–46;
class, 99–100, 102–6, 303–4; clothing,
280–281; colonial criticism, 284–85,
300–1; consumer goods, 139, 143;

desegregation, 250–53; education,
302–3; feminism, 185–86; frontier
philosophy, 32–33; frontier process,
297–98; frontier product, 24–25,
293–94, 298–300; gender, 3–4; interracial marriage, 221–24; kipande,
282–83; labor systems, 107–8, 112–18;
marriage, 218–20; politics, 184,
189–90; segregation, 87, 90–91,
139–41, 185–86, 194–96; sports, 136,
195–96; violence in Kenya, 273–78;
violence in the American West,
267–71; women's fears, 188–89;
women travel writers, 238–42
railroads, 59–60, 72, 77–78. *See also*
Uganda Railway
religion. *See* missionaries
resistance to whites: by Asian Indians,
215; by black Kenyans, 106, 114,
215–17, 284, 288–89; kipande, 282–83;
Mau Mau Rebellion, 15, 291–92; and
mission reforms in Kenya, 210; by
Native Americans, 192, 214–15; and
segregation in Kenya, 196–97; Sepoy
Rebellion, 193

Salter, Meodra, 177
Sandbach-Baker, Mrs., 91
San Francisco, 61–62
Scott, Lord and Lady Francis, 45, 96
Sepoy Rebellion, 193
settlement, 12, 13–14, 17, 18–19. *See also*
migration
settlers, 26, 27
Sidpra, Freny Mehenwanji, 52
slavery: in Africa, 206–7; in the American
West, 34, 203–5; in California,
189–90; and Great Britain, 34–35; and
violence, 268–69
Social Darwinism, 6, 7–8, 39, 221–22. *See
also* race
social networks, 119, 132–38
South Africans, 64
de Souza, Dr. Mary, 52
sports, 133, 136, 195–96
Stephani, Sister Irene, 212–13
suffragists, 175–77, 179, 186

Swahili women, 50, 102

Tate, Fred, 167
teachers, 49. *See also* employment
technology: in the American West, 15–16;
and colonization, 303; and domestic
space, 121–22; industrialization, 35; in
Kenya, 16, 127
temperance movement, 217–18
Thomas Cook & Son, 78
Thuku, Harry, 106
Todd, Jean, 35
tourists: in the American West, 77–78,
159, 190–93; and indigenous people,
191–93; in Kenya, 78, *159*; and racial
segregation, 190–91; women travel
writers, 233–36, 238
towns and cities, *150*; in the American
West, 86–88; entrepreneurs in Kenya,
166–70; entrepreneurs in the
American West, 164–65; in Kenya,
88–93
Tules, Doña, 99–100

Uganda Railway: introduction of, 38–39,
45; labor force, 50, 51–52; land acquisition, 108–9; and tourists, 78
urban areas. *See* towns and cities

violence, 262–78

Waciuma, Charity, 109–10
Waterhouse, Dr. Lavinia Goodyear, 35
Watkins, Olga, 169
Welch, Josephine, 165
Wilson, Florence Kerr, 167–68
world systems, 4, 301
World War I: Kenyan soldiers, 287–88;
Kenya's labor system, 111; soldier-
settlement in Kenya, 46, 65–66; travel
to Kenya, 73; women in Kenya, 129